D1496387

NELSON

SCIENCE & TECHNOLOGY
PERSPECTIVES (7)

GRADE 7 AUTHOR TEAM

Roberta Oswald
Toronto Catholic District School Board

Jeffrey Major
Thames Valley District School Board

Douglas Hayhoe, Ph.D.
Bachelor of Education Program,
Tyndale University College

Christy Hayhoe
Science Writer and Editor

Martin Gabber
Durham District School Board

Douglas Fraser
District School Board Ontario North East

Maurice DiGiuseppe, Ph.D.
Formerly Toronto Catholic District School
Board

SENIOR PROGRAM CONSULTANT

Maurice DiGiuseppe, Ph.D.
Formerly Toronto Catholic District School Board

PROGRAM CONSULTANT

Jeffrey Major
Thames Valley District School Board

NELSON EDUCATION

NELSON **EDUCATION**

Nelson Science and Technology Perspectives 7

Senior Program Consultant
Maurice DiGiuseppe

Program Consultant
Jeffrey Major

Authors
Roberta Oswald
Jeffrey Major
Douglas Hayhoe
Christy Hayhoe
Martin Gabber
Douglas Fraser
Maurice DiGiuseppe

Contributing Writers
Al Hirsch
Julia Lee
Rachelle Redford

Director of Publishing
Kevin Martindale

General Manager, Mathematics, Science, and Technology
Lenore Brooks

Publisher, Science
John Yip-Chuck

Associate Publisher, Science
David Spiegel

Managing Editor, Development
Susan Ball

General Manager Marketing, Math, Science, and Technology
Paul Masson

Program Manager
Lee Ensor

Developmental Editors
Christina D'Alimonte
Julia Lee
Louise MacKenzie
Lina Mockus
Rachelle Redford

Contributing Editor
Caroline Winter

Assistant Editor
Sarah Tanzini

Editorial Assistant
Jessica Fung

Executive Director, Content and Media Production
Renate McCloy

Director, Content and Media Production
Linh Vu

Content Production Manager, Science
Sheila Stephenson

Copy Editor
Linda Szostak

Proofreader
Judy Sturrup
Linda Szostak

Indexer
Jin Tan

Production Manager
Helen Jager-Locsin

Senior Production Coordinator
Sharon Latta Paterson

Design Director
Ken Phipps

Interior Design
Media Services
Bill Smith Studios

Cover Design
Peggy Rhodes
Ken Phipps

Cover Image
Image Source Photography / Veer

Asset Coordinators
Renee Forde
Suzanne Peden

Illustrators
Greg Banning
Steve Corrigan
Deborah Crowle
Renee Forde
Steven Hall
Stephen Hutchings
Sam Laterza
Dave McKay
Brian McLachlan
Allan Moon
Sue Peden
David Schuppert
Bart Vallecoccia

Compositors
Zenaida Diores
Nelson Gonzalez
Courtney Hellam

Photo Shoot Coordinator
Lynn McLeod

Studio Photographer
Dave Starrett

Photo/Permissions Researcher
Mary Rose MacLachlan

Printer
Transcontinental Printing Inc.

On the cover: Even though you may not realize it, science and technology are a huge part of your everyday life. The food you eat is a pure substance or a mixture. You are a part of complex ecosystems. The things you do can affect even the smallest living things, like the beetle on the cover. What would your life be like without heat and our ability to control it? You interact with different structures everyday—your home is a structure, but so are tables and MP3 players. Throughout this text you will learn about these four topics—Pure Substances and Mixtures, Interactions in the Environment, Heat in the Environment, and Form and Function—and how they apply to your everyday life.

Reviewers

Accuracy Reviewers

James Conners, P.Eng.
Structural Manager, VE Collective Inc.

Roberta Fulthorpe, Ph.D.
Professor, Division of Physical and
    Environmental Sciences, University
    of Toronto

David Naylor, Ph.D., P.Eng.
Professor, Department of Mechanical
    and Industrial Engineering,
    Ryerson University

Heather A. Phillips, Ph.D.
Department of Chemistry, McGill
    University

Assessment Consultants

Damian Cooper
Nelson Education Author

Liza Karunakaran
Toronto Catholic DSB

Catholicity Reviewer

Ted Laxton
Wellington Catholic DSB

Combined Grades Consultant

Mary Rome
Toronto DSB

Environmental Education Consultant

Dr. Allan Foster
Working Group on Environmental
    Education, Ontario
Former Director of Education,
    Kortright Centre for Conservation

ESL/Culture Consultant

Vicki Lucier, B.A., B.Ed., Adv. Ed.
ESL Specialist Simcoe County DSB

Literacy Consultants

Jennette MacKenzie
Education Consultant

Nancy Reid
Ottawa-Carleton DSB

Thérèse McNamara
Simcoe County DSB

Numeracy Consultant

Melanie Quintana
Dufferin-Peel Catholic DSB

Safety Consultant

Jim Agban
Science Teachers' Association of
    Ontario (STAO)

STSE Consultant

Jasodhara Bhattacharya
Peel DSB

Technology/ICT Consultant

Luciano Lista
Toronto Catholic DSB

Advisory Panel and Teacher Reviewers

Diane Aitken
Hamilton-Wentworth DSB

Hanali Atkinson
Rainbow DSB

Rosanna Romano Baldassarra
York Region Catholic DSB

Ron Ballentine
Halton DSB

Sharon Butler
Simcoe County DSB

Mark Cassar
Dufferin-Peel Catholic DSB

Cathy Chaput
Wellington Catholic DSB

Charles J. Cohen
TanenbaumCHAT Kimel Campus

Paul Coulter
Algonquin and Lakeshore Catholic DSB

Richard DeMarchi
Dufferin-Peel Catholic DSB

Kristine Denomme
Sudbury Catholic DSB

Xavier Fazio
Brock University

Donna Forward
Ottawa Catholic SB

Sharon Gillies
London District Catholic SB

Cathy Hall
Ottawa-Carleton DSB

Robert P. Hartnett
Ottawa-Carleton DSB

Steve Hedderson
Limestone DSB

Patrick Hogan
Catholic DSB of Eastern Ontario

Kathy Holvey
Ottawa-Carleton DSB

Shawna Hopkins
DSB of Niagara

Chris Hristow
York Region DSB

Janet Jackowski
Peel DSB

Pamela Jacob
Limestone DSB

Richard LaChapelle
Toronto Catholic DSB

Heather MacLeod
Ottawa-Carleton DSB

Kerri Monaghan
Rainbow DSB

Scott Moore
Thames Valley DSB

Bob Moulder
Halton DSB

Pietrina Orlandi
York Region Catholic DSB

Leda Ostafichuk
Toronto Catholic DSB

RoseMarie Owen
Simcoe County DSB

Brad Parolin
Toronto DSB

Kathryn Perino
Halton Catholic DSB

Lisa Pilgrim
Halton DSB

Tara Potter
Ottawa Catholic SB

Rajeev Puri
Toronto DSB

Tiffany Rainville
Ottawa Catholic SB

Margaret Ramsay
Dufferin-Peel Catholic DSB

Nancy Reid
Ottawa-Carleton DSB

Mirella Sanwalka
York Region DSB

Carl Twiddy
Formerly York Region DSB

Students
Nelson Education Ltd. would like to
thank all the students who participated
in focus groups and field tests of this
resource.

Table of Contents

UNIT D: FORM AND FUNCTION

This textbook will be your guide to the exciting world of science and technology. On the following pages is a tour of important features that you will find inside. **GET READY** includes all the features of the introductory material that come before you begin the first chapter of each unit. Under **GET INTO IT** you will find all the features within the sections of each chapter. Finally, **WRAP IT UP** shows you the features in the Chapter Summary and Chapter Review, and the Unit Review and Unit Task. Try the **Go Discover** activity on page xix to become familiar with the features in your new textbook.

Get Ready

Unit Opener

Each of the four units has a letter and a title. There is also a large photo. Look at this photo and think about what you might be learning in the unit.

Discover Science and Technology

Read these stories at the start of every unit to discover an interesting topic related to the learning in the unit.

Unit Preview and Big Ideas

The Unit Preview introduces you to what you will learn in the unit. The Big Ideas provide a quick summary of the main topics covered.

Chapter Titles

The titles of the three chapters in the unit are listed here.

Linking to Literacy

Get the most out of your reading by using the strategies described in this feature.

Let's Get Started
This fun activity will help you to review what you already know (or do not know) about the topics in the unit.

Unit Task Preview
Find out about the task that you will complete at the end of each unit.

Unit Task Icon
Look for this icon throughout the unit. When you see this icon, you will know that you have just learned skills or knowledge that will help you to complete the Unit Task.

Assessment Box
This box lists some of the skills and knowledge you should be using to complete the Unit Task.

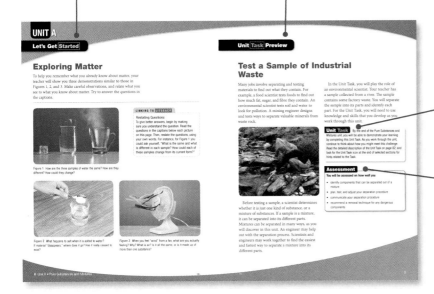

Chapter Opener
Each Chapter has a number, a title, and a Key Question.

Reading Science and Technology
Read a comic, story, photo essay, or article related to the topics covered in the chapter. Use the strategies in the Linking to Literacy box to interpret and understand your reading.

Looking Ahead
These statements outline the new concepts and skills you will learn by the end of the chapter.

Vocabulary
This is a list of the key terms you will learn in the chapter.

Get Into It

Vocabulary
You will come across many new and unfamiliar terms. These key terms are in bold print and highlighted. Definitions of key terms are in the margins and in the glossary at the back of the book.

Weblink Icon
This icon lets you know that you can find more information on the Nelson Science website.

Linking to Literacy
These boxes contain tips to help you understand and interpret the text, images, and other features in the textbook.

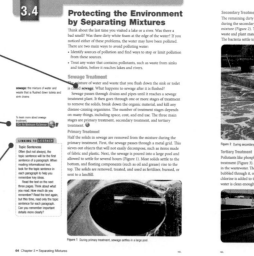

Equation Box
Important equations are highlighted in a red box.

Sample Problems
This feature shows you how to solve numerical problems using the GRASS method. Make sure to complete Practice problems to check your learning.

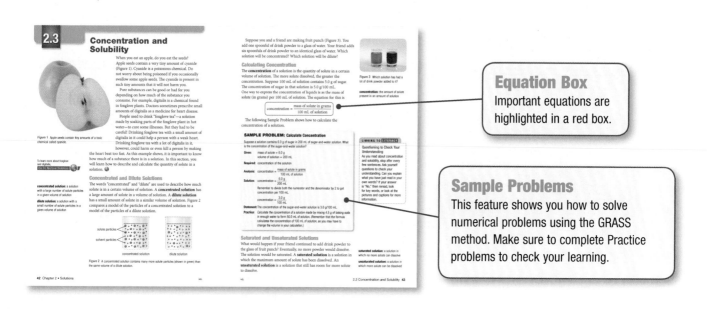

Try This Activity

These are quick, fun activities designed to help you understand concepts and improve your science skills.

Skills Handbook Icon

The Skills Handbook Icon appears in Sample Problems and other activities. It directs you to the section of the Skills Handbook that contains helpful information and tips.

Unit Task Icon

This icon lets you know that what you have learned in the section will be helpful to you as you complete the Unit Task.

Check Your Learning

This box appears at the end of each content section. Complete these questions to make sure you understand the concepts you have learned.

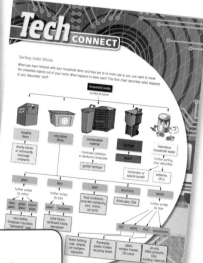

Magazine Features

Look for these special feature sections in each unit to learn about exciting developments in science, cool new technology, or how science relates to your everyday life.

NEL

Discover Your Textbook **xv**

Perform an Activity

These are active hands-on activities that allow you to explore the science and technology you are learning.

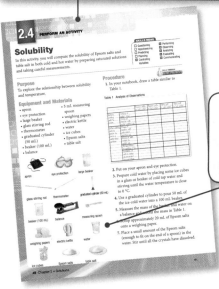

Explore an Issue Critically

These activities allow you to examine social and environmental issues related to the topics you are learning in the unit.

Equipment and Materials

These photos help you to identify all the items you will need to complete the activity or investigation.

Conduct an Investigation

These investigations are an opportunity to apply your scientific inquiry skills.

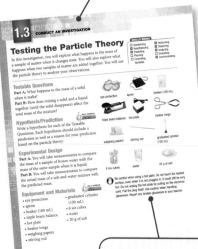

Solve a Technological Problem

These activities require you to use technological problem-solving skills to find a solution to a human need or want.

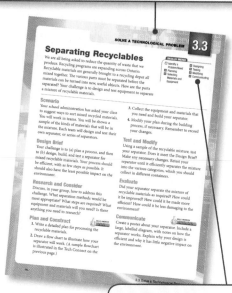

Safety Precautions

Look for these warnings about potential safety hazards in investigations and activities. They will be in red type with a STOP icon.

Skills Menu

The Skills Menu in each activity lists the skills that you will use to solve the problem or reach a conclusion.

Wrap It Up

Chapter Summary
This is a study guide that will help you to summarize and review your learning.

Looking Back
Review the Looking Ahead statements from the beginning of the chapter. The concepts you have covered are summarized here.

Big Ideas
The Big Ideas covered in the chapter are checked off.

Vocabulary
This feature lists all the key terms you have learned and the page number where the term is defined.

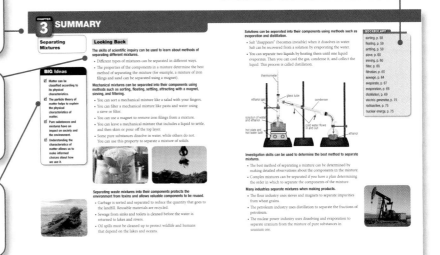

Achievement Icons
Review questions are tagged with icons that identify the types of knowledge and skills you must use to answer the question.

Self-Quiz Icon
There is an online study tool for each chapter on the Nelson Science website.

Chapter Review
Complete these questions to check your learning and apply your new knowledge.

Unit Task

The Unit Task requires you to apply the skills and knowledge you have learned in the unit to complete a challenge.

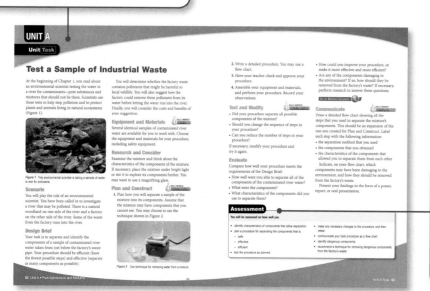

Assessment Box

This feature lists the criteria that your teacher will use to evaluate your Unit Task. Read these criteria carefully before completing the task.

Unit Review

Complete the Unit Review questions to check your learning of all the concepts and skills in the unit.

Make a Summary

This is a quick activity to help you summarize your learning of the entire unit.

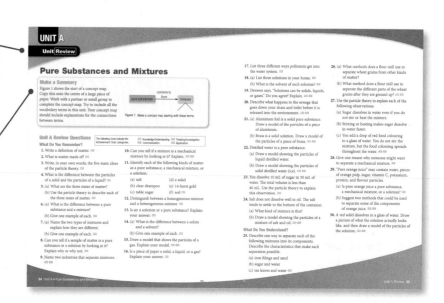

Glossary

This is a list of all vocabulary terms in your book in alphabetical order.

Pronunciation Key

Keys are provided for words that are difficult to read or pronounce.

Page References

The page on which a glossary term first appears is provided at the end of each definiton.

Glossary

A

abiotic [ay-bye-AW-tik] element any non-living component of the environment (p. 98)

active solar energy system a device that harnesses radiant energy from the Sun and converts it into a more useful form of energy (p. 244)

aesthetics [es-THET-iks] the concept of how visually attractive or beautiful something is (p. 325)

alternative energy source a source of energy that is not as common as conventional sources; alternative energy sources tend to be renewable and have few negative impacts on the environment (p. 242)

arch a curved structure used to span a space while supporting a load (p. 301)

bar graph [GRAFF] a type of graph used to make comparisons when one variable is in numbers and the other is not; useful for showing how data are distributed across categories (p. 400)

beam a horizontal structure designed to support a load (p. 295)

biodiversity [BYE-oh-dih-VUR-sih-tee] the variety of plant and animal life in an ecosystem (p. 152)

biofuel [BYE-oh-fyoo-uhl] a liquid fuel, such as ethanol, produced from plant or animal material (p. 248)

biotic [bye-AW-tik] element any living thing found in the environment (p. 97)

bubble [BUH-bul] map a graphic organizer that shows properties or characteristics (p. 409)

C

cantilever [KAN-tuh-LEE-ver] a beam supported at only one end (p. 297)

carnivore [KAHR-nuh-vawr] an organism that eats other animals only (p. 123)

cause-and-effect question a type of question that asks whether something is causing something else (p. 357)

cause variable see independent variable

centre of gravity the point around which an object's mass is equally balanced in all directions; the point where the mass seems to be concentrated (p. 290)

chemistry [KEH-muh-stree] the study of matter and its changes (p. 10)

circle [SER-kuhl] graph a type of graph that shows the whole of something divided into all of its parts; shows how different things compare in size or quantity; also known as pie graph (p. 401)

closed system a system in which the amount of matter remains constant over time (p. 135)

community a group of populations of different species in a given area (p. 97)

compare and contrast chart a graphic organizer that shows similarities and differences (p. 408)

comparison matrix [MAY-triks] a graphic organizer used to record and compare observations or results (p. 408)

competition [kawm-puh-TIH-shun] occurs when more than one organism tries to obtain the same basic resources in the same habitat (p. 107)

compression [kuhm-PREH-shun] an internal force that presses or squeezes the particles of an object together (p. 279)

concentrated solution [KAWN-suhn-TRAY-tid sub-LOO-shun] a solution with a large number of solute particles in a given volume of solution (p. 42)

concentration [kawn-suhn-TRAY-shun] the amount of solute present in an amount of solution (p. 43)

concept [KAWN-sept] map a graphic organizer that shows relationships between ideas; the ideas are connected by arrows and words or expressions that explain the connections (p. 406)

condensation [kawn-duhn-SAY-shun] the change in state of a substance from gas to liquid (p. 138)

conduction [kun-DUHK-shun] the transfer of thermal energy through a substance, or between substances in contact, by the collision of particles (p. 207)

consumer an organism that eats other living things for energy (p. 123)

controlled variable a condition that remains unchanged in an investigation; does not affect the outcome (p. 357)

convection [kun-VEK-shun] the transfer of thermal energy from one part of a fluid to another by a circulating current of faster-moving and slower-moving particles (p. 210)

conventional energy source a source of energy that has been widely used for many years (p. 234)

corrugation [kor-uh-GAY-shun] multiple folds in a material that provide additional strength (p. 296)

cycle [SYE-cuhl] a pattern in nature that repeats over time (p. 135)

cycle map a graphic organizer that shows cycles in nature (p. 405)

D

dead load a type of static load caused by the weight of the structure itself (p. 273)

decomposer [dee-kuhm-POH-zer] an organism that consumes and breaks down dead organisms or waste matter into simple substances (p. 124)

dependent variable the variable that is affected by a change in an investigation; the variable measured to see how it is affected by the independent variable; also known as effect variable (p. 357)

detritivore [DET-rih-vohr] an organism that feeds on large parts of decaying plant and animal matter and on waste material (p. 124)

dilute [dye-LOOT] solution a solution with a small number of solute particles in a given volume of solution (p. 42)

dissolve [dih-ZOHLV] to mix one type of matter into another type of matter to form a solution (p. 36)

dissolving mixing completely with a solvent to form a solution (p. 36)

distillation [dih-still-AY-shun] the process of separating liquids in a solution by heating the solution, trapping and cooling the gas, and collecting the resulting pure liquid (p. 69)

Skills Handbook

The Skills Handbook is your resource for useful science and technology skills and information. It is divided into numbered sections. Whenever you see a Skills Icon, you can use the numbers in the icon to find the relevant section of the Skills Handbook. For example, Section 3.J.2. Researching, is found in Section 3. Scientific Research, subsection 3.J. Exploring an Issue Critically.

SKILLS HANDBOOK

Contents

GO DISCOVER

Complete the following activity to check out the different features of your textbook.

1. What is the title of the second chapter in Unit C?
2. How many Try This activities are there in Unit B?
3. What are the five headings under which the Chapter Review questions are organized?
4. There are two Skills Handbook Icons in Section 1.6. On which pages will you find the sections of the Skills Handbook that these icons refer to?
5. Locate the glossary at the back of your textbook. What is the definition of "solubility"? In which section will you find this vocabulary term?
6. What skills will you use in Section 2.4?
7. Which Big Ideas are covered in Chapter 2?
8. What are the skills that your teacher will be assessing as you complete the Unit A Unit Task?

UNIT

A

PURE SUBSTANCES AND MIXTURES

Chocolate chip cookies are made from many different ingredients. Some of the ingredients, such as sugar and salt, look very similar. However, each ingredient has a different purpose in the recipe. Sugar makes the cookies sweet. Butter keeps the cookies soft after they are baked.

Each ingredient in the recipe looks like just one type of material. The sugar is made up of small, white crystals. The butter is a soft, yellow solid. When you mix the ingredients, however, you get chocolate chip cookie dough. You can see some of the different ingredients in the dough, like chocolate chips and small pieces of butter. Cookie dough is a particular kind of mixture.

In this unit, you will learn about different pure substances and mixtures in the world around you. You will investigate how to separate mixtures, and what the benefits of separation might be. You will consider the choices involved in making, using, and disposing of many pure substances and mixtures. Finally, you will apply what you learn to help you solve a pollution problem.

BIG Ideas

☐ Matter can be classified according to its physical characteristics.

☐ The particle theory of matter helps to explain the physical characteristics of matter.

☐ Pure substances and mixtures have an impact on society and the environment.

☐ Understanding the characteristics of matter allows us to make informed choices about how we use it.

CHAPTER 1 Classifying Matter

CHAPTER 2 Solutions

CHAPTER 3 Separating Mixtures

PROTECTING A RIVER

Raven and Matt like to spend time with their friends in the woodland not far from their school. They enjoy climbing the trees, lounging in the grass, watching the insects, and listening to the birds. Across the river, at the bottom of the woodland, there are factories.

One day, Raven noticed that the river looked different: it was soapy, with white bubbles floating on it. Matt found a dead fish lying on the shore.

Raven and Matt were worried. Unsure what to do, they talked to their teacher at school. The teacher had a suggestion. "We can call the Ministry of the Environment. They will send an environmental scientist to test the river water for pollution. If the river is polluted, they may be able to find out where the problem is, and figure out how to fix it."

LINKING TO LITERACY

Reading Visual Information: Illustration
Examine the illustration on this page. Where are the scientist and students located? Refer to the map on the previous page to help you determine their location. Which way are they facing? What are they standing or sitting next to?

A couple of days later, the environmental scientist came to the school and asked Raven, Matt, and their teacher to come with her to the river. They pointed out the dead fish and the pipes pouring waste water from the factories into the river. "Is the waste water killing the fish?" Matt asked.

"Could be," replied the scientist. "Some chemicals can harm the environment. We need to make sure that the factories remove any harmful material from their wastewater before they let it flow into the river."

The scientist collected samples of water from different parts of the river, and took samples of the waste coming out of each factory pipe.

"I'll take these samples to the lab to figure out what's in each one," she explained. "We will find out if any of them contain harmful substances."

A few weeks later, the environmental scientist came back to update Matt and Raven on what had happened. "One of the factories was letting toxic substances flow out in their waste water. We found out which factory it was and fined them. They have figured out a way to remove those substances from their waste mixture, so that they are not polluting anymore. The river is already starting to recover. I'm going to check on it for the next few months to make sure that it stays clean. Thanks for letting us know about the problem. If we work together, we can help protect the environment from pollution."

Exploring Matter

To help you remember what you already know about matter, your teacher will show you three demonstrations similar to those in Figures 1, 2, and 3. Make careful observations, and relate what you see to what you know about matter. Try to answer the questions in the captions.

Figure 1 How are the three samples of water the same? How are they different? How could they change?

LINKING TO LITERACY

Restating Questions
To give better answers, begin by making sure you understand the question. Read the questions in the captions below each picture on this page. Then, restate the questions, using your own words. For instance, for Figure 1 you could ask yourself, "What is the same and what is different in each sample? How could each of these samples change from its current form?"

Figure 2 What happens to salt when it is added to water? If material "disappears," where does it go? Has it really ceased to exist?

Figure 3 When you feel "wind" from a fan, what are you actually feeling? Why? What is air? Is it all the same, or is it made up of more than one substance?

Test a Sample of Industrial Waste

Many jobs involve separating and testing materials to find out what they contain. For example, a food scientist tests foods to find out how much fat, sugar, and fibre they contain. An environmental scientist tests soil and water to look for pollution. A mining engineer designs and tests ways to separate valuable minerals from waste rock.

Before testing a sample, a scientist determines whether it is just one kind of substance, or a mixture of substances. If a sample is a mixture, it can be separated into its different parts. Mixtures can be separated in many ways, as you will discover in this unit. An engineer may help out with the separation process. Scientists and engineers may work together to find the easiest and fastest way to separate a mixture into its different parts.

In the Unit Task, you will play the role of an environmental scientist. Your teacher has a sample collected from a river. The sample contains some factory waste. You will separate the sample into its parts and identify each part. For the Unit Task, you will need to use knowledge and skills that you develop as you work through this unit.

Unit Task By the end of the Pure Substances and Mixtures unit, you will be able to demonstrate your learning by completing this Unit Task. As you work through the unit, continue to think about how you might meet this challenge. Read the detailed description of the Unit Task on page 82, and look for the Unit Task icon at the end of selected sections for hints related to the Task.

Assessment

You will be assessed on how well you

- identify components that can be separated out of a mixture
- plan, test, and adjust your separation procedure
- communicate your separation procedure
- recommend a removal technique for any dangerous components

1 Classifying Matter

KEY QUESTION: What kinds of matter are around us?

Looking Ahead

- Human production, use, and disposal of pure substances and mixtures have both benefits and costs.

- The particle theory explains the behaviour of particles of matter.

- The skills of analysis can be used to apply the particle theory to changes in matter.

- A pure substance contains only one kind of particle, but a mixture contains more than one kind of particle.

- The skills of scientific inquiry can be used to classify matter as a pure substance or a mixture.

- A mechanical mixture contains different components that you can see.

- A solution is a mixture that looks like a pure substance.

VOCABULARY

matter	gas
chemistry	pure substance
particle theory of matter	mixture
	mechanical mixture
solid	heterogeneous mixture
volume	solution
liquid	homogeneous mixture

Take Our Kids to Work Day

Today was Take Our Kids to Work Day. Instead of going to school, Jiao was going to work with her mom.

Jiao's mom had already told Jiao something about her job. "I work in a lab where we design artificial flavours. Remember the strawberry yogurt you had for breakfast? It had real strawberries in it, but it also had artificial strawberry flavour. That flavour was designed by scientists in my lab!"

"How did they do it?" Jiao had wanted to know.

"Strawberries are a mixture of many different substances," said her mom. "The scientists analyzed real strawberries to see which chemicals give the strawberry its smell and taste. Then, they figured out how to make similar chemicals in the lab. The right mixture of chemicals tastes and smells like real strawberries."

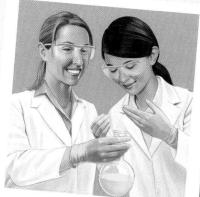

When they arrived, Jiao and her mom went into a special room where they both tied their hair back. They put on white lab coats, eye protection, and gloves. Then, they went into the lab.

The lab smelled delicious! Jiao could smell bananas and cherries, and a yummy caramel smell that made her mouth water.

Jiao noticed rows of bottles sitting on shelves all around the room. "What's in all those bottles?" she asked.

"The small bottles hold all the flavours we have designed. It's not safe to taste things in the lab, but you can smell them," said her mom.

Jiao's mom took the lids off two small bottles. Jiao sniffed the first one carefully, wafting the air as her mom had shown her. It smelled like apples. The second smelled like pineapple. "Wow!" said Jiao. "I like your job. Maybe I'll design flavours, too, when I grow up."

LINKING TO LITERACY

Gaining Meaning from Context
You can learn about new or difficult words from the story you are reading without using a dictionary. See if you can figure out what a new word means by using information from the sentence or paragraph.

1 In this story, Jiao learns about substances and chemicals. Read the information in the paragraph that begins with, "Strawberries are a mixture…" Can you tell what the word "substances" means? What might be a good synonym for this word?

2 What other new words did you learn from this story? Work with a partner to compare words you learned about by using information from the text.

What Is Matter?

You have probably seen, touched, and tasted hundreds of different things in your life. You have touched wood, steel, and ice. You use shampoo, and you drink milk. You breathe air. Have you ever wondered what all these things are made of?

The examples listed above are all made of matter. In fact, all of the objects around you are made of matter (Figure 1). **Matter** is anything that has mass and takes up space. Remember the chocolate chip cookies at the beginning of the unit? All of the ingredients are examples of matter. A mixing spoon is an example of matter. Your entire body is made of matter!

matter: anything that takes up space and has mass

LINKING TO LITERACY

Before Reading: Skimming and Scanning
To improve your understanding of informational text, think of it as a puzzle in which you need to put all of the pieces together. Start by looking at the title. Then, skim and scan the page for more information. Are there captions you can read? Are there subtitles or headings? What about pictures? Are there words that are highlighted or bolded, and that jump out at you from the page? Take a moment to connect all of your thoughts. What have you learned about this text even before beginning to read it?

Figure 1 What examples of matter can you see?

The Science of Matter

The study of matter and its changes is called **chemistry**. Scientists who work in chemistry are called chemists. The photograph at the beginning of this chapter shows chemists working in a lab. Knowledge of chemistry is useful in many different careers. People who work in medicine, cooking, art, photography, and solving crimes all use chemistry in some way.

chemistry: the study of matter and its changes

Some chemists use their knowledge about matter to develop new kinds of matter. Often, scientists study matter that is found in nature, and then imitate it. These human-made chemicals are sometimes better than chemicals found in nature. For example, natural almond extract comes from wild almonds. It contains tiny amounts of a dangerous poison called cyanide. Human-made almond extract is a mixture of substances made in a chemistry lab (Figure 2). It is similar to the natural flavour, but it does not contain poisonous cyanide. Human-made chemicals are also sometimes cheaper to obtain than chemicals found in nature.

Human-made chemicals, however, are not always better than natural ones. Lemonade made with real lemons includes lots of vitamin C. Lemonade made with artificial flavour may taste almost the same, but will probably not have the same vitamin content.

Figure 2 Artificial almond extract is a kind of matter that chemists copied from nature.

To learn more about artificial flavours,
Go to Nelson Science

The Makeup of Matter

What makes up matter? To help us think about matter, we will look at something made of just one type of matter: aluminum foil (Figure 3). Imagine using stronger and stronger microscopes to examine the foil. What would you see?

With the first microscope, you would see the smooth, shiny surface of the foil, perhaps with some little scratches or marks (Figure 4). With a stronger microscope, the marks would be more visible, but you could still recognize the material as aluminum foil.

What if you used the most powerful kind of microscope available—a scanning probe microscope? You might be surprised at what you would see. Figure 5 shows what a piece of aluminum foil looks like through a scanning probe microscope. The surface is not smooth or silver-coloured. Instead, it is made of many tiny bumps. These bumps show the presence of aluminum particles.

Figure 3 Aluminum foil is made of just one kind of matter: aluminum.

Figure 4 If you look at aluminum foil through a microscope, it still looks like a smooth, silver-coloured metal.

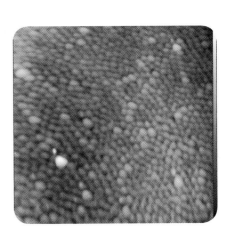

Figure 5 A scanning probe microscope allows you to see the aluminum particles in the foil.

A small piece of aluminum foil contains billions of tiny aluminum particles. All matter is made of particles that are too small to be seen, except through powerful microscopes. These particles of matter are tinier than the smallest thing you can imagine. Imagine a piece of aluminum foil that is 1 cm by 1 cm. If each particle in that piece of foil were expanded to the size of an egg, the eggs would cover the entire surface of Earth to a depth of several metres.

The Particle Theory of Matter

All matter is made of tiny particles. Different kinds of matter are made of different kinds of particles. The particles themselves do not look like the kind of matter they make up. For example, a single particle of aluminum does not look the same as a piece of aluminum. A single particle of water does not look or behave like the water in a lake. Only when large numbers of particles are together do aluminum particles behave like aluminum, or water particles behave like water.

The **particle theory of matter** (also known as "particle theory") helps to explain what scientists have learned about these tiny particles of matter. The main ideas of the particle theory are listed in Table 1.

particle theory of matter:
an explanation of what matter is made of and how it behaves; the particle theory states that all matter is made up of tiny particles that are always moving, that attract each other, and that have space between them

Table 1 The Particle Theory

Main idea	Illustration
1. All matter is made up of tiny particles.	
2. Particles have empty spaces between them.	
3. Even though you cannot see them, particles are moving randomly all the time.	
4. Particles move faster and spread farther apart when they are heated.	
5. Particles attract each other, so they tend to stay together rather than fly apart.	

Using the Particle Theory

You can use the particle theory to explain many of the things you observe in everyday life. The following sample problem shows how to use the particle theory to explain an observation.

SAMPLE PROBLEM: Explain an Observation Using the Particle Theory

If you placed a few drops of food colouring in a container of water without stirring, what do you think you would see (Figure 6)?

Solution: Particles of food colouring and particles of water are moving and bumping into each other all the time. This causes the food colouring particles and the water particles to mix together, even without stirring.

Figure 6

Look at the paper in this textbook. Is it hard to believe that the paper is made of billions of invisible particles? If you answered yes, you are not alone. For thousands of years, people did not know that matter is made of particles. Today, we accept the particle theory because it helps scientists to explain many puzzling observations.

TRY THIS: Explain Observations Using the Particle Theory

SKILLS HANDBOOK 2.B.5., 2.B.7.

SKILLS MENU: performing, observing, analyzing, communicating

In this activity, you will make observations and use the particle theory to explain your observations. You may want to review the main ideas of the particle theory in Table 1.

Equipment and Materials: tablespoon; ceramic coffee mug; timing device; sugar; room-temperature water; cold water; ice; hot water

 Never taste anything in the science lab. Use care when working with hot water.

1. Stir a level spoonful of sugar into a mug of water at room temperature. At the same time, start timing. Keep stirring until you can no longer see the crystals of sugar. Measure the time it takes for the sugar to completely disappear. Record your observations.

2. Empty the sugar water into the sink and rinse the mug.

3. Repeat steps 1 and 2 using cold water with a couple of ice cubes in it.

4. Repeat steps 1 and 2 using hot water.

A. What did you observe in all three mugs of water?

B. Use the particle theory to explain your observations.

C. In which mug of water did the sugar crystals disappear most quickly?

D. Use the particle theory to explain your observations in part C.

✔ CHECK YOUR LEARNING

1. **(a)** In this section, you learned that matter is made of very tiny particles. Do you find this idea easy or difficult to understand? Explain why.
   (b) What can you do to help you understand this idea better?

2. **(a)** What is matter?
   (b) Give three examples of things that are made of matter.

3. In point form, list the five main ideas of the particle theory. You may use diagrams.

More About Matter

Have you ever seen a snowflake under a microscope? Look at the beautiful snowflake in Figure 1. Can you tell what kind of matter it is made of? If not, how could you find out?

Figure 1 If you held this snowflake in your hand, it would melt into a drop of water. The snowflake is made of the same kind of matter as a drop of water.

Three States of Matter

Snowflakes are a form of solid water. Water particles are always water particles, whether water is in solid (ice), liquid (water), or gas (water vapour) form. All forms of matter, including water, can exist in three different states: solid, liquid, and gas. The particles are exactly the same in each state. Individual particles do not freeze or melt. Instead, their movement changes. Also, the arrangement of particles is different in each state. Matter also behaves differently in each state.

Solids

solid: a state of matter with a definite volume and a definite shape

volume: a measure of the quantity of space occupied by an object

A **solid** has a definite shape and a definite volume. **Volume** is the quantity of space something occupies. For example, a coin is made of metal. The metal is in the solid state. Therefore, the coin's shape and volume remain constant (if the coin's temperature does not change).

Liquids

liquid: a state of matter with a definite volume, but no definite shape; a liquid takes the shape of its container

A **liquid** has a definite volume, but does not have a definite shape. Instead, a liquid takes the shape of its container. Milk is an example of a liquid. If you have 250 mL of milk in a carton, the milk's volume will be 250 mL. The volume does not change if you pour the milk into a cylindrical glass, but the shape will change.

Gases

A **gas** does not have a definite volume or a definite shape. Instead, a gas takes the shape and volume of its container. When a deflated basketball is filled with air, the air particles occupy a spherical space and a volume equal to the volume of the inflated ball.

gas: a state of matter that does not have a definite volume or a definite shape; a gas takes the shape and volume of its container

Particles of Solids, Liquids, and Gases

The particles of a sample of matter always stay the same, whether the matter is solid, liquid, or gas. The difference is in the movement and arrangement of the particles. Particles move differently in solids, liquids, and gases.

The particles of a solid are like students sitting in a movie theatre watching a movie (Figure 2). The students have a bit of distance between them, they can fidget in their seats, but they cannot move around very much.

The particles of a liquid are like students moving through a crowded shopping mall (Figure 3). The students can walk around, but they are still close together.

The particles of a gas are like students running out of the school building on the last day of school (Figure 4). The students can move quickly, and in all different directions.

LINKING TO LITERACY

Synthesizing Information
When you read text that presents new information, you compare it to what you have already read or already know. Use the text on this page, the diagrams, and what you already know to help you understand particles in solids, liquids, and gases.

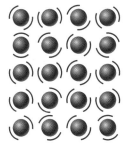

particles of a solid

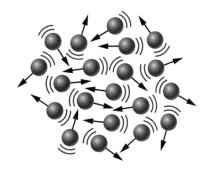

particles of a liquid

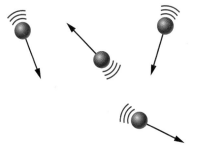

particles of a gas

Figure 2 The particles of a solid are closely packed together. The particles stay in the same positions, but they vibrate all the time.

Figure 3 The particles of a liquid are still close together, but they can move around each other in all directions.

Figure 4 The particles of a gas are very far apart. They have lots of energy and move very fast in all directions. The particles can even leave their container if it is not sealed.

The particles are also arranged differently in each state of matter. Particles are closer together in solids and liquids than in gases. Because of this closeness, the forces of attraction among the particles hold the particles together. This explains why the volume of a solid or a liquid does not change much. The particles of gases are farther apart, so the forces of attraction cannot hold the particles together in a fixed volume. 🌐

To learn more about the particle theory and the states of matter,

Go to Nelson Science 🌐

Changes in State

Matter can change from one state to another. A change in state can happen when a sample of matter is heated or cooled.

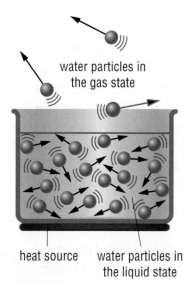

water particles in the gas state

heat source   water particles in the liquid state

Figure 5 Water changing state from liquid to gas

When ice is heated, the water particles move faster, so the water changes from solid to liquid. More heating makes the particles move even faster and farther apart, so the liquid water changes to a gas. The particles of a gas are much farther apart than the particles of a solid or a liquid.

If the gas is cooled, the attractive forces pull the particles closer together, and the gas changes back into a liquid. What would happen if you cooled the liquid water even more by placing it in a freezer? The particles would slow down: the water would change from a liquid to a solid. When a sample of matter changes state, the particles themselves remain the same. The number of particles also remains the same. It is the arrangement and speed of the particles that changes. Figure 5 shows water changing state from liquid to gas. As liquid water is heated, water particles start to move faster. They leave from the surface moving very quickly. (This is shown by longer arrows.) As more and more particles leave from the surface, the liquid water becomes water vapour.

CHECK YOUR LEARNING

1. In this section, you learned that particles are moving all the time, even in the solid state. Do you find this easy or difficult to believe? Discuss this with a classmate or your teacher, and explain why or why not.

2. What are the three states of matter?

3. In your own words, use the particle theory to explain why water changes from a solid (ice) to a liquid (water) when it is heated.

4. Identify the state of each of the following materials:
   (a) a rock
   (b) grape juice
   (c) air

5. Draw a diagram that shows particles of a solid, a liquid, and a gas. Your labels should describe the motion of the particles in each state and the attraction among the particles.

AWESOME SCIENCE

Other States of Matter

You have just learned about solids, liquids, and gases. Scientists have found other states of matter that have unique properties.

A gas that is electrically charged is called plasma. Plasma is sometimes considered to be a fourth state of matter. It is found mainly in stars and nebulas in outer space.

Plasma (which is different from blood plasma) has fascinated people for thousands of years. The northern lights are an example of plasma in nature (Figure 1). Traditionally, Inuit have believed that the northern lights were the torches of spirits guiding souls to a land of happiness and plenty.

Figure 1 The northern lights (aurora borealis)

Today, you can find plasma in many manufactured items, such as fluorescent lights, neon signs (Figure 2), and plasma television screens.

Figure 2 Neon lights contain plasma.

According to the particle theory, particles move more slowly when they are cooled. Experiments have shown that this is true. Scientists have cooled particles until they almost stopped moving completely. If you drew a graph showing the movement of particles against temperature, the graph would indicate that the particles would stop moving at approximately −273 °C. This temperature is called absolute zero. Absolute zero is the coldest possible temperature that could ever exist. Scientists believe that even the coldest places in our universe are warmer than absolute zero.

In 1924, Albert Einstein predicted that if you cooled particles down to absolute zero, a new state of matter would form. In 1995, scientists Eric Cornell and Carl Wieman finally managed to cool down a sample of particles to a temperature very close to absolute zero. Einstein was right: the particles formed a new state of matter!

This exciting new state of matter is called a Bose–Einstein condensate. Scientists think that this discovery may lead to very tiny computer chips in the near future.

To read more about these strange states of matter,
Go to Nelson Science

Testing the Particle Theory

In this investigation, you will explore what happens to the mass of a sample of matter when it changes state. You will also explore what happens when two samples of matter are added together. You will use the particle theory to analyze your observations.

Testable Questions

Part A: What happens to the mass of a solid when it melts?

Part B: How does mixing a solid and a liquid together (until the solid disappears) affect the total mass of the mixture?

Hypothesis/Prediction

SKILLS HANDBOOK 2.B.3.

Write a hypothesis for each of the Testable Questions. Each hypothesis should include a prediction as well as a reason for your prediction based on the particle theory.

Experimental Design

Part A: You will take measurements to compare the mass of a sample of frozen water with the mass of the same sample when it is liquid.

Part B: You will take measurements to compare the actual mass of a salt-and-water mixture with the predicted mass.

Equipment and Materials

SKILLS HANDBOOK 5.B.

- eye protection
- apron
- beaker (100 mL)
- triple beam balance
- hot plate
- beaker tongs
- weighing papers
- stirring rod
- graduated cylinder (100 mL)
- 6 ice cubes
- water
- 20 g of salt

 eye protection
 apron
beaker (100 mL)

 triple beam balance
 hot plate
 beaker tongs

 weighing papers
 stirring rod
 graduated cylinder (100 mL)

 6 ice cubes
 water
 20 g of salt

 Be careful when using a hot plate. Do not touch the heated surface, even when it is not plugged in; it could still be very hot. Do not unplug the hot plate by pulling on the electrical cord. Pull the plug itself. Use caution when handling glassware. Report any broken glassware to your teacher.

Procedure

SKILLS HANDBOOK
6.A.3., 6.D.1.

Part A: Melting Ice

1. Read the complete investigation and construct a suitable table called Table 1 for recording your observations. Ask your teacher to approve your table before you continue.

2. Put on your eye protection and apron. Measure and record the mass of an empty, dry beaker.

3. Add one piece of ice to the beaker. Measure and record the total mass.

4. Place the beaker on the hot plate, and then turn the heat to low. Allow the ice to melt completely. Do not let the water boil. Remove the beaker from the hot plate using beaker tongs. (It could still be hot.) Measure and record the total mass of the beaker and melted ice.

5. Pour the water into the sink and dry the beaker completely.

6. Repeat step 4 using the same beaker. This time, use five pieces of ice all at once, instead of one piece. Again, record your observations.

Part B: Salt in Water

7. Read the rest of the investigation and construct a suitable table called Table 2 for recording your observations. Ask your teacher to approve your table before you continue.

8. Measure and record the mass of an empty, dry beaker.

9. Measure 50 mL of water into a graduated cylinder, and then pour the water into the beaker. Measure and record the total mass.

10. Measure and record the mass of a weighing paper. Add 5 g of salt to the weighing paper. Add the salt to the water and stir. Measure and record the total mass of the beaker, water, and salt.

11. Pour the salt water into the sink. Rinse and dry the beaker.

12. Repeat steps 8 to 11, but this time using 100 mL of water and 10 g of salt.

Analyze and Evaluate

SKILLS HANDBOOK
2.B.7., 2.B.8.

(a) Using your measurements in steps 2 and 3, calculate the mass of the single piece of ice. Record this value in Table 1.

(b) Using your measurement in step 4, calculate the mass of the melted ice. Record this value in Table 1.

(c) Repeat (a) and (b) for the five pieces of ice.

(d) Using your measurements in steps 8 and 9, calculate the mass of 50 mL of water. Record this value in Table 2.

(e) Calculate the total mass of the beaker, the water, and the salt before mixing. Record this value in Table 2.

(f) Using your measurements in step 10, calculate the mass of the beaker, the water, and the salt after mixing. Record this value in Table 2.

(g) Repeat (d), (e), and (f) for 100 mL of water and 10 g of salt.

(h) Use your results to answer the Testable Questions. Compare your answers to your Hypothesis/Prediction. Account for any differences.

(i) Why do you think you repeated each experiment with different masses?

Apply and Extend

(j) If you froze the water in Part A and then determined its mass again, what would you observe?

(k) If you left the mixed liquid in Part B in a warm place for a long time and then measured the mass, what would you observe?

Pure Substances and Mixtures

Figure 1 Does "100 % pure apple juice" contain only one type of particle?

Figure 2 Aluminum foil, table sugar, and distilled water are pure substances and are each made of one kind of particle.

pure substance: matter that contains only one kind of particle

mixture: matter that contains two or more pure substances mixed together

The apple juice in Figure 1 is labelled as 100 % apple juice. Does this mean that the juice is made of only one kind of matter? Does it have only one kind of particle in it?

Apple juice is actually a mixture of water particles, sugar particles, flavour particles, and vitamin particles. Apple juice may look like one kind of matter, but it contains many kinds of particles all mixed together.

Pure Substances

Most examples of matter in everyday life contain more than one kind of particle. Some types of matter, however, do contain only one kind of particle (Figure 2). A piece of aluminum foil contains only one kind of particle. Each aluminum particle is the same as every other aluminum particle. White table sugar is made of only sugar particles.

Aluminum and table sugar are both examples of pure substances. A **pure substance** is a type of matter that contains only one kind of particle (Figure 3(a)). Other examples of pure substances include distilled water and salt. Uranium, used in nuclear power stations to produce electricity, is another pure substance.

Water from your tap is not a pure substance. It contains water particles and a number of other kinds of particles, too. Distilled water, however, has had all of the "non-water" particles removed: it is pure water.

Mixtures

When you stir a spoonful of sugar into a glass of distilled water, the sugar disappears and the water tastes sweet. Now there are two kinds of particle in the glass. The sweetened water is not a pure substance anymore. It is a mixture containing sugar particles and water particles.

A **mixture** is a type of matter that contains more than one kind of particle. A mixture is made of two or more pure substances mixed together (Figure 3(b)).

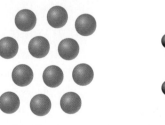

(a) pure substance   pure substance   **(b)**   mixture

Figure 3 (a) Pure substances contain identical particles. (b) Mixtures contain more than one kind of particle.

SKILLS MENU: performing, observing, analyzing

You can test the ink in a black marker to determine if it is a pure substance.

Equipment and Materials: water-soluble black marker; colourless drinking glass or beaker; 10 cm strip of filter paper; tap water

1. Use the marker to draw a horizontal black line about 3 cm from the bottom of the strip of filter paper.

2. Pour water into the glass to a depth of about 1 cm.

3. Carefully stand the strip of filter paper in the glass of water. The black line should be close to the water, but not touching it (Figure 4).

A. What happens to the black line on the paper after 1 min? After 5 min?

B. Is the ink in a black marker a pure substance or a mixture? What evidence supports this?

marker
clear glass
filter paper
black marker line
1 cm water

Figure 4 Use the clip on the marker lid to hold the paper away from the side of the glass.

Mixtures can be solids, liquids, or gases, or even combinations of these. Steel, batteries, and cookies are all mixtures in the solid state. Antifreeze and milk are mixtures in the liquid state. The air you breathe is a mixture of gases.

Many mixtures that we use, such as the mixtures inside compact fluorescent light bulbs (CFLs) and batteries, include some pure substances that can be harmful if they escape into the environment. CFLs contain mercury. Some batteries contain cadmium while others contain lead. Mercury, cadmium, and lead are all pure substances that are toxic to both animals and people. We should not dispose of CFLs and batteries in the regular garbage. We should carefully collect them and deposit them at special recycling stations, where their components can be separated out and recycled. 🌐

LINKING TO LITERACY

After Reading: Summarizing
After you finish reading the section "Pure Substances and Mixtures," work with a partner to summarize all of the key ideas. The text subheadings will help to guide your thinking. Develop one sentence for each of the subheadings in the text.

To learn more about disposing of dangerous substances,
Go to Nelson Science

Unit Task Think about the Unit Task. How will this information about pure substances and mixtures be useful as you work on the task?

✔ **CHECK YOUR LEARNING**

1. (a) What is a pure substance? Give three examples.
   (b) What is a mixture? Give three examples.

2. In your notebook, draw a sample of matter that is a pure substance. Make sure you show the types of particles present in the pure substance. Explain why your drawing shows a pure substance and not a mixture.

3. Is milk a pure substance or a mixture? Explain how you know.

4. (a) Why should you not place used batteries in the regular garbage?
   (b) How should you dispose of batteries?

Identifying and Classifying Matter

All samples of matter are either pure substances or mixtures. Sometimes, two pure substances mix so completely that the resulting mixture looks like a pure substance. In this activity, your teacher will give you six samples of matter labelled A, B, C, D, E, and F. You will use information about the different types of matter, and design your own tests to identify the six samples. Some of your tests will involve making mixtures. Using the equipment and materials listed, you will perform your tests. When you have tested and identified each sample, you will examine the mixture(s) that you made. You may discover that there are different types of mixtures.

Purpose

To plan and perform tests to identify six unknown samples of matter.

Equipment and Materials

SKILLS HANDBOOK
5.B.

- eye protection
- apron
- gloves
- 6 test tubes with stoppers
- test-tube rack
- spoon
- beaker (250 mL)
- magnifying glass
- 6 samples of matter (labelled A, B, C, D, E, and F)
- water

eye protection

apron

gloves

6 test tubes with stoppers

test-tube rack

spoon

beaker (250 mL)

magnifying glass

6 samples of matter

water

 Never taste anything in the science lab. Some of the samples could be toxic. Handle glassware carefully. Report any broken or chipped glassware to your teacher. Use rubbing alcohol very carefully.

Procedure

Part A: Identify the Samples

1. Samples A to F are the six substances listed in Table 1. You will use the information in Table 1 to identify the six unknown samples. Design at least one test for each sample. (Hint: Your tests might involve mixing pairs of the samples. See Figure 1. Do not mix more than two samples together.) Write the steps of your procedure. Include any safety precautions you will need to take. Create a table in which to record your observations.

Table 1

Sample of matter	Properties
distilled water	• colourless liquid • mixes completely with sugar
rubbing alcohol	• colourless liquid • does not mix completely with sugar
glycerol	• thick, colourless liquid • mixes completely with water
castor oil	• thick, pale yellow liquid • does not mix completely with water
sugar	• white powder • mixes completely with water
flour	• white powder • does not mix completely with water

Figure 1 To mix samples in a test tube, fill the tube no more than halfway. Put a stopper in the test tube, and put your thumb firmly over the stopper. Holding the test tube away from you, gently turn it upside down two or three times. Wear gloves when mixing samples this way.

2. When your teacher has approved your procedure, perform the tests. Record your observations as you go along.

3. Keep the mixtures in the test tubes. You will need them for the next part of the activity.

Part B: Examine the Mixtures

4. Use a magnifying glass to examine each mixture that you made in Part A. Record your observations.

Analyze and Evaluate

SKILLS HANDBOOK
2.B.7.

(a) Identify each sample of matter in Part A.

(b) Was any sample of matter particularly easy to identify? Why?

(c) Was any sample of matter particularly difficult to identify? Why?

(d) Using your observations in Part B, classify the mixtures into groups.

(e) How did you classify the mixtures into groups?

(f) Not all of the samples were pure substances. Explain how you can tell which ones were mixtures.

(g) Can you always tell the difference between a pure substance and a mixture? Explain why or why not.

Apply and Extend

SKILLS HANDBOOK
2.B.

(h) Imagine that you are a scientist in a forensics lab. You have a beaker with a clear, colourless liquid. Suggest a test that might help to identify the liquid. Remember: You should *never* taste anything in a lab.

(i) Make a list of what you have learned in this chapter about safety in the science lab. Include a description of the following:

• wearing protective clothing
• caution around glassware
• checking labels for warning symbols

Mechanical Mixtures and Solutions

Mixtures are an important part of food preparation. Figure 1 shows a mixture of eggs, vegetables, and cheese cooking on a stove to make an omelette. Figure 2 shows a glass of grape juice. How are these mixtures the same? How are they different?

Figure 1 This omelette is a mixture of eggs, vegetables, and cheese. You can see the different parts of this mixture.

Figure 2 Grape juice is a mixture of water, sugar, and flavour particles. This mixture looks like just one kind of matter.

Scientists classify mixtures into two main groups: mechanical mixtures and solutions. Both are mixtures because both are made up of two or more different kinds of particles.

Mechanical Mixtures

Sometimes it is easy to tell whether something is a mixture, but at other times it is more difficult. You can tell that the soil in Figure 3 is a mixture because you can see the different parts. If you can see different kinds of matter in a mixture, it is called a **mechanical mixture**. Mechanical mixtures are also called **heterogeneous mixtures**.

mechanical mixture or **heterogeneous mixture:** a mixture with different parts that you can see

LINKING TO LITERACY

During Reading: Monitoring Comprehension
As you read through this page, stop from time to time to think about what you are reading. Can you put the pieces of information together to make sense? Good readers stop to think when something does not make sense. They look for key words to help their understanding. Often they reread text and locate information from titles, pictures, captions, and tables.

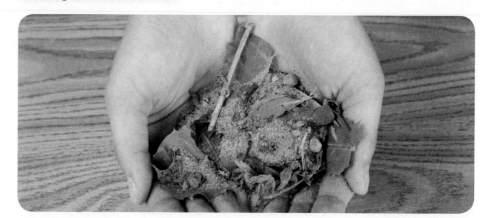

Figure 3 You can see sand, little stones, twigs, and bits of leaves mixed together in this mechanical mixture.

You see and use mechanical mixtures almost every day. To find a mechanical mixture, you could look inside your closet at home or inside your pencil case at school. Maybe you ate a mechanical mixture for breakfast, such as cereal and milk, or a raisin bran muffin. Figure 4 shows three more examples of mechanical mixtures.

Figure 4 How can you tell that each example is a mechanical mixture?

Solutions

Some mixtures do not look like mechanical mixtures. They look like pure substances. Like the grape juice in Figure 2, clear shampoo looks like only one kind of matter. However, both grape juice and clear shampoo are mixtures. Grape juice contains water particles, sugar particles, and flavour particles. Shampoo contains water particles, detergent particles, colour particles, and scent particles.

Mixtures that look as though they are pure substances are called solutions. A **solution** contains more than one kind of particle, but it looks like a pure substance. Solutions are sometimes called **homogeneous mixtures**. Both steel and seawater are solutions. Think back to the black marker ink that you tested in Section 1.4. What evidence do you have that marker ink is a solution, rather than a pure substance or a mechanical mixture?

Clear apple juice is a solution. The air you breathe is also a solution. More examples of solutions are shown in Figure 5. Try to think of three solutions that you have seen today.

solution or **homogeneous mixture:** a mixture that looks like a single pure substance; a uniform mixture of two or more pure substances

Figure 5 Stainless steel is made of iron, chromium, and nickel particles. Tea is made of water, caffeine, and flavour particles. Clear nail polish is made of nitrocellulose, resin, colour, and acetate particles.

1.6 Mechanical Mixtures and Solutions **25**

You have probably realized that homogeneous mixtures, or solutions, can be in any of the three states: solid, liquid, or gas. However, in any one solution, there is only one state visible. This is not the case for heterogeneous mixtures, which can include different states in one mixture.

Particles of Mixtures

Maybe it surprises you that clear apple juice, air, and steel are homogeneous mixtures, and not pure substances. The different kinds of matter are not visible in a solution like apple juice. Why not? Figure 6 may help you to answer this question. It compares the distribution of the particles of a solution with the distribution of the particles of a mechanical mixture.

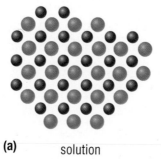
(a) solution

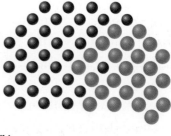
(b) mechanical mixture

Figure 6 (a) The different particles of a solution are evenly mixed. (b) The different particles of a mechanical mixture are unevenly mixed.

In a solution, the different kinds of particles are mixed together evenly. Individual particles are too small to see, so when you look at a solution, it looks like just one kind of matter. You will learn more about the particles of solutions in Chapter 2.

In a mechanical mixture, the different kinds of particles are not mixed evenly. Instead, they stay together in groups and are distributed unevenly. As a result, when you look at a mechanical mixture, you can usually see the different kinds of matter.

To learn more about mechanical mixtures and solutions,
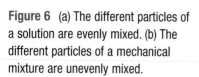
Go to Nelson Science ▶

TRY THIS: Make a Mixture

SKILLS MENU: observing, analyzing, communicating

In this activity, you will make your own mixture and observe its properties.

Equipment and Materials: apron; clear drinking glass or beaker; spoon; water; cooking oil; food colouring; liquid dish detergent

1. Put on your apron. Pour water into a glass until it is half full.
2. Add a spoonful of oil to the water and stir. Record your observations.
3. Add a few drops of food colouring to the mixture and stir. Record your observations.
4. Add a few drops of dish detergent to the mixture and stir. Record your observations.

A. In step 2, what kind of mixture did you make?

B. In step 3, did the food colouring mix with the water or the oil? What kind of mixture did the food colouring form?

C. What happens to the mixture when the dish detergent is added in step 4?

Classifying Matter

You have learned that matter can be classified as either a pure substance or a mixture. Mixtures can be further classified as mechanical mixtures or solutions. Pure substances can combine to form mixtures. Figure 7 summarizes what you have learned about classifying matter.

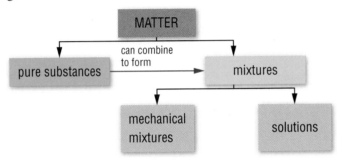

Figure 7 Classification of matter

Unit Task How do you think this information about mechanical mixtures and solutions will be useful as you work on the Unit Task?

✔ CHECK YOUR LEARNING

1. (a) Which ideas did you find easiest to understand as you learned about the arrangements of the particles of mixtures?
   (b) Which ideas did you find most difficult to understand as you learned about the arrangements of the particles of mixtures? Explain why.
   (c) Suggest a strategy to help you better understand the arrangement of the particles of mixtures.

2. Describe each of the following types of mixture:
   (a) a mechanical mixture
   (b) a solution

3. Copy Figure 7 (above) into your notebook. Add two examples of each type of mixture and two examples of a pure substance.

4. (a) What is the difference between the arrangement of the different particles of a mechanical mixture and the arrangement of the different particles of a solution?
   (b) Draw diagrams of the particles of a mechanical mixture and the particles of a solution.

5. Identify each of the following as a mechanical mixture or a solution:
   (a) stainless steel
   (b) a granola bar
   (c) clear apple juice
   (d) an omelette
   (e) soil from your backyard

SKILLS MENU

☐ Defining the Issue
☑ Researching
☑ Identifying Alternatives
☑ Analyzing the Issue
☑ Defending a Decision
☑ Communicating
☑ Evaluating

Using Compact Fluorescent Light Bulbs

Pure substances and mixtures affect the world around you. Using pure substances and mixtures involves both benefits and costs. A benefit is a good or positive result. A cost is a bad or negative result. Some pure substances are harmful to the environment or to human health. Some mixtures contain pure substances that could pollute the air, soil, or water. Often, a mixture or a product containing a mixture has both benefits and costs associated with it. For example, compact fluorescent light bulbs (CFLs) use much less energy than incandescent bulbs (Figure 1). However, CFLs contain a mixture of gases and mercury—a toxic pure substance that can pollute the environment when the bulb is thrown away (Figure 2). Are the benefits of using CFLs worth the costs?

Figure 1 A compact fluorescent light bulb (CFL)

Figure 2 Heavy metals, such as mercury, can pollute both land and water.

LINKING TO LITERACY

Organize Your Thinking
As you read, make a t-chart to show the benefits (column 1) and costs (column 2) of using CFLs. When you have completed your chart, reflect on what the chart shows. You can use this information to conduct your cost-benefit analysis.

The Issue

The town council of a small Ontario town is having a meeting to discuss whether to promote the use of energy-saving CFLs and how to handle the disposal of CFLs. You are a concerned resident in the town. You and a small group of townspeople have been asked by the town council to research these issues. Your group has been asked to summarize your research and present it at the town council's next meeting. You are also expected to recommend a position on each issue.

To prepare for the meeting, you will research the benefits and costs of using CFLs in place of incandescent light bulbs. You should also research the disposal options for CFLs.

Goal

To research CFLs, and to develop and present a cost-benefit analysis of the use and disposal of CFLs.

Gather Information

Working as a group, you will gather information on the issue. Use newspapers and books, as well as the Internet, to find information. Remember that when searching for information using the Internet, some sites will be more trustworthy than others. It is important to seek accurate information when doing research. Educational or government sites are often good places to start.

Identify Solutions

SKILLS HANDBOOK
3.J.4., 3.J.6.

The following questions may help you to conduct your cost-benefit analysis and to find possible solutions:

- What are the benefits of using CFLs?
- How can the benefits of using CFLs be maximized?
- What are the costs, or drawbacks, of using CFLs?
- How can the costs of using CFLs be minimized?
- What are the disposal options (both safe and dangerous) for CFLs (Figure 3)?
- What are the best available alternatives?

Figure 3 If your town decides to promote CFLs, how will you dispose of used or broken bulbs?

Make a Decision

Are the benefits of using CFLs worth the costs? Is there a safe way to dispose of broken CFLs? How did you decide?

Communicate

SKILLS HANDBOOK
3.J.7., 8.

With your group, prepare a presentation on the issues. Decide how you will make your presentation: a brochure, an audiovisual presentation, a poster, a video, or something else. Your report should include the following information:

- benefits and costs of CFLs
- information on the safe disposal of CFLs
- your opinion on what the town should do about the issue

Present your report at a town meeting. Other groups will also present their reports. Together, you will decide what the town will do about the issue.

Classifying Matter

BIG Ideas

- ☑ Matter can be classified according to its physical characteristics.
- ☑ The particle theory of matter helps to explain the physical characteristics of matter.
- ☑ Pure substances and mixtures have an impact on society and the environment.
- ☑ Understanding the characteristics of matter allows us to make informed choices about how we use it.

Looking Back

Human production, use, and disposal of pure substances and mixtures have both benefits and costs.

- We use pure substances and mixtures in everything we do.
- Some mixtures contain pure substances that are harmful to people and the environment.
- Some pure substances are beneficial but are also potentially dangerous.

The particle theory explains the behaviour of particles of matter.

- Everything that has mass and takes up space is made of matter.
- The particle theory states that all matter is made up of tiny particles that are separated by empty spaces. These particles are attracted to one another.
- The particle theory states that particles are in constant motion, and move faster and farther apart when they are heated.
- Three states of matter are solid, liquid, and gas.

The skills of analysis can be used to apply the particle theory to changes in matter.

- Changes in mass observed during investigations can be explained using the particle theory.

A pure substance contains only one kind of particle, but a mixture contains more than one kind of particle.

- Aluminum, table sugar, salt, and distilled water are all examples of pure substances.
- The particles of pure substances do not change, regardless of their state of matter.
- Mixtures can be mechanical mixtures (heterogeneous mixtures) or solutions (homogeneous mixtures).
- Chocolate chip cookies, steel, salad dressing, pop, and ketchup are examples of mixtures.

VOCABULARY

matter, p. 10
chemistry, p. 10
particle theory of matter, p. 12
solid, p. 14
volume, p. 14
liquid, p. 14
gas, p. 15
pure substance, p. 20
mixture, p. 20
mechanical mixture, p. 24
heterogeneous mixture, p. 24
solution, p. 25
homogeneous mixture, p. 25

The skills of scientific inquiry can be used to classify matter as a pure substance or a mixture.

- Pure substances and mixtures can be identified using observation skills.
- Different properties of pure substances and mixtures can be determined by mixing them together.

A mechanical mixture contains different components that you can see.

- A granola bar, cooking oil with herbs, and a children's ball room are all examples of mechanical mixtures.
- A mechanical mixture is also called a heterogeneous mixture.

A solution is a mixture that looks like a pure substance.

- Stainless steel, clear tea, and clear nail polish are all solutions.
- A solution is also called a homogeneous mixture.

CHAPTER
1 REVIEW

The following icons indicate the Achievement Chart categories:
K/U Knowledge/Understanding **C** Communication **T/I** Thinking/Investigation **A** Application

What Do You Remember?

1. What is matter? **K/U**

2. (a) List the five main ideas of the particle theory. **K/U**

   (b) Choose one idea of the particle theory. Draw a diagram that illustrates this idea. **C**

3. (a) List, compare, and contrast the three states of matter.

   (b) Give an example of matter in each of the three states. **K/U**

4. What are the main differences between the particles of a solid and the particles of a gas? **K/U**

5. (a) What is a pure substance?

   (b) What is a mixture? **K/U**

6. Draw a picture to show the difference between the particles of a pure substance and the particles of a mixture. **K/U** **C**

7. Is clear apple juice (Figure 1) a pure substance or a mixture? Explain your answer. **K/U**

Figure 1

8. Tap water contains small amounts of minerals and other chemicals. Is tap water a pure substance or a mixture? **K/U**

9. (a) What is a mechanical mixture?

   (b) How is a mechanical mixture different from a solution? **K/U**

10. Classify each of the following mixtures as a mechanical mixture or a solution:

    (a) a fruit salad

    (b) clear liquid hand soap

    (c) an oil-and-vinegar salad dressing **K/U**

11. List two solutions that you can drink. **K/U**

12. Use the particle theory to explain why you can see the different parts of a mechanical mixture, but not the different parts of a solution. **K/U**

13. Draw a picture to show the difference between the arrangement of particles of a mechanical mixture and the arrangement of particles of a solution. **K/U** **C**

14. Based on what you learned in this chapter, list three things that a piece of wood, a bowl of salad, and your body all have in common. **K/U**

What Do You Understand?

15. Classify the following materials into three groups: pure substances, mechanical mixtures, and solutions.

    (a) copper wire   (d) fruit salad

    (b) iced tea   (e) table sugar

    (c) seawater   (f) salad dressing **K/U**

16. Jonas blew up a balloon in his room. When he took the balloon outside, it got bigger. Was it hotter or colder outside than in his room? Use the particle theory to explain your answer. **K/U** **A**

17. When an ice cube melts, do the particles of the ice cube change to a different type of particle? Explain why or why not. **K/U**

18. Janice says that a glass of orange juice with pulp in it is a solution. Pedro says that it is a mechanical mixture. Do you agree with Janice or Pedro? Explain why. **K/U**

19. Can you tell if a liquid is a pure substance or a solution by looking at it? Explain why or why not. K/U

20. Madur stirred together flour, oil, green peas, chopped onion, and some spices to make dough for pakoras. Is the final mixture a mechanical mixture or a solution? Explain why. K/U

21. (a) Jing has a brand-new, unopened bottle of ginger ale. Is the pop a solution or a mechanical mixture? Explain.

    (b) Jing opens the bottle, and the pop starts to fizz (Figure 2). Is the pop a solution or a mechanical mixture now? Explain why. A

Figure 2

22. Ken added a spoonful of salt to a glass of water. He stirred until the water was clear again. What kind of mixture did Ken make? Explain your answer. K/U A

23. Tina says, "A solution can have only two different kinds of particles." Deepa says, "A solution can have many different kinds of particles." Whom do you agree with? Explain why. K/U A

24. Lakisha says, "You can have a mechanical mixture that has both solids and liquids in it." Kris says, "A mechanical mixture has to be all solids or all liquids, not both." Whom do you agree with? Give an example to explain why. K/U A

Solve a Problem!

25. Jayzee's old kettle developed a crusty white layer on the inside after years of boiling tap water (Figure 3). The white solid would not wash out, even with soap and water.

Figure 3

    (a) What may have caused the white solid to build up on the inside of the kettle? T/I

    (b) If Jayzee buys a new kettle, what could she do to prevent the same white solid from building up in this kettle as well? A

Create and Evaluate!

26. Create a rap, rhyme, or jingle describing the particle theory, then explain how well your rap, rhyme, or jingle describes the particle theory. K/U A C

Reflect on Your Learning

27. In this chapter, you learned about pure substances, mechanical mixtures, and solutions.

    (a) Which of these three things do you find the easiest to understand? Explain why.

    (b) Which of these three things do you find the hardest to understand? Explain why.

    (c) What can you do to help you understand these three things better?

28. Think back to the Key Question on the first page of this chapter.

    (a) In a brief paragraph, answer the Key Question. You may use diagrams.

    (b) Write one or two more questions about the topic of this unit that you would like to explore.

2 Solutions

KEY QUESTION: What are the parts of a solution, and how do the particles of a solution behave?

Looking Ahead

● Solutions are composed of a solvent and one or more solutes.

● Water is called "the universal solvent" because it can dissolve many different kinds of matter.

● The particle theory can be used to explain how a solute dissolves in a solvent.

● "Concentration" describes a solution, and "solubility" describes a solute.

● The skills of scientific inquiry can be used to compare the solubilities of different samples of matter.

● Experimentation skills can be used to determine how to increase the rate at which matter dissolves.

VOCABULARY

dissolve	concentrated solution
solvent	dilute solution
solute	concentration
dissolving	saturated solution
pollution	unsaturated solution
soluble	solubility
insoluble	

A Canadian Tradition

Maple syrup is a traditional Canadian topping for pancakes and French toast. Maple syrup comes from the sap of sugar maple trees. People collect the sap and boil off most of the water. As the water evaporates, the sap becomes thicker, darker, and very sweet.

The First Nations peoples of North America have many stories about maple syrup.

Story 1: Glooskap and the Lazy People

Long ago, the Creator made sugar maple trees. At that time, the sap of the trees was thick and sweet. All you had to do was cut the bark, and syrup dripped out.

One day, the great lord Glooskap walked into a village. To his surprise, it was empty! Glooskap found all the people of the village lying under sugar maple trees, drinking the sweet sap.

"Get up!" said Glooskap. "You need to work!" But everyone ignored him. So Glooskap got water from the river and poured it over the sugar maple trees. The water made the sap thin and not very sweet.

"You are too lazy," Glooskap told the people. "Now you have to work to get maple syrup. You must boil the sap to make it good to eat."

Story 2: The Discovery of Maple Syrup

Many years ago, a man came home from hunting. He threw his hunting axe into a maple tree nearby and went to sleep. While he slept, thin, watery sap dripped into a cooking bowl that was sitting on the ground. The next day, the man's wife began to make stew for dinner. She saw the bowl of sap and added it to her stew. She cooked her stew for a long time.

When the man and woman ate the stew, they were amazed! The stew was sweet and delicious. From that day on, the woman collected the sap from the sugar maple tree and used it in her cooking.

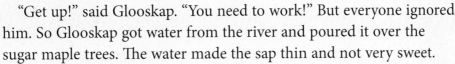

LINKING TO LITERACY

Making Connections

To gain deeper meaning from your reading, make connections to what you have read before and to your own experiences.

1 Read the introductory paragraph and then describe the process that is used to make maple syrup.

2 What connections can you make between the process used for making maple syrup and each of the myths?

3 What connections can you make to your own experiences? Describe meals or desserts you have tried that were made with maple syrup.

Solutes and Solvents

Have you ever made iced tea by mixing a powder and water (Figure 1)? If so, did you use more powder or more water to make the drink? You probably mixed a lot of water with a small amount of powder. What kind of mixture is iced tea? It looks like a pure substance, but you know that it contains at least two components (water and tea). It is a homogeneous mixture, or solution. The powder mixes evenly, or **dissolves**, into the water to make the solution.

Most solutions are made by dissolving a small quantity of one type of matter into a much larger quantity of another type of matter. The part that is present in the larger quantity is called the **solvent**. The part that is present in the smaller quantity is called the **solute**. The solutes are the parts of the solution that dissolve. Solutions are generally made by **dissolving** one or more solutes in a solvent.

Liquid Solutions

You are probably most familiar with solutions that are liquids. These all have liquid solvents. In food preparation, the solvents are usually liquids like water or vegetable oil. In iced tea, water is the solvent. Water is the most common solvent on Earth.

Other solvents, besides water, are also useful. Ethanol is the solvent in perfume. Turpentine is a solvent that is used with paints. Ethyl acetate is one of the solvents in nail polish (Figure 2).

Figure 1 This iced tea was made by dissolving iced tea powder in water.

dissolve: to mix one type of matter into another type of matter to form a solution

solvent: the larger part of a solution; the part of a solution into which the solutes dissolve

solute: the smaller part of a solution; the part of a solution that dissolves in the solvent

dissolving: mixing completely with a solvent to form a solution

LINKING TO LITERACY

During Reading: Comparisons
Comparisons are used to make clear what is the same and what is different about two or more items. As you read this section, compare characteristics of solvents and solutes. How are they similar? How are they different? How does making comparisons help you to better understand solvents and solutes?

Figure 2 Ethanol, turpentine, and ethyl acetate are useful solvents for matter that does not dissolve in water.

The solutes that dissolve in liquids may be solids, liquids, or gases. Salt and sugar are common solid solutes. Acetic acid is a liquid solute that can be added to water to form vinegar. Gases such as carbon dioxide and nitrogen dissolve in our blood and are carried around our bodies. Can you think of other solids, liquids, and gases (solutes) that dissolve in liquids to form solutions?

Water: The Universal Solvent

The water from your tap probably looks and tastes like pure water. Tap water is a solution that contains many solutes. These solutes include iron, aluminum, salt, fluorine, calcium, magnesium, and chlorine. How did they get into your tap water? As water flows in rivers and lakes and underground, it comes into contact with many types of matter (Figure 3). Gases from the air and minerals from the rocks and soil dissolve in the water. Pollutants may also dissolve in the water.

Figure 3 As water flows in a stream, it dissolves many substances.

Before water reaches your tap, it is cleaned to make it safe for drinking. Chlorine and fluorine are sometimes added to the water. Chlorine kills bacteria, and fluorine may help keep your teeth healthy.

Water probably dissolves more different substances than any other solvent. For this reason, water is sometimes called "the universal solvent." Water is the solvent in many important solutions. 🌐

To learn more about "the universal solvent,"

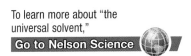
Go to Nelson Science

Water in Your Body

Your body is about 70 % water. All this water dissolves many different solutes, making a variety of solutions. The solutes include salt, oxygen, sugars, and mineral components such as calcium and potassium. These solutes are able to travel around your body because they are dissolved in water. Blood plasma, sweat, urine, and tears are common solutions produced by your body. Water is the solvent in all of these solutions.

Water around Earth

About 70 % of Earth's surface is covered by water. There is always about the same amount of water on Earth. Water from rivers and oceans evaporates into the air and then condenses to form clouds and precipitation (rain and snow). As water moves around Earth, it dissolves many different solutes. These solutes are transported to almost every part of the world. Figure 4 shows that solutes in water can be absorbed by living things.

Figure 4 Plants absorb the minerals and nutrients dissolved in water through their roots.

Solid Solutions

Not all solutions are liquids. Solutions can also be solids. In a solid solution, both the solvent and the solute are solids. The gold used to make jewellery is often called "14-karat gold." Pure gold is 24-karat gold, so 14-karat gold is made up of 14 parts of gold to 10 parts of other metals—generally silver, copper, nickel, or palladium (Figure 5). In this case, gold is the solvent and the other metals are the solutes.

Solid solutions are called "alloys" when they contain two or more metals. To make alloys, the metals are heated until they melt, and then they are mixed together and allowed to cool. Brass is an alloy of copper and zinc (Figure 6). Bronze is an alloy of copper and tin. In both brass and bronze, copper is the solvent. What are the solutes?

Figure 5 Yellow gold is a solid solution of solutes (silver and copper) in a solvent (gold).

Figure 6 Brass is an alloy (a solid solution) of copper and zinc.

LINKING TO LITERACY

During Reading: Comparisons
You have now read about three different types of solutions: liquid, solid, and gas. How are these similar? How are they different? How does making comparisons help you to deepen your understanding of solutions?

Gas Solutions

The air you breathe is about 78 % nitrogen gas, 21 % oxygen gas, and 1 % argon gas, along with smaller amounts of other gases like carbon dioxide. Air is therefore a solution that is a gas. What is the solvent of this solution? What are the solutes?

In all gas solutions, both the solvent and the solutes are gases. Other gas solutions include the gasoline–air mixture in a car engine, and the perfume that you may smell in the air as someone walks by you.

 TRY THIS: Identify Solutions at Home

SKILLS MENU: observing, analyzing, communicating

SKILLS HANDBOOK
5.F., 6.D.1.

There are many household products that you use everyday. Can you tell which ones are solutions?

1. Search at home for two liquid solutions, two solid solutions, and two gas solutions. Examples might include clear shampoo, cleaning products, medicines, clear juices, gold jewellery, objects made of brass, bronze, or steel, and anything that you can smell!

   To smell any substance, hold it away from you and, using your hand, waft the scent toward your nose. Never directly inhale an unknown substance.

A. Try to identify the solvent and the solute for each solution. If they are not listed on a label, use the Internet to help you find out. Remember that the solvent is always the largest ingredient in a solution. To learn more about the contents of household products,

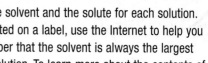 Go to Nelson Science

B. Present your discoveries in a table.

Water Pollution

Plants and animals get some of the nutrients they need from water. However, water can dissolve pollutants, too. **Pollution** includes any pure substance or mixture that contaminates the natural environment. Polluted water is a mixture of pure water and pollutants. Figure 7 shows how pollutants can enter water from various sources.

It is very important to keep the water in our lakes, rivers, and oceans clean, so that organisms can grow and live there normally. We all have to be careful not to let contaminants get into our water.

pollution: contaminants in the environment that could harm living things

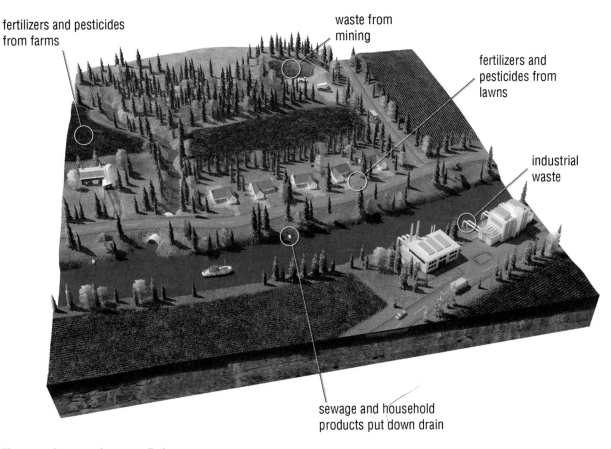

fertilizers and pesticides from farms

waste from mining

fertilizers and pesticides from lawns

industrial waste

sewage and household products put down drain

Figure 7 Sources of water pollution

Unit Task How will you use the information about solutes and solvents in this section when you start to work on the Unit Task?

✔ CHECK YOUR LEARNING

1. In your own words, define solute and solvent.

2. Ocean water is a solution. It contains about 96 % water, 4 % salt, and very small amounts of other salts and minerals.
   (a) What is the solvent in ocean water?
   (b) What are the solutes in ocean water?

3. (a) List one solution that is a solid, one solution that is a liquid, and one solution that is a gas.
   (b) For each solution, describe the solvent and the solute(s).

4. A sealed bottle of soda water contains carbon dioxide gas dissolved in water. When you open the bottle, the gas bubbles out of the solution.
   (a) What is the solvent in soda water? How do you know?
   (b) What is the solute?

5. How is water an important solvent in the body?

6. (a) What is pollution?
   (b) Name four ways that pollutants enter water.

2.2 Dissolving and the Particle Theory

Figure 1 You can add a lot of popcorn to a full glass of milk.

Here is a demonstration you can try at home. Fill a glass with milk. Next, slowly add popped corn to the milk, one piece at a time. How much popcorn can you add before the milk overflows? Figure 1 shows that you can add a lot! Why is the volume almost the same even though you are adding more matter to the glass?

TRY THIS: Where Does the Sugar Go?

SKILLS MENU: performing, observing, analyzing, evaluating

SKILLS HANDBOOK
2.B.7., 6.A.2.

In this activity, you will observe what happens to the volume of mixtures when two substances are combined together.

Equipment and Materials: graduated cylinder (100 mL); 50 mL measuring cup; plastic graduated cylinder (250 mL); stirring rod; sugar; water; sand; marbles

1. Predict the total volume of a mixture of 50 mL of sugar with 100 mL of water.

2. Measure 50 mL of sugar into a 250 mL graduated cylinder. Measure 100 mL of water in the smaller graduated cylinder.

3. Add the water to the sugar. Stir for 1 to 2 min. What is the total volume?

4. Repeat this activity using sand to represent water particles and marbles to represent sugar particles.

A. Explain what you think happened to the water and sugar particles when they were mixed.

B. How does the sand and marble model help you explain what happened to the sugar and water particles?

You can use the particle theory to help explain what happens when solutes dissolve. Go back and reread the particle theory in Table 1 in Section 1.1. The particle theory states that there are spaces between all particles. This means that, in a sample of water, there are many water particles, but also many empty spaces. The same is true in a sample of sugar. When you look at sugar, you can see many grains, or crystals, of sugar. Each sugar crystal contains enormous numbers of invisible sugar particles. When sugar dissolves, the sugar particles separate and mix with the water particles.

Figure 2 shows a model of sugar particles dissolving in water particles. As the sugar particles separate, the smaller water particles fit into the spaces between the larger sugar particles. The water and sugar particles are attracted to each other, so they move closer together when they are mixed. This is why the total volume is often slightly less than the volumes of the two separate components.

Figure 2 The sugar particles are attracted to the water particles, so the sugar particles separate and mix with the water particles. There is less space between the particles when sugar and water are mixed.

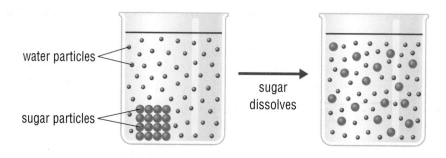

water particles

sugar particles

sugar dissolves

Sugar particles are attracted to water particles, but what happens if the particles of one pure substance are not attracted to the particles of another pure substance? For example, will sugar dissolve in other solvents as easily as it dissolves in water (Figure 3)? You can explore this question in the following activity.

Figure 3 Does sugar dissolve equally well in all solvents?

 TRY THIS: Compare Different Solvents

SKILLS HANDBOOK
2.B.5., 2.B.7.

SKILLS MENU: performing, observing, analyzing, evaluating, communicating

In this activity, you will compare how sugar dissolves in three different liquids: water, rubbing alcohol, and oil.

If a solid dissolves in a liquid, then you have a solute and a solvent. This tells you that the solute and solvent particles are strongly attracted to each other—even more strongly than the particles of the solute are attracted to each other. What will happen if the particles are not strongly attracted to each other?

Equipment and Materials: apron; small clear glass; small spoon; 3 liquids (water, rubbing alcohol, oil); sugar

 Rubbing alcohol is poisonous and flammable. Do not sniff or taste it! Make sure there is no open flame in the room.

1. Put on your apron. Pour water into a clear glass to a depth of about 3 cm. Add about half a spoonful of sugar to the water. Stir the mixture. Record your observations.

2. Rinse out the glass. Repeat step 1 using rubbing alcohol instead of water.

3. Rinse out the glass. Repeat step 1 using oil instead of water.

A. Did all of the sugar dissolve in each of the three liquids? How were you able to tell?

B. Which solute and solvent particles are most strongly attracted to each other? How do you know?

C. Which solute and solvent particles are not very strongly attracted to each other? How do you know?

In the Try This activity, you discovered that sugar dissolves better in some solvents than in others. If a solute dissolves in a particular solvent, we say that it is **soluble** in that solvent. If a solute does not dissolve, it is **insoluble**. Sugar, for example, is soluble in water but insoluble in vegetable oil. Think of one solute that is insoluble in water. What does this tell you about the particles of this solute in water?

soluble: able to dissolve in a specified solvent

insoluble: unable to dissolve in a specified solvent

Unit Task How will you use your new knowledge of how solutes dissolve in the Unit Task?

✔ CHECK YOUR LEARNING

1. Use the particle theory to explain what happens when solutes dissolve. Use a diagram in your explanation.

2. Sundeep mixed 300 mL of water with 100 mL of sugar. She says, "The total volume is 300 mL + 100 mL = 400 mL." Do you agree with Sundeep? Explain why or why not.

3. Define the terms "soluble" and "insoluble." Give one example of each.

4. Drink crystals are a mixture of sugar, flavour particles, and colouring particles. The crystals dissolve in water.
   (a) What is the solute in this solution? What is the solvent?
   (b) What happens to the different particles as the crystals dissolve in water particles?

Concentration and Solubility

Figure 1 Apple seeds contain tiny amounts of a toxic chemical called cyanide.

To learn more about foxglove and digitalis,

Go to Nelson Science

concentrated solution: a solution with a large number of solute particles in a given volume of solution

dilute solution: a solution with a small number of solute particles in a given volume of solution

When you eat an apple, do you eat the seeds? Apple seeds contain a very tiny amount of cyanide (Figure 1). Cyanide is a poisonous chemical. Do not worry about being poisoned if you occasionally swallow some apple seeds. The cyanide is present in such tiny amounts that it will not harm you.

Pure substances can be good or bad for you depending on how much of the substance you consume. For example, digitalis is a chemical found in foxglove plants. Doctors sometimes prescribe small amounts of digitalis as a medicine for heart disease.

People used to drink "foxglove tea"—a solution made by soaking parts of the foxglove plant in hot water—to cure some illnesses. But they had to be careful! Drinking foxglove tea with a small amount of digitalis in it could help a person with a weak heart. Drinking foxglove tea with a lot of digitalis in it, however, could harm or even kill a person by making the heart beat too fast. As this example shows, it is important to know how much of a substance there is in a solution. In this section, you will learn how to describe and calculate the quantity of solute in a solution.

Concentrated and Dilute Solutions

The words "concentrated" and "dilute" are used to describe how much solute is in a certain volume of solution. A **concentrated solution** has a large amount of solute in a volume of solution. A **dilute solution** has a small amount of solute in a similar volume of solution. Figure 2 compares a model of the particles of a concentrated solution to a model of the particles of a dilute solution.

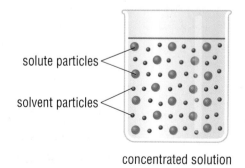

solute particles

solvent particles

concentrated solution   dilute solution

Figure 2 A concentrated solution contains many more solute particles (shown in green) than the same volume of a dilute solution.

Suppose you and a friend are making fruit punch (Figure 3). You add one spoonful of drink powder to a glass of water. Your friend adds six spoonfuls of drink powder to an identical glass of water. Which solution will be concentrated? Which solution will be dilute?

Calculating Concentration

The **concentration** of a solution is the quantity of solute in a certain volume of solution. The more solute dissolved, the greater the concentration. Suppose 100 mL of solution contains 5.0 g of sugar. The concentration of sugar in that solution is 5.0 g/100 mL. One way to express the concentration of liquids is as the mass of solute (in grams) per 100 mL of solution. The equation for this is

$$\text{concentration} = \frac{\text{mass of solute in grams}}{100 \text{ mL of solution}}$$

The following Sample Problem shows how to calculate the concentration of a solution.

Figure 3 Which solution has had a lot of drink powder added to it?

concentration: the amount of solute present in an amount of solution

SAMPLE PROBLEM: Calculate Concentration

Suppose a solution contains 6.0 g of sugar in 200 mL of sugar-and-water solution. What is the concentration of the sugar-and-water solution?

Given: mass of solute = 6.0 g
volume of solution = 200 mL

Required: concentration of the solution

Analysis: $\text{concentration} = \dfrac{\text{mass of solute in grams}}{100 \text{ mL of solution}}$

Solution: $\text{concentration} = \dfrac{6.0 \text{ g}}{200 \text{ mL}}$

Remember to divide both the numerator and the denominator by 2 to get concentration per 100 mL.

$\text{concentration} = \dfrac{3.0 \text{ g}}{100 \text{ mL}}$

Statement: The concentration of the sugar-and-water solution is 3.0 g/100 mL.

Practice: Calculate the concentration of a solution made by mixing 4.5 g of baking soda in enough water to form 50.0 mL of solution. (Remember that the formula calculates the concentration of 100 mL of solution, so you may have to change the volume in your calculation.)

LINKING TO LITERACY

Questioning to Check Your Understanding
As you read about concentration and solubility, stop after every few sentences. Ask yourself questions to check your understanding. Can you explain what you have just read in your own words? If your answer is "No," then reread, look for key words, or look at the pictures and captions for more information.

Saturated and Unsaturated Solutions

What would happen if your friend continued to add drink powder to the glass of fruit punch? Eventually, no more powder would dissolve. The solution would be saturated. A **saturated solution** is a solution in which the maximum amount of solute has been dissolved. An **unsaturated solution** is a solution that still has room for more solute to dissolve.

saturated solution: a solution in which no more solute can dissolve

unsaturated solution: a solution in which more solute can be dissolved

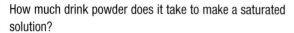
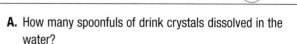

TRY THIS: Make a Saturated Solution

SKILLS MENU: performing, observing, analyzing

SKILLS HANDBOOK
6.A.2.

How much drink powder does it take to make a saturated solution?

Equipment and Materials: apron; graduated cylinder (100 mL) or measuring cup; clear glass; 5 mL measuring spoon; water at room temperature; drink crystals

1. Put on your apron. Measure 100 mL of water into the glass. Add exactly 1 spoonful of drink crystals (5 mL), and stir.

2. Continue adding spoonfuls of crystals, stirring after each one. Count the number of spoonfuls you add. Stop adding crystals when no more will dissolve.

A. How many spoonfuls of drink crystals dissolved in the water?

B. One spoonful of drink crystals has a mass of about 4 g. Calculate the mass of the crystals that dissolved in 100 mL of water to form a saturated solution.

C. If you had 200 mL of water, what mass of drink crystals would you need to make a saturated solution?

Solubility

solubility: a measure of how much solute can dissolve in a certain solvent to form a saturated solution at a particular temperature and volume

You now know that there is a limit to the amount of solute that can dissolve in a solvent. Chemists call this amount the **solubility** of a solute: the maximum amount of solute that will dissolve in a given volume of solvent at a particular temperature. When this amount of solute has dissolved, a saturated solution has been formed. Solubility can be measured in grams of solute per 100 mL of solvent at room temperature. The mathematical equation is

$$\text{solubility} = \frac{\text{maximum mass of solute that will dissolve, in grams}}{\text{100 mL solvent at a certain temperature}}$$

Table 1 Solubility Table

Solute	Solubility in water at 20 °C
sugar	204 g/100 mL of water
salt	36 g/100 mL of water

Remember the distinction between concentration and solubility. Concentration is measured in grams of solute per 100 mL of *solution* (g/100 mL solution), but solubility is measured in grams of solute per 100 mL of *solvent* (g/100 mL solvent). Different solutes have different solubilities, as Table 1 shows. The solubility of a solute changes depending on different factors. In the next section, you will investigate some of the factors that affect solubility.

✔ CHECK YOUR LEARNING

1. You learned several new terms in this section.
   (a) Which term was the easiest for you to remember? Why?
   (b) Which term was the hardest for you to remember? Why?
   (c) How can you make the term (your answer to (b)) easier to remember? Share your strategy with a classmate.

2. Define each of the following terms in your own words:
   (a) concentrated solution
   (b) dilute solution
   (c) saturated solution
   (d) unsaturated solution
   (e) solubility

3. How are the terms "solubility" and "saturated" similar? How are they different?

4. What is the important difference between how concentration and solubility are measured?

5. Which solute is more soluble: sugar or salt? (Refer to Table 1.)

6. Kai has 200 mL of water at room temperature. How much salt can she dissolve in the water? (Refer to Table 1.)

SCIENCE WORKS

Pharmaceuticals

Have you taken any medicine recently? A spoonful of cough syrup, some antacid for an upset stomach, or a traditional herbal infusion? All liquid medicines are solutions. Usually, the active ingredient in the medicine is the solute. The solvent is just there to keep the medicine well mixed, easy to measure, and easy to swallow (Figure 1).

Figure 1 Children often find it easier to swallow medicine as a liquid than as a pill.

Until the early twentieth century, most medicines were made by pharmacists in their own shops. Now, big drug companies have taken over this role. These companies employ teams of doctors, pharmacists, chemical engineers, and lab technicians to develop and manufacture the medicines (Figure 2).

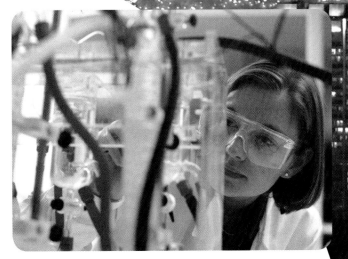

Figure 2 The development team makes sure that it is easy to take the correct dose.

Many liquid medicines contain water as the solvent. Sometimes, however, an active ingredient does not dissolve well in water. In that case, a different solvent has to be used, such as ethanol. The pharmaceutical industry selects solvents very carefully. They must dissolve the active ingredient without changing it, and the solvent must not be harmful to the person taking the medicine.

Besides medicines that you take by mouth, you might have seen pharmaceuticals in liquid form that can be administered in other ways: by injection, as topical applications, in eye drops or ear drops, or through nasal sprays or inhalers. For example, creams and ointments like sunscreen are often made with oily solvents. These solvents help the active ingredients to stay on your skin longer than they would if the solvent were water.

The pharmaceutical industry and Health Canada closely monitor the components and concentrations of most pharmaceutical solutions. This assures us that the medicines are safe and effective.

To learn more about pharmaceuticals and careers in this field,

Go to Nelson Science

Solubility

In this activity, you will compare the solubility of Epsom salts and table salt in both cold and hot water by preparing saturated solutions and taking careful measurements.

SKILLS MENU

☐ Questioning ☑ Performing
☐ Hypothesizing ☑ Observing
☐ Predicting ☑ Analyzing
☐ Planning ☑ Evaluating
☑ Controlling ☑ Communicating
　 Variables

Purpose

To explore the relationship between solubility and temperature.

Equipment and Materials

- apron
- eye protection
- large beaker
- glass stirring rod
- thermometer
- graduated cylinder (50 mL)
- beaker (100 mL)
- balance
- 5 mL measuring spoon
- weighing papers
- electric kettle
- water
- ice cubes
- Epsom salts
- table salt

apron　　　eye protection　　　large beaker

glass stirring rod　　thermometer　　graduated cylinder (50 mL)

beaker (100 mL)　　balance　　measuring spoon

weighing papers　　electric kettle　　water

ice cubes　　Epsom salts　　table salt

Procedure

SKILLS HANDBOOK
6.A.3., 6.A.4.

1. In your notebook, draw a table similar to Table 1.

Table 1　Analysis of Observations

		Epsom salts in cold water	Epsom salts in hot water	Table salt in cold water	Table salt in hot water
Before adding salt to water	Volume of water (mL)				
	Mass of beaker with water added (g)				
After adding salt to water to form a saturated solution	Mass of beaker with saturated solution (g)				
	Mass of salt added to water (g)				
	Temperature of solution (°C)				
	Solubility of salt in water at recorded temperature				

2. Put on your apron and eye protection.

3. Prepare cold water by placing some ice cubes in a glass or beaker of cold tap water and stirring until the water temperature is close to 0 °C.

4. Use a graduated cylinder to pour 50 mL of the ice-cold water into a 100 mL beaker.

5. Measure the mass of the beaker and water on a balance and record the mass in Table 1.

6. Scoop approximately 20 mL of Epsom salts onto a weighing paper.

7. Place a small amount of the Epsom salts (enough to fit on the end of a spoon) in the water. Stir until all the crystals have dissolved.

8. Repeat step 7 until some crystals remain at the bottom of the beaker, no matter how thoroughly you stir. The solution is now saturated.

9. Measure the temperature of the saturated solution. Record your observation in Table 1.

10. Measure the mass of the beaker, water, and dissolved Epsom salts using the balance and record in Table 1.

11. Dispose of the solution according to your teacher's instructions. Return any unused Epsom salts to your teacher. Rinse and dry the beaker.

12. Use a graduated cylinder to obtain 50 mL of hot water from the kettle. Pour the hot water into the dry beaker.

🤚 Use care when handling containers with hot water.

13. Repeat steps 5 to 11 using the beaker of hot water instead of ice-cold water, and record your observations in Table 1.

14. Repeat steps 3 to 13 using table salt instead of Epsom salts. Record your data in Table 1.

Analyze and Evaluate

SKILLS HANDBOOK
2.B.7., 2.B.8.

(a) Complete your observations by calculating the mass of Epsom salts and table salt in each case. Record the masses in Table 1. Calculate the solubility of Epsom salts and table salt in cold and hot water.

(b) How did you find the mass of the salt that dissolved in the water, without measuring the mass of the salt on the balance? What assumption did you make in finding the mass of the salt in this way?

(c) Compare the solubility that you calculated for Epsom salts in cold water and in hot water. What do you conclude about how the solubility of Epsom salts changes with temperature?

(d) Compare the solubility that you calculated for table salt in cold water and in hot water. What can you conclude?

(e) Compare the solubility of Epsom salts with the solubility of table salt in cold water and in hot water.

(f) What kind of mixture was in the beaker just before you emptied it? Name the components of the mixture.

(g) How could you improve the accuracy of your measurements in this activity?

(h) When you compare the solubility of table salt in water with the solubility of Epsom salts in water, the one variable that you are changing is the type of salt. You must control all other variables. Which variables were not controlled very well? How could you control these variables better?

Apply and Extend

(i) Apply the particle theory to your observations in this activity. Can the particle theory help you to predict the differences that you observed between the solubilities of table salt and Epsom salts? What do you think are some of the problems in using the particle theory to explain solubility?

(j) Think about the results of your investigations for the solubility of table salt and Epsom salts. Suppose you made a saturated solution of table salt in hot water and then cooled the water down. What do you think might happen? Suppose you made a saturated solution of Epsom salts in hot water and then cooled it. What do you think might happen?

Dissolving Solutes Faster

Can you change the speed with which sugar dissolves? What can you do to make a sugar cube dissolve faster in water?

SKILLS MENU

☐ Questioning   ☐ Performing
☐ Hypothesizing   ☐ Observing
☐ Predicting   ☐ Analyzing
☐ Planning   ☐ Evaluating
☐ Controlling   ☐ Communicating
   Variables

Testable Question

SKILLS HANDBOOK
2.B.1.

Write two testable questions that investigate how quickly sugar cubes dissolve in water.

Hypothesis/Prediction

SKILLS HANDBOOK
2.B.3.

For each testable question, make a hypothesis. Your hypothesis should include both a prediction and reasons for your prediction. Use the particle theory to provide a reason for each prediction.

Experimental Design

Think about how you will design your experiment. To conduct a fair test, you should only change one variable at a time. For each question, write the one variable that you will change, and the other variables that you will keep constant.

Equipment and Materials

You will use sugar cubes and water. Make a list describing what else you will need to test the hypothesis for each of your questions. Figure 1 and Figure 2 might give you some ideas.

Figure 1 Change one variable at a time to see how it affects the dissolving rate of sugar.

Figure 2 Useful equipment and materials for testing the dissolving rate of sugar

Procedure

SKILLS HANDBOOK
2.B.4., 5.

1. With your partner, brainstorm how you will investigate each of your testable questions. Write the steps of your procedure.

2. Add to your procedure any necessary safety precautions.

3. Create a table in which to record your observations.

4. Ask your teacher to check and approve your procedure before you continue, and then perform your procedure. Record your observations.

Analyze and Evaluate

SKILLS HANDBOOK
2.B.7., 2.B.8.

(a) Analyze your results and answer your testable questions.

(b) Did your observations support your hypotheses? What happened in each experiment?

(c) Use the particle theory to explain what you observed in each experiment.

(d) Evaluate your experimental design. What would you change if you were going to repeat the experiment?

(e) Suggest another testable question to investigate, relating to speed of dissolving.

Apply and Extend

(f) In this investigation, you found ways to make solutes dissolve faster. Describe how you use one of these ways in your everyday life.

(g) Think of one way in which your discovery could be used by an industry making products.

(h) You may sometimes want a solute to dissolve slowly instead of quickly (Figure 3). For example, when you take a pill, you may want it to dissolve in your stomach and not in your mouth. Think about the last time you took medicine in the form of a pill. What did the pill manufacturer do to keep the pill from dissolving too quickly?

Figure 3 Some pills dissolve quickly. What would you do if you wanted the pill to dissolve slowly?

Unit Task You have now learned about the speed at which solutes dissolve, and what factors change this speed. How might this be useful when you start to work on the Unit Task?

Solutions

BIG Ideas

☐ Matter can be classified according to its physical characteristics.

☑ The particle theory of matter helps to explain the physical characteristics of matter.

☑ Pure substances and mixtures have an impact on society and the environment.

☑ Understanding the characteristics of matter allows us to make informed choices about how we use it.

Looking Back

Solutions are composed of a solvent and one or more solutes.

- Solutions may be solids, liquids, or gases.
- Examples of common solvents include water, ethanol, copper, and nitrogen gas.
- Examples of common solutes include sugar, salt, tin, and oxygen gas.

Water is called "the universal solvent" because it can dissolve many different kinds of matter.

- Water is the solvent in many solutions produced by the body, including blood plasma, tears, and urine.
- Water dissolves minerals and nutrients, making them available to plants and animals.

The particle theory can be used to explain how a solute dissolves in a solvent.

- The particle theory states that matter is made up of tiny, invisible particles, and that particles have empty spaces between them.
- When a solute dissolves in a solvent, the particles of the solute separate from each other and become evenly mixed with the particles of solvent.
- The particle theory states that particles attract each other. The attraction between solute and solvent particles explains why solutes dissolve.

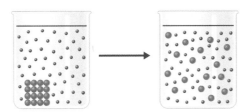

"Concentration" describes a solution, and "solubility" describes a solute.

- Concentration is a measure of the quantity of solute in a given volume of solution, often expressed as

$$\frac{\text{mass of solute (g)}}{100 \text{ mL of solution}}$$

- Solubility is a measure of the quantity of solute that can be dissolved in a given volume of solvent at a certain temperature, often expressed as

$$\frac{\text{mass of solute (g)}}{100 \text{ mL of solvent}}$$

- A concentrated solution contains more solute than does the same volume of a dilute solution.
- Solubility is different for different pure substances and at different temperatures.

The skills of scientific inquiry can be used to compare the solubilities of different samples of matter.

- Solubility can be determined by creating saturated solutions and taking careful measurements.
- Solubility can be affected by changing the temperature of the solvent.

Experimentation skills can be used to determine how to increase the rate at which matter dissolves.

- The rate at which matter dissolves can be investigated by changing one variable (such as temperature or speed of stirring), while keeping all other variables constant.

dissolve, p. 36

solvent, p. 36

solute, p. 36

dissolving, p. 36

pollution, p. 39

soluble, p. 41

insoluble, p. 41

concentrated solution, p. 42

dilute solution, p. 42

concentration, p. 43

saturated solution, p. 43

unsaturated solution, p. 43

solubility, p. 44

The following icons indicate the Achievement Chart categories: **K/U** Knowledge/Understanding **C** Communication **T/I** Thinking/Investigation **A** Application

What Do You Remember?

1. Use each of the following terms appropriately in a sentence. (Write one sentence for each term.)

   (a) dissolve   (d) concentrated

   (b) solute   (e) dilute

   (c) solvent   (f) solubility **K/U** **C**

2. (a) List three examples of common solvents.

   (b) List three examples of common solutes. **K/U**

3. Which of the solutions in Figure 1 is concentrated? Which solution is dilute? Explain. **K/U**

(a)   (b)

Figure 1

4. Hassan dissolved a spoonful of salt in a glass of water.

   (a) Draw a labelled diagram showing the particles in Hassan's solution.

   (b) Explain your picture.

   (c) What is in the space between the particles? **K/U** **C**

5. Figure 2 shows a green solid in a glass of water. After a while, the green solute dissolves in the water.

   (a) Draw a picture of the final solution. **C**

   (b) Explain your drawing. **K/U**

Figure 2

6. Ling is dissolving some sugar cubes in water. List three things Ling can do to dissolve the sugar cubes faster. **K/U** **A**

What Do You Understand?

7. Look back at the information about maple syrup in the chapter opening.

   (a) Why is maple syrup an example of a solution?

   (b) What is the solvent in maple syrup?

   (c) What are some of the solutes in maple syrup?

   (d) Is maple syrup more or less concentrated than maple sap? Explain why. **K/U** **A**

8. Jordan's iced tea contains 96 % water, 3 % sugar, and 1 % caffeine and other tea flavours.

   (a) What is the solvent of this solution?

   (b) What are the solutes in this solution? **K/U**

9. Why is water "the universal solvent"? **K/U**

10. Malcolm dissolves 50 mL of drink powder in 150 mL of water. He is surprised that the final volume is only 170 mL.

    (a) Why do you think Malcolm is surprised at the final volume? **K/U**

    (b) Use the particle theory to explain Malcolm's observation. **A**

11. Your teacher gives you a solution of salt in water. How can you find out if it is a saturated solution? **T/I**

12. Raven is vigorously stirring a mixture of sand and water. She says, "As long as I keep stirring, the sand stays dissolved in the water." Do you agree with Raven? Explain why or why not. **K/U**

13. Mohan dissolved a lot of sugar in a glass of water until no more sugar would dissolve. Mohan says, "This is a saturated solution." Raven says, "It is a concentrated solution." Are both correct? Explain your answer. K/U

14. Matt thought of a model to help explain concentrated and dilute solutions. He said, "A concentrated solution is like a swimming pool full of people. A dilute solution is like the same swimming pool with only a few people in it."

    (a) What part of Matt's model represents the solute particles?

    (b) What part of Matt's model represents the solvent?

    (c) Do you think Matt's model does a good job of explaining concentrated and dilute solutions? Explain why or why not. T/I

Solve a Problem!

15. The solubility of sugar in water at room temperature is 204 g/100 mL.

    (a) How much sugar will dissolve in 100 mL of water at room temperature?

    (b) How much sugar will dissolve in 2000 mL of water at room temperature? K/U T/I

16. A coffee shop attendant added instant coffee powder to hot water until no more would dissolve. He added 30 g of powder to 100 mL of water. What is the solubility of the instant coffee powder in hot water? K/U T/I

17. Malcolm added table salt to water until no more would dissolve. He added 108 g of salt to 300 mL of water. What is the solubility of the table salt in water at that temperature? K/U T/I

18. Calculate the concentration (in g/100 mL) of each of the following solutions: K/U T/I

    (a) 3 g of sugar in 100 mL of solution

    (b) 10 g of sugar in 50 mL of solution

    (c) 54 g of sugar in 200 mL of solution

Create and Evaluate!

19. A vegetable soup recipe requires one teaspoonful of salt. A chef accidentally puts in one tablespoonful. Now the soup is much too salty.

    (a) What can the chef do to reduce the salty taste of the soup?

    (b) What effects would your suggestion in (a) have on the soup? T/I A

20. Think back to Matt's models of solutions in question 14.

    (a) Create your own model to help explain concentrated and dilute solutions. Here are a few ideas you could use:

       • cereal flakes in milk
       • people in a park
       • leaves on a tree

    (b) Evaluate your model. T/I

Reflect on Your Learning

21. In this chapter, you learned a lot about solutions.

    (a) Create a t-chart with the headings "Easy to Understand" and "Hard to Understand."

    (b) Which of the ideas in this chapter were the easiest to understand? List these in your t-chart.

    (c) Which of the ideas were the hardest to understand? List these in your t-chart.

    (d) Draw pictures of one idea that you found easy to understand, and one idea that you found difficult to understand. Share your drawings with the class.

22. Think back to the Key Question on the first page of this chapter.

    (a) In a brief paragraph, answer the Key Question. You may use diagrams.

    (b) Write one or two more questions about the topic of this unit that you would like to explore.

3 Separating Mixtures

KEY QUESTION: How can we separate the components of a mechanical mixture or solution?

Looking Ahead

- The skills of scientific inquiry can be used to learn about methods of separating different mixtures.

- Mechanical mixtures can be separated into their components using methods such as sorting, floating, settling, attracting with a magnet, sieving, and filtering.

- Separating waste mixtures into their components protects the environment from toxins and allows valuable components to be reused.

- Solutions can be separated into their components using methods such as evaporation and distillation.

- Investigation skills can be used to determine the best method to separate mixtures.

- Many industries separate mixtures when making products.

VOCABULARY

sorting	sewage
floating	evaporate
settling	evaporation
sieve	distillation
sieving	electric generator
filter	radioactive
filtration	nuclear energy

LINKING TO LITERACY

Critical Literacy

When you read something critically, you analyze the text and look for underlying messages. As you read the cartoon, think about the author's viewpoint.

1 The characters are faced with a dilemma. Describe the choice they must make. What does this tell you about their beliefs? Are they believable characters? Why or why not?

2 If you were to encounter this dilemma, how would you react? What could you do to make the situation better?

3 What message is the author trying to relate to readers?

3.1 PERFORM AN ACTIVITY

Separating Mechanical Mixtures

There are different ways to separate the parts of a mechanical mixture. In this activity, you will explore some of these methods.

SKILLS MENU

- ☐ Questioning
- ☐ Hypothesizing
- ☐ Predicting
- ☐ Planning
- ☐ Controlling Variables
- ☑ Performing
- ☑ Observing
- ☑ Analyzing
- ☑ Evaluating
- ☑ Communicating

Purpose

To separate mechanical mixtures using different methods.

Equipment and Materials

- apron
- eye protection
- spoon
- 2 beakers
- 3 watch glasses
- magnet and paper
- sieve
- funnel
- plastic container
- wash bottle containing water
- 3 mystery mixtures
- paper towels
- coffee filter

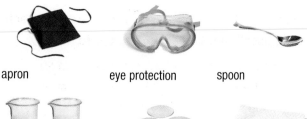

apron

eye protection

spoon

2 beakers

3 watch glasses

magnet and paper

sieve

funnel

plastic container

wash bottle containing water

3 mystery mixtures

paper towels

coffee filter

Procedure

SKILLS HANDBOOK
2.B.5., 2.B.6.

Part A: Floating and Settling

1. Put on your apron and eye protection. Use the spoon to stir mixture #1. After stirring, examine the mixture and record your observations.

2. Let the mixture sit for 15 min. (You can work on Parts B and C while you wait.)

3. Examine the mixture. What parts floated to the top? What parts settled to the bottom? Record your observations.

4. Use the spoon to skim off the floating parts of the mixture (Figure 1). Put them onto a watch glass.

Figure 1 Separating the parts of mixture #1 by floating

5. Pour the liquid part of the mixture into an empty beaker, leaving the settled solids behind.

Part B: Magnetism

6. Examine mixture #2. Record your observations.

7. Wrap the magnet in paper towel. Use it to separate the mixture (Figure 2). Put the different parts on two clean watch glasses.

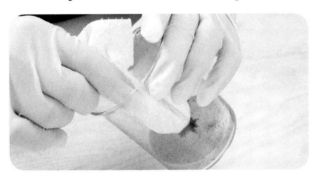

Figure 2 Separating the parts of mixture #2 by magnetism

Part C: Sieving and Filtering

8. Examine mixture #3. Record your observations.

9. Place the sieve over the plastic container.

10. Stir the mixture. Pour it through the sieve. Use the wash bottle to wash any remaining mixture from the beaker into the sieve. Put the sieve and its contents to one side, resting on paper towels. Record your observations.

11. Fold the filter paper into a cone and place it in a funnel. Put the cone in the top of an empty beaker.

12. Slowly pour the contents of the container through the filter paper (Figure 3). Use water to wash any remaining mixture from the container into the filter. Record your observations.

Figure 3 Separating the parts of mixture #3 by filtering

Analyze and Evaluate

SKILLS HANDBOOK
2.B.8.

(a) In Part A, how well did floating and settling work to separate a mixture? How could you do it better?

(b) What kinds of mixtures can effectively be separated using floating and settling?

(c) In Part B, how well did magnetism work to separate a mixture? How could you do it better?

(d) Why were you instructed to wrap the magnet in paper before using it? What might have happened if you had not done this?

(e) What kinds of mixtures can effectively be separated using magnetism?

(f) In Part C, how well did sieving and filtering work to separate a mixture? How could you do it better?

(g) What kinds of mixtures can effectively be separated by sieving? By filtering?

(h) Which method was the most effective? Why?

(i) What method would you use to separate each of the following mixtures? Explain why.

   i) iron filings   ii) sand and gravel
       and water   iii) sand and water

Apply and Extend

SKILLS HANDBOOK
2.B.4.

(j) You work in a factory that makes three different sizes of glass marbles. A problem results in all the different-sized marbles getting mixed up. Plan how to separate the marbles by size. Describe the equipment you would need.

(k) Imagine you have a mixture of paper clips, sand, pebbles, and water. Create a flow chart to show how you would separate the mixture.

(l) How could any of the techniques in this activity be used to sort recyclable waste?

Unit Task How will you apply the skills learned in this section to the Unit Task?

3.2

Separating Mechanical Mixtures

People work with mixtures every day, even though they may not know it. Here are three examples. What does each one have to do with mixtures?

- Kalia likes lettuce, onions, and red peppers in her salad, but she does not like tomatoes. Kalia always picks the tomatoes out of her salad before she eats it.
- One of Ali's chores is to sort the laundry before washing. He separates the laundry into a pile of light colours and a pile of dark colours.
- Jen boils pasta in water for lunch. Once the pasta is cooked, Jen pours it through a colander to separate the pasta from the water (Figure 1).

Figure 1 A colander separates a mechanical mixture of solid pasta and liquid water.

Kalia, Ali, and Jen are all separating mechanical mixtures. Think of the last time you separated a mechanical mixture. Maybe you took the mushrooms off of a slice of pizza before eating it. Perhaps you took the loonies and toonies out of a mixture of coins and put them in a jar. What kind of mixture did you separate? How did you do it?

Sorting

The simplest way of separating mechanical mixtures is by sorting. Sorting is used when the two (or more) types of matter are in fairly large pieces. **Sorting** simply involves looking at the various pieces and physically moving one or more of the pieces into a different container.

The parts of many mechanical mixtures, however, are in pieces that are too small to separate by sorting. For these mixtures, you have to find other ways of separating the parts. This often involves finding a way in which the parts of the mixture are different from each other.

sorting: physically separating large pieces of a mechanical mixture so that similar pieces are together

Floating and Settling

Some parts of a mechanical mixture may float or sink in water. If one part of a mixture is **floating**, you can skim it off the top using a spoon or a scoop. If one part of a mixture sinks (settles) in water, you can pour the water off, and then collect the part at the bottom. This method is called **settling**. Sand and cocoa powder both settle in water.

A mechanical mixture might include two or more different liquids, one of which floats on top of the other. In this case, the floating layer could be carefully skimmed or poured off, just as melted chicken fat is skimmed off a pot of hot chicken soup (Figure 2).

During the Gold Rush era, thousands of miners headed to Western Canada to search for gold. Many of them used the technique of settling to separate gold dust from rock dust. A miner would grind up rocks, or just pick up gravel and sand from riverbeds, and swirl the solids around in a pan full of water. Gold dust is heavier than rock dust. If there were any gold dust mixed with the rock dust, the gold dust would sink to the bottom faster than the rock dust. The swirling water would then wash the rock dust away.

The technique of settling is used on a huge scale to treat water waste (sewage) in wastewater treatment facilities. You will learn more about this process in Section 3.4.

floating: a separation technique in which a "lighter" component rises to the top of a liquid where it can be skimmed or poured off

settling: a separation technique in which a "heavier" component sinks to the bottom of a liquid, and the liquid can be poured off

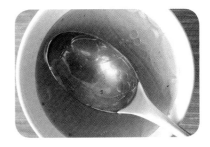

Figure 2 The melted fat can be skimmed off the rest of the soup because the fat floats on top of the broth.

Complex Mixtures

Some mixtures are complex. This means that they are mechanical mixtures that include solutions. Blood, for example, is a complex mixture. Blood contains a solution of water with dissolved nutrients (called plasma) and red blood cells. However, the blood cells are very small and can only be seen with a microscope.

Medical laboratories commonly separate the components of blood. If a blood sample is taken from a patient and left for several hours, the blood cells gradually sink to the bottom of the container (Figure 3). This leaves the clear, yellowish plasma solution at the top. The solution can then be poured off, separate from the blood cells.

This ability to separate blood into its different components has important applications. People who require blood transfusions may need only one component of blood and not the others. For example, a patient may need a transfusion of only red blood cells or only the plasma component of blood due to his or her particular illness or injury.

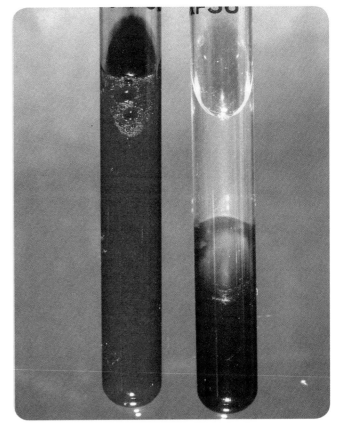

Figure 3 The test tube on the right shows how blood separates.

Figure 4 Many medical and veterinary labs have centrifuges.

The settling process can be sped up by the use of a centrifuge (Figure 4). A centrifuge is a piece of equipment that holds test tubes containing mixtures to be separated. The centrifuge spins the test tubes around very quickly to make the heavier components sink rapidly to the bottom of the tubes. Centrifuges are used in many labs to separate mechanical mixtures.

Using a Magnet

Some metals and alloys, such as iron and steel, are attracted to magnets. Other metals (for example, silver and aluminum) and most non-metals (for example, plastic and glass) are not attracted to magnets. If only one part of a mechanical mixture is attracted to magnets, a magnet can be used to separate that part from the rest of the mixture (Figure 5).

Figure 5 This magnet separates scrap metal so that it can be recycled and reused.

Using Sieves and Filters

Sometimes, different parts of a mechanical mixture contain pieces of different sizes. For example, the material extracted from a gravel pit includes both sand and gravel. The gravel company can get a better price for the gravel if it can first remove the sand. A sieve can separate mixtures like this. A **sieve** is a device with many visible holes in it that can be used to separate the components of a mixture. The smaller pieces in the mixture fall through the holes, while the bigger pieces stay on top.

This method—known as **sieving**—also works when a mechanical mixture has solid and liquid parts. The liquid parts, and perhaps some smaller solid pieces, pass through the holes, but the sieve traps the larger solid pieces. An example of a household sieve is a colander.

A **filter** is a device, with many small holes or channels, that can be used to separate a mixture. **Filtration** is similar to sieving, but it is used to remove tiny pieces of solids from a liquid or a gas. The holes through a filter are usually too small to see, so large and small solid pieces become trapped and cannot pass through.

sieve: a device used to separate the components of a mixture, with many visible holes that allow smaller solid pieces and liquids to pass through while blocking the larger solid pieces

sieving: the process of passing a mechanical mixture through a sieve to separate the larger pieces of matter

filter: a device with many small holes that trap solid pieces of a mixture but allow liquids and gases to pass through

filtration: the process of passing a mechanical mixture through a filter to separate solid pieces from a liquid or gas

Household filters include air filters (in furnaces and air conditioners) and coffee filters. Figure 6 shows an air filter from a furnace. As air is drawn into the furnace, it first passes through the filter. The filter traps dust and other small pieces of solids in the air. This helps the furnace work better. Air filters are also used in air circulation systems to clean the air in homes, offices, and hospitals.

Figure 6 An air filter removes small pieces of solids from the air.

Dissolving Soluble Components

If one part of a mechanical mixture dissolves easily in a solvent, you can separate this part from the rest of the mixture using dissolving. For example, suppose you had a mixture of salt and sand, and you wanted to separate the sand. You could mix the mechanical mixture with water. The salt would dissolve in the water, and the sand would settle to the bottom of the container. After a short period of time, you could pour the salt-and-water solution off the sand. Alternatively, you could stir the whole mixture and pour it through a filter. The filter would trap the sand, but allow the solution (containing the dissolved salt) to run through.

To learn more about separating mechanical mixtures,

Go to Nelson Science

TRY THIS: Separate a Mixture by Dissolving

SKILLS HANDBOOK
2.B.4.

SKILLS MENU: planning, performing, observing, analyzing, evaluating

Some kinds of matter dissolve in water. Other kinds do not. You can use this property to separate a mixture of salt and pepper.

Equipment and Materials: apron; 2 clear plastic cups; spoon; 1 large spoonful of salt; 1 large spoonful of pepper; warm water; filter paper (coffee filter)

1. Put on your apron. Mix the salt and pepper together in a cup. Examine the mixture. Think about how you could separate this mixture.

2. Add warm water to the salt-and-pepper mixture. Stir for 30 seconds. Record your observations.

3. Fold the filter paper into a cone. Put it in the top of an empty cup.

4. Stir the mixture. Pour it slowly through the filter. Use more water to rinse out any mixture sticking to the cup.

A. Does the pepper dissolve in the water? How can you tell?

B. What part(s) pass through the filter? What part does the filter catch?

C. Suggest what you could do next to separate the parts of the salt-and-water solution.

Unit Task How will you use what you have learned about separating mechanical mixtures when you start to work on the Unit Task?

✓ CHECK YOUR LEARNING

1. What are four methods of separating a mechanical mixture?

2. Describe one way to separate each of the following mechanical mixtures:
   (a) metals in a scrap yard
   (b) salt and sand
   (c) sand and gravel
   (d) sand and water

3. Some air purification systems include filters. How do air filters make the air healthier for people to breathe?

4. What is the difference between a filter and a sieve?

Sorting Solid Waste

When you have finished with your household items and they are of no more use to you, you want to move the unwanted objects out of your home. What happens to them next? This flow chart describes what happens to your discarded "stuff."

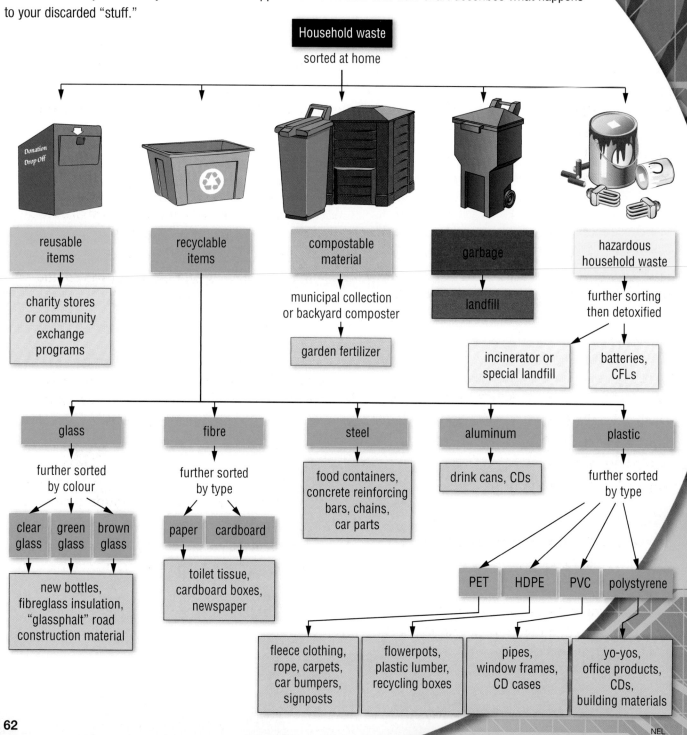

Household waste
sorted at home

| reusable items | recyclable items | compostable material | garbage | hazardous household waste |

charity stores or community exchange programs

municipal collection or backyard composter

garden fertilizer

landfill

incinerator or special landfill

further sorting then detoxified

batteries, CFLs

| glass | fibre | steel | aluminum | plastic |

further sorted by colour

further sorted by type

food containers, concrete reinforcing bars, chains, car parts

drink cans, CDs

further sorted by type

clear glass | green glass | brown glass

paper | cardboard

PET | HDPE | PVC | polystyrene

new bottles, fibreglass insulation, "glassphalt" road construction material

toilet tissue, cardboard boxes, newspaper

fleece clothing, rope, carpets, car bumpers, signposts

flowerpots, plastic lumber, recycling boxes

pipes, window frames, CD cases

yo-yos, office products, CDs, building materials

Separating Recyclables

We are all being asked to reduce the quantity of waste that we produce. Recycling programs are expanding across Ontario. Recyclable materials are generally brought to a recycling depot all mixed together. The various parts must be separated before the materials can be turned into new, useful objects. How are the parts separated? Your challenge is to design and test equipment to separate a mixture of recyclable materials.

SKILLS MENU

- ☐ Identify a Problem/Need
- ☑ Planning
- ☑ Selecting Materials and Equipment
- ☑ Designing
- ☑ Testing
- ☑ Modifying
- ☑ Communicating

Scenario

Your school administration has asked your class to suggest ways to sort mixed recycled materials. You will work in teams. You will be shown a sample of the kinds of materials that will be in the mixture. Each team will design and test their own separator, or series of separators.

Design Brief

Your challenge is to (a) plan a process, and then to (b) design, build, and test a separator for mixed recyclable materials. Your process should be efficient, with as few steps as possible. It should also have the least possible impact on the environment.

Research and Consider

Discuss, in your group, how to address this challenge. What separation methods would be most appropriate? What steps are required? What equipment and materials will you need? Is there anything you need to research?

Plan and Construct

SKILLS HANDBOOK 4.B.4.

1. Write a detailed plan for processing the recyclable materials.

2. Draw a flow chart to illustrate how your separator will work. (A sample flowchart is illustrated in the Tech Connect on the previous page.)

3. Collect the equipment and materials that you need and build your separator.

4. Modify your plan during the building process, if necessary. Remember to record your changes.

Test and Modify

Using a sample of the recyclable mixture, test your separator. Does it meet the Design Brief? Make any necessary changes. Retest your separator until it efficiently separates the mixture into the various categories, which you should collect in different containers.

Evaluate

Did your separator separate the mixture of recyclable materials as required? How could it be improved? How could it be made more efficient? How could it be less damaging to the environment?

Communicate

SKILLS HANDBOOK 4.B.7., 4.C.

Create a poster about your separator. Include a large, labelled diagram, with notes on how the separator works. Explain why your design is efficient and why it has little negative impact on the environment.

Protecting the Environment by Separating Mixtures

Think about the last time you visited a lake or a river. Was there a bad smell? Was there dirty white foam at the edge of the water? If you noticed either of these problems, the water may have been polluted. There are two main ways to avoid polluting water:

- Identify sources of pollution and find ways to stop or limit pollution from these sources.
- Treat any water that contains pollutants, such as waste from sinks and toilets, before it reaches lakes and rivers.

Sewage Treatment

The mixture of water and waste that you flush down the sink or toilet is called **sewage**. What happens to sewage after it is flushed?

Sewage passes through drains and pipes until it reaches a sewage treatment plant. It then goes through one or more stages of treatment to remove the solids, break down the organic material, and kill any disease-causing organisms. The number of treatment stages depends on many things, including space, cost, and end use. The three main stages are primary treatment, secondary treatment, and tertiary treatment. 🌐

Primary Treatment

Half the solids in sewage are removed from the mixture during the primary treatment. First, the sewage passes through a metal grid. This sieves out objects that will not easily decompose, such as items made of fabric and plastic. Next, the sewage is poured into a large pool and allowed to settle for several hours (Figure 1). Most solids settle to the bottom, and floating components (such as oil and grease) rise to the top. The solids are removed, treated, and used as fertilizer, burned, or sent to a landfill.

Figure 1 During primary treatment, sewage settles in a large pool.

sewage: the mixture of water and waste that is flushed down toilets and sink drains

To learn more about sewage treatment,

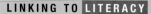
Go to Nelson Science

Secondary Treatment

The remaining dirty water passes through tanks containing bacteria during the secondary treatment. Oxygen gas is bubbled through the mixture (Figure 2). The bacteria break down any remaining human waste and plant material. Next, the water is allowed to settle again. The bacteria settle to the bottom and are removed.

Figure 2 During secondary treatment, bacteria remove any wastes left in the liquid mixture.

Tertiary Treatment

Pollutants like phosphorus and nitrogen are removed during the tertiary treatment (Figure 3). Various kinds of bacteria are encouraged to grow in the wastewater. The water may also pass through filters, have ozone bubbled through it, or be exposed to ultraviolet radiation. Finally, chlorine is added to the water to kill any remaining organisms. Now the water is clean enough to be returned to the ocean, lake, or river.

Figure 3 During some tertiary treatments, chemicals are added to the water. The water may also be filtered.

3.4 Protecting the Environment by Separating Mixtures **65**

Figure 4 Once a bird's feathers are coated in oil, the bird quickly loses body heat and dies.

To learn more about oil spill cleanup,

Keeping Our Water Clean

As you learned in Section 2.1, polluted water is a mixture of contaminants and pure water. Besides sewage, the contaminants can get into water from

- waste produced by manufacturing or processing factories
- fertilizers, pesticides, or salt from farms, golf courses, or roads
- accidental spills and leaks

Clean water is important to everyone, and we must work together to keep pollutants out of the water.

Mixtures of dirty water can be very difficult to separate. Petroleum and petroleum products are transported on ships around the world, including around the Great Lakes. If an oil-carrying cargo ship leaks or sinks, the oil escapes into the ocean or lake water. Some of the substances in oil sink and contaminate the lake or sea bed. Other parts float and spread over the surface, affecting the wildlife that live on or near the water (Figure 4). It is very difficult to separate oil from water once they are mixed. Oil spill clean-up operations are time-consuming, costly, and usually only partly successful.

TRY THIS: Clean Up an Oil Spill

SKILLS HANDBOOK
4.B., 3.I.

SKILLS MENU: planning, performing, evaluating, communicating

In this activity, you will plan and investigate different methods of removing oil from water.

Equipment and Materials: apron; shallow container; spoon; medicine dropper; water; cooking oil; paper plate; cotton balls; straws; detergent; other materials of your choice

1. Put on your apron. Run water into the container until it is a few centimetres deep.

2. Pour a small amount of oil on the water. Wait until the oil spreads over the water, and then pour another small amount. Keep pouring until about half the water is covered with a thin layer of oil.

3. Use the spoon, cotton balls, medicine dropper, straws, detergent, and any other material you choose to clean up the "oil spill." Try at least three different methods. For example:

   - Use the cotton balls or paper towels to soak up the oil.
   - Use the medicine dropper to suck up oil.
   - Use the straws to move the oil to one corner.
   - Add drops of detergent to the oil.

A. Which method was the most successful? Why?

B. Do you think this method could be used to clean up a real oil spill? Explain your answer.

C. Research ways of cleaning up an oil spill on the ocean. Are any of these ways similar to what you did in this activity? Explain how.

Unit Task   As you work on the Unit Task, you will have to think about the environmental considerations that were mentioned in this section.

✔ CHECK YOUR LEARNING

1. What are the two main ways to avoid water pollution?

2. How is settling used in sewage treatment?

3. Briefly outline the main steps of the sewage treatment process.

4. List some ways in which pollutants can get into water.

5. Why is it particularly difficult to separate oil and water once they are mixed?

6. Give at least one example of how oil spills can endanger wildlife.

Separating Solutions

Have you ever been swimming in the ocean (Figure 1)? Once you dry off, you may notice that your skin feels strange. Maybe you licked your fingers and tasted salt. Where did the salt come from?

The ocean is a solution of salt and other solutes in water. After you swim in the ocean, the water on your skin **evaporates**. This means that the water on your skin is heated by the warm skin and changes from the liquid state to the gas state. As a gas, the water dissolves in the air and "disappears." The salt does not evaporate, so it gets left behind on your skin. What does this have to do with separating a solution?

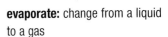

evaporate: change from a liquid to a gas

Figure 1 Ocean water contains salt. The salt dries on your skin when the water evaporates.

As you know, solutions are mixtures in which the particles of the different components are so completely mixed that the mixture appears to be a single pure substance. How can you separate a solution into its components? To answer this question, you need to think about how the particles of a solution behave.

Particles of a Solution

Figure 2 shows sugar and water being mixed together. What happens to the sugar particles when they are mixed with the water particles? Think back to the model of dissolved particles in a solution (Figure 6 in Section 1.6). Remember that the particles of a solution are evenly mixed.

The sugar particles are still in the solution. They have not changed into something different. If you were to make a solution of sugar and water in your kitchen at home, you could tell that the sugar is still there because the solution would taste sweet.

Figure 2 How can we get the sugar back from a sugar-and-water solution?

Separating Solutions by Evaporation

How could you reclaim the sugar from a water-and-sugar solution? Think about some of the differences between sugar and water. When you heat liquid water, it evaporates quite easily. Sugar does not evaporate so easily. You can use this difference to remove the water from the sugar-and-water solution, leaving the sugar behind. **Evaporation** occurs when a liquid changes into a gas. The solid (or a more concentrated solution) is left behind.

Evaporation is often used to remove the liquid from a solution made of a liquid and a solid. This is how maple syrup is made from maple sap. The process of making maple syrup only releases water into the air, so it is not directly damaging to the environment. However, burning wood or natural gas to heat the sap releases gases that cause pollution.

evaporation: the process by which a sample of matter changes from a liquid to a gas

---

⏱ TRY THIS: Make a Stalactite

SKILLS MENU: performing, observing, analyzing, communicating

SKILLS HANDBOOK
2.B.7.

Look at the cave in Figure 3. When water evaporates, it leaves its dissolved solutes behind. You can use this fact to make your own cave formations!

Equipment and Materials: apron; large bowl; spoon; piece of cardboard; 2 clear plastic cups; warm water; Epsom salts; 50 cm of cotton string or wool yarn

1. Put on your apron. Pour about 400 mL of warm water into the large bowl. Add large spoonfuls of Epsom salts and stir until you get a saturated solution (until no more will dissolve).

2. Choose a place in your classroom or home where the experiment can stay for about a week. Put the cardboard on a flat surface.

3. Pour half of the solution into each cup. Place one cup at each side of the piece of cardboard, about 15 cm apart.

4. Rinse the string in tap water. Next, soak the string in the saturated solution for a few seconds.

5. Hang the string between the two cups as shown (Figure 4). Let the string sag in the middle, but do not let it touch the cardboard.

6. Wait for several days. Be careful not to touch your experiment.

A. Was your experiment successful? What happened?

B. Explain your observations.

C. Explain how the stalactites you made are similar to, or different from, the rock formations in Figure 3.

Figure 3 Dripping water evaporates, leaving behind the mineral solutes. Over thousands of years, the minerals form stalactites hanging from the roof and stalagmites on the ground below.

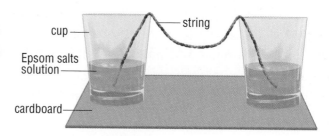

Figure 4 Creating stalactites

Separating Solutions by Distillation

Is there a way of separating two liquids that are mixed together without losing either of them? There is a way if one of the liquids evaporates more easily than the other. **Distillation** is the process of heating a solution of two or more liquids until one liquid evaporates into a gas. The gas is then trapped and cooled until it becomes a liquid again (Figure 5).

distillation: the process of separating liquids in a solution by heating the solution, trapping and cooling the gas, and collecting the resulting pure liquid

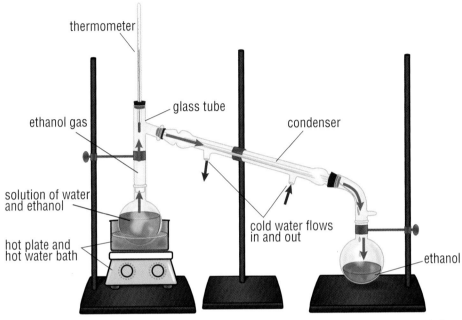

Labels: thermometer, glass tube, ethanol gas, condenser, solution of water and ethanol, cold water flows in and out, hot plate and hot water bath, ethanol

LINKING TO LITERACY

Locating Information
Think about the concept map you created in Section 3.2. What connections can you make between concepts learned in that section and in this one (Section 3.5)? What two additional methods of separation can you now add to your concept map?

Figure 5 To separate ethanol and water using distillation, the solution is heated to just below 78 °C. The ethanol evaporates rapidly at this temperature. As a gas, it travels to the condenser where cold water cools it. The ethanol then cools to become a liquid again. As a liquid, it drips into the collecting flask on the right. Most of the water stays behind in the round-bottomed flask on the left.

If you had a liquid solution with more than two liquid components, you could repeat the distillation process to separate all the liquid parts of the solution. You would have to use a different collecting flask for each component that evaporated and then cooled to become a liquid again.

To learn more about evaporation and distillation,

Go to Nelson Science

Unit Task How can you use information about separating solutions as you work on the Unit Task? Can you use evaporation or distillation?

✔ CHECK YOUR LEARNING

1. Describe one way to separate sugar from a sugar-and-water mixture.
2. Explain, using a labelled diagram, how the process of distillation works.

3. The sap from a sugar maple tree is a mixture of sugar dissolved in water.
   (a) What method is used to make maple syrup?
   (b) When you boil maple sap, something leaves the mixture. What is it? Is this process likely to be harmful to the environment?

Separating a Solution

Once a solute is dissolved in water, can you get it all back again? In this investigation, you will make a salt-and-water solution using measured quantities of salt and water. Next, you will plan and perform your own procedure to reclaim the salt from the mixture. You will determine whether the quantity of solute changes after it dissolves into a solution.

SKILLS MENU

- ☐ Questioning
- ☑ Hypothesizing
- ☑ Predicting
- ☑ Planning
- ☐ Controlling Variables
- ☑ Performing
- ☐ Observing
- ☑ Analyzing
- ☑ Evaluating
- ☐ Communicating

Testable Question

How is the quantity of salt affected when the salt is reclaimed from a salt-and-water solution?

Hypothesis/Prediction

 SKILLS HANDBOOK 2.B.3.

Make a hypothesis based on the Testable Question. Your hypothesis should include a prediction and a reason for your prediction based on the particle theory.

Experimental Design

In this investigation, you will plan your own procedure to reclaim the salt in a solution made of 5 g of salt and 100 mL of warm water. You will compare the mass of the salt before and after to determine whether or not the amount of salt changes during the investigation.

Equipment and Materials

- eye protection
- apron
- oven mitts
- balance
- weighing papers
- large beaker
- graduated cylinder
- stirring rod
- hot plate
- wire gauze with ceramic centre
- salt
- warm water

eye protection

apron

oven mitts

balance

weighing papers

large beaker

graduated cylinder

stirring rod

hot plate

wire gauze with ceramic centre

salt

warm water

Procedure

Part A: Planning

SKILLS HANDBOOK
2.B.4.

1. Read through the whole investigation.
2. With your partner, brainstorm how you will separate the solution and collect the salt.
3. Write the steps of your procedure. You may use a flowchart. Your procedure should include
   - steps you will follow to separate the solution
   - safety precautions
   - a way to measure the amount of salt obtained after the separation
4. Create a table in which to record your observations.
5. Have your teacher check your procedure before you continue.

Part B: Making the Solution

6. Measure and record the mass of an empty beaker.
7. Measure out 5 g of salt. Pour the salt into the empty beaker. Measure and record the total mass of the beaker and salt.
8. Add 100 mL of warm water to the beaker. Stir until you cannot see any solid salt.

Part C: Separating the Solution

9. Perform the procedure you planned, using the prepared salt-and-water solution. Record your observations in your table.

Analyze and Evaluate

SKILLS HANDBOOK
2.B.7.

(a) Calculate the mass of the salt used to make your solution in Part B.
(b) Calculate the mass of the salt that is left behind in Part C.
(c) Answer the Testable Question.
(d) Where is the water at the end of the procedure? Use the particle theory to explain your answer.

(e) When you make a solution of salt and water, does the salt cease to exist? Use the particle theory to explain your answer.
(f) When you separate a salt-and-water solution using your procedure, what happens to the salt? Use the particle theory to explain your answer.

Apply and Extend

(g) To make candy, sugar is mixed with water and flavourings (Figure 1). The mixture is then heated for several minutes. Use what you have learned in this investigation to explain the purpose of these two steps.

Figure 1 Making candy requires a knowledge of chemistry

Unit Task How will you use the skills you learned in this investigation when you work on the Unit Task?

3.7

Mixtures in Industry

Many industries separate mixtures to produce pure products. In this section, you will learn about three industries that separate mixtures: the flour industry, the petroleum industry, and the nuclear power industry. As you read through this section, ask yourself these questions:

- What are the components of the mixture?
- Is the mixture a mechanical mixture or a solution?
- What method is used to separate the mixture into its pure components?
- How does the separation method work?

Making Wheat Flour

Bread, cake, cookies, and many other baked goods are made from wheat flour. How are the grains of wheat in Figure 1 made into flour?

Figure 1   Wheat grains are crushed and separated into their components.

Purifying the Wheat Grains

Wheat flour must be made from ground wheat grains and nothing else. Wheat grains arriving at a flour mill may be mixed with dust, sand, metal splinters, or parts of other plants. Figure 2 shows how the wheat is separated from the rest of this mixture.

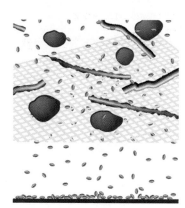

Wheat grains pass through metal sieves. Sticks and stones are caught by the sieve.

A vacuum extractor sucks up the impurities that are lighter than wheat grains, such as dust and leaves.

Magnets pick out any pieces of iron and steel in the mixture.

Figure 2   Methods used to purify wheat grains

Grinding the Wheat Grains

A wheat grain has three main parts: endosperm, bran, and wheat germ (Figure 3). In a process called "milling," metal rollers break open the wheat grains (Figure 4). The milled mixture is passed through a series of sieves to separate the endosperm, bran, and germ from each other. The endosperm is used to make white flour.

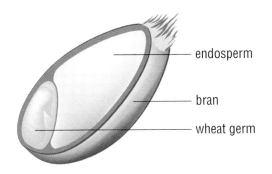

Figure 3 Parts of a grain of wheat

— endosperm

— bran

— wheat germ

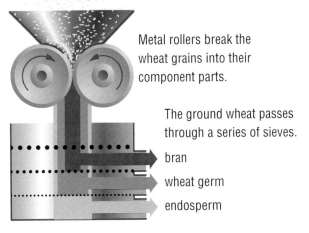

Wheat grains enter the mill.

Metal rollers break the wheat grains into their component parts.

The ground wheat passes through a series of sieves.

bran

wheat germ

endosperm

Figure 4 Grinding and sieving the wheat grains

The bran and wheat germ are often sold separately from the endosperm. Bakers sometimes add bran and wheat germ to breads, muffins, and other baked goods. This adds fibre and nutrients. Whole-wheat flour is a mixture of all three parts of the wheat grain. Eating products made from whole-wheat flour, rather than white flour, is often a healthy choice because whole-wheat is less processed and contains more nutrients.

Refining Petroleum

Petroleum, or crude oil, is a homogeneous mixture of many pure substances found deep in the ground (Figure 5). Many products in your everyday life are made from petroleum, including plastics, asphalt, many medicines, synthetic fibres, and fertilizers. Most of the fuels that power cars, trucks, trains, and airplanes also come from petroleum.

To learn more about refining petroleum,

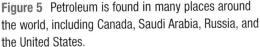

Figure 5 Petroleum is found in many places around the world, including Canada, Saudi Arabia, Russia, and the United States.

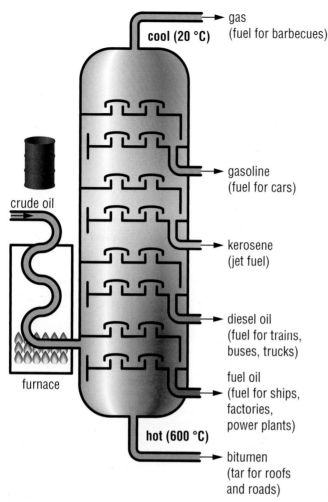

gas
(fuel for barbecues)

cool (20 °C)

crude oil

gasoline
(fuel for cars)

kerosene
(jet fuel)

diesel oil
(fuel for trains,
buses, trucks)

fuel oil
(fuel for ships,
factories,
power plants)

hot (600 °C)

furnace

bitumen
(tar for roofs
and roads)

Figure 6 Crude oil is purified in a
fractional distillation column.

Petroleum comes out of the ground as a thick, liquid mixture of many different substances. Each component of the mixture boils at a different temperature. Engineers have developed a technology to separate the various components (Figure 6). First, a furnace heats petroleum until its components begin to evaporate. The hot gases rise through a tall column that cools the gases. This column is called a "fractional distillation column." Different components of the gas mixture cool (becoming liquids) at different temperatures. The liquids produced settle at different levels in the column. The liquid collected at each level of the column is called a "fraction." Each fraction can be further purified.

Benefits of Refining Petroleum

Natural petroleum is not very useful because it contains many chemicals that behave in different ways. When petroleum is refined, however, you can take advantage of the special characteristics of each fraction. If you need a material for surfacing a road, you would select the heaviest fraction: bitumen. Bitumen is thick and sticky, and good for making asphalt and roadways. If you need a liquid fuel for vehicles, you would choose a lighter fraction such as diesel. You could use the lightest fractions, such as gasoline and propane, as fuels for cars and barbecues, and to make paints, plastics, and medicines.

Petroleum Refining and the Environment

Refining petroleum has risks. Raw petroleum is piped or shipped to oil refineries, and the refined products are transported away again. Leaks and spills sometimes occur during transportation (Figure 7). These can seriously damage the environment, both land and water, and cause health problems for plants and animals. Leaks during the refining process may cause air pollution. The lighter fractions of petroleum catch fire easily, so explosions and fires are a risk. Refining petroleum also produces bad smells and noise. For these reasons, most petroleum industries are located away from areas where people live.

Figure 7 Petroleum spills are difficult to clean up. This petroleum was spilled when a wind storm split an oil tanker in two.

Uranium and Nuclear Power

Ontario uses a lot of electricity for heating, cooling, and powering machines and electrical devices. Ontario's electricity is produced using several energy sources. These include the energy of falling water, the energy in fossil fuels such as natural gas and coal, and the energy in the particles of special pure substances such as uranium. In each case, a machine called an **electric generator** converts the energy into electricity.

Uranium is a **radioactive** substance. This means that, unlike most pure substances, uranium's particles break apart into smaller particles. As uranium particles split, they release a burst of energy called **nuclear energy**. This energy is used to generate electricity in a nuclear power plant.

Uranium occurs naturally in rocks called uranium ore. Uranium is separated from the ore by crushing the ore and adding a solution that dissolves the uranium. The waste rock is sieved out and the uranium-containing solution is collected. When the water evaporates from the solution, a solid remains. This solid is further processed into pure uranium and shaped into small pellets.

Inside a nuclear power plant, the uranium pellets are placed in the centre, or core, of a nuclear reactor (Figure 8). There, the uranium particles split apart and release energy in the form of intense heat and radiation. This energy heats water surrounding the core, and the water evaporates. As the hot water vapour expands, it turns the blades of large, fan-like turbines. The spinning turbines then turn generators that produce electricity.

electric generator: a machine with moving parts that produce electricity when they spin

radioactive: a term used to describe pure substances whose particles naturally split into smaller particles, releasing energy as they break apart

nuclear energy: the energy released when the particles of pure substances like uranium split apart

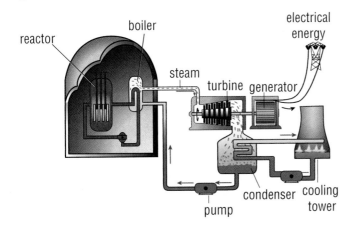

Figure 8 A nuclear power reactor

When a certain fraction of uranium particles has split, the energy production slows down and the "used" uranium has to be replaced with new pellets. Over 90 % of the used uranium is reprocessed and used again in a nuclear reactor. The remainder must be disposed of.

Figure 9 Areas surrounding Chernobyl were deserted after the accident in 1986 due to high levels of radiation.

Nuclear power has two big advantages over energy from petroleum and petroleum products: it does not produce pollution that can lead to acid rain, and it does not release carbon dioxide that causes climate change. So, why do many people oppose nuclear power? There are two main reasons.

First, people are concerned that something could go wrong with the nuclear reactor and radioactive particles could be released into the environment. This happened in 1986 in Chernobyl, Ukraine, when a reactor core exploded and radioactive material contaminated much of eastern and northern Europe (Figure 9). High levels of radiation from radioactive substances can cause serious diseases, like cancer, and can even cause death.

Second, disposing of the used uranium is a problem. Used uranium is still radioactive and continues to release radiation and thermal energy for thousands of years. It cannot just be buried in a landfill, as the surrounding rock, soil, and water would be contaminated. One method of disposal involves mixing used uranium with a form of melted glass, cooling it, and burying the solid mixture in a deep, closed mine. There is still the concern that earthquakes may disturb mines such as these, or that people may accidentally rediscover the buried waste in future centuries. The nuclear waste disposal problem has not yet been resolved, and the debate goes on. Meanwhile, about half of Ontario's electricity continues to come from nuclear power plants.

LINKING TO LITERACY

Compare and Contrast
Comparing and contrasting helps to identify similarities and differences. Create a t-chart to compare and contrast the refining of petroleum and the separation of uranium. How are they the same? How are they different?

To learn more about nuclear power,

Go to Nelson Science

CHECK YOUR LEARNING

1. There were several diagrams in this section.
   (a) Which diagram did you find the hardest to understand? Explain why.
   (b) Where can you find help to understand the diagram?

2. Describe one way to separate each of the following mixtures:
   (a) wheat grains mixed with stones and large sticks
   (b) wheat grains mixed with pieces of metal
   (c) a mixture of different oil components that evaporate at different temperatures

3. List three methods of separating mixtures that are used in the flour industry.

4. (a) Why can uranium be used to produce electricity?
   (b) How is uranium used to produce electricity?

5. What is uranium ore, and how is uranium obtained from it?

6. (a) Why can waste uranium not be treated the same as regular garbage?
   (b) Describe one way in which uranium is disposed of.

7. List two risks and two benefits of nuclear power.

Separating a Complex Mixture

SKILLS MENU

- ☐ Questioning
- ☐ Hypothesizing
- ☐ Predicting
- ☑ Planning
- ☐ Controlling Variables
- ☑ Performing
- ☑ Observing
- ☐ Analyzing
- ☑ Evaluating
- ☐ Communicating

In this activity, you will be given a complex mechanical mixture that has four different components that you must separate.

Purpose

To plan and perform a series of steps to separate the components of a complex mechanical mixture.

Equipment and Materials

- eye protection
- apron
- small beakers
- plastic container
- magnet
- spoon
- sieve

- a pre-mixed mechanical mixture
- water in a wash bottle
- filter paper
- other equipment and materials that you will need

eye protection   apron   small beakers

plastic container   magnet   spoon

sieve   mechanical mixture   water in a wash bottle

filter paper

Procedure

SKILLS HANDBOOK
2.B.4., 2.B.5.

1. Look closely at your mixture to identify the various components. Plan how you will separate each component.

2. Decide in which order you will separate the components. Create a flow chart outlining your plan.

3. Write a detailed procedure, including necessary safety precautions.

4. With your teacher's approval, perform your procedure and collect the separate components of your mixture.

Analyze and Evaluate

SKILLS HANDBOOK
2.B.8.

(a) What components did your mixture contain? How do you know?

(b) Which separation method did you choose for each component? Were these methods appropriate? Why or why not?

(c) If you were to repeat this activity, what would you do differently?

(d) If you had been given the same mixture but with water added, would you have been able to collect all the components? Explain.

Apply and Extend

(e) Suggest an industrial process in which a complex mixture has to be separated. What separation methods could be used?

Unit Task The skills you used in this activity will be useful when you work on the Unit Task.

Separating Mixtures

BIG Ideas

- ☑ Matter can be classified according to its physical characteristics.
- ☑ The particle theory of matter helps to explain the physical characteristics of matter.
- ☑ Pure substances and mixtures have an impact on society and the environment.
- ☑ Understanding the characteristics of matter allows us to make informed choices about how we use it.

Looking Back

The skills of scientific inquiry can be used to learn about methods of separating different mixtures.

- Different types of mixtures can be separated in different ways.
- The properties of the components in a mixture determine the best method of separating the mixture (for example, a mixture of iron filings and sand can be separated using a magnet).

Mechanical mixtures can be separated into their components using methods such as sorting, floating, settling, attracting with a magnet, sieving, and filtering.

- You can sort a mechanical mixture like a salad with your fingers.
- You can filter a mechanical mixture like pasta and water using a sieve or filter.
- You can use a magnet to remove iron filings from a mixture.
- You can leave a mechanical mixture that includes a liquid to settle, and then skim or pour off the top layer.
- Some pure substances dissolve in water, while others do not. You can use this property to separate a mixture of solids.

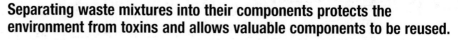

Separating waste mixtures into their components protects the environment from toxins and allows valuable components to be reused.

- Garbage is sorted and separated to reduce the quantity that goes to the landfill. Reusable materials are recycled.
- Sewage from sinks and toilets is cleaned before the water is returned to lakes and rivers.
- Oil spills must be cleaned up to protect wildlife and humans that depend on the lakes and oceans.

Solutions can be separated into their components using methods such as evaporation and distillation.

- Salt "disappears" (becomes invisible) when it dissolves in water. Salt can be recovered from a solution by evaporating the water.

- You can separate two liquids by heating them until one liquid evaporates. Then you can cool the gas, condense it, and collect the liquid. This process is called distillation.

VOCABULARY

sorting, p. 58
floating, p. 59
settling, p. 59
sieve, p. 60
sieving, p. 60
filter, p. 60
filtration, p. 60
sewage, p. 64
evaporate, p. 67
evaporation, p. 68
distillation, p. 69
electric generator, p. 75
radioactive, p. 75
nuclear energy, p. 75

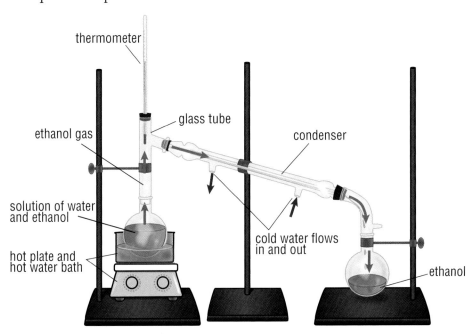

Investigation skills can be used to determine the best method to separate mixtures.

- The best method of separating a mixture can be determined by making detailed observations about the components in the mixture.

- Complex mixtures can be separated if you have a plan determining the order in which to separate the components of the mixture.

Many industries separate mixtures when making products.

- The flour industry uses sieves and magnets to separate impurities from wheat grains.

- The petroleum industry uses distillation to separate the fractions of petroleum.

- The nuclear power industry uses dissolving and evaporation to separate uranium from the mixture of pure substances in uranium ore.

CHAPTER 3 REVIEW

The following icons indicate the Achievement Chart categories: **K/U** Knowledge/Understanding   **C** Communication   **T/I** Thinking/Investigation   **A** Application

What Do You Remember?

1. Describe one method used to separate the following mixtures into the products indicated:

   (a) sewage → cleaner water

   (b) wheat grains → white flour

   (c) petroleum (crude oil) → gasoline **K/U**

2. (a) Name a way to separate a solution that contains two liquids.

   (b) Name a way to reclaim solid solute from a solution. **K/U**

3. Suggest a mechanical mixture (not already mentioned) that could be separated into its parts by each of the following methods: **K/U**

   (a) sorting

   (b) floating or settling

   (c) using a magnet

   (d) using a filter or a sieve

   (e) dissolving soluble parts of the mixture

4. How does a filter work to separate the components of a mechanical mixture? **K/U**

5. Could you use a magnet to separate any kind of mixture? Why or why not? **K/U**

6. Draw a diagram showing how you would reclaim salt from a salt-and-water solution. Explain your diagram. **K/U** **C**

7. Why is it important to remove harmful materials from waste before putting the waste in the environment? **K/U**

What Do You Understand?

8. Describe one way to separate each of the following mechanical mixtures:

   (a) air and dust

   (b) paper clips and erasers

   (c) mud (soil and water)

   (d) sugar and sand

   (e) sawdust and sand **T/I** **A**

9. Which methods of separating mechanical mixtures do you think would be most useful in separating garbage that includes compost, waste paper, steel cans, and plastic bottles? Explain why. **K/U** **A**

10. (a) Wheat grains might arrive at a flour mill mixed up with stones, sticks, and so on. What kind of mixture is this?

    (b) When the wheat grains have been crushed, what kind of mixture is this?

    (c) When petroleum arrives at an oil refinery, what kind of mixture is this? **K/U**

Solve a Problem!

11. Joshua mixed sand with water. Describe two ways to separate Joshua's mixture. **C** **A**

12. The town of Sunnydale is on an ocean coast. The sewage from the town is dumped directly into the ocean with no treatment. Today, Sunnydale is having a meeting about whether to start sewage treatment. There are three speakers at the meeting:

    Speaker 1: The mayor of Sunnydale is worried that if they put a lot of money into expensive sewage treatment, there may not be enough money for the town's hospital.

    Speaker 2: A local scientist says that the sewage is harming the environment. The number of fish in the ocean nearby is decreasing.

    Speaker 3: A sewage treatment expert says that Sunnydale has two options: primary treatment, or both primary and secondary treatment. Just primary treatment is less expensive, but only removes 60 % of the waste. Using both treatments is more expensive, but will purify the water better.

    Do you think Sunnydale should start sewage treatment? If so, which kind? Explain your answer. **T/I** **A** **C**

13. Chang poured salt into his glass of juice by accident. Can Chang remove all the salt by pouring his juice through a filter? Explain why or why not. A T/I

14. Jayanthy has a mixture of sawdust, gravel, and salt. Create a flow chart to describe how Jayanthy can separate her mixture. T/I A

15. Perform research to find out

    (a) what is, and what is not, recycled in your home town (Figure 1)

    (b) how you can reduce the quantity of waste material that is sent to landfills A

Figure 1

16. Millions of people around the world, including some in parts of Canada, do not have easy access to clean, fresh water. Research answers to the following questions. Present your findings to your class as a speech, song, story, electronic presentation, or in some other way:

    (a) Where, on Earth, is there no access to clean water?

    (b) Why is clean water not available?

    (c) How does this relate to pure substances and mixtures?

    (d) What, if anything, is being done to solve the problem? K/U T/I C

Go to Nelson Science

Create and Evaluate!

17. Create a flow chart to show the changes that happen to uranium, from when it is mined to when it is finally disposed of. Evaluate this process in terms of potential hazards to the environment and living things, and its cost. Is nuclear power a benefit to society? A T/I C

18. "People often separate mechanical mixtures in their daily lives." Do you agree or disagree with this statement? Explain why. A

Reflect on Your Learning

19. There were three main concepts in Chapter 3:

    • You can separate mechanical mixtures using sorting, sieving/filtration, settling, floating, and magnetism.

    • You can separate solutions using distillation, and reclaim solid solutes by evaporation.

    • Industries separate mixtures to process raw materials and make new products.

    (a) Which of these concepts was the easiest to understand?

    (b) Which concept was the hardest to understand?

    (c) List one thing you can do to help you understand this concept better.

    (d) Did anything not make sense to you in this chapter?

    (e) Explain your answer to part (d) to a classmate or your teacher. Do they agree, or do they have a different opinion?

20. Think back to the Key Question on the first page of this chapter.

    (a) In a brief paragraph, answer the Key Question. You may use diagrams.

    (b) Write one or two more questions about the topic of this unit that you would like answered.

Test a Sample of Industrial Waste

At the beginning of Chapter 1, you read about an environmental scientist testing the water in a river for contaminants—pure substances and mixtures that should not be there. Scientists use these tests to help stop pollution and to protect plants and animals living in natural ecosystems (Figure 1).

Figure 1 This environmental scientist is taking a sample of water to test for pollutants.

Scenario

You will play the role of an environmental scientist. You have been called in to investigate a river that may be polluted. There is a natural woodland on one side of the river and a factory on the other side of the river. Some of the waste from the factory runs into the river.

Design Brief

Your task is to separate and identify the components of a sample of contaminated river water taken from just below the factory's waste pipe. Your procedure should be efficient (have the fewest possible steps) and effective (separate as many components as possible).

You will determine whether the factory waste contains pollutants that might be harmful to local wildlife. You will also suggest how the factory could remove these pollutants from its water before letting the water run into the river. Finally, you will consider the costs and benefits of your suggestion.

Equipment and Materials

SKILLS HANDBOOK
4.B.3.

Several identical samples of contaminated river water are available for you to work with. Choose the equipment and materials for your procedure, including safety equipment.

Research and Consider

Examine the mixture and think about the characteristics of the components of the mixture. If necessary, place the mixture under bright light or stir it to explore its components further. You may want to use a magnifying glass.

Plan and Construct

SKILLS HANDBOOK
4.B.2., 4.B.4

1. Plan how you will separate a sample of the mixture into its components. Assume that the mixture may have components that you cannot see. You may choose to use the technique shown in Figure 2.

Figure 2 One technique for removing water from a mixture

2. Write a detailed procedure. You may use a flow chart.

3. Have your teacher check and approve your procedure.

4. Assemble your equipment and materials, and perform your procedure. Record your observations.

Test and Modify

SKILLS HANDBOOK
4.B.5., 4.B.6.

- Did your procedure separate all possible components of the mixture?
- Should you change the sequence of steps in your procedure?
- Can you reduce the number of steps in your procedure?

If necessary, modify your procedure and try it again.

Evaluate

Compare how well your procedure meets the requirements of the Design Brief:

- How well were you able to separate all of the components of the contaminated river water?
- What were the components?
- What characteristics of the components did you use to separate them?

- How could you improve your procedure, or make it more effective and more efficient?
- Are any of the components damaging to the environment? If so, how should they be removed from the factory's waste? If necessary, perform research to answer these questions.

Go to Nelson Science

Communicate

SKILLS HANDBOOK
4.B.7., 8.

Draw a detailed flow chart showing all the steps that you used to separate the mixture's components. This should be an expansion of the one you created for Plan and Construct. Label each step with the following information:

- the separation method that you used
- the components that you obtained
- the characteristics of the components that allowed you to separate them from each other

Indicate, on your flow chart, which components may have been damaging to the environment, and how they should be removed from the factory's waste.

Present your findings in the form of a poster, report, or oral presentation.

Assessment

You will be assessed on how well you

- identify characteristics of components that allow separation
- plan a procedure for separating the components that is
  - safe
  - effective
  - efficient
- test the procedure as planned

- make any necessary changes to the procedure, and then retest
- communicate your best procedure as a flow chart
- identify dangerous components
- recommend a technique for removing dangerous components from the factory's waste

Pure Substances and Mixtures

Make a Summary

Figure 1 shows the start of a concept map. Copy this onto the centre of a large piece of paper. Work with a partner or small group to complete the concept map. Try to include all the vocabulary terms in this unit. Your concept map should include explanations for the connections between terms.

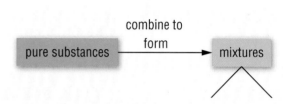

Figure 1 Make a concept map starting with these terms.

Unit A Review Questions

What Do You Remember?

The following icons indicate the Achievement Chart categories: **K/U** Knowledge/Understanding **C** Communication **T/I** Thinking/Investigation **A** Application

1. Write a definition of matter. **K/U**

2. What is matter made of? **K/U**

3. Write, in your own words, the five main ideas of the particle theory. **K/U**

4. What is the difference between the particles of a solid and the particles of a liquid? **K/U**

5. (a) What are the three states of matter?

   (b) Use the particle theory to describe each of the three states of matter. **K/U**

6. (a) What is the difference between a pure substance and a mixture?

   (b) Give one example of each. **K/U**

7. (a) Name the two types of mixtures and explain how they are different.

   (b) Give one example of each. **K/U**

8. Can you tell if a sample of matter is a pure substance or a solution by looking at it? Explain why or why not. **K/U**

9. Name two industries that separate mixtures. **K/U** **A**

10. Can you tell if a mixture is a mechanical mixture by looking at it? Explain. **K/U** **C**

11. Identify each of the following kinds of matter as a pure substance, a mechanical mixture, or a solution:

    (a) salt   (d) a salad

    (b) clear shampoo   (e) 14-karat gold

    (c) table sugar   (f) soil **K/U**

12. Distinguish between a homogeneous mixture and a heterogeneous mixture. **K/U**

13. Is air a solution or a pure substance? Explain your answer. **K/U**

14. (a) What is the difference between a solute and a solvent?

    (b) Give one example of each. **K/U**

15. Draw a model that shows the particles of a gas. Explain your model. **K/U** **C**

16. Is a piece of paper a solid, a liquid, or a gas? Explain your answer. **K/U**

17. List three different ways pollutants get into the water system. K/U

18. (a) List three solutions in your home. A

    (b) What is the solvent of each solution? A

19. Devawn says, "Solutions can be solids, liquids, or gases." Do you agree? Explain. K/U C

20. Describe what happens to the sewage that goes down your drain and toilet before it is released into the environment. K/U A

21. (a) Aluminum foil is a solid pure substance. Draw a model of the particles of a piece of aluminum.

    (b) Brass is a solid solution. Draw a model of the particles of a piece of brass. K/U C

22. Distilled water is a pure substance.

    (a) Draw a model showing the particles of liquid distilled water.

    (b) Draw a model showing the particles of solid distilled water (ice). K/U C

23. You dissolve 10 mL of sugar in 30 mL of water. The total volume is less than 40 mL. Use the particle theory to explain this observation. K/U

24. Salt does not dissolve well in oil. The salt tends to settle to the bottom of the container.

    (a) What kind of mixture is this?

    (b) Draw a model showing the particles of a mixture of salt and oil. K/U C

What Do You Understand?

25. Describe one way to separate each of the following mixtures into its components. Describe the characteristics that make each separation possible.

    (a) iron filings and sand

    (b) sugar and water

    (c) tea leaves and water T/I

26. (a) What methods does a flour mill use to separate wheat grains from other kinds of matter?

    (b) What method does a flour mill use to separate the different parts of the wheat grains after they are ground up? K/U A

27. Use the particle theory to explain each of the following observations:

    (a) Sugar dissolves in water even if you do not stir or heat the mixture.

    (b) Stirring or heating makes sugar dissolve in water faster.

    (c) You add a drop of red food colouring to a glass of water. You do not stir the mixture, but the food colouring spreads throughout the water. T/I C

28. Give one reason why someone might want to separate a mechanical mixture. A

29. "Pure orange juice" may contain water, pieces of orange pulp, sugar, vitamin C, potassium, protein, and flavour particles.

    (a) Is pure orange juice a pure substance, a mechanical mixture, or a solution? K/U

    (b) Suggest two methods that could be used to separate some of the components of orange juice. T/I A

30. A red solid dissolves in a glass of water. Draw a picture of what the solution actually looks like, and then draw a model of the particles of the solution. K/U C

31. Figure 2 shows one step in the process of refining sugar. Research and report on the process of refining table sugar from raw materials. c A

Go to Nelson Science

Figure 2

32. Explain why water is an important solvent in
   (a) your body
   (b) the environment K/U A

33. (a) When you boil a mixture of sugar maple sap to make maple syrup, what part of the mixture are you removing?
   (b) Is the process of making maple syrup likely to harm the environment? Explain why or why not. K/U c A

34. Uranium is a pure substance that is radioactive. Use the Internet to research uranium. K/U T/I A
   (a) Why is uranium harmful to humans?
   (b) What is uranium used for?
   (c) What are the benefits of using uranium?
   (d) How do people dispose of uranium?
   (e) Do you think humans should continue to use uranium? Explain why or why not.

Go to Nelson Science

35. Jason says, "I can separate a solution of sugar and water even though I can't see the different parts of the mixture." Yousif says, "I can only separate a mixture if I can see the different parts." Do you agree with Jason or with Yousif? Explain your answer. K/U

36. (a) Matt mixes 5 g of sugar with 10 g of water. Can he accurately predict the total mass of the mixture? Explain.
   (b) Raven mixes 5 mL of sugar with 10 mL of water. Can she accurately predict the total volume of the mixture? Explain. K/U T/I A

37. (a) Kemisha's glass of ice water has a mass of 35 g. Will the mass change as the ice melts? Explain.
   (b) Kemisha left her glass of water outside in the sun for the whole day. Will the mass of the water in the glass change? Explain. K/U T/I

38. (a) How does the petroleum industry separate petroleum into different parts? K/U
   (b) What effects does the petroleum industry have on the environment? K/U
   (c) Would you want a petroleum refinery near your home? Why or why not? A

39. *Exxon Valdez* was a ship carrying oil across the ocean. Use the Internet to research what happened to *Exxon Valdez* in 1989.
   (a) What happened to *Exxon Valdez*?
   (b) What did people do to solve the problem?
   (c) How well did the solution(s) work?
   (d) What were the long-term effects?
   (e) Do you think oil should be carried across oceans in ships? Why or why not? Suggest alternatives to ocean transport of oil. K/U

Go to Nelson Science

Solve a Problem!

40. The town of Jonesburg is considering building a petroleum refinery in the middle of town. You have been asked to advise the city on the best path to take. Write a report to the city, outlining the pros and cons of this proposal, and make your recommendation. `T/I` `A` `C`

41. Ali dissolves 3 g of sugar in water to make 10 mL of solution. What is the concentration of Ali's solution in grams per 100 mL? `K/U`

42. Ling left a glass with some water in it on a counter overnight. The next day, the glass was empty.

  (a) What happened to the water?

  (b) Ling noticed a tiny bit of white solid left in the bottom of the glass. Where might the white solid have come from?

  (c) What could Ling have done to prevent the glass of water from emptying? `T/I` `A`

43. At 20 °C, you can dissolve no more than 36 g of salt in 100 mL of water.

  (a) How many grams of salt can you dissolve in 50 mL of water?

  (b) If you dissolve 20 g of salt in 100 mL of water, is the solution saturated or unsaturated? Explain.

  (c) If you dissolve 1 g of salt in 100 mL of water at 20 °C, is the solution concentrated or dilute? Explain why. `K/U` `A`

Create and Evaluate!

44. Sugar dissolves easily in water. It does not dissolve easily in ethanol.

  (a) Write a short story that explains why sugar dissolves in water but not in ethanol.

  (b) Does your story describe the dissolving process accurately? Explain.

  (c) Modify your story so that it describes the dissolving process better. `K/U` `C`

45. "Mixtures have benefits and costs." Write a short paragraph explaining what this sentence means. Provide examples of the benefits and costs of using specific mixtures. `K/U` `C` `A`

Reflect on Your Learning

46. Review the particle theory in Section 1.1.

  (a) How well do you think you understand the particle theory?

  (b) How much does the particle theory help you to understand dissolving?

  (c) Here are some things you can do to understand the particle theory better:

- Read Section 1.1 again.
- Discuss the particle theory with a friend.
- Review all the diagrams showing models of particles in this unit.
- Use a physical model to help you think about particles.
- Draw a picture (model) that shows the particles of a solution. Carry out two of the ideas listed. Did the ideas help? Why or why not?

"We are part of the earth and it is part of us.... This we know: the earth does not belong to man, man belongs to the earth. This we know: all things are connected like the blood which unites one family. All things are connected. Whatever befalls the earth befalls the sons of the earth. Man did not weave the web of life; he is merely a strand in it. Whatever he does to the web, he does to himself."

—Chief Sealth (excerpt from *The Land is Sacred to Us*)

Better known today as Chief Seattle, Chief Sealth was the leader of the Suquamish and Duwamish, two First Nations that lived on the West Coast, near what is now the state of Washington, U.S.A. It is believed that he gave the speech on the previous page in 1854 as a warning to people that Earth cannot be exploited forever. His message continues to have profound meaning today.

Every day we receive warnings about the state of our planet. Greenhouse-gas emissions, climate change, energy and water shortages, and severe weather events dominate the news. However, if we act responsibly today, we can save the planet from a bleak future. As First Nations peoples have traditionally taught, "we are a part of Earth and it is part of us."

In this unit, you will learn how living things depend on each other and how they interact with their environment. You will learn how Earth supports life. Most importantly, you will discover how humans fit into the natural world and the important role you play in keeping our planet healthy.

BIG Ideas

☐ Ecosystems are made up of biotic (living) and abiotic (non-living) elements, which depend on each other to survive.

☐ Ecosystems are in a constant state of change. The changes may be caused by nature or by human intervention.

☐ Human activities have the potential to alter the environment. Humans must be aware of these impacts and try to control them.

CHAPTER 4   Healthy Ecosystems

CHAPTER 5   Interactions within Ecosystems

CHAPTER 6   Organisms Depend on a Healthy Environment

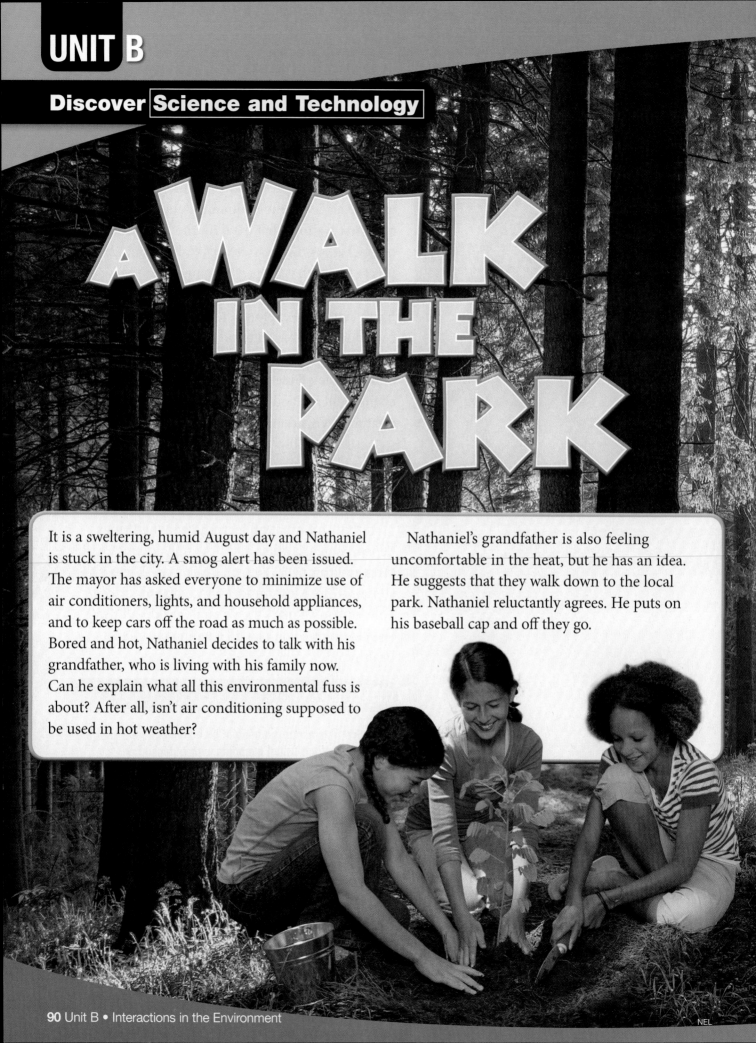

A WALK IN THE PARK

It is a sweltering, humid August day and Nathaniel is stuck in the city. A smog alert has been issued. The mayor has asked everyone to minimize use of air conditioners, lights, and household appliances, and to keep cars off the road as much as possible. Bored and hot, Nathaniel decides to talk with his grandfather, who is living with his family now. Can he explain what all this environmental fuss is about? After all, isn't air conditioning supposed to be used in hot weather?

Nathaniel's grandfather is also feeling uncomfortable in the heat, but he has an idea. He suggests that they walk down to the local park. Nathaniel reluctantly agrees. He puts on his baseball cap and off they go.

As they walk to the park, Grandpa reflects on Nathaniel's question. "Where I spent my childhood, there was no need to worry about water, air, or heat. We could drink out of the river, and the air was fresh and clean. Cool breezes and large trees in our backyard kept us comfortable in the summers. We were surrounded by nature." Nathaniel and his grandfather finally reach the park. Nathaniel immediately feels cooler as soon as they walk into the wooded area. The hum of traffic and loud noises are replaced by the sound of their breathing and an occasional bird call.

They find a secluded place to sit and Grandpa continues. "The last couple of generations have been unkind to the environment. People thought that technology would solve all our problems and took nature for granted. Instead, we have created new problems. We are creating too much waste, polluting the air, and ruining the land."

Grandpa says, " Do you know that this area used to be covered in weeds and grass? There were no trees. Now, it has become a park, thanks to some very dedicated volunteers. They planted native vegetation and returned the land to its original, natural state. Insects, birds, and wild animals have returned here. People enjoy this place."

"But there is nothing to do here," responds Nathaniel.

"This may not have the excitement of a computer game, or the action of a mall," continues Grandpa, "but if you are quiet enough and you take the time to observe, there is actually quite a bit happening here."

Sure enough, after several minutes of gazing at the trickling river, Nathaniel spots a muskrat swimming by! He has never seen one before!

"I wonder if I could join the volunteer group that helps keep this place so beautiful?" he asks. Nathaniel has totally forgotten about the heat.

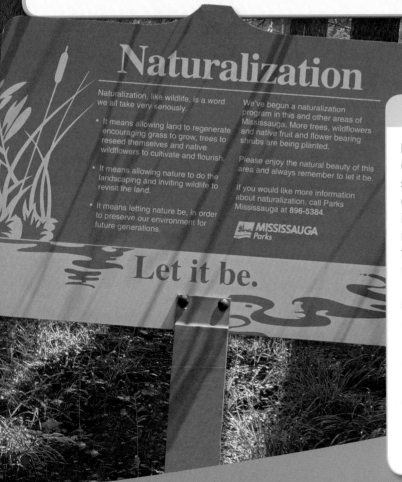

Naturalization

Naturalization, like wildlife, is a word we all take very seriously.

- It means allowing land to regenerate encouraging grass to grow, trees to reseed themselves and native wildflowers to cultivate and flourish.

- It means allowing nature to do the landscaping and inviting wildlife to revisit the land.

- It means letting nature be, in order to preserve our environment for future generations.

We've begun a naturalization program in this and other areas of Mississauga. More trees, wildflowers and native fruit and flower bearing shrubs are being planted.

Please enjoy the natural beauty of this area and always remember to let it be.

If you would like more information about naturalization, call Parks Mississauga at **896-5384.**

MISSISSAUGA
Parks

Let it be.

LINKING TO LITERACY

Environmental Print

Our environment "speaks" to us through signs and symbols everywhere: signs on stores, menu boards in drive-throughs, billboards, road signs, and even signs in natural settings like parks and nature trails. Readers need to be able to read messages in all places so that they can follow directions, instructions, and rules and regulations.

Read the sign on this page. Discuss the following with a partner or small group:

- How is this sign related to what Grandpa talks about in the story?

- After reading the sign, describe in your own words what naturalization means to you.

- What other signs might be posted in the park? Think about messages for park users to protect the environment, learn about plants and animals, and help them enjoy the park.

What Is the Connection?

In Grade 6, you learned about plants, animals, and the relationship between living things and the natural environment. You have also experienced these things in your daily life. In any natural environment, each component is important and affects the other components. Components of a natural environment include sunlight, soil, water, air, plants, animals, and other living things.

1. Select one of the components listed above. In your notebook, explain how the component affects the other components.

2. Form a group of six. As a group, create a concept map showing the connections between the different components (Figure 1). Once you have marked a connection, include a label indicating what the connection is. For example, in Figure 1 the label "plants need sunlight to grow" indicates the connection between sunlight and plants. Each component may have more than one arrow.

3. Each group will then share their ideas with the rest of the class. You may want to show your concept map to the class and act out your findings in a skit. Your teacher will record all the ideas.

4. Based on the ideas from the concept maps, write a paragraph explaining how the different components in a natural environment depend on each other. Be sure to use what you learned in previous grades in addition to what you noted from the concept maps.

LINKING TO LITERACY

Concept Maps

A concept map helps you make connections between words, pictures, and concepts or ideas. Connect these with arrows. Next, add words along the arrows to explain each connection.

Concept maps are used for different purposes. On this page, you are asked to create a concept map to brainstorm what you already know about a topic. Can you think of other reasons for using a concept map?

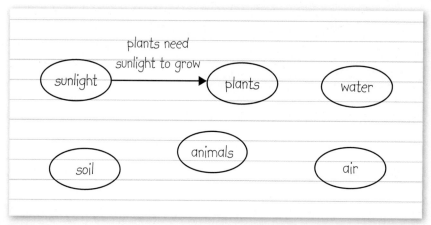

Figure 1

Naturalizing Your Community

Natural environments benefit all living things. Sometimes we do not take care of our natural environment as much as we should. How do you think you can help a natural environment near your home or school? Can you help an environment like the volunteers did in "A Walk in the Park"?

It is important for you to start thinking like a naturalist while you read through this unit. Naturalists defend and protect nature, and they also educate others about ways they can help preserve local species and habitats. Thinking like a naturalist will help you to prepare for the Unit Task.

In this Unit Task, you will select an area in your community that would benefit from "naturalization"—adding plants and changing the landscape in a way that will attract local animals and also make it attractive to humans.

You will analyze the area you select and create a plan to naturalize the area in a way that reflects the local natural environment. You will study your selected area and identify factors that must be considered to ensure the plan will be successful. The plan must involve both living and non-living elements, as well as the needs of the people in the area.

Unit Task By the end of the Interactions in the Environment unit, you will be able to demonstrate your learning by completing this Unit Task. As you work through the unit, continue to think about how you might meet this challenge. Read the detailed description of the Unit Task on page 168, and look for the Unit Task icon at the end of selected sections for hints related to the task.

Assessment

You will be assessed on how well you

- show your knowledge and understanding of the local ecosystem
- develop a reasonable plan to naturalize your area
- propose practical solutions for naturalizing your area
- evaluate the impact your plan will have on living things that will inhabit the area, as well as on humans living nearby

4 Healthy Ecosystems

KEY QUESTION: What are the essential elements of a healthy ecosystem?

Looking Ahead

- Ecosystems are made up of living and non-living elements.

- The living things in an ecosystem depend on each other and on non-living elements for survival.

- Living and non-living elements interact with each other in many different ways.

- The skills of scientific inquiry can be used to investigate the living and non-living elements in a model ecosystem.

- Humans are part of ecosystems and affect ecosystems.

VOCABULARY

biotic element	ecology
organism	habitat
micro-organism	nutrient
species	competition
population	predator
community	prey
abiotic element	mutualism
ecosystem	

GETTING A CHUCKLE FROM THE ENVIRONMENT

"Of course our company cares about the environment! We just switched our entire factory to energy-efficient bulbs."

LINKING TO LITERACY

Text Genres: The Comic Strip

Comic strips can be written as very sophisticated texts. They require readers to make connections between illustrations, text, and what they already know about a topic. Sometimes a message is hidden and the reader must "read between the lines," or make an inference to figure out the comic strip's meaning.

Read each of the comic strips on this page.

1 How does the cartoonist use humour in each comic strip?

2 Read the words in the last comic strip. What message does the written text give you? How does the picture help you to "read between the lines" to see a different message?

3 What is Milton's opinion of zoos? Whose point of view might be in favour of the benefits of zoos?

What Is an Ecosystem?

Point Pelee National Park, located at the southernmost tip of Ontario, is one of the smallest national parks in Canada (Figure 1). Although the park covers only 15 km², it contains many different types of plants and animals. Thousands of monarch butterflies stop and feed in the park before continuing their migration to Mexico in the fall (Figure 2). Many birds also stop in the park during migration. The park receives over 350 000 human visitors a year, all eager to discover its treasures. People visit from around the world to see the birds that come to the park each year.

To learn more about Point Pelee,

Go to Nelson Science

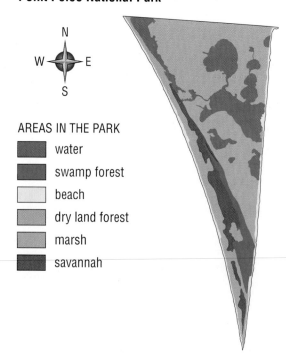

Point Pelee National Park

N
W   E
S

AREAS IN THE PARK

- water
- swamp forest
- beach
- dry land forest
- marsh
- savannah

Figure 1 Point Pelee is a sand spit that juts out into Lake Erie.

Figure 2 A monarch butterfly feeding before travelling south to Mexico

Why is Point Pelee so attractive to both wildlife and people? For wildlife, the park provides food and shelter. For humans, it is a place to watch birds, hike, and enjoy nature. This tiny area of land has a mixture of forests, woodland, and swamps. It also has an untouched marsh full of cattails, dragonflies, and other plants and animals. The beach area is home to hop trees and shorebirds. Finally, there are grasslands filled with milkweeds, wildflowers, birds (such as the savannah sparrow), and even prickly pear cacti. Like other parks throughout Ontario, Point Pelee is not only a place where living things can find food and shelter, but it is also a place where humans can learn more about nature.

The Living Parts of the Environment

Living and non-living things can be found almost everywhere on Earth. The living parts of an environment, such as plants and animals, are **biotic elements**. Biotic elements in an environment affect one another. For example, the plants that grow in a particular environment will affect the survival of other living things. Living things are also known as **organisms**. Organisms that can only be seen with a microscope, such as bacteria and some algae, are known as **micro-organisms**.

Organisms that look similar to one another and that can mate to produce more of the same type of organism are called a **species**. An individual monarch butterfly is a member of the monarch butterfly species (Figure 3(a)). All the members of one species in an area are called a **population**. The thousands of monarch butterflies that fly to Point Pelee in the fall form a population (Figure 3(b)). When populations of different species live in the same area, they form a **community**. For example, the grassland community of Point Pelee includes the monarch butterfly population, as well as common milkweed, Eastern kingbird, and American coyote populations (Figure 3(c)). Each species within this community plays an important role.

biotic element: any living thing found in the environment

organism: a living thing

micro-organism: a living thing that is small and must be viewed with the help of a microscope

species: a group of similar organisms that can mate and reproduce more of the same type of organism

population: a group of organisms of the same species in a given area

community: a group of populations of different species in a given area

LINKING TO LITERACY

Word Origins: Roots, Suffixes, and Prefixes
Knowing what words mean can help you to better understand science texts. For instance, the roots *bio-* and *biotic* mean "life." When you read about biotic elements, you will know that these are living things. *Micro-* means "small," therefore a micro-organism is a small organism. *Eco-* means "to do with the environment" and *-logy* refers to a field of study. See if you can use these terms to help define words found later in Section 4.1.

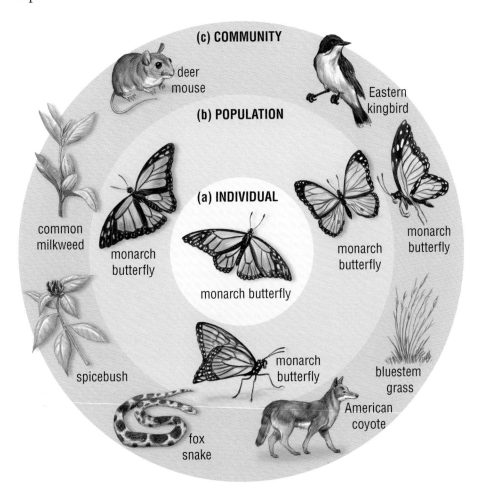

(c) COMMUNITY

deer mouse

Eastern kingbird

(b) POPULATION

(a) INDIVIDUAL

common milkweed

monarch butterfly

monarch butterfly

monarch butterfly

monarch butterfly

monarch butterfly

spicebush

monarch butterfly

bluestem grass

fox snake

American coyote

Figure 3 This nested circle diagram shows how each individual of a species is part of a population, and each population is part of a community.

The Non-Living Parts of the Environment

abiotic element: any non-living component of the environment

The non-living things in parts of an environment are **abiotic elements**. They include sunlight, air, rain, snow, sand dunes, rock, and water (Figure 4). Abiotic elements provide many of the things that organisms need to survive. Plants, for example, need air, water, and sunlight to grow.

Figure 4 What abiotic elements on the beach of Point Pelee can you identify from this photo?

Abiotic and Biotic Elements Interact to Form Ecosystems

The biotic elements in an environment constantly interact with each other and with the abiotic elements of the environment. A fox snake eating an Eastern mole is an example of an interaction between two biotic elements. Wind that changes the shapes of sand dunes on the beach is an interaction between two abiotic elements. A sunfish making its nest on the bottom of a marsh is an interaction between a biotic and an abiotic component of the marsh. The interactions among the biotic and abiotic parts of an environment are called an **ecosystem**. The grasslands, beach, and marsh and the living things in these areas form different ecosystems in Point Pelee.

ecosystem: the network of interactions that link the living and non-living parts of an environment

An ecosystem can be large or small, but the abiotic and biotic parts always interact. For example, a rotting log is an ecosystem. All the organisms living in, or on, the log interact with each other and with the log itself. A forest is also an ecosystem, but it is large. It is made up of all the organisms living in it and the abiotic elements of the forest that affect them.

A large ecosystem often contains many smaller ecosystems (Figure 5). All the ecosystems that exist within a larger ecosystem are interconnected. For example, a deer that lives in a forest ecosystem might get its water from a creek ecosystem.

The study of relationships between living things, non-living things, and their environment is called **ecology**.

ecology: the study of relationships between organisms, and between organisms and their environment

LINKING TO LITERACY

Main Ideas
Readers who recognize main ideas and keep them in mind as they read are more successful at understanding the text that they are reading.

Read the last paragraph on the previous page and the text on this page, and look at the illustration and photo. Then re-read the first line of the last paragraph on the previous page. What main idea is discussed in that paragraph? What is the main idea in the last paragraph on this page?

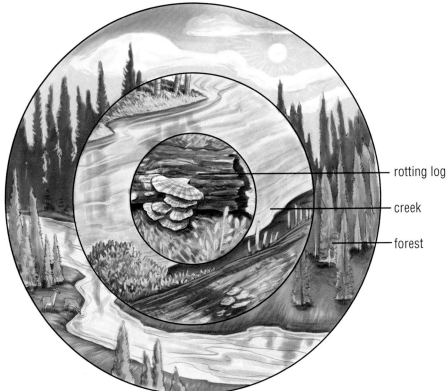

rotting log

creek

forest

Figure 5 Ecosystems often contain smaller ecosystems.

Humans are also part of ecosystems. Visitors entering Point Pelee (Figure 6) may accidentally introduce things into the environment, such as trash, or they may tread on plants by mistake. Visitors may also scare away animals by making too much noise. People may also bring seeds, plant parts, and insects into ecosystems on their shoes or clothing. This can introduce new species. You will learn more about introduced species in Chapter 6.

Figure 6 Humans can affect the ecosystems that they interact with.

Unit Task Ecosystems have abiotic and biotic elements that interact. How can this knowledge help you with the Unit Task?

✔ CHECK YOUR LEARNING

1. Draw diagrams of some of the living and non-living elements of Point Pelee. Draw lines to indicate the interactions between the living and non-living parts. Describe those interactions.

2. Describe in your own words the difference between species, population, and community. Give examples.

3. Name three human interactions that may happen in an environment such as Point Pelee.

4. Explain how a rotting log can be an ecosystem.

5. Give an example of a smaller ecosystem existing within a larger ecosystem.

4.2

The Needs of Living Things

LINKING TO LITERACY

Scanning
Scanning is a way of previewing the section to get an idea of what it is about. Look at the title of this section. Now look at the subheads. What do you think are the needs of living things?

habitat: the environment where an organism lives

Can organisms live in every environment found on Earth (Figure 1)? Think of what you need to survive. You need a warm place to live, food, water, and air. All organisms have basic survival needs. If these needs are not met within their environment, the organism cannot live there. The physical space where an organism lives is called its **habitat**. An organism can only live in a habitat where its basic needs are met.

Figure 1 Death Valley National Park in California is one of the hottest and driest places in North America. How do living things survive in such a harsh environment?

Sunlight

Sunlight is a basic need for life. Most of the energy that makes life possible comes from the Sun (Figure 2). Plants and animals need energy to grow and reproduce. Plants use sunlight to make their own food (sugars), which are then used to perform life functions. The amount of sunlight that an area receives can determine what is able to live there. For example, dandelions grow best in bright sunlight (Figure 3(a)), while ferns prefer shade (Figure 3(b)). Sunlight can shine through water only to a certain depth. Therefore, plants can only exist close to the surface in underwater ecosystems because they need sunlight to produce food.

Figure 2 Almost all the energy that makes life possible on Earth comes directly or indirectly from the Sun.

Figure 3 Different organisms have different needs. Dandelions require lots of sunlight to grow (a), whereas ferns grow best in shade (b).

Animals obtain energy indirectly from sunlight. Some animals consume plants, which have already produced energy-rich sugars using sunlight. Eating plants provides the animals with energy. These animals may then be consumed by larger animals, and energy is transferred. In this way, the energy produced in a plant may be transferred to a plant-eating animal, such as a deer, and then to another animal that consumes the deer.

Sunlight heats Earth's surface and provides warmth. Many animals such as snakes depend on this warmth to raise their body temperature so they can move more quickly. In Canada, there are more hours of sunlight in the summer than there are in the winter. Changes in the number of hours of sunlight trigger seasonal events such as bird migration and the flowering of plants.

Air

Air is another basic need for life. Air is made up of many gases, including oxygen, carbon dioxide, and nitrogen. Humans and many other organisms breathe in air to obtain oxygen, which they need to perform life processes (Figure 4). Plants absorb carbon dioxide from the air. They need carbon dioxide to produce sugars. In addition to sugars, plants produce oxygen. Oxygen production by plants is one of the most important processes on Earth. Without the oxygen input from plants, there would not be enough oxygen in the air for most organisms to perform their life functions. In one way or another, all organisms depend on the oxygen produced by plants. You will learn more about this in Chapter 5.

The gases found in air are critical for living things to survive. Canadian environmentalist Dr. David Suzuki stresses the importance of air: "You can't see it or grab it or hear it, but it's just about the most precious thing in the world." 🌐

To learn more about the David Suzuki Foundation,

Go to Nelson Science

Figure 4 This moose cow is breathing air to obtain the oxygen its body needs.

Water

All organisms need water to survive (Figure 5). Animals need water to digest food and to form body fluids, such as blood, that distribute water, minerals, gases, and food particles throughout their bodies. Plants need water to grow and produce their food. Organisms vary in their need for water. Some need salt water, while others need fresh water. Some need very little water and others need a lot.

Many organisms live in water. Water contains dissolved oxygen and carbon dioxide. Water plants, such as seaweed and pond lilies, absorb carbon dioxide from the water, and animals, such as lake trout and clams, absorb oxygen from the water.

Figure 5 Water covers 74 % of Earth's surface. Adult humans are composed of about 60 % water.

Food

nutrient: a substance that an organism needs to grow and maintain its body

Food provides organisms with nutrients (Figure 6). A **nutrient** is a substance that an organism needs for energy and to grow and maintain itself. Nutrients include sugars and starches, fats, proteins, vitamins, and minerals, such as phosphates and nitrogen. Plants that live on land absorb nutrients from the soil and surrounding environment. Animals obtain nutrients from the food they eat as well as from the environment.

Figure 6 Plants obtain nutrients from the soil and surrounding environment. Humans can obtain nutrients from the plants they grow as crops.

Ideal Temperature Range

In everyday terms, temperature is a measure of the warmth or coolness of a place or object. Temperature is affected by the interactions of sunlight, soil, air, and water.

Temperatures on Earth can range from −88 °C to 50 °C. Most organisms have an ideal temperature range in which they can live. If temperatures are too hot or too cold for any length of time, then the organism may not be able to survive. For example, brook trout prefer water temperatures between 4 °C and 20 °C and will only lay eggs when the water temperature is below 13 °C (Figure 7).

Figure 7 Brook trout will lay eggs only when the water temperature is ideal.

TRY THIS: Identify the Best Living Conditions

SKILLS MENU: performing, communicating

When you purchase a plant from a store, the plant comes with instructions on how to care for it (Figure 8). You can use this information to determine the best growing conditions for the plant. Visit a plant nursery or pet store or conduct research on the Internet to help you with the following activity.

Equipment and Materials: markers; scissors; bristol board

1. Choose an organism to study. This organism could be a plant or animal from an ecosystem in your area, or a pet.

2. Research the needs of the organism you have chosen.

   Go to Nelson Science

A. Design a "best living conditions" list of instructions for your organism.

B. What are the most important considerations you have to take into account?

C. Are conditions for plants and animals similar? Explain.

Figure 8 Plant tags provide information on how to care for the plant.

Many abiotic elements determine which organisms can live in a particular location. For example, few plants can survive in Canada's Arctic because of the cold temperatures, long periods without sunlight, and lack of nutrients in the soil.

Unit Task Living things need sunlight, air, water, food, and ideal temperatures to survive. How might this information help you in the Unit Task?

CHECK YOUR LEARNING

1. (a) List the basic needs of all living things.
   (b) Explain why organisms need these factors to survive.

2. Explain why sunlight is a basic need for both plants and animals.

3. Describe the different ways that different organisms need water to survive.

4. Name two ways that plants affect human survival.

Designing Your Own Model Ecosystem

An ecosystem exists in an area when the living (biotic) and non-living (abiotic) parts of the environment interact. In this activity, you will study biotic and abiotic elements by creating your own model ecosystem (Figure 1). You will observe any changes that occur in your model ecosystem, as well as any interactions among the biotic and abiotic elements.

Figure 1 A model ecosystem

Purpose

To design and build an ecosystem and observe the interactions among the living (biotic) and non-living (abiotic) elements.

Equipment and Materials

- clear plastic container, such as an aquarium, large jar, or 2 L plastic drink bottle
- light source
- hand lens or magnifying glass
- thermometer
- gravel
- aquarium-grade charcoal
- garden soil
- 2 to 4 small plants
- small animals such as earthworms and isopods (pillbugs)
- water
- dry leaves

 Notify the teacher of any allergies that you have. Wash your hands upon completing your ecosystem. Treat animals with care and respect. Do not use mercury thermometers.

 clear plastic container

 light source

 hand lens or magnifying glass

 thermometer

 gravel

 aquarium-grade charcoal

 garden soil

 2 to 4 small plants

 small animals such as earthworms and isopods (pillbugs)

 water

 dry leaves

Procedure

SKILLS HANDBOOK
2.B.6.

1. Use the equipment and materials listed to design a model ecosystem. You can use other items if they are necessary for your design.

2. Make sure that your ecosystem includes the following: good soil drainage, plants and animals, adequate space for the organisms, moisture (water), a way for fresh air to enter and leave, a means of recording temperature, and a way to keep the animals from escaping from the container.

3. Have your teacher approve your design before you begin constructing your model.

4. Build your ecosystem. Record the number and type of plants and animals that you place in your ecosystem.

5. Place the container in a sunny location or under artificial light. Your ecosystem should receive 6 to 8 hours of light per day.

6. Observe your ecosystem regularly. Use a table similar to Table 1 to record your observations. In addition to completing Table 1, use diagrams to illustrate your observations. Describe any changes seen in the organisms or in the activities that the organisms are doing. Record the temperature of the soil, as well as its condition (dry, moist). You may need to add water to maintain moisture in the ecosystem.

Table 1   Ecosystem Observations

Date	Temperature	Soil condition	Changes

7. Continue observing and maintaining your ecosystem for at least three weeks. Add water as needed.

8. At the end of three weeks, take apart your ecosystem. Release any animals into an appropriate natural habitat, and clean up the remaining materials.

Analyze and Evaluate

(a) What are the abiotic elements in your ecosystem? What are the biotic elements?

(b) Use your observations to explain the interactions between the biotic and abiotic elements in your ecosystem.

(c) Was your model ecosystem design successful? Explain. How might you design it differently?

(d) Using your inference skills, describe three interactions that you believe were occurring in your model ecosystem, but that you did not observe directly.

(e) Is your classroom an ecosystem? Explain.

Apply and Extend

(f) Study your observations and diagrams of your ecosystem. What might happen to the ecosystem if you removed it from the light source for a long period of time? Stopped watering it for a long period? Took away another biotic or abiotic element?

(g) Using the Internet and other sources, research *Biosphere 2*. Imagine that you are designing a similar project. What types of organisms would you include in your biosphere? How would you provide for the needs of all living things in your biosphere?

Go to Nelson Science

Unit Task   Now that you have designed your own model ecosystem, how might you use this new knowledge in completing the Unit Task?

4.4 Interactions among Living Things

Recall from Section 4.1 that a population is all the members of a particular species found in one area. Biological populations vary in size. They can be large, such as an ant colony (Figure 1), or small, such as a single pair of breeding woodpeckers in a woodlot (Figure 2).

Figure 1 The tens of thousands of ants that live in this ant nest are an example of a large population.

Figure 2 The two red-bellied woodpeckers shown here represent a small population.

TRY THIS: Counting Populations

SKILLS MENU: performing, observing, analyzing, communicating

SKILLS HANDBOOK
2.B.7.

The size of populations and number of populations in a specific area can vary greatly. In this activity, you will compare the size and number of plant populations on your school grounds.

Equipment and Materials: metre stick; plant identification guide (optional)

1. In groups of three or four, measure out an area of 1 m² on your school grounds where vegetation is growing. This will be your study plot. All of the class study plots should be close together and in the same general location.

2. Find three plant species growing on your plot. Draw a sketch of each of these plant species. If you know the names of your selected plants, record them on your drawings. Your teacher may provide you with identification guides to help you identify the plants.

3. For each species of plant, count the number of individuals on your plot. Record your totals.

4. Compare your findings with other groups. Use information from your classmates' drawings to fill in the names of any species that are missing from your own drawings.

5. Create a master list of plants and their populations for the total area (all study plots) covered by your class.

A. Which plant species in your plot had the largest population? Which plant species had the smallest population?

B. When you compared your findings with other groups, were there any plant species that were found on all or most of the study plots? If so, name them.

C. Were there any plants on your study plot that were not found on other study plots? If so, name them.

D. When all the study plots were compared, which plant species was the most common? How do you know this?

E. Which plant, or plants, was the least common over all the study plots?

Although ecosystems vary in size, there is a limit to the number of organisms an ecosystem can support. Abiotic factors limit the number of organisms that can live in an ecosystem. For example, if there is little water, then only a few plants can grow. How organisms interact within an ecosystem also limits the number of organisms in an ecosystem. Two important biotic interactions are competition and predation.

Competition

Competition is the struggle that happens when organisms in the same habitat try to use the same resources. For example, plants that grow close together in one area compete for the same water, sunlight, and nutrients (Figure 3). If these resources are limited, some plants may become small and thin, and some may die. This leaves more water, sunlight, and nutrients for the remaining plants, which survive and grow strong. Competition controls the population size by limiting the number of organisms that can survive on the resources in the area.

competition: occurs when more than one organism tries to obtain the same basic resources in the same habitat

Figure 3 All these plants are competing for the same resources.

Animals also compete for resources. A pond may only be able to provide enough food and water for a certain number of frogs. If too many frogs live in the same area and compete for resources, there will not be enough food and water. Some frogs will move to another area or some may die. Humans are an example of an organism that competes with other organisms for resources. When farmers grow crops, they spray pesticides on the crops to stop other organisms from eating them. Farmers are able to control, or even eliminate, competing organisms.

Predation

An animal that hunts other animals for food is called a **predator**. The animal that is hunted by the predator is called the **prey**. A wolf (predator) eating a moose (prey) is an example of a predator–prey relationship (Figure 4). A moose eating grass is not an example of a predator–prey relationship because the moose does not need to hunt the grass.

The population of predators is affected by the population of prey and vice versa. The number of predators can only increase if there is enough food to eat. If a predator population is increasing in size, the prey population will decrease in size because more predators are eating prey. Hence, predators keep the number of prey from increasing. However, if the prey population gets too low, there is not enough for the predators to eat. The predator population decreases; some individuals die from starvation and others may be too weak to produce young. As the predator population decreases, the prey population increases because there are fewer predators hunting them. This results in an up-and-down pattern of predator and prey populations in a particular habitat over time (Figure 5).

predator: an organism that hunts other living things for food

prey: an animal that is hunted by a predator

Figure 4 These wolves are feeding on a moose they have hunted.

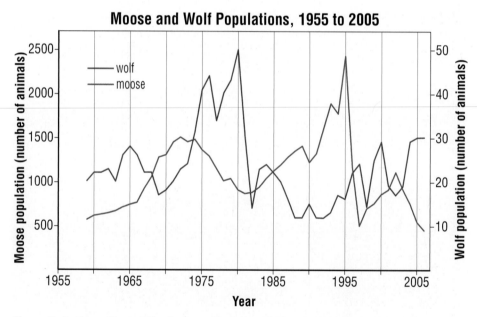

Figure 5 As the wolf population increased between 1970 and 1980, the moose population decreased in size. When the wolf population decreased in size, the moose population recovered.

The predator–prey cycle also affects plant populations. Most prey animals, such as moose and rabbits, feed on plants. When the prey population is large, the prey animals eat all of the available plants in the habitat. The plant population gets smaller, which can lead to starvation of the prey animals. Predators can now easily catch the weakened prey, which reduces the prey population. The plants then have a chance to recover because there are fewer prey animals eating them.

Mutualism

In competition and predation, one organism usually "wins" while another "loses." However, there are some interactions between organisms in which both organisms "win." **Mutualism** is an interaction between individuals of different species in which both individuals benefit. An example of mutualism can be seen when a bee visits a flower. The bee takes nectar from the flower for food, and picks up pollen from the flower while doing so. The pollen is then transferred to the next flower the bee visits. This transfer of pollen allows plants to reproduce. The nectar benefits the bee and the transfer of pollen benefits the flower. 🌐

Another example of mutualism occurs between plants of the legume family and bacteria in the soil. Peas, beans, peanuts, and other legumes have swellings on their roots (Figure 6). These swellings contain special bacteria. The bacteria provide the plants with nitrogen, and the plants provide the bacteria with several nutrients that the bacteria need to survive. Both the bacteria and the legume plants benefit from the interaction.

mutualism: an interaction between individuals of different species that benefits both individuals

To try an interactive pollination activity,
Go to Nelson Science 🌐

Figure 6 The swellings on the roots of this field bean plant contain bacteria. The process by which bacteria provide plants with nitrogen is called "nitrogen fixation." The bacteria that do this are called "nitrogen-fixing bacteria."

Unit Task The interactions among living things affect their ability to survive. How might this knowledge help you with the Unit Task?

✔ CHECK YOUR LEARNING

1. In your own words, explain competition.

2. Explain how competition affects the number of organisms that can live in a habitat.

3. (a) Give an example of a predator.
   (b) Give an example of a prey animal.

4. (a) Look at Figure 5. Describe what is happening to the wolf population and the moose population between 1985 and 1990.
   (b) In your own words, explain why this is happening.

AWESOME SCIENCE

Living Walls

You walk into one of the many tall buildings in the "concrete jungle" of a typical urban centre. As you enter, you hear cascading water, feel and smell the cool, fresh air, and then you see a green wall. Are those plants growing up the wall? Welcome to the world of living walls (Figure 1)!

Figure 1 The living wall at the University of Guelph contains over 1000 plant species.

When we think of air pollution, we usually think of the air outdoors. Indoor air can also be polluted. Sources of indoor air pollution include moulds, pet dander, plant pollen, and chemicals from paints and furniture. Living walls are an environmentally friendly way to improve the air quality inside office buildings. A living wall can remove up to 90 % of over 300 different pollutants from indoor air.

A typical living wall (Figure 2) is made of a material that allows air and water to flow through it. Two layers of this material are attached to each other and mounted on the wall. Plants are placed into holes in the material, where their roots grow and hold them in place. The bottom edge of the living wall sits in a pool of water. The water is pumped to the top of the wall where it trickles down. Fans placed behind the living wall pull air through the wall and send it to different parts of the building.

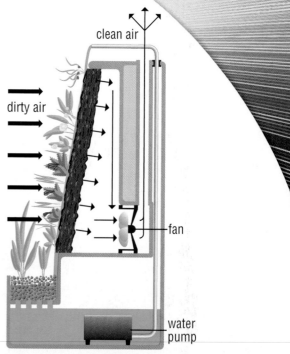

Figure 2 Cross-section of a living wall

How does a living wall clean the air? Most of the work is done by micro-organisms, which live on the plants' roots. As air passes through the wall, the micro-organisms consume the pollutants in the air and break them down into harmless substances. This process is known as biofiltration. For this reason, living walls are sometimes called "biowalls." In addition to providing a habitat for the micro-organisms, the plants also remove carbon dioxide, another indoor pollutant, from the air.

To learn more about living walls,

Go to Nelson Science

How Do Humans Fit into Ecosystems?

The girl in the *Tina's Groove* cartoon on page 95 said, "A healthy atmosphere, clean water—that's not very good evidence of human habitation." Humans have a bad reputation when it comes to protecting the environment.

A healthy ecosystem consists of interactions among living and non-living elements. Different species, including humans, interact with each other. Although we do not always interact directly with the natural environment, we are still part of ecosystems. We depend on resources such as sunlight, soil, water, and air for our survival, and we also depend on other species.

Humans tend to change the ecosystems they live in. For example, most of southern Ontario used to be forested land. When European settlers arrived, they cut down most of the forests to clear land for farms and towns. The wood was used for building materials and firewood. Today, southern Ontario is mostly made up of urban areas and farmland. Only a small amount of forest remains (Figure 1).

> **LINKING TO LITERACY**
>
> **During Reading: Asking Questions**
> Good readers ask questions as they read to make sure that they understand a topic. Sometimes these questions lead to learning more about a topic. As you read about how humans fit into ecosystems, try to be an active reader. Ask questions and think about how you fit into ecosystems.

Figure 1 Humans have changed ecosystems to meet their needs. Much of the land in this photograph was once forest.

Like all organisms, humans compete with other species for basic needs in an ecosystem. Humans usually succeed because they have developed technology to help them. Humans change ecosystems to meet their needs. They take things from the environment to meet these needs. As a result, some species can no longer live in the same environment as humans. Humans have also introduced new elements to ecosystems, such as pollution. Pollution can affect all of the organisms in an ecosystem.

Farming

Humans can create ecosystems to grow food crops. Many technologies have been developed over the years to increase food production. For example, farmers often use fertilizers to promote plant growth. Many farmers also use pesticides to stop insects and other pests from eating the plants they grow (Figure 2).

These farming methods have other consequences. The excess nutrients from fertilizers and the toxic chemicals in pesticides can pollute the soil and water. Also, pesticide use harms other organisms in the ecosystem. For example, using pesticides to kill "pest" insects removes a food source for birds that feed on these insects. This causes bird populations to decrease. This, in turn, affects organisms that feed on the birds. Humans have also developed machines to help grow and harvest crops. Farm machinery contributes to air pollution. 🌐

To learn more about the impact of farming on the environment,

Go to Nelson Science 🌐

Figure 2 Although pesticides help remove insects from crops, they can also have negative effects on ecosystems.

Mining

Can you imagine a world without metal? Metals such as iron, steel, and aluminum are commonly used in farm machinery, automobiles, and household appliances. We rely on the use of metals in many areas of technology and industry. Nickel, for example, is a metal that is used in many different everyday items from batteries to braces (Figure 3).

We obtain metals by extracting metal ores (rocks that contain metal) from the ground. This is known as mining. Once a metal has been extracted, tailings (the remaining rock material) are left in large piles. Mine tailings contain toxic substances that can damage ecosystems. Tailings left out in the open after mining can release toxic chemicals into the surrounding soil. Over time, rain will carry these substances into nearby lakes, rivers, and oceans. This has a negative impact on the organisms living in those ecosystems.

Figure 3 The archwire in orthodontic braces is made of a mixture of nickel and titanium metals.

Nickel has been mined near Sudbury for over 100 years. Sulfur dioxide is one of the many toxic substances released in the mining process. Over the years, sulfur dioxide released from mine tailings caused severe damage to the land and water surrounding Sudbury (Figure 4). By the 1960s, the ground was so polluted that almost no native plants could grow in the soil. Without these plants, the native animals could not survive there either.

The mining companies reduced their emissions of sulfur dioxide and other toxic substances such as arsenic, cadmium, and mercury. By the late 1990s, sulfur dioxide emissions were reduced by 75 %. Since then, the land around Sudbury has started to recover, and native plants and animals have returned to the area. However, even at lower levels, sulfur dioxide and other toxic substances continue to pollute the air, water, and land. ⊕

To learn more about how Sudbury is recovering from environmental damage,

Figure 4 Toxic substances can wash out of mine tailings and pollute the local water and land, which can poison local plants and animals.

Humans have developed many different technologies to make life easier and more comfortable. However, making and using these technologies often creates pollution. For example, automobiles, trains, and airplanes provide great benefits by transporting people and goods all over the world. However, they also pollute the air and water, and add solid waste to the environment. Humans have come to realize that current methods of making and using technologies are not healthy for the environment or for living things. Humans are now working hard to reduce the amount of pollution we produce. We are developing "green" technologies to help protect our environment.

✔ CHECK YOUR LEARNING

1. Describe how humans change the ecosystems they live in.

2. What are the benefits and drawbacks of using fertilizers?

3. What are the benefits and drawbacks of using pesticides?

4. Mining has costs and benefits. Give examples of both the costs (disadvantages) and benefits (advantages) of mining.

SKILLS MENU
- ☐ Defining the Issue
- ☑ Researching
- ☑ Identifying Alternatives
- ☑ Analyzing the Issue
- ☑ Defending a Decision
- ☑ Communicating
- ☐ Evaluating

The Impact of Vehicles on the Environment

Vehicles, such as cars, vans, and trucks, have had an enormous impact on how we live our lives. Without automobiles, travelling even a few kilometres would take a very long time. We depend on emergency services to arrive within minutes (Figure 1(a)). Vehicles also provide many jobs to people, from those who make them to the mechanics who repair them. However, vehicles also cause air and water pollution (Figure 1(b)). Building roads for vehicles also contributes to the destruction of natural habitats for living things.

(a) (b)

Figure 1 Vehicles can literally save lives (a), but they can also cause air pollution (b).

The Issue

An environmental organization wants to bring attention to how vehicles affect the environment, including ways they may benefit society and hurt the environment. They have hired you as a consultant. You have been asked to create a public awareness campaign presenting the impact of vehicles on the environment's ability to support life. Your campaign should address benefits, problems, and possible solutions.

To prepare for your campaign, you will research the impacts of vehicles on the environment. You will then select three impacts that most affect the ability of the environment to support life. These three impacts will be the basis for your campaign.

Goal

To research the impacts that vehicles have on the environment and to create and present a public awareness campaign outlining these impacts.

LINKING TO LITERACY

Critical Literacy
Describe the environmental organization's point of view. Is there a point of view that will not be represented by your work? Who is the audience that will be targeted by this campaign? Think of reasons why people might be resistant to your project.

Gather Information

Working in groups, investigate the impact vehicles have on the environment. In what ways do vehicles help us in our daily lives? What are the environmental impacts of building, using, and disposing of vehicles? What natural resources are used at any of these stages of a vehicle's life? What effects do vehicles have on the water, land, and air? Is habitat destruction involved at any stage?

Use the Internet, newspaper and magazine articles, conservation groups, and local community members to find information.

Go to Nelson Science

Identify Solutions

As you conduct your research, consider both the positive and negative effects that vehicles have on society. Research possible solutions to the negative effects of vehicles on the environment. Depending on the effect, possible solutions may include

• starting anti-idling campaigns
• choosing energy-efficient vehicles (hybrids, hydrogen fuel cells)
• promoting walking and biking when travelling short distances
• introducing stronger pollution controls
• introducing "no-vehicle" zones in cities

Make a Decision

Review the research of everyone in your group. Decide which three impacts most affect the ability of the environment to support life. Then, decide how best to communicate these impacts to a general audience in a public awareness campaign.

Communicate

Create a public awareness campaign to show your findings. The campaign can take the form of a commercial, brochure or pamphlet, public service announcement, billboard, or multimedia presentation. The campaign should clearly show each impact of vehicles on the environment. The campaign should also inform the public about what they can do to reduce the impact of vehicles on the environment.

Your class will represent the environmental group that hired you. Present your campaign to them, and explain why you chose the three impacts that you did. Be prepared to answer any questions they may have.

Healthy Ecosystems

BIG Ideas

☑ Ecosystems are made up of biotic (living) and abiotic (non-living) elements, which depend on each other to survive.

☐ Ecosystems are in a constant state of change. The changes may be caused by nature or by human intervention.

☑ Human activities have the potential to alter the environment. Humans must be aware of these impacts and try to control them.

Looking Back

Ecosystems are made up of living and non-living elements.

- Biotic elements in ecosystems are living things, such as plants, animals, and micro-organisms.

- Abiotic elements in ecosystems are non-living things, such as sunlight, air, water, and temperature.

- Within ecosystems, living things can be organized into individual species, populations, and communities.

- All ecosystems, whether large or small, are interconnected. Some ecosystems contain smaller ecosystems within them.

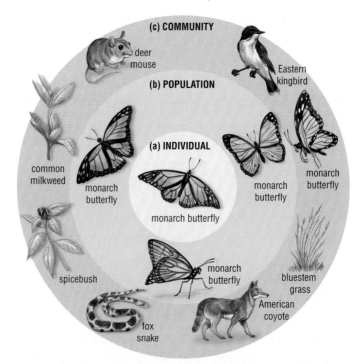

The living things in an ecosystem depend on each other and on non-living elements for survival.

- All organisms have basic needs. An organism can only live in a habitat where its basic needs are met.

- The abiotic elements in a habitat often determine which organisms can live in that particular location. These include sunlight, water, air, and an ideal temperature range.

Living and non-living elements interact with each other in many different ways.

- Some organisms in an ecosystem compete for the same resources. Competition limits the number of organisms that can live in an ecosystem.

- The number of prey affects the number of predators that can live in an ecosystem. In a similar way, the number of predators affects the number of prey in the ecosystem.

- Mutualism is an interaction between two species in an ecosystem in which both species benefit from the relationship.

The skills of scientific inquiry can be used to investigate the living and non-living elements in a model ecosystem.

- Model ecosystems can be designed and built using everyday equipment and materials.

- Model ecosystems can be used to observe biotic and abiotic elements and the interactions between these elements.

Humans are part of ecosystems and affect ecosystems.

- Humans interact with living and non-living elements of the environment. They compete with other organisms for resources.

- Humans often win competitions with other organisms because humans can develop technology to help them survive. Farming and mining are two common techniques humans use to obtain resources from the environment.

- When humans take resources from ecosystems, they often leave pollution, which affects other organisms.

CHAPTER 4 REVIEW

The following icons indicate the Achievement Chart categories: | K/U Knowledge/Understanding | T/I Thinking/Investigation | C Communication | A Application

What Do You Remember?

1. For each of the following, explain the difference between the two terms:

   (a) biotic and abiotic

   (b) individual and population

   (c) predator and prey K/U

2. Give two examples of biotic–abiotic interactions. K/U

3. (a) What is an ecosystem?

   (b) How is an ecosystem different from a habitat? Give an example of each. K/U

4. (a) What do all of the ecosystems in Table 1 have in common?

   (b) How are they different? K/U

Table 1 Ecosystems and Their Populations

Ecosystem	Some populations in the ecosystem
frozen ocean in Hudson Bay	polar bears, ringed seals, beluga whales, Arctic cod, Arctic char, krill, algae, plankton, Arctic terns, Arctic foxes
rotting log	salamanders, toads, millipedes, centipedes, bacteria, fungi, woodpeckers, earthworms, snails, bark beetles, mosses, lichens
urban vacant lot	dandelions, crab grass, thistles, clover, cats, deer mice, dogs, house sparrows, starlings, pigeons

What Do You Understand?

5. List all the biotic and abiotic elements in an area near you. Explain why this area may be an ecosystem. A

6. (a) Give an example of a predator–prey relationship that may exist in the ecosystem you studied in question 5.

   (b) Give an example of competition from your ecosystem. A

7. List some populations that form the community in the area you studied in question 5. A

8. Use an example to explain how competition limits the number of organisms that can survive in an ecosystem. A

9. (a) The graph in Figure 1 indicates that as snowshoe hare populations rise, lynx populations also rise. Between 1925 and 1930, the population of snowshoe hares dropped to a very low level. Explain how this might have happened.

   (b) Explain why the hare population then increased so dramatically. A

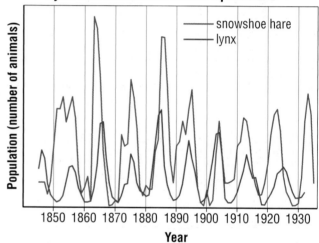

Lynx and Snowshoe Hare Populations

Figure 1

10. Humans are able to live in more types of environments than any other species. Explain this statement. A

11. (a) Make a list of organisms in your environment that you compete with. Explain how you compete with them.

   (b) Are humans as susceptible to environmental influences as other organisms are? Defend your answer. A

12. (a) Describe three human activities that can have a negative effect on an ecosystem.

   (b) For each negative effect that you described in part (a), describe a human activity that can reduce the negative effect. A

Solve a Problem!

13. Imagine you are a gardener. You are having trouble growing a certain species of plant in the area where you live (Figure 2).

    (a) Suggest possible reasons why this type of plant will not grow in your area.

    (b) What steps could you take to solve the problem? T/I A

Figure 2

14. You are the Environment Club team captain and your project is to help your school become certified as a "green" school. You notice that there are lots of old computers lying around that must be disposed of.

    (a) Investigate how computers are used in your school and how they make life easier for students and teachers.

    (b) Investigate the environmental issues around the production and disposal of computers.

    (c) Create a set of standards for your School Board that outlines how computers should be purchased, used, and disposed of. These standards should balance the needs of students and teachers, as well as the needs of the environment. A

Create and Evaluate!

15. (a) Research several First Nations stories (myths and legends) that promote the importance of the four elements—sunlight, water, earth, and air. Summarize these stories and create a visual display promoting the need to look after these elements.

    (b) Write your own legend or myth that promotes the idea that it is important to look after the environment. Exchange your legend/myth with a friend and evaluate each other's work objectively. How well does the legend/myth get your message across? C

16. Select an ecosystem found in Ontario. Your ecosystem can be an urban one (something found in a city) or a rural one (something found outside of the city or in the country). The ecosystem can be one planned by humans or a natural one. Create a poster about the ecosystem, identifying all of the abiotic and biotic elements in it. You should also identify the interactions between the different elements. Your classmates will then evaluate your poster and add any elements or interactions you may have missed. A C

Reflect on Your Learning

17. Think about the Big Ideas that you learned about in this chapter. List three questions that you still have about these Big Ideas.

18. List the three most important ideas you have learned about your local ecosystem. What is the most fascinating idea you discovered? Why?

19. Think back to the Key Question on the first page of this chapter.

    (a) In a brief paragraph, answer the Key Question. You may use diagrams.

    (b) Write one or two more questions about the topic of this unit that you would like to explore.

5 Interactions within Ecosystems

KEY QUESTION: How are all of the parts within an ecosystem connected?

Looking Ahead

- Organisms have different roles in ecosystems.

- Food chains and food webs show how energy from the Sun is passed from one organism to another in an ecosystem.

- The skills of scientific inquiry can be used to model and investigate food webs.

- Matter is constantly recycled in an ecosystem.

- Investigation skills can be used to examine the biotic and abiotic interactions in a composter.

VOCABULARY

photosynthesis	food chain
producer	food web
consumer	pyramid of numbers
herbivore	closed system
carnivore	cycle
scavenger	sustainable
omnivore	evaporation
detrivore	condensation
decomposer	precipitation

Rocks that Teach

Deep within a forest near Peterborough is the largest known collection of First Nations rock carvings in Canada. These carvings, known as "petroglyphs," were carved into limestone rock hundreds of years ago. There are several hundred petroglyphs depicting turtles, snakes, birds, and humans. The rock is a sacred place to the First Nations peoples and is known as "Kinomagewapkong," which means "the rocks that teach." The carvings show the history of the people who first settled this area and their sacred traditions. They also teach of the interactions between humans and the environment.

David Johnson, a council member of Curve Lake reserve, is an artist who has spent a great deal of time learning from the "rocks that teach." He now educates others about their significance. Johnson has learned that from a First Nations perspective, humans are an integral part of nature and cannot separate themselves from "Mother Earth." The Sun, soil, water, and air are sacred gifts to be cared for and treated with respect. All living beings have lessons to teach us and help humanity co-exist with nature.

Every component in an ecosystem has an important role to play and is affected by the other components in the ecosystem. This is why many First Nations communities believe in the saying "in every deliberation we must consider the impact of our decisions on the next seven generations." In other words, for every decision we make, we must think of how it will affect the world one hundred, or even two hundred, years from now.

Figure 1 The limestone petroglyphs northeast of Peterborough are generally believed to have been carved by the Algonquins between 900 and 1400 CE.

LINKING TO LITERACY

Making Connections

To gain deeper meaning from your reading, practise making connections between what you are reading and what you have read before, what you know about similar topics or elements in the world, and your own life experiences.

1 How do First Nations petroglyphs compare to Egyptian hieroglyphics? Consider composition, creation, and purpose.

2 Discuss the following with a partner: What did you already know about First Nations' beliefs? How does this text add to your knowledge about these people?

3 Examine the photo of the petroglyphs on this page. What do you see? What do you think it means? Write a short summary of your interpretation.

The Roles of Organisms in an Ecosystem

You, like all members of human communities, play several roles. At school you are a student, after school you may be on a sports team, at home you are part of a family. Organisms in a natural community also play different roles within their ecosystem. An organism's role within an ecosystem depends on how it obtains its food. Plants and animals obtain their food in very different ways, so they have very different roles in an ecosystem. The way in which an organism obtains food also affects its interactions with other organisms in the ecosystem.

Producers

Plants have the ability to make their own food through a process called **photosynthesis**. In photosynthesis, plants use energy that they absorb from the Sun, water that they absorb from the soil, and carbon dioxide that they absorb from the air to make food in the form of sugar (Figure 1). Because plants produce their own food through photosynthesis, they are known as producers. **Producers** are organisms that are able to make their own food using abiotic elements in the ecosystem. Plants use only some of the food they make to perform life processes. Any food that they do not use is stored in the form of starch.

photosynthesis: a process by which plants use water, carbon dioxide, and sunlight to produce sugars (food)

producer: an organism that makes its own food from non-living materials

LINKING TO LITERACY

Summarize Your Understanding
In your own words, summarize the process of photosynthesis. Refer to the diagram to support your understanding.

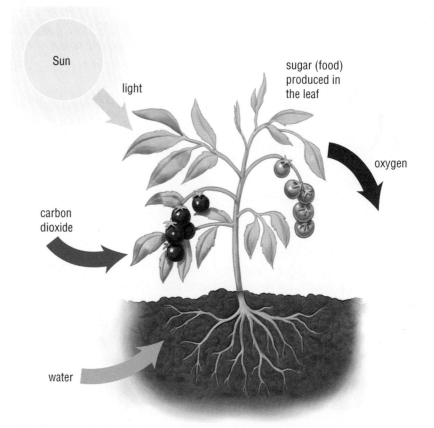

Figure 1 In photosynthesis, energy from the Sun, carbon dioxide, and water combine to produce sugars that the plant can use for food.

The process of photosynthesis can also be written as a word equation:

Sun's energy + water + carbon dioxide → food (sugar) + oxygen

Oxygen is another product of photosynthesis. Plants need oxygen to help perform life processes, but they produce more oxygen than they need. They release the excess oxygen into the air where it can be used by humans and other organisms. 🌐

To learn more about photosynthesis,

Go to Nelson Science 🌐

Consumers

Animals cannot make their own food. They must obtain their energy by eating, or consuming, other organisms. An organism that eats other organisms for energy is called a **consumer**. There are different types of consumers. Consumers that eat only plants are called **herbivores**. Deer (Figure 2(a)) and beavers are examples of herbivores.

Consumers that eat only animals are called **carnivores**. Ospreys (Figure 2(b)), wolves, and bass are all examples of carnivores. One group of carnivores, called **scavengers**, feed on already dead animals (they do not usually kill their own food). Coyotes and ravens are scavengers, but also occasionally prey on living things.

A consumer that eats both plants and animals is called an **omnivore**. For example, raccoons are omnivores because they eat fish and frogs but also seeds. Bears are omnivores because they eat fish as well as blueberries. Humans are generally omnivores (Figure 2(c)); they can eat chicken, sheep, and many other animals. Humans also eat different types of plant seeds (grains), which are ground up to make flour for use in breads, pastas, and many other foods. In addition, humans eat a wide variety of fruits and vegetables.

consumer: an organism that eats other living things for energy

herbivore: an organism that eats plants only

carnivore: an organism that eats other animals only

scavenger: an organism that eats already dead animals

omnivore: an organism that eats both plants and animals

Figure 2 (a) Deer are herbivores. (b) Ospreys and other hawks are carnivores. (c) Although some humans eat only vegetable products, most are omnivores.

Detrivores and Decomposers

detrivore: an organism that feeds on large parts of decaying plant and animal matter and on waste material

Earth would soon be covered in dead organisms if there were not some way of disposing of all the dead plants and animals. **Detrivores** are organisms that obtain nutrients by feeding on large parts of decaying animals and plants, and on waste material. Earthworms, many types of beetles (Figure 3), and some sea birds are detrivores.

Figure 3 In addition to eating living plants, this darkling beetle feeds on decaying vegetation.

decomposer: an organism that consumes and breaks down dead organisms or waste matter into simple substances

Detrivores leave behind their own waste material and small pieces of decaying plant and animal matter. **Decomposers** feed on any remaining decayed matter and waste left behind by consumers and detrivores. Decomposers break these parts down into simpler substances. Bacteria and fungi, such as mould (Figure 4), are common decomposers.

Figure 4 The mould on this bread is a decomposer.

✓ CHECK YOUR LEARNING

1. Explain the differences between producers and consumers.

2. (a) What are the raw materials of photosynthesis?
   (b) What are the products of photosynthesis?
   (c) What happens to the products of photosynthesis?

3. What is the difference between detrivores and decomposers?

4. (a) What are the similarities between omnivores and carnivores?
   (b) What are the differences between omnivores and carnivores?

5. What role do scavengers play in ecosystems?

Food Chains and Food Webs

How did you get to school today? Did you walk, ride your bike, or take a bus (Figure 1)? Did you walk from class to class during the day? Did you write in your notebook today? All of these activities require energy. We obtain energy from the food we eat. But how did energy get into our food in the first place?

Figure 1 You obtain the energy you need to get to school from the food you eat.

The path energy takes in an ecosystem begins with the Sun. All plants grow by absorbing energy from the Sun and turning it into foods such as sugars and starches. The energy of the Sun is stored in the plant. When an animal such as a chicken eats grain (seeds of various grass plants), the energy stored in the plant is transferred from the starches in the grain to the chicken (Figure 2). When you eat chicken for dinner, some of the energy is passed on to you. So, energy starts from the Sun and passes from producers to consumers.

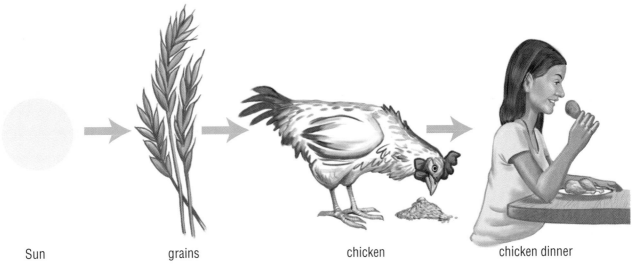

Sun   grains   chicken   chicken dinner

Figure 2 The energy from the Sun is stored by producers in the form of high-energy sugars and starches. When an organism consumes grain, some of the Sun's energy is passed on.

Food Chains

A **food chain** is a model that shows how energy and nutrients flow from one organism to another in an ecosystem. Arrows show the direction of the energy and nutrient flow. The number of "links" in a food chain can vary, but the food chain always starts with a producer and ends with a consumer. A food chain can have just two components, a producer and a consumer (Figure 3(a)). Other food chains are more complicated (Figures 3(b) and (c)). A producer may be consumed by a herbivore (primary consumer), which is then eaten by a carnivore (secondary consumer). In some cases, another carnivore (tertiary consumer) eats the first carnivore.

(a)   blueberry bush   bear

(b)   dandelion plant   aphid   ladybug   robin   hawk

(c)   algae   mosquito larva   sunfish   smallmouth bass

Figure 3 Three food chains: (a) a forest, (b) a school ground, (c) a small lake. The length of a food chain depends on the number of organisms. The flow of energy through a food chain is in one direction, from producers (on the far left) to consumers (to the right of the producer).

Food Webs

Food chains show one producer being eaten by one consumer and perhaps another consumer eating the first consumer. Food chains are not that simple in real ecosystems. Producers are usually eaten by many different consumers, and most consumers are eaten by more than one predator. For example, a squirrel eats several different types of seeds, fruits, and nuts. The squirrel may be eaten by a fox, a hawk, or a raccoon. The raccoon also feeds on frogs, clams, birds' eggs, and corn. The fox will also eat mice and grasshoppers; the hawk will also eat frogs, mice, and snakes. Most organisms are part of several food chains. A model that shows the connections between several different food chains is called a **food web** (Figure 4). A food web starts with the producers in the ecosystem and then branches off into interconnected food chains that show who eats whom in the ecosystem. Food webs can quickly become very complex.

food web: a model that shows how food chains in an ecosystem are connected

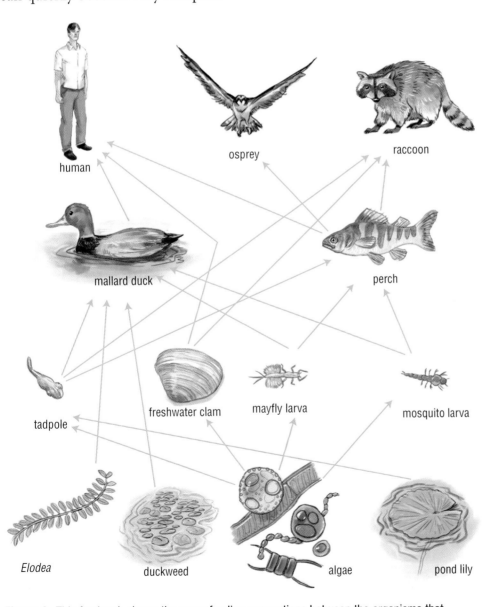

Figure 4 This food web shows the many feeding connections between the organisms that live in and around a small lake.

Changes in Food Chains and Food Webs

If one species is eliminated from a food chain or web, it affects the other species in that chain or web. For example, consider the simple food chain: clover → rabbit → fox. If rabbits are removed from the food chain, then the population of foxes in that ecosystem will decrease because they will have no food (Figure 5). If one species disappears from a food chain, organisms that eat that species may eat other species instead. This will also affect the food web that the food chain is part of. The foxes, for example, may begin to eat mice and insects instead. When any part of a food web changes, it affects the flow of energy throughout the web.

To learn more about food chains and food webs,
Go to Nelson Science

Figure 5 Foxes rely on rabbits as a source of food. If rabbits are not available to feed on, the population of foxes must find other organisms for food, or they will die.

Unit Task A food web shows how energy flows through an ecosystem. The food chains within a food web show the feeding relationships among species in a community. How will your knowledge of food chains and food webs help you with the Unit Task?

CHECK YOUR LEARNING

1. Create two food chains from the following list. Use Figure 4 to help you.

   - raccoon
   - mallard duck
   - mosquito larva
   - algae
   - *Elodea*
   - freshwater clam
   - human
   - duckweed

2. What is the role of producers in food chains and food webs?

3. **(a)** What are the similarities between food webs and food chains?

   (b) What are the differences between food webs and food chains?

4. In your own words, explain what may happen to a food web if one of the species of the web is removed.

5. What is the initial source of the energy in all food webs and food chains?

SCIENCE WORKS

Bridget Stutchbury—Renowned Ecologist

What do Canadian forests, South American rainforests, coffee, and songbirds have in common? Bridget Stutchbury (Figure 1), ecologist, author, and professor at York University, believes they have a lot in common. Everything is connected in ecosystems, and what humans do in one place can have a tremendous impact in other places. To illustrate this point, Professor Stutchbury and her students are currently studying the effects of habitat loss on forest songbirds. These songbirds spend the summer in Canadian forests and then migrate to South American rainforests in winter.

Figure 1 Dr. Stutchbury uses a variety of methods to study the effects of habitat loss on forest songbirds.

"I became a biologist by accident," says Stutchbury. "As a kid I loved the outdoors. My dad… always encouraged me to take science in high school and in university. My lucky break came in my third year at Queen's University, when I was hired by a professor to work on a project involving birds. I learned to catch birds, check their nests, and study their breeding behaviour. I was hooked for life!"

According to Stutchbury, ecology will play a huge role in our future. "Ecologists and environmental scientists are going to be needed more than ever to keep Earth's life-sustaining ecosystems functioning. Biology students need to understand ecology and the threats to our environment. As an ecologist at York University, I don't just explain the problems to people; I am figuring out solutions through my own research."

"Field biologists today need more than a good pair of binoculars and a notebook; my research involves DNA testing, physiological tests of health, and miniature tracking devices that allow us to follow birds on migration. All these projects have a common goal: find out why bird populations are declining."

Professor Stutchbury has some advice on how to help songbirds:

- Buy toilet paper (and other paper products) made from 100 % post-consumer waste. It does not make sense to destroy our forests on Earth to make toilet paper!
- Plant fruit trees, shrubs, or sunflowers in your backyard. During migration, these plants provide tired and hungry songbirds safe places to rest and eat.

What is the connection between coffee and birds? "Shade-grown" coffee is grown in the shade of tropical trees. Keeping these trees means that songbirds have a winter habitat. If you can convince your parents to buy shade-grown coffee, you will be helping Canadian songbirds!

To learn more about songbirds,
Go to Nelson Science

The Great Web of Life

What happens when a food web, or a part of a food web, is weakened? Think of a chainlink fence. If one or two links are broken, the chain still works. However, as more links are removed, the entire fence becomes weaker until it can no longer do its job. The same relationship happens in an ecosystem. An ecosystem consists of many interactions among the various elements. If one of these elements is weakened or removed, the ecosystem changes, but can accommodate the loss. However, a major disruption will affect the entire system. In this activity, you will model what happens to food chains when changes occur.

Purpose

To investigate interactions within an ecosystem and to determine what happens when these interactions are weakened.

Equipment and Materials

- coloured cards
- tape or pins
- string or yarn

coloured cards   tape or pins   string or yarn

LINKING TO LITERACY

Understanding Text Patterns: Procedural Text
The text on this and the next page is a procedure, or a type of text that explains, step by step, how something is made or done. Procedures can include a purpose, equipment and materials, steps to the procedure, and analysis questions. Many procedures also include an extension where you are asked to think about other ways to apply what you have learned.

Knowing more about this text pattern will help you to better understand your reading and what you are asked to do when following a procedure.

Procedure

1. Each of the following will already be printed on a coloured card, with each colour representing different biotic and abiotic elements in a water ecosystem:
   - blue: sunlight, air, water, soil (abiotic elements)
   - green: algae, *Elodea*, duckweed, cattails, willow, pond lilies (producers)
   - yellow: tadpoles, mosquito larvae, beaver, snails, *Daphnia* (herbivores)
   - red: raccoon, black bear, clams, mallard duck (omnivores)
   - orange: loon, osprey, perch, sunfish, otter, bullfrog (carnivores)
   - brown: herring gull (scavengers), bacteria (decomposers)

2. Select one of the cards. Research or review the biotic or abiotic element on your card.

3. Attach the card to your shirt.

4. As a class, form a large circle. Make sure that the different coloured cards are dispersed throughout the circle. For example, all students with yellow cards should not be standing side by side.

5. The student with the "sunlight" card begins the next part of the activity by holding the end of the yarn. The student then names another card and states his or her connection to that card. For example, "I provide energy for duckweed to make its own food." The student then passes the ball of yarn to the student with the "duckweed" card, but keeps holding the end of the yarn.

6. That second student then names another card and states his or her card's connection to it. The second student passes the yarn while holding on to his or her piece of the yarn at the same time (Figure 1).

Figure 1 Step 6

7. Continue stating connections and passing the ball of yarn until each card has at least one connection to another card. There may be several connections to any one card. Make sure that you hold on to the yarn.

8. Once all the connections have been made, gently tug on the yarn you are holding. Count how many people in the circle feel the tug.

9. Repeat step 8 for each member of the circle.

10. Determine which component of the web seems least important. Remove it from the web by having the person with that card drop the yarn.

11. Repeat step 10 with the remaining elements. From time to time, tug on the yarn and note any difference in the sensation.

Analyze and Evaluate

(a) What happens as the web becomes less complex? Are changes more dramatic as the web has fewer elements? Explain.

(b) Which cards (species) had more impact on the web? Which had less impact?

(c) What do you think would happen if the water in this model ecosystem became badly polluted?

(d) Why are the scavengers and decomposers necessary in the food web?

Apply and Extend

(e) What do you think would happen if more cards (more species) were added to the circle?

(f) Is there anything that was left out of the circle that you might include? Explain why or why not.

(g) Come up with another creative way to model the interactions within an ecosystem. Try it out with your group.

(h) Describe in your own words what the term "interdependence" means.

5.4 Energy Flow in an Ecosystem

Food chains and food webs show how energy moves from one organism to another. They do not show how each organism uses the energy or how much is used. Different organisms need different amounts of energy. This can depend on what the energy is being used for. For example, we eat more food when we have been very active because we need energy. The energy comes from the food.

To understand how energy flows in an ecosystem, you need to know how each organism in a food chain uses the energy it obtains. You also need to understand how much energy passes between levels in the food chain or food web. In this section, you will learn how ecologists study energy flows within and between organisms.

Energy Use within an Organism

An organism obtains energy when it makes its own food or eats a plant or animal. Some of the energy fuels the organism's normal life functions and is used up and released as heat. Some of the energy is stored in the organism for growth, maintenance, and repair. Finally, some of the energy is not useable. Unused energy passes out of the organism as waste. Only the energy stored in the organism is available to the next organism in the food chain. Figure 1 shows the breakdown of energy. In general, only about 10 % of the energy that an organism eats is passed on to the next organism in the food chain.

LINKING TO LITERACY

Summarize
Summarizing will help you check your understanding of the information in this section. Read the subsection "Energy Use within an Organism" on this and the following page. Before moving onto the next part of the section, stop and think about what you have read. Work with a partner to summarize, in your own words, how energy is used within an organism. Refer to Figure 1 to explain your thinking.

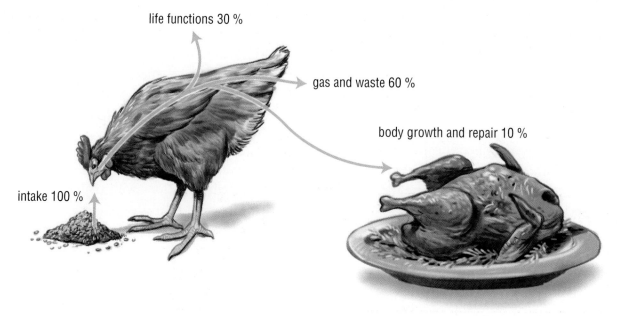

life functions 30 %

gas and waste 60 %

body growth and repair 10 %

intake 100 %

Figure 1 Only a small portion of the energy that the chicken receives from consuming the grain ends up on our plates.

At each level in a food chain or food web, the amount of available energy is much smaller than in the level below it. The amount of energy left for the top consumers in a food web is just a tiny portion of the energy that was in the producers. As a result, there are usually no more than four levels in a food chain or food web. There is not enough energy left to feed consumers at higher levels.

Pyramid of Numbers

An ecological pyramid shows the effects of energy loss at each level in a food chain. Ecologists use ecological pyramids to show this energy loss in a visual way. Each level in the pyramid represents a level in the food chain or food web. One way that ecologists measure the amount of energy available at different levels is by comparing the total mass of all organisms at each level. As you move higher in the food web, there is less mass and, therefore, less energy. The levels in the energy pyramid get smaller.

Another way to show the amount of energy available at each level of a food web is by constructing a pyramid of numbers. A **pyramid of numbers** shows the total number of organisms at each level of a food chain or food web (Figure 2). In a healthy ecosystem, there are usually more producers than consumers. The producers form a broad base, while the number of consumers at each level above gets smaller. This gives the diagram its "pyramid" shape. Each level of consumers above the producers has fewer individuals because there is less energy available. For example, in a lake ecosystem, hundreds of tadpoles need to eat thousands of duckweed plants to get enough energy to survive and grow. These tadpoles only provide enough energy to support one or two snapping turtles.

LINKING TO LITERACY

Summarize
Read the subsection called "Pyramid of Numbers." Before moving onto the next section, work with a partner to summarize how and why numbers are different from one level of the pyramid to the next. Refer to Figure 2 to help explain your thinking.

pyramid of numbers: a model that shows the number of individuals at each level in a food chain or food web

To learn more about pyramids used by ecologists, **Go to Nelson Science**

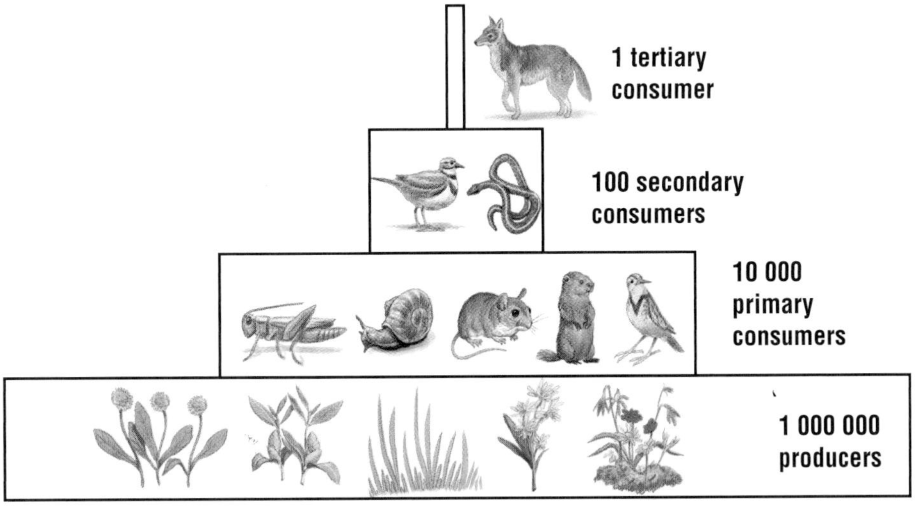

Figure 2 A pyramid of numbers for a grassland food web

1 tertiary consumer

100 secondary consumers

10 000 primary consumers

1 000 000 producers

TRY THIS: Dealing Out a Pyramid of Numbers

SKILLS MENU: performing, observing, analyzing, evaluating

A pyramid of numbers illustrates the number of different organisms at each level of a food chain or food web. In this activity, you will make your own pyramid of numbers using playing cards to represent organisms.

Equipment and Materials: playing cards; field guide (optional); paper; pencil

1. Write down the name of a plant or animal on a piece of paper. Do not show it to anyone.

2. As a class, collect all the papers and classify them as producers, primary consumers, secondary consumers, or tertiary consumers. Create a tally for each category. If you are unsure about which category an organism should be in, use a field guide to determine what that organism eats.

3. For each category, deal out the same number of playing cards as the tally number for that category. For example, if the tally showed four tertiary consumers, there should be four playing cards in that pile.

4. Use the four piles of cards to build a card tower. Use only the producer cards for the bottom level, only the primary consumer cards for the next level, only the secondary consumer cards for the next level, and the tertiary consumer cards for the top level.

5. If you cannot build a stable tower from the piles, start again using as many cards as you need to create a stable tower with four levels.

6. As you build, count the number of cards you use for each level. Record the numbers for each level in your notebook.

A. Were you able to create a card tower using the tally totals? Discuss the reasons why or why not.

B. In step 5, what adjustments had to be made to the numbers of cards at each level before a stable tower could be created?

C. If the cards in the card tower represent individual producers and consumers in a pyramid of numbers, what does the card tower tell you about the number of individuals at each level?

D. Does a card tower adequately represent the idea of a numbers pyramid? Explain why or why not.

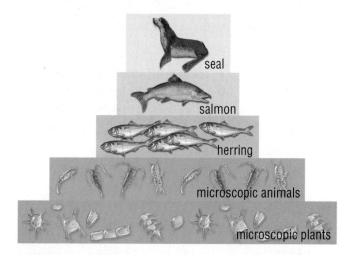

Figure 3 A pyramid with a wide base can support a stable population of consumers.

To maintain stable populations in an ecosystem, there must be a large number of producers to provide enough food energy for primary, secondary, and tertiary consumers. The wider the base of the pyramid, the more consumers can live in the ecosystem. Now, consider Figure 3. What do you think would happen if the microscopic plants level of the pyramid was only half the width it is in the diagram? What would happen to the microscopic animals level? Changes to the number of organisms at any level in the pyramid will affect the number of organisms at other levels.

CHECK YOUR LEARNING

1. A chicken eats some grain. In your own words, describe what happens to the energy in the food once the chicken eats it.

2. What is a pyramid of numbers? How does it relate to a food chain?

3. How is a pyramid of numbers different from an ecological pyramid?

4. (a) What happens to the total number of organisms at each level of a pyramid of numbers?
   (b) Explain in your own words why this occurs.

5. What type of organisms always occupy the first level of an ecological pyramid or a pyramid of numbers?

Matter Cycles

5.5

Food chains, food webs, and ecological pyramids show how energy moves in one direction in ecosystems. Matter also moves in ecosystems. What happens to matter—the leaves, roots, bones, hair, muscles, and every other part of an organism—in an ecosystem?

Earth is a closed system. A **closed system** is one in which no new matter can enter and no matter can leave. (On Earth, the only exception to this is when meteorites hit the surface of the planet.) The amounts of carbon, water, oxygen, hydrogen, and nitrogen on Earth are the same now as they were when dinosaurs were alive. However, organisms are continuously using these materials to stay alive. How do the amounts of matter on Earth remain the same over long periods of time? The answer is through recycling. Matter is taken up from the environment, used in life processes, and eventually returned to the environment where it can be used again. Ecologists call this repeating pattern a **cycle**.

closed system: a system in which the amount of matter remains constant over time

cycle: a pattern in nature that repeats over time

The Cleanup Squad

Detrivores and decomposers recycle in an ecosystem. They are essential to any ecosystem. As you have already learned, detrivores and decomposers eat the remains of dead plants and animals that scavengers and other consumers have left behind (Figure 1). Detrivores and decomposers also feed on animal wastes. Detrivores break up organic matter into smaller pieces. When decomposers feed, they break down these smaller pieces into simple substances such as minerals, nitrates, and phosphates. These substances are left in the soil as nutrients that plants can absorb. This is nature's way of recycling matter. Decomposers play a critical role in any ecosystem. They convert biotic elements, such as plant and animal matter, into abiotic elements, such as minerals. They allow matter to be recycled and reused by other organisms in the ecosystem.

LINKING TO LITERACY

Synthesizing Information
Synthesizing means to summarize what you read, reflect on your learning, and make connections with what you already know to form new opinions, apply your learning, or construct new ideas. Use the text on this and the next page to help you understand decomposers and detrivores.

Figure 1 (a) Scavengers like this turkey vulture feed on already dead animals and leave behind decaying matter. (b) Detrivores such as earthworms break down the organic matter into smaller pieces. (c) Decomposers like this fungus break down the remaining matter, releasing nutrients back into the ecosystem.

A composter is a perfect example of matter being recycled. Food and plant wastes are put into a container. Earthworms and other detrivores break down large pieces of decaying matter into smaller pieces. Bacteria, fungi, and other decomposers then further break down these pieces into nutrient particles. The final product is compost. Gardeners mix nutrient-rich compost into the existing soil. Garden plants then use these nutrients to grow.

To learn more about composting,

Go to Nelson Science

TRY THIS: Discovering Interactions in a Rotting Log

SKILLS MENU: performing, observing, analyzing

It generally takes 10 years for a rotting log (Figure 2) to break down completely into soil. In this activity, you will investigate the interactions in a rotting log that will cause it to decompose.

Equipment and Materials: rotting log; gloves; hand lens; forceps; water in a spray bottle; small shovel; plastic containers with lids; field guides (optional)

Figure 2 There are many hidden interactions happening within a rotting log.

1. Find a rotting log in your neighbourhood. It might be in a park or even on your school grounds.

2. Put on your gloves. Using the hand lens and forceps, carefully observe the log. Look for any signs of life. Use the spray bottle to keep the log moist. You may want to use field guides to identify what you see. Place any living things you find into plastic containers for temporary observation.

3. In your notebook, record any observations, along with any questions that arise from your investigation.

4. Return any organisms to where you found them on the log. Wash your hands when you are finished.

A. What evidence did you observe that indicates that the log is decomposing?

B. Is the rotting log an ecosystem? Use your evidence to explain.

Ecosystems Are Sustainable

Without scavengers, detrivores, and decomposers, Earth would be piled high with dead organisms. For example, the leaves that fall from trees would still be there in the spring, continuing to pile up year after year. With no new nutrients being added to the soil, plants would slowly starve and die. As a result, animals would also starve and die.

sustainable: something that can be maintained and used indefinitely

Healthy ecosystems are **sustainable**, which means that they can be maintained indefinitely. They can replenish resources by continuously recycling matter. For example, a bear catches a fish, eats most of it, and leaves the carcass to rot into the soil. The nutrients in the carcass are released by decomposers. Forest trees use these nutrients to grow and stay healthy. The healthy forest provides a home and food for the bear.

The Carbon Cycle

Carbon is found in many places on Earth. It is found in abiotic elements, such as coal, oil, and natural gas, and in the air as carbon dioxide. Carbon is also found in all living things.

Carbon has a predictable cycle (Figure 3). Plants use carbon dioxide in photosynthesis to produce sugars. When animals and other organisms break down these sugars to obtain energy, they produce water and carbon dioxide. Animals also release waste carbon dioxide when they exhale, or breathe out. When decomposers break down dead plants and animals, they too release carbon dioxide. All of the carbon dioxide released into the air by these processes is available to plants for photosynthesis. The cycle starts again.

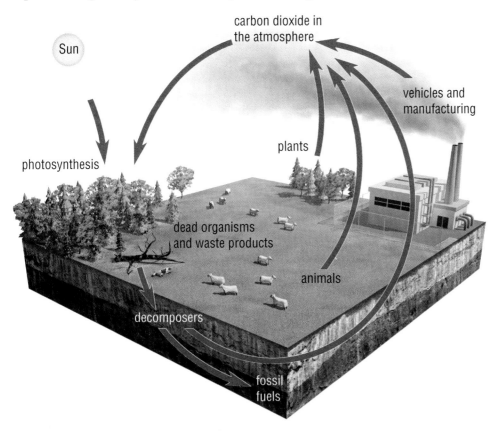

Figure 3 The carbon cycle

Carbon in dead plants that are buried in soil may not decompose completely. This organic matter remains underground for millions of years where it undergoes chemical changes to form fossil fuels such as coal, oil, and natural gas. When humans burn fossil fuels, most of the carbon quickly enters the atmosphere as carbon dioxide. Carbon dioxide is a gas that stays in Earth's atmosphere and absorbs the energy radiated by Earth and the Sun. This contributes to the warming of Earth's surface. Gases that trap energy in Earth's atmosphere are known as greenhouse gases. Earth would be a frozen world without greenhouse gases. However, humans have burned so much fossil fuel that there is about 30 % more carbon dioxide in the air today than there was 150 years ago.

All this extra carbon dioxide in the atmosphere has affected where organisms can live. Some locations are now too warm to meet the ideal temperature ranges of the organisms. These temperature changes have become a growing concern for society.

The Water Cycle

Water keeps all living things alive. Most living things are made largely of water. Water also moves in a cycle.

The water cycle begins with evaporation (Figure 4). **Evaporation** is the change in state of a substance from liquid to gas. As the Sun's energy warms up oceans, lakes, and rivers, some of the water evaporates to form water vapour. Large amounts of water vapour also escape from plant leaves. The water vapour rises in the atmosphere, contracting as it cools to form tiny water droplets. The change of state from a gas to a liquid is called **condensation**. The tiny water droplets that result from the condensation of water vapour form clouds. As more and more droplets condense, they fall back to Earth as rain or snow, also called **precipitation**. Precipitation can run off of the surface of Earth and into bodies of water. Precipitation may also seep into the ground and remain trapped there for years as groundwater. Groundwater also eventually seeps into large bodies of water. At any stage in the cycle, the water may evaporate back into the atmosphere. Nature recycles water so that it can be used again and again!

evaporation: the process in which a substance changes state from liquid to gas

condensation: the change in state of a substance from gas to liquid

precipitation: water in the liquid or solid state that falls to Earth

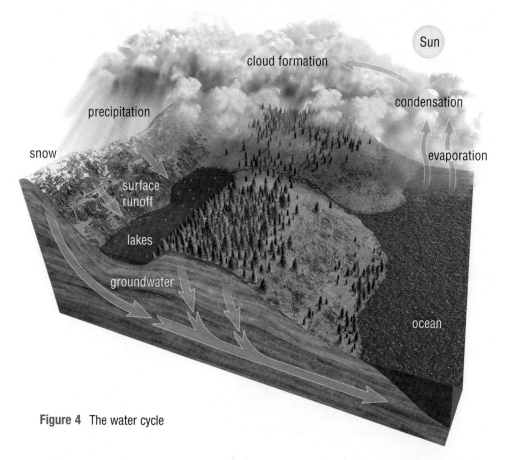

Figure 4 The water cycle

We all need clean fresh water to survive, but the supply of fresh water on Earth is limited. Agriculture and industry use large amounts of fresh water to irrigate crops and for industrial processes. Humans use water faster than it can be replenished by the water cycle because the demand has increased with the growth of the human population. Also, pollutants from agriculture, mine tailings, and other industrial processes can seep into local groundwater and make it unsafe to drink (Figure 5). We have to use water more carefully and protect it from pollution. This is the only way to ensure a supply of clean fresh drinking water in the future.

To learn more about the water cycle,

Go to Nelson Science

Figure 5 Smoke and steam are released from this paper mill near an Ontario lake. Pollutants that enter the water from industrial plants such as this are cycled through ecosystems and affect organisms.

In the same way that changes in food chains can affect an entire food web, changes to one of nature's cycles can affect other cycles. For example, Earth's temperature increases when more carbon enters the atmosphere. This can affect the water cycle. Higher temperatures affect precipitation patterns and the amount of water humans take from lakes and groundwater sources. It is important to think about the effects that different cycles in nature can have on each other.

Unit Task When you complete the Unit Task, think about whether your plan for naturalizing your area is sustainable.

✔ CHECK YOUR LEARNING

1. What is a cycle?

2. Explain how detrivores and decomposers recycle matter.

3. What is meant by the statement "Ecosystems are sustainable"?

4. In your own words, describe the carbon cycle.

5. In your own words, describe the water cycle.

6. Describe some of the ways that the supply of fresh water on Earth is at risk.

Breaking Down the Waste Barrier

You create waste when you prepare a meal, such as vegetable peels or leftover chopped greens. Most kitchen waste can be composted. Decomposers in compost break down wastes so that the nutrients they contain can be released into the soil. What kinds of materials break down? Which do not? In this investigation, you will examine the processes of composting and observe decomposers at work.

SKILLS MENU

☐ Questioning   ☑ Performing
☑ Hypothesizing   ☑ Observing
☑ Predicting   ☑ Analyzing
☐ Planning   ☑ Evaluating
☑ Controlling   ☑ Communicating
   Variables

Testable Question

What types of household materials decompose when buried in moist soil?

Hypothesis/Prediction

SKILLS HANDBOOK 2.B.3.

Read the Experimental Design and Procedure, and then formulate a hypothesis based on the Testable Question. Your hypothesis should include a prediction and reasons for your prediction.

Experimental Design

In this investigation, you will determine whether or not decomposition occurs (dependent variable) depending on the kinds of materials you choose to test (independent variable). The materials you choose will be the only things different in each container. All other materials and conditions used will be the same in each container; they will be controlled variables. You can then determine which materials decompose and which do not.

markers

scissors

rubber bands

water in a spray bottle

6 bottoms of clear 2 L plastic bottles

garden soil

garden waste

raw vegetable and fruit peels

paper, aluminum foil, plastic wrap

masking tape

window screening

Equipment and Materials

- markers
- scissors
- rubber bands
- water in a spray bottle
- 6 bottoms of clear 2 L plastic bottles
- garden soil
- garden waste
- raw vegetable and fruit peels
- paper, aluminum foil, plastic wrap
- masking tape
- window screening

Procedure

1. Place a 2 cm layer of garden soil at the bottom of each of the six bottles.

2. Add a 5 cm layer of garden waste on top of the soil layer in each of the six bottles.

3. Place a different vegetable or fruit scrap into each of the first three bottles. For example, place some banana peel into one, some potato peel into the next, and some orange peel into the third.

4. Place pieces of paper, aluminum foil, and plastic wrap into the remaining three bottles. Put only one type of material into each bottle.

5. Make sure that there are similar amounts of each material in each bottle.

6. Add garden soil to each bottle until half full. Label each bottle to indicate what materials it contains.

7. Add enough water to each bottle to make the mixture inside moist, but not wet. Cover the bottle opening with window screening and secure it with a rubber band.

8. Place the bottles in a warm location for one week. Use a spray bottle to moisten the contents of each bottle every couple of days.

9. After one week, remove the screening. Move the soil in each container aside so that you can view the materials. In your notebook, record any observations, including how the materials look and smell. Describe the degree of decomposition of each of the test materials.

    Minimize the amount of time that the materials in the bottle are exposed to air. Do not breathe in too deeply when smelling the contents. Be sure to wash your hands after you observe your bottles.

10. Push the soil back over, moisten the contents of the bottles, and set aside for another week.

11. Repeat steps 8 to 10 for two more weeks.

Analyze and Evaluate

(a) Which materials decomposed? Which did not? Did your observations support your hypothesis?

(b) Answer the Testable Question.

(c) Of the materials that decomposed, which decomposed fastest? Which decomposed slowest?

(d) What may have enabled some of the materials to decompose?

(e) Why were both garden waste and soil added to the compost?

Apply and Extend

SKILLS HANDBOOK
2.B.2., 2.B.4.

(f) Consider the health of our environment. What should be done with those materials that did not break down easily?

(g) Design your own experiment to determine what effect, if any, temperature would have on the rate of decomposition. Make sure that your experiment is a fair test (your hypothesis should state whether you expect one variable, such as the rate of decomposition, to change when you alter another variable, such as temperature).

(h) Conduct research on vermicomposting and red wrigglers. What is the advantage of each? With permission from your teacher, set up a vermicomposter in your classroom to compost any vegetable and fruit waste you may have.

Go to Nelson Science

Interactions within Ecosystems

BIG Ideas

- ☑ Ecosystems are made up of biotic (living) and abiotic (non-living) elements, which depend on each other to survive.
- ☑ Ecosystems are in a constant state of change. The changes may be caused by nature or by human intervention.
- ☑ Human activities have the potential to alter the environment. Humans must be aware of these impacts and try to control them.

Looking Back

Organisms have different roles in ecosystems.

- The role each organism plays is related to the way in which it obtains energy.
- Producers make their own food. Consumers must eat other organisms to obtain energy.
- Herbivores eat plants; carnivores eat animals; omnivores eat both plants and animals.
- Scavengers eat dead animals; detrivores and decomposers eat dead plants and animals and their wastes.

Food chains and food webs show how energy from the Sun is passed from one organism to another in an ecosystem.

- Food chains start with a producer and end with a consumer. Food chains show the feeding patterns of organisms in an ecosystem.
- Food webs show how the food chains in an ecosystem are interconnected. A food web may contain several food chains.
- Changing any part of a food chain or food web affects all the organisms in that chain or web.
- Energy is lost at each level in a food chain.
- Ecological pyramids are visual representations of the loss of energy at each level in a food chain. Number pyramids show the number of organisms at each level of a food chain or web.

The skills of scientific inquiry can be used to model and investigate food webs.

- A model food web can be used to investigate the interactions between the biotic and abiotic elements in an ecosystem.
- Changes in food webs can be observed by using a model ecosystem.

Matter is constantly recycled in an ecosystem.

- Carbon, water, and oxygen are recycled in ecosystems. Both detrivores and decomposers are critical to the recycling of matter.
- Detrivores break down decaying plant and animal matter into small pieces. Decomposers further break down the matter, releasing nutrients back into the environment for use by organisms.
- The continuous recycling of matter makes ecosystems sustainable.

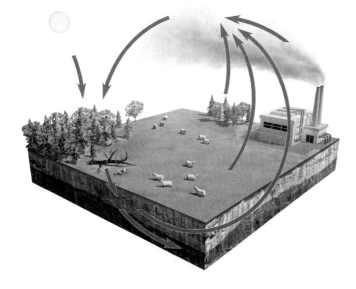

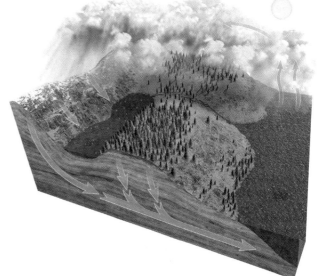

Investigation skills can be used to examine the biotic and abiotic interactions in a composter.

- Only certain types of matter decompose in a composter.
- Biotic elements help matter in a composter decompose.

What Do You Remember?

1. What are the "ingredients" of photosynthesis? **K/U**

2. Create a food chain that has four organisms. **K/U**

3. What would happen to ecosystems if dead organisms did not decompose? **K/U**

4. Decomposers play an important role in which matter cycle? **K/U**

5. Give two examples of each of the following: producer, herbivore, carnivore, omnivore, scavenger, detrivore, and decomposer. Organize your answers in a table. **K/U** **C**

6. Explain the difference between a producer and a consumer. **K/U**

7. For each of the following, explain the difference between the two terms: **K/U**

   (a) food chain, food web

   (b) carnivore, scavenger

   (c) detrivore, decomposer

   (d) primary consumer, secondary consumer

8. If you found bald eagles, algae, mosquito larvae, and salmon within the same ecosystem, what role would each organism most likely play? **K/U**

9. Explain what is meant by "Energy flows and matter cycles." **K/U**

10. Explain why each level in a pyramid of numbers is smaller than the one below it. **K/U**

11. List four different roles organisms play within an ecosystem. Include examples. **K/U**

12. Why are long food chains less effective in transferring energy than short food chains? Explain your answer using a diagram of an energy pyramid. **K/U**

13. Based on Figure 1, use your own words to explain what is happening at each arrow. **K/U**

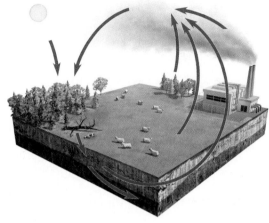

Figure 1

What Do You Understand?

14. Some people promote vegetarianism as a way of helping the environment.

    (a) Explain how vegetarianism can help the environment in terms of what you have learned in this chapter.

    (b) Do you agree or disagree that vegetarianism is a good way to help the environment? Explain. **A**

15. A rotting log is an ecosystem. Create a food web for a rotting log that may be found in your local area. **A**

16. Composting has become popular in urban communities. What are the benefits of putting kitchen wastes into a composter or green bin? **A**

Solve a Problem!

17. An average tree can remove about 9 kg of carbon dioxide per year from the air.

    (a) Why might tree-planting campaigns be useful in urban areas?

    (b) Suggest other ways to reduce the amount of carbon in the air. **A**

18. Read situations i, ii, iii, iv, and v.

    (a) Indicate whether the carbon cycle, water cycle, or both are affected in each situation.

    (b) Predict the changes that might happen in the carbon and water cycles if the situation actually occurred. T/I A

    i)   An oil spill occurs.

    ii) Heavy rains wash pesticides and toxins on our roads down the sewers.

    iii) Carbon dioxide gas emissions into the air continue to increase.

    iv) No garden waste is placed into garden beds.

    v)   There are no plants in a given area.

19. You have just consumed a ham and cheese sandwich and a glass of milk. T/I C

    (a) List all the organisms needed to produce your lunch.

    (b) Draw a food chain for each item, with you at the top. (Hint: break down each part of the lunch to create your chains. For example, create separate chains for bread, cheese, and so on.)

20. Trace the water cycle within your community. In your area, are there any human-made structures or mechanisms to deal with the water cycle? T/I A

21. Many communities are concerned about West Nile disease, which is spread by mosquitoes, and want to add chemical pesticides to the local pond to destroy all the mosquito larvae.

    (a) Create a typical food web for a pond. Include all the links that mosquito larvae may have in that ecosystem.

    (b) Use this drawing to explain how using pesticides affects the food web.

    (c) Provide some alternative ways to control the mosquito population. T/I A C

22. Gulls and raccoons are often looked down upon by humans because they eat garbage.

    (a) What is your view of the situation?

    (b) What might our beaches and cities be like if this did not occur?

    (c) What role do these animals play within an ecosystem that includes humans?

    (d) What can you do to help people live in greater harmony with wildlife in cities and towns? T/I A

Create and Evaluate!

23. You are a nature interpreter at a local park.

    (a) Create a poster for visitors to the park that shows what happens to dead material and illustrates how it helps promote sustainability in the ecosystem.

    (b) Have your classmates evaluate the effectiveness of your poster. Evaluate their suggestions and make any changes that you think will improve the poster. K/U C

24. Collect several pictures of Native artwork that focus on nature. Discuss your interpretation of these artworks with a partner. Create a visual display of what you believe the paintings show about ecosystems. A C

Go to Nelson Science

Reflect on Your Learning

25. Has your understanding of human and nature interactions changed from the concepts introduced in this chapter? Explain why or why not.

26. Think back to the Key Question on the first page of the chapter.

    (a) In a brief paragraph, answer the Key Question. You may use diagrams.

    (b) Write one or two more questions about the topic of this unit that you would like to explore.

6 Organisms Depend on a Healthy Environment

▶ **KEY QUESTION:** What impacts do humans have on the environment, and what can we do to keep the environment healthy?

Looking Ahead

- Ecosystems change naturally over time.

- Human activities can alter the environment.

- The skills of scientific inquiry can be used to investigate factors that affect local ecosystems.

- Humans can do many things to protect the environment.

- The skills of scientific inquiry can be used to assess how technology affects the environment.

VOCABULARY

succession	extinction
primary succession	invasive species
secondary succession	native species
biodiversity	steward
endangered species	

Words of Wisdom

"Take care of the Earth and she will take care of you."
—Unknown

"Humankind has not woven the web of life. We are but one thread within it. Whatever we do to the web, we do to ourselves. All things are bound together. All things connect."
—Chief Sealth

"Never doubt that a small group of thoughtful, committed citizens can change the world. Indeed, it is the only thing that ever has."
—Margaret Mead

"We do not inherit the Earth from our ancestors, we borrow it from our children."
—Aboriginal proverb

"Our personal consumer choices have ecological, social, and spiritual consequences. It is time to re-examine some of our deeply held notions that underlie our lifestyles."
—David Suzuki

"If you talk to the animals they will talk with you and you will know each other. If you do not talk to them you will not know them, and what you do not know you will fear. What one fears one destroys."
—Chief Dan George

"Those who contemplate the beauty of the Earth find reserves of strength that will endure as long as life lasts."
—Rachel Carson

"When one tugs at a single thing in nature, he finds it attached to the rest of the world."
—John Muir

LINKING TO LITERACY

Critical Literacy

Critical literacy is about the power of language. It involves using language to improve people's lives and to question unfairness in the world. Authors express their beliefs about the world through their writing; readers can analyze these messages by asking themselves why, how, and for whom a text was written. The reader can also look to see whose point of view is represented, and whose point of view is silent.

1 Read the quotes on this page. Work with a partner or a small group to analyze and critique each one. You may draw a table or chart to explain your thinking. Allow one column for each of the following headings:

- Quote
- Logic (How logical is the quote? Does it make sense?)
- Accuracy (How accurate is the quote?)
- Bias (Does the quote support one person or group more that another? Whose voice is not heard?)
- Comments (What are your personal thoughts or feelings about each quote?)

6.1

The Dynamics of Nature: Succession

Figure 1 This parking lot has become overgrown with vegetation.

succession: a series of gradual changes that result in the replacement of one community of plants and animals by another

primary succession: succession that develops a community of plants and animals in an area where no living things existed before

LINKING TO LITERACY

Marking the Text
You can use sticky notes to help you stay focused and reflect on your reading. As you read the following three pages, make note of key ideas, words you need to check for meaning, or questions you have about the topic. Write your thoughts on sticky notes. Place the sticky notes on each page alongside the text.

When you have finished reading, follow up on your notes. Is there information that you have to learn more about?

When you mark up your text and follow up on your notes, you develop a deeper, more complete understanding of a topic.

Have you ever noticed grasses or other plants growing in a vacant lot (Figure 1)? Eventually, bushes and trees will begin to grow, and animals will make their homes in the lot. Over time, ecosystems change.

Ecological **succession** is the predictable and orderly change over time in the types of organisms in an ecosystem. In succession, the dominant plant and animal species living in an ecosystem are gradually replaced by new species. This occurs in stages over many years. Plants play a key role in succession because they provide food and shelter for animals. The new, changed environment creates conditions that are ideal for new species. Over time, the community becomes more stable and succession slows down. Eventually, the community remains as is and simply renews itself.

Primary Succession

Primary succession happens in areas where there has never been any life. Imagine that a volcano, landslide, or earthquake has created a large area of newly exposed bare rock. Lichens are the first organisms to "colonize" the bare rock (Figure 2). They begin the process of building soil. Lichens use photosynthesis to make food and to grow, and they produce acids that help them to absorb nutrients from the rock and the air. These acids break down the rock into soil. Lichens pick up some of the newly formed soil particles and other bits of debris as the wind blows over them. Once lichens are thick enough, mosses can live in the area. The death and decay of lichens and mosses also help build new soil. When enough soil gathers, small plants begin to grow. Plant roots continue to break up the rock and keep the existing soil in place. Eventually, the area develops enough soil for grasses and weeds to grow.

Figure 2 Lichens form because of the interaction of an alga and a fungus. Lichens are the first organisms to appear in primary succession.

As each generation of plant grows and dies, more soil is created. This allows plants to grow even taller, and shrubs and other bushes begin to grow. As more shrubs grow, they out-compete the shorter plants, such as grasses, for resources. Shorter plants die out because they no longer receive enough sunlight to grow. The shrubs provide shade and more stable, moist soil for tree seedlings to develop. As the tree population expands, the trees out-compete the shrub species, and only shade-loving plants remain. The area eventually develops into a forest.

As each new plant species begins to grow, consumers that feed on that species move into the community (Figure 3). Grasshoppers and groundhogs feed on the grasses in the early stages of succession, but are replaced as more dominant species, such as shrubs and trees, cover the area and grasses die out. Caterpillars and squirrels move in to feed on the trees. Foxes, which feed on grassland animals, are replaced by wolves, which feed on forest animals. Grass-nesting birds such as sparrows are replaced by tree-nesting birds such as orioles.

In succession, early communities are quite simple, with few species interacting. As succession progresses, communities become more complex and contain many interactions.

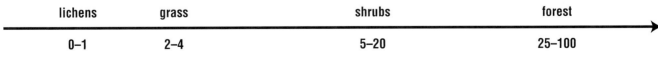

lichens	grass	shrubs	forest
0–1	2–4	5–20	25–100

Time (years)

Figure 3 Succession is gradual; as plants change, so do the animals. Succession can take more than a hundred years.

Secondary Succession

Secondary succession is the slow change in species in an established community after the community has been disturbed. Examples of natural disturbances include forest fires and strong winds. Examples of human-made disturbances include cutting down forests for agriculture or urban development.

In secondary succession, soil already exists and needs to be revitalized. First, seeds from grasses and wildflowers blow in from neighbouring communities. The seeds grow on the exposed soil, enriching it over time. This enriched soil promotes the growth of bigger plants, such as blackberry bushes and birches (Figure 4). These plants provide food and shelter for animals such as deer mice, nesting birds, and garter snakes, which begin to move into the community. Eventually, larger trees begin to grow and out-compete the bushes and birches, pushing them out. Animals that prefer tall trees move in. Succession continues until the community re-establishes itself.

However, humans often interfere with succession. For example, clear-cutting a forest eliminates the entire forest ecosystem. Left alone, this area can recover through succession, eventually returning to a complex forest ecosystem. However, humans often replace complex ecosystems with simple ones designed for their own needs. These ecosystems tend not to be sustainable. For example, reforestation companies may plant only one tree species in an area that has been clear-cut (Figure 5). One tree species results in a less complex food web. Fewer organisms can be supported in the ecosystem, and it is more likely that problems will occur. Planting only one tree species instead of allowing succession to occur naturally also increases the risk of the forest being wiped out by disease or insect invasion.

Figure 4 This area has been abandoned for some time. It is at the stage of succession where shrubs are starting to grow.

Figure 5 Christmas trees often come from fir tree farms, such as this one. However, relatively few other organisms can live here.

✔ CHECK YOUR LEARNING

1. **(a)** What is primary succession?
   (b) Why are lichens so vital for primary succession?

2. What is the difference between primary and secondary succession?

3. A forest is clear-cut and left to regrow naturally. Describe the pattern of succession for the area.

4. Explain how humans interfere with succession. How does this negatively affect ecosystems?

Human Impact on Ecosystems

What effects do human activities have on nature? Like all other living things, people can be in balance or out of balance with an ecosystem.

Habitat Loss

Humans use land in many ways. Farming, building cities, mining, and even travelling can result in loss of habitat for other living things. Consider, for example, shopping malls. They are often built on farm fields or on "undeveloped" land (Figure 1). All the vegetation is cleared from the land so that it can be paved over or built on. The habitat for species in the local ecosystem is destroyed. The products sold in the mall are manufactured in other parts of Canada or the world. Manufacturing also contributes to habitat loss because factories all around the world destroy local habitats. In addition, some manufactured goods contain metal, which is obtained by mining. Mining can alter or destroy habitats. Humans pave over local habitats to build roads to transport goods and customers to the mall. You can see the impact that a shopping mall can have on an ecosystem!

Figure 1 This shopping mall is sitting on prime farming land.

When forests are clear-cut, wetlands are drained, or meadows are paved over, habitat is lost. Habitat loss means that organisms that lived in these habitats have nowhere to go. Plants die because they cannot uproot and move. Some animals may die because they may not be able to travel far enough to find a suitable habitat. Animals that move to new communities may not be able to compete with the organisms already living there and may die. The end result of habitat loss is fewer organisms.

Land-use issues are complicated. It can be difficult to balance the needs of ecosystems and the needs and wants of humans. Humans need places to live, farmland on which to grow food, and jobs that may come from development. Our standard of living in Canada is very high compared to the rest of the world. It is time to think about how we can get what we want in ways that cause as little damage to ecosystems as possible.

LINKING TO LITERACY

Topic Sentences
Locate the topic sentence in the paragraph under "Habitat Loss." Often, the topic sentence will be the first sentence of the paragraph. In this case it is, "Humans use land in many ways." This sentence tells you that the paragraph will be describing ways in which humans use land. Together, the subtitle and topic sentence give you a clue that the paragraph will also tell you about some of the ways in which habitat is lost.

When reading informational text, practise looking for the topic sentence in each paragraph. It will help you make a prediction about what you will be reading in the paragraph and remember key ideas.

SKILLS MENU: analyzing, communicating

There are many organizations in Ontario and Canada working to protect habitat for future generations. In this activity, you will research some of these organizations to discover what they are doing to protect habitats.

Equipment and Materials: computer with Internet access

1. Select one of the following organizations to research: Greenbelt of Ontario, Ducks Unlimited, Nature Conservancy of Canada, World Wildlife Fund.

2. Use the Internet to research the organization you have chosen.

Go to Nelson Science 🌐

A. Choose an appropriate method to share your findings with the class, for example, a poster, multimedia presentation, or an oral report.

Habitat Loss and Biodiversity

biodiversity: the variety of plant and animal life in an ecosystem

endangered species: species that are at risk of becoming extinct due to either reduction in numbers or an environmental threat

extinction: the complete disappearance of a species from anywhere on Earth

For more information on at-risk species in Ontario,

Go to Nelson Science 🌐

For an ecosystem to be healthy, it needs a large variety of plant and animal life. The variety of organisms in an ecosystem is called **biodiversity**. Biodiversity can be used to measure the health of an ecosystem: the more varied the organisms in an ecosystem, the more interactions will take place. Loss of habitat can place a species at risk of becoming endangered (Figure 2). **Endangered species** are species that are in danger of becoming extinct. **Extinction** occurs when a species no longer exists anywhere on Earth! A species may become endangered because its population has been reduced, or because its population is being threatened by elements of the ecosystem (Figure 3). Loss of biodiversity can threaten the sustainability of ecosystems. 🌐

Figure 2 The Eastern Massasauga rattlesnake was commonly found in southern Ontario 50 years ago. Development and urbanization has endangered this species.

Figure 3 The American chestnut has almost disappeared from eastern North America due to a fungus that was accidentally introduced into the population.

Earth's biodiversity provides many of the things humans need to live and enjoy life. For example, plants provide the raw material for a wide range of products. They also provide us with pleasant surroundings, and they help remove carbon dioxide from the atmosphere.

So far, scientists have identified close to 1.75 million species of living things. Most of these are small organisms, such as micro-organisms and invertebrates. Scientists estimate that there are between 5 and 30 million different species of organisms on Earth!

Invasive Species and Biodiversity

Invasive species are species that are not normally found in a particular area. In most cases, they have been introduced into an area by human activities. Sometimes they are introduced by accident, and sometimes they are introduced purposely. Invasive species may be introduced into an ecosystem in many different ways. Invasive species can arrive on boats (Figure 4), trucks, or even people's shoes! They may also escape or be released from farms and pet collections (Figure 5). Common invasive species include pigeons and house sparrows. These birds were intentionally brought over to North America from Europe.

invasive species: a species that has been introduced into an area (accidentally or purposely) where it did not exist before; often reproduces so aggressively that it replaces some of the original species

Figure 4 These zebra mussels were accidentally introduced to Lake Erie from Eastern Europe in the 1980s. Today, zebra mussels have spread to all the Great Lakes and are one of the worst invasive species in Ontario waters.

Figure 5 The red-eared slider turtle was introduced to the Rideau River due to pet owners dumping their unwanted turtles. This invasive turtle species competes with native species for food and habitat.

When invasive species move into an area, they generally have a negative impact on the organisms in that ecosystem. Invasive species are not part of the existing food chains. They grow quickly and have few or less effective natural predators. They compete for the same resources as native species. **Native species** are species that have lived in an area for a long time and have adapted to the other organisms in the ecosystem. Because invasive species have few predators, native species are pushed out and the biodiversity of the area decreases. Kentucky bluegrass, for example, was introduced by American settlers for use in lawns. It spread into other communities and is now widespread in North American grasslands. A related species of bluegrass has become so common in Canada that it is known as "Canada bluegrass," even though it is not a native species.

native species: species that occur naturally in an area

Table 1 shows other common invasive species in Ontario.

Table 1 Some Invasive Species in Ontario and the Effects They Have on Local Ecosystems

Invasive species	Effects on ecosystems
Asian longhorn beetle	• This wood-boring insect from China attacks healthy hardwood trees. It was introduced from wood packing material brought over in ships. • Infested trees must be destroyed to prevent the beetle's spread.
Garlic mustard	• Garlic mustard competes with wildflowers that flower in the spring, such as spring beauty, wild ginger, and trilliums, stealing light, moisture, nutrients, soil, and space. • Organisms that depend on these early plants for food soon disappear.
Zebra mussels	• Zebra mussels carried by ocean ships clog water intakes at treatment plants. • They remove much of the plankton and other essential food sources at the bottom of the food web. • Populations of native mussels, clams, and small fish disappear.
Purple loosestrife	• This garden plant was introduced from Europe by ships crossing the ocean. • It out-competes native plants in wetlands and wild meadows. • It clogs up irrigation systems and interferes with the recreational enjoyment of ponds and lakes.

Fortunately, many people are trying to control the spread of non-native species. Volunteers spend many weekends removing invasive plant species from sensitive habitats. Creating your own natural habitat at school or home, if done carefully, can give back valuable resources to the original plants and animals that used to live there.

To learn more about invasive species,

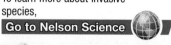

CHECK YOUR LEARNING

1. What is habitat loss?

2. (a) What is biodiversity?
   (b) How are habitat loss and biodiversity connected?

3. (a) Define invasive species and native species.
   (b) How do invasive species cause harm to the environment?
   (c) Name two invasive species found in Ontario and explain how they harm the environment.

The Trouble with Invasive Species

In this activity, you will research invasive species in Ontario and determine an action plan to help control, or eliminate, that species.

SKILLS MENU

- ☐ Questioning
- ☐ Hypothesizing
- ☑ Predicting
- ☑ Planning
- ☐ Controlling Variables
- ☑ Performing
- ☑ Observing
- ☑ Analyzing
- ☑ Evaluating
- ☑ Communicating

Purpose

To investigate an invasive species in your area and develop a plan to lessen the impact of that species on the environment.

Equipment and Materials

- map of Ontario
- computer with Internet access
- field guide to invasive species (optional)

map of Ontario

computer with Internet access

field guide to invasive species

Procedure

1. Obtain a map of Ontario from your teacher. Working in groups, use the map to select an area close to your community. Try to choose an area that you can visit and study first-hand.

2. Find out which invasive species are found in your selected area, including species found in lakes or rivers. You can use field guides or the Internet to identify invasive species in your selected area.

Go to Nelson Science

3. Once you have identified the invasive species in your area, choose one that is both common and destructive. Research how to recognize it, how it was introduced to the area, how it affects the balance within the ecosystem, and how well-established it is.

4. Research solutions that have been suggested to remove your invasive species from the area. Local naturalists' clubs, hunters' and anglers' associations, plant nurseries, Aboriginal Elders, farmers, and Conservation Authorities may provide you with information.

5. Create a three- to five-point plan of action to eliminate the species from the area, or to slow its spread. Make sure your solutions do not cause harm to the environment.

6. Create a brochure for the community that summarizes your research. It should also provide information about what people can do to eliminate the species or stop or slow its spread.

Analyze and Evaluate

(a) Why has your selected invasive species been able to become so established in the environment?

(b) Predict which of the points in your action plan will be most successful. Explain.

(c) Why might it be more effective to stop invasive species from entering a specific habitat as opposed to trying to remove such a species once it is already established?

Apply and Extend

(d) Determine if there is a group that you can contact to put your plan into action. How might you encourage them to take action?

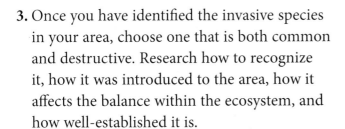
Unit Task Can you use any of the points in your action plan in the Unit Task?

6.4 Protecting the Environment

We depend on healthy ecosystems to meet our basic needs: to grow our food, to provide us with clean water, and to supply us with building materials and clothing. We also need someplace to put our waste. We use Earth's resources to provide us with energy. We use this energy for heating, transportation, manufacturing, and many other things.

We also use Earth's resources to make many things that we want, but do not necessarily need. How much we take from nature depends on our daily habits and the choices we make. How can we satisfy both our needs and wants in a way that does not hurt our environment? How can we live in a sustainable way?

Ecological Footprints

In 1996, Matthias Wackernagel and William Rees, two researchers at the University of British Columbia, developed a way to measure human demand on Earth's ecosystems. They called this measure the "ecological footprint." An ecological footprint estimates the amount of land and water needed to regenerate the resources a human consumes, as well as to absorb the waste produced. Ecological footprints are used to make people aware of how much of Earth's resources we use. The more we consume, use, and throw out, the larger our individual footprint (Figure 1). The more we conserve and use only what we need, the smaller our individual footprint. The impact that humans have on the environment is a product of our population size and the total of our individual footprints.

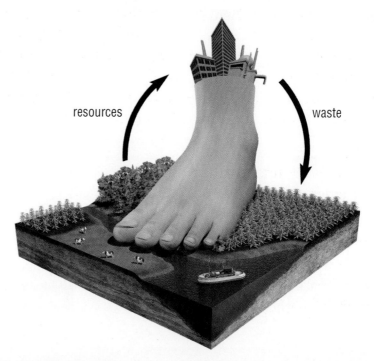

resources   waste

Figure 1 An ecological footprint compares human demand on nature with the ability of Earth's ecosystems to regenerate those resources.

North Americans have extremely large individual footprints. The average North American requires 12.4 hectares of Earth's space to support his or her lifestyle. Based on current consumption and population trends, Earth can provide only two hectares for every person on the planet. If everyone lived the way people in North America do, we would need at least three more planets to sustain the human population!

We need to be willing to decide which is more important: our wants, or our need for a healthy planet. Making this decision is part of becoming a responsible environmental citizen. We can all do things to reduce our ecological footprint. Making changes will then lessen our impact on ecosystems.

To learn more about ecological footprints and ways to reduce them,

TRY THIS: Determining Your Ecological Footprint

SKILLS MENU: predicting, evaluating

In this activity you will determine your ecological footprint and explore ways to reduce your footprint.

Equipment and Materials: computer with Internet access; chart paper; markers

1. Find an ecological footprint calculator on the Internet and use it to determine the size of your ecological footprint.

2. Compare your results with others in your group.

A. Create a list of ten practical things that you and your peers can do to reduce the size of your ecological footprint.

B. Some of the ways of reducing your footprint are harder to accomplish than others. Select one or two ways that would be difficult for you to do and explain why.

C. How might the adults in your life score on this? Explain.

D. Is there one thing that your entire class could commit to doing that would lessen your ecological footprint?

Stewardship of Earth

More and more people are concerned about the negative effects that humans have on ecosystems. They want to do something to help. People can become stewards of the environment. A **steward** is a person who carefully manages a resource. To become stewards, we first have to learn about the environment. Secondly, we have to change some of our behaviours in order to care for the environment. Thirdly, we have to tell others about what we have learned and how they can help, too. An acronym for STEWARD is someone who does the following:

steward: a person who carefully manages a resource by taking responsibility for their actions and educating others

Sustainably uses resources.
Trains others to become stewards.
Educates himself or herself about environmental concerns.
Works to repair damage to the natural environment.
Acts to save the environment and change policies.
Reflects on her or his behaviour and personal impact.
Decides to get involved!

Preserving, Conserving, and Restoring Ecosystems

Preserve

Stewardship means taking responsibility for your own actions. People across Ontario and Canada recognize the need to preserve areas that have not yet been damaged by humans. There are some areas of untouched boreal forest in northern Ontario that should be protected from being logged in the future (Figure 2).

Figure 2 Preserving areas of untouched wilderness helps to maintain Earth's biodiversity.

Conserve

Conserving ecosystems means using ecosystems wisely. Traditional farming methods use chemical fertilizers and pesticides on soil and crops to help grow as much as possible. Organic farming methods use compost and biological pest control techniques to keep soil productive without destroying the natural balance in the soil. Conventional farmers can also be environmental stewards of their land. They can reduce the amounts of chemical fertilizer that they use. They can also use farming practices that help protect the soil.

We create a lot of waste that we usually put into landfill sites. These sites displace natural habitats. Garbage in landfill sites can contribute to air, water, and soil pollution. In improperly built landfills, water from rain and snow soaks through the waste, carrying contaminants into the soil and groundwater. The solutions are not simple. Still, there is something we can do to help. The "3 Rs" is a simple method of addressing the amount of garbage we produce: reduce, reuse, and recycle. We can reduce the amount of garbage we produce by buying goods that have little or no packaging. We can also buy fewer unnecessary things. Household items such as jars, boxes, paper, and clothing can be reused. Towns and cities have recycling programs (Figure 3). Glass and aluminum are melted down and reused. Paper is recycled into cardboard. Some plastics can be made into other products. We can recycle food waste using a backyard composter or by using the green bin recycling programs that some municipalities offer.

Figure 3 The more we recycle, the more we help conserve ecosystems.

Restore

We can restore ecosystems by taking steps to repair the damage done by human activity. Restoration projects can be as simple as planting trees to repair soil erosion, or as involved as building nest sites for birds such as loons, ospreys, and terns (Figure 4).

Figure 4 (a) An osprey lands on a human-made platform. Osprey populations have increased as a result of these platforms. (b) People built artificial islands for terns, who like to nest on outcroppings in the water.

Biodiversity is important to healthy ecosystems. Homes and businesses displace plants and animals in local ecosystems. This means that there are fewer plants available to take up carbon dioxide from the air. Many towns and cities are finding ways to restore ecosystem biodiversity by creating more green spaces. Individuals can promote biodiversity by replacing lawns with a wider variety of plant species (Figure 5). This provides food and shelter for local wildlife. Using native plants in gardens also improves local biodiversity.

There are many small steps you can take to make big changes to the impact you have on Earth. Turn off lights and computers when you have finished using them. Shut off the water while you brush your teeth. Support environmental projects to save endangered species or to prevent pollution. All the steps you take will help you to become a "Steward of Earth."

Figure 5 Gardens with lots of different plants provide a better habitat for local birds and insects.

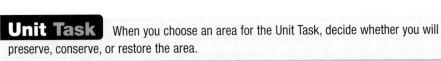

Unit Task When you choose an area for the Unit Task, decide whether you will preserve, conserve, or restore the area.

✔ CHECK YOUR LEARNING

1. **(a)** What is an ecological footprint?
   (b) How many hectares of land does a North American need to sustain him or herself?
   (c) How many hectares are available for each human on Earth?

2. What is meant by conserving ecosystems?

3. How does organic farming help to conserve ecosystems?

4. What problem is created by improperly built landfill sites?

5. Name two ways in which people can help restore ecosystems.

Traditional Knowledge and Stewardship of Earth

Poems are often used in Traditional Knowledge to express connections between humans and nature. Read the following poem.

> The old man
> Must have stopped our car
> Two dozen times to climb out
> And gather into his hands
> The small toads blinded
> By our lights and leaping, live drops of rain.
> The rain was falling,
> A mist about his white hair
> And I kept saying
> You can't save them all,
> Accept it, get back in
> We've got places to go.
> But, leathery hands full
> Of wet brown life,
> Knee deep in the summer
> Roadside grass,
> He just smiled and said
> They have places to go to
> Too.
>
> — Joseph Bruchac,
> "Entering Onondaga"

What Is Traditional Knowledge?

Traditional Knowledge is the experience, wisdom, and practices gained by Aboriginal peoples over many generations. It is developed from centuries of close interaction with the local environment. Traditional Knowledge includes such areas as farming, fishing, health, forestry, hunting, and environmental management. It is passed from generation to generation through stories, poems, music, art, rituals, and laws.

Aboriginal peoples share knowledge by telling stories. These stories help explain complex relationships found in nature (Figure 1). Many of the stories show the relationships among living things and their environment. Traditional Aboriginal peoples understand very well how all things are interconnected. They also understand how important it is for humans to live in harmony with nature. This knowledge can help us change our attitudes and behaviour in order to protect our planet.

Figure 1 Passing down stories from generation to generation is one form of Traditional Knowledge.

The Value of Traditional Knowledge

Today more and more people are recognizing the value of Traditional Knowledge. This knowledge is valuable not only to those who depend on it in their daily lives, but to modern industry, farming, and society. It has also begun to play a key role in public education.

Many Aboriginal communities are located in areas that have large amounts of natural resources. These communities have cultivated and used the local land and organisms in a sustainable way for thousands of years. Because their way of life is so connected to the land, they work hard to maintain healthy ecosystems. We can learn from their skills and techniques for managing the land and its resources. For example, the Ontario Ministry of Natural Resources and the Anishinabek Nation have agreed to work together to help manage the Great Lakes water systems in a sustainable way. The Anishinabek Nation includes seven different First Nations that live in Ontario.

On a more local level, the Willow Beach Field Naturalists and the Alderville First Nation have teamed up to restore and manage the Alderville Black Oak Savannah, an area south of Peterborough. This fragile and rare area consists of grassland with oak and pine trees scattered through it. The Alderville Savannah was once a vast grassland with many wild blue lupine flowers. The Karner Blue butterfly (Figure 2), which depends on this flower for survival, was once common in the savannah. However, much of the savannah has been lost to development. As a result, the Karner Blue butterfly has not been seen in Ontario since 1979. The First Nation and the naturalists are planting blue lupines in an effort to restore the ecosystem. They hope that the Karner Blue will return to the area. The Willow Beach Naturalists and the Alderville First Nation have the same goal: to protect Ontario's unique natural habitat, as well as species at risk.

Figure 2 The Karner Blue butterfly is a small butterfly about the size of a nickel. The female will only lay her eggs on blue lupines.

To learn more about the Alderville Savannah and the Karner Blue,

Go to Nelson Science

✓ CHECK YOUR LEARNING

1. **(a)** What is Traditional Knowledge?
   (b) How is Traditional Knowledge passed on from generation to generation?

2. In what ways can Traditional Knowledge help Ontario strive toward sustainability?

3. What is the message in the poem at the beginning of this section?

SKILLS MENU
- ☐ Defining the Issue
- ☐ Researching
- ☐ Identifying Alternatives
- ☐ Analyzing the Issue
- ☐ Defending a Decision
- ☐ Communicating
- ☐ Evaluating

Potential Solutions to Traffic

Traffic congestion in our urban centres gets worse every year (Figure 1). It takes drivers more time to get to where they are going, and it costs more to drive their cars. Drivers are frustrated. More time spent on the road also means that cars use more gas and produce more exhaust, which causes more air pollution.

Solving traffic problems is not easy. People depend on cars to get to work or school, and most of the goods we buy are shipped to stores in trucks. What changes can we make to help solve the traffic problem without inconveniencing people or denying them basic needs? How do we make those changes? Which solution is better for the environment or local ecosystems? If a solution is good for the environment but inconvenient for people, what compromises should we make?

Figure 1 How do we relieve the amount of traffic congestion in our urban centres?

The Issue

You have been hired by your city council to propose solutions to traffic congestion in and around your city. Currently, the roads and highways cannot handle the amount of traffic, and the public transportation system is not big enough to meet people's needs. Pollution from vehicles is affecting people's health, especially the young and the elderly. Your job is to find possible solutions, analyze their costs and benefits, and determine which solution solves the traffic problem and has the least impact on the local environment.

Goal

To recommend a method, or methods, of reducing traffic congestion that is both effective and environmentally friendly.

Gather Information

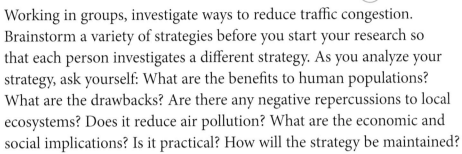

SKILLS HANDBOOK
3.J., 7.C.

Working in groups, investigate ways to reduce traffic congestion. Brainstorm a variety of strategies before you start your research so that each person investigates a different strategy. As you analyze your strategy, ask yourself: What are the benefits to human populations? What are the drawbacks? Are there any negative repercussions to local ecosystems? Does it reduce air pollution? What are the economic and social implications? Is it practical? How will the strategy be maintained?

The Internet, local police or traffic control centres, local transit commissions, and newspaper articles may provide you with more information. If you are doing an Internet search, what key words can you use?

Go to Nelson Science

LINKING TO LITERACY

Critical Literacy: Taking Social Action

Critical literacy text gives readers an opportunity to look at ways of taking action on important social issues. Explain why you believe traffic to be a social issue.

What is the purpose of the research activity outlined here? Who stands to benefit from your presentation? Whose opinions might not be represented? How might you use what you learned from this activity to take action on an important social issue in your community?

Identify Solutions

Once you have finished your research, discuss which strategy is the most effective and the most environmentally friendly. You may decide to combine some of the strategies.

Consider the following ideas to help identify possible solutions:

- widening highways and major roads
- increasing access to public transit
- imposing a higher tax on gasoline
- introducing toll roads and dedicated lanes for carpooling
- introducing bylaws that stop vehicles from entering urban areas on certain days
- increasing the cost of parking

Make a Decision

Upon reviewing your group's research, what will you recommend to city council? Be sure to support your position with evidence.

Communicate

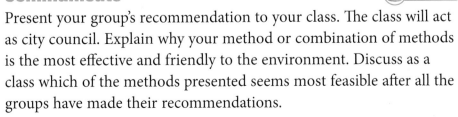

SKILLS HANDBOOK
8.

Present your group's recommendation to your class. The class will act as city council. Explain why your method or combination of methods is the most effective and friendly to the environment. Discuss as a class which of the methods presented seems most feasible after all the groups have made their recommendations.

Organisms Depend on a Healthy Environment

BIG Ideas

☐ Ecosystems are made up of biotic (living) and abiotic (non-living) elements, which depend on each other to survive.

☑ Ecosystems are in a constant state of change. The changes may be caused by nature or by human intervention.

☑ Human activities have the potential to alter the environment. Humans must be aware of these impacts and try to control them.

Looking Back

Ecosystems change naturally over time.

- Succession is the slow and predictable process in which the dominant species in an ecosystem are replaced by new species.
- Primary succession is succession that happens in places where no living things have existed previously.
- Secondary succession is succession that happens when an existing habitat has been disturbed by a natural or human-related event such as a forest fire or logging.

Human activities can alter the environment.

- When humans develop land and take resources from the environment, it results in habitat loss for local species. This alters, and sometimes destroys, the local ecosystem. Habitat loss can reduce biodiversity. Some species may become endangered or even extinct.
- Species that are introduced into areas where they are not normally found can become invasive species. They can reduce local biodiversity by out-competing native species.

The skills of scientific inquiry can be used to investigate factors that affect local ecosystems.

- Research skills can be used to learn more about the effects of invasive species on local ecosystems.
- Research skills can be used to learn more about ways to control or eliminate invasive species in an ecosystem.

Humans can do many things to protect the environment.

- We can measure our ecological footprint to learn how our consumption of natural resources affects the environment.
- By becoming stewards of the environment, we can preserve, conserve, and restore ecosystems.
- Buying less reduces the amount of waste we produce. Recycling waste and reusing items are ways to help the environment.
- We can help restore ecosystems and increase biodiversity by planting native species and building habitats for local species.
- Using the Traditional Knowledge of Aboriginal peoples can help us to be better stewards of the environment.

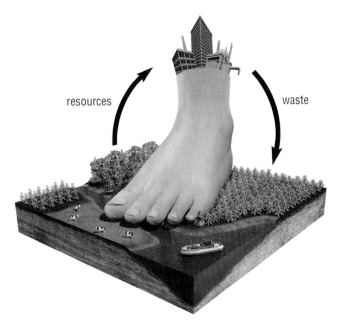

resources   waste

The skills of scientific inquiry can be used to assess how technology affects the environment.

- Research skills can be used to determine how traffic, and factors associated with traffic, affect the environment.
- Research skills can be used to learn about ways to solve problems associated with traffic.

CHAPTER 6 REVIEW

The following icons indicate the Achievement Chart categories: **K/U** Knowledge/Understanding **C** Communication **T/I** Thinking/Investigation **A** Application

What Do You Remember?

1. What is the difference between an endangered species and an extinct species? **K/U**

2. What is an "ecological footprint"? **K/U** **C**

3. Preserving, conserving, and restoring are three methods of helping to prevent habitat loss. Give an example of each. **K/U**

4. (a) What are the environmental "three Rs"?

   (b) Explain how each one helps the environment. **K/U**

5. Explain in your own words the meaning of "sustainability." **K/U** **C**

6. Define "succession" in your own words. **K/U**

7. Why is the grass in a garden lawn considered an invasive or non-native species? **K/U**

8. How does Traditional Knowledge help us to live in a more sustainable way? **K/U**

9. Why is biodiversity so important to healthy ecosystems? **K/U**

What Do You Understand?

10. List three human activities that have reduced biodiversity in your area. Explain how they have reduced biodiversity. **A**

11. (a) Are humans the only species that harm the environment?

    (b) Make a list of other organisms that may cause harm.

    (c) Under what circumstances might other organisms harm an ecosystem? **A**

12. Why has the expansion of urban centres become a concern? **A**

13. List some of the ways that we can protect our natural habitats from invasive species. **A**

14. A mnemonic is a strategy that helps you remember something. Make up your own environment-based mnemonic for STEWARD. **A** **C**

Solve a Problem!

15. Drinking bottled water has become a growing trend in the last several years. Is it safer than tap water? Should companies be allowed to sell water? Use the Internet to research the pros and cons of bottled water. Decide whether this is a good thing for the planet. Be sure to justify your decision. **A**

 Go to Nelson Science

16. Taxing items is a way for governments to get people to stop or reduce harmful activities. Both cigarettes and alcohol are heavily taxed for this reason. Suggest some things that could be taxed to help us decrease our ecological footprint. For each one, explain how the tax might help. **A**

17. We have to make some changes in our daily lives to live in a more sustainable way.

    (a) What changes are you willing to make to ensure a healthier planet for the future? Explain why each of the changes would be effective.

    (b) Share your "top 10" list with your classmates.

    (c) Note changes that others have placed on their lists that do not appear on your list. Will you keep your list the same or will you change it? Follow through with your decision. **T/I** **A**

18. Changing attitudes and behaviours is not easy to do. It helps if making a change is a positive experience. From all that you have learned in this chapter, particularly about our ecological footprint, create two lists with the titles "Top Ten Changes for Students" and "Top Ten Changes for Adults." These changes should help promote a healthier planet and be reasonable to make. **T/I** **A**

19. Urban sprawl is what occurs as cities increase in size. Urban sprawl results in a loss of biodiversity.

    (a) Outline a plan to increase biodiversity in a nearby natural setting (for example, a lawn consisting of grass and one tree, or the front of a building with a few trees).

    (b) What effect would adding a bird feeder or a water feature such as a birdbath or pond have on the area you selected?

    (c) What are some of the advantages of biodiversity? A C

20. Revisit the quotes at the beginning of the chapter.

    (a) What is the value of quotes such as these?

    (b) Create your own environmental saying that summarizes the chapter. Write it on a sheet of paper and display it in the classroom. You may want to add diagrams or pictures. A C

21. Every year, there are fewer and fewer monarch butterflies (Figure 1). Use the Internet to research the plight of the monarch butterfly.

    (a) Devise a plan to help restore monarch populations in your area.

    (b) Devise a campaign strategy to promote your monarch rehabilitation plan. A

Figure 1

22. Using carpools and taking public transportation would certainly help reduce our ecological footprint by reducing fuel consumption. Make a list of the pros and cons of these two methods of reducing fuel use. Should there be laws to make people carpool or take the bus? Explain. A C

Create and Evaluate!

23. (a) Write a poem that expresses your views about sharing this planet with other species.

    (b) Share your poem with a friend or your family.

    (c) Why is writing a poem about the environment and sharing it with friends and family a good thing to do? C

24. The energy bills in your school have increased tremendously in the past few years. Develop a plan to reduce the school's energy bill. Find out what types of energy are being used in the school and what they are being used for. Devise ways to reduce energy consumption. Once the school starts following your plan, how will you know if your plan was effective? T/I A

25. What is your "wish list" for a healthy planet? Create a poster or collage to express your views. Invite others to evaluate the ideas you have represented and to make suggestions for what they think could be missing. What can you do with your poster to help others become better stewards of the environment? Why would this have an effect? A C

Reflect on Your Learning

26. Think back to the Key Question on the first page of this chapter.

    (a) In a brief paragraph, answer the Key Question. You may use diagrams.

    (b) Write one or two more questions about the topic of this unit that you would like to explore.

Naturalizing Your Community

You have learned about interactions that take place within ecosystems and how all living and non-living things are interconnected. You have also learned that humans have positive and negative effects on ecosystems. All organisms depend on healthy ecosystems for survival. If we can increase the natural habitats in our neighbourhoods, both humans and other organisms will benefit.

"Naturalizing" means improving an area to increase its beauty and its usefulness to wildlife. This is done by planting vegetation and making changes to the area that will attract organisms. More and more people are seeing the value of naturalizing their communities (Figure 1).

Figure 1 (a) Sudbury was one of the first communities in Ontario to restore the local environment. (b) Sudbury looked very different in the 1970s before the local ecosystems were restored.

Purpose

To select an area in your neighbourhood and prepare an action plan to naturalize that area.

Equipment and Materials

Read the Procedure carefully. Write a list of Equipment and Materials that you will need to perform the Task.

Procedure

SKILLS HANDBOOK
7.C.

1. Working in groups of four, investigate the community around your school or home to find an area that can be naturalized. This area can be any size and may include your school grounds, an empty lot, a neighbourhood street, or even an existing park.

2. Before beginning step 2, make sure you have a notebook to record all of your information and steps in planning. Determine which environmental factors affect the area you have chosen. For example, is there a source of water? Is there enough soil to encourage plant growth? If there is a human influence, where is it most visible? Make a list of these factors.

3. Describe the ecosystem(s) that you want to protect, restore, or enhance in this area. Include the biotic and abiotic elements, and interactions within the ecosystem, that your plan will encourage.

4. A natural habitat includes native species. Make a list of native plants currently growing in your area and plants that you would like to plant in your area. Determine whether there are any invasive species currently in your area.

5. Draw possible food webs and food chains for your area.

6. How is the area currently being used? Will naturalizing this area encourage human activity or will it reduce it? What rules for using the area might be needed?

7. What safety issues need to be considered? How can you attract individual species and keep the human population safe?

8. Determine whether your plan for your area will preserve, conserve, or restore an ecosystem.

9. Use the information you have gathered to create a plan for your area. Draw a diagram that shows what the area would look like if your plan were completed. Include a picture of what the area currently looks like. Include a way to represent the organisms that you expect to inhabit the area. Also, indicate the abiotic elements of the area and any other important landscape features.

10. Your plan should include the possible new (or changed) food chains or food webs that could occur in the area.

11. If invasive species are a problem, indicate how you will address the problem.

12. Develop a plan to maintain the health of this ecosystem for future generations.

Analyze and Evaluate

(a) Describe your plan's benefits to the organisms that will inhabit the area.

(b) How will your plan benefit humans today and in the future?

(c) Will your plan have any negative effects? If so, what are they?

(d) Describe how completing this activity has affected your understanding of ecosystems.

Apply and Extend

SKILLS HANDBOOK
8.

(e) Prepare a summary of your plan in the form of a presentation.

(f) Present your plan to your class and discuss whether you have missed or neglected anything. Determine how your plan is similar to and different from the other plans.

(g) How has this project influenced your class?

(h) Discuss next steps. What might your class do to put your plans into action?

Assessment

You will be assessed on how well you

- show your knowledge and understanding of the local ecosystem
- observe your area and gather evidence about what types of organisms can live in your area
- develop a reasonable plan to naturalize your area

- organize your ideas in your plan
- propose practical solutions for naturalizing your area
- evaluate the impact that your plan will have on organisms that will inhabit the area, as well as on humans living nearby

Interactions in the Environment

Make a Summary

Each Chapter Review lists the new words and terms that were introduced in the chapter. Use these vocabulary lists to help you complete the following activity.

Equipment and Materials

- sticky notes or small pieces of paper
- markers
- chart paper

Procedure

1. In groups of three or four, write each of the vocabulary words from each chapter on the sticky notes (or paper). Write one word (or one term) only on each note.

2. Copy the fishbone organizer in Figure 1 onto the chart paper. The fishbone organizer in Figure 1 is just a start. Other "bones" could include "limiting factors," "benefits of protecting the environment," "energy and food chains/webs," "human activity and perspectives," and "cycles and sustainability."

3. Organize the words on the sticky notes onto the chart paper under the appropriate headings.

4. Below each group of words, write one sentence that describes an important idea from the unit that is associated with that group of words.

5. Use these sentences as the basis of one or two paragraphs that summarize your learning.

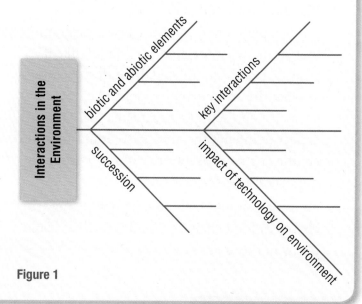

Figure 1

Unit Review Questions

What Do You Remember?

The following icons indicate the Achievement Chart categories:
- **K/U** Knowledge/Understanding
- **T/I** Thinking/Investigation
- **C** Communication
- **A** Application

1. What are the essential abiotic elements of an ecosystem? **K/U**

2. What is the difference between a habitat and an ecosystem? **K/U**

3. For each of the following, state two ways that they are important to life: sunlight, earth (soil), water, air. **K/U**

4. What role does temperature play in an ecosystem? **K/U**

5. Select a natural habitat in your area. Give two examples of each of the following:
   (a) an interaction between living things
   (b) an interaction between a living thing and a non-living thing **K/U**

6. (a) Give an example of a producer and a consumer.

   (b) Describe three differences between producers and consumers. K/U

7. Create a simple food chain with four species involved. K/U C

8. Describe two factors that limit the number of living things in a given ecosystem. K/U

9. Explain how decomposers recycle nutrients within ecosystems. K/U

10. Water and carbon are two essential substances that cycle through ecosystems. Describe the cycles and explain how the two cycles are connected to each other. K/U

11. Explain how the energy you obtain from eating a hamburger originally came from the Sun (Figure 2). K/U

Figure 2

12. Plants play a key role within an ecosystem. Explain this statement. K/U

13. Predator–prey interactions are very important to a healthy ecosystem. Demonstrate this using a specific example. K/U

14. What is meant by a "closed system"? How is Earth a closed system? K/U

15. Describe the flow of energy in the food chain that you created in question 7. What would happen to this flow if any part of the food chain were eliminated? K/U

16. Matter cycles through our environment. Explain how this promotes sustainability. Give a clear example of this. K/U

17. Predict what would happen if earthworms disappeared from the soil. T/I

What Do You Understand?

18. Find out which provincial or national park is closest to your home.

    (a) What makes the park environmentally special?

    (b) What ecosystems are being protected?

    (c) Are there any human economic activities going on in the park?

    (d) How can humans enjoy the park?

    (e) What can people learn about ecosystems from this park?

    (f) Is the land worth keeping as a park, or should some of it be sold to developers to build low-cost housing? T/I

Go to Nelson Science 🌐

19. "You have a very important role to play in keeping our planet healthy." Explain what this statement means using ideas you have learned in this unit. K/U

20. The buildings in an entire city block have been demolished and the rubble has been removed.

(a) What will happen on the bare soil over the next few years?

(b) What type of succession is this? Explain. K/U A

21. The use of technology has a great impact on our environment, both positive and negative. How has the use of automobiles affected ecosystems? A

22. How might Traditional Knowledge about the environment help with efforts to conserve and preserve habitats and wildlife? A

23. Human activity often alters the interactions in ecosystems. Select one example from below and describe the effects it can have: A

- clear-cutting a forest
- extensive overuse of chemicals in farming
- overuse of motorized vehicles
- increasing the number and size of roads

24. Select a habitat in your area. This could be part of the school grounds, a vacant lot, or a natural habitat in your neighbourhood. It could also be a small ecosystem like a rotting log or backyard pond. Describe the importance of sunlight, soil, water, air, and temperature on that habitat. A

25. "We are part of the Earth and it is part of us…. This we know." Refer back to the quote attributed to Chief Sealth on the first page of Unit B. From what you have learned in this unit, explain the significance of this quote. Write your own quote or find a similar quote from another culture. K/U A

26. Loss of jobs is often a reason given for not protecting a habitat or ecosystem. For example, protecting a forest may interfere with logging jobs and result in unemployment for some loggers. Write a one-page supported opinion essay in which you evaluate the loss of jobs that may be caused by activities aimed at protecting the environment. T/I A

Solve a Problem!

27. In many urban areas, there are too many of some species and not enough of others. For example, the city of Windsor has many squirrels (Figure 3). Using the concepts of food chains and food webs, explain why these imbalances occur and provide solutions to help solve the problem. Be sure to provide solutions that will not harm other parts of the ecosystem. T/I A

Figure 3

28. In recent years, young people have been exposed to fewer natural habitats.

(a) With the help of other classmates, create a list of suggestions to encourage youth to "get back to nature."

(b) Suggest an effective way to communicate this information. With your teacher's permission, perform your plans. T/I A C

29. It is said that by the age of six, most children can recognize 1000 company logos but they cannot name 10 species that share their neighbourhood. Research 10 species in your neighbourhood. Create a pamphlet to educate your neighbours about these species. [A] [C]

Go to Nelson Science

30. A vegetarian diet is considered by some people to be more "Earth-friendly" than a diet that contains lots of meat. Use what you know about energy flow to explain how our environment would be healthier if people ate less meat. [A]

Create and Evaluate!

31. Matter constantly cycles through an ecosystem. How well does your school recycle materials?

    (a) Determine what materials are recycled and how much of the waste produced in the school is actually recycled.

    (b) Devise a plan to reduce the amount of waste produced in your school. Include strategies for the classroom, lunchroom, office, and staff room.

    (c) Exchange your plan with a classmate. Evaluate each other's ideas, and then produce a plan that incorporates only the ideas that you both consider to be the best. [T/I] [A]

32. Your friend wants to start a club called "Lunch Room Litter Vigilantes."

    (a) What do you think the goal of the club is? Is this a good idea?

    (b) Is this a good name for the club? Why?

    (c) Suggest ways to improve on this idea. [A]

33. Traditional Knowledge is becoming very important to groups trying to understand the complexities of ecosystems and to protect them from further abuse. Think of an area in your neighbourhood that could use human protection or care. Create a story or legend similar to Aboriginal stories to give people a new respect for that area. Have a classmate read your story, and evaluate his or her reaction to it. [C]

Reflect on Your Learning

34. As you finish learning the content in this unit, reflect on what you have learned. Are there any questions that you still have on this topic? What can you do to ensure your questions are answered? Is this a strategy you can use after you finish every new unit of learning?

35. Real learning happens when you take what you learn in the classroom and allow it to change the way you live and think everyday. To what degree have you done this with what you learned in this unit? What does your answer show you about what you believe and how much you understand about what you learned?

Canadian educator and environmentalist David Suzuki once described Earth as "a tiny blue and green oasis in a cold universe." This description reminds us that our planet is a unique and fragile place. It is the only planet we know of that can provide the necessities of life.

Earth's main source of energy is the Sun. All living things need energy to grow, move, and stay warm. Living things also use energy to move objects and build structures. Energy from the Sun even affects non-living things. Although Earth absorbs a lot of energy from the Sun, it maintains a balance by transferring some of this energy back into space.

Recently, scientists have noticed that Earth's climate is changing. They have evidence suggesting that the changes are due to human activities. Concern about climate change is making societies think about how to live in ways that take Earth's energy balance into account.

In this unit, you will learn about energy. How does the transfer of energy as heat affect life on Earth? How do humans use energy? What are some of the positive and negative impacts of energy use on society and on the environment?

BIG Ideas

☐ Heat is a form of energy that can be transformed and transferred. These processes can be explained using the particle theory of matter.

☐ There are many sources of heat.

☐ Heat has both positive and negative effects on the environment.

CHAPTER 7 Heating and Cooling

CHAPTER 8 Energy Transfer and Conservation

CHAPTER 9 Heat Sources in the Environment

LIVING IN A GIANT FOAM COOLER!

On the way home from a trip to Ottawa, Tara and her mom, Gatleen, stopped in Brockville to visit some friends. Their friends, the Narangs, were building a new home. Soon after arriving at the apartment, Tara and Gatleen were ushered into the Narang family car and taken to the construction site. When they arrived, Tara was surprised by what she saw. On a patch of muddy ground was a framework of walls made entirely of pure white foam. There were none of the typical building materials that Tara had seen before on construction sites—no bricks, no cement blocks, and no wood frames. It looked as if the Narangs were going to live in a giant foam cooler!

Fascinated by what she saw, Tara watched as a construction worker built a wall. He stacked foam blocks, one on top of the other. The blocks were about the size of backpacks, and they were light enough for the worker to stack them with one hand. Tara wondered why the Narangs were building their home with such lightweight materials. Could such a house ever withstand strong wind, rain, and heavy snow?

The Narangs explained that the workers were using Polystyrene Block Form Construction to build the house. They said that this type of construction would help keep the house warm in the winter and cool in the summer. Mr. Narang explained that the blocks are hollow. They are filled with concrete once the wall is built.

Tara was not sure how the foam and concrete walls would help keep the Narangs' house warm in winter and cool in summer. She did remember learning in science class that polystyrene is a plastic that may harm the environment. She asked the Narangs why they were using so much plastic in the construction of their home. The Narangs explained that the environmental benefits of using less fuel and electricity to heat and cool their home justified the use of the foam blocks in the walls. Tara thought about that, but was not convinced. How could having foam walls be so good for the environment? She planned to do some research on the Internet when she got home to find out if the Narangs were right.

LINKING TO LITERACY

Asking Questions

When you do not know the answer to something, you ask a question. The same is true for reading. But in reading, you end up answering most of the questions yourself. Questions can be asked before you start reading, while you are reading, or after you are finished reading.

1. Talk to a partner about the questions you had when you were reading about the Narangs' new home.
   - Which questions were answered for you as you read more?
   - What questions do you still have?
   - Pick one question that you can do further research on to find the answer.

Feeling Cool

During this activity, you will explore the effect of heat on ice when the ice is placed on two different surfaces. You will then be asked to describe your observations in an expository paragraph. An expository paragraph is one that presents information, explains facts, or provides an opinion. This textbook contains many expository paragraphs. For example, see the paragraphs on page 182. The list of science terms on the right has been provided to help you write your paragraph.

Equipment and Materials: dry metal surface (metal kitchen sink); dry plastic surface (plastic countertop or plastic plate); 2 ice cubes

> ### Science Terms
> warm
> cold
> heat
> steel
> plastic
> conductor
> insulator
> temperature
> melt

1. Place yourself so that a dry metal surface (for example, a metal kitchen sink) and a dry plastic surface (for example, a plastic countertop) are both within reach.

2. Touch your fingers to the metal surface and the plastic surface at the same time (Figure 1). Do they feel different?

Figure 1 Touch both surfaces at the same time.

3. Predict which ice cube will melt faster if you place one ice cube on the metal surface and another on the plastic surface at the same time. Using your observations from step 2, state your prediction in the form of a hypothesis.

4. Test your prediction by placing one ice cube on the dry metal surface and the other ice cube on the dry plastic surface. Observe both ice cubes for 3 min, especially where the ice cubes touch the surfaces.

A. Describe what you felt in step 2.

B. Brainstorm possible reasons why the two ice cubes melted at different rates.

C. Write an expository paragraph to describe your observations from step 2, your hypothesis from step 3, and your observations from step 4.

D. Evaluate your hypothesis. Did your observations support your prediction, and your reasons for it?

E. Use what you have just discovered to predict whether hot chocolate will remain hot longer in a plastic cup or in a metal cup. Give reasons for your prediction.

Designing an Energy-Efficient Doghouse

Most living things need to stay warm in the winter and cool in the summer. Humans, in particular, control the transfer of energy to stay comfortable year round. As you progress through this unit, you will learn about different sources of energy and how we can control them.

The K-9 Doghouse Company is interested in building a new doghouse that it can sell to dog owners in Ontario. The company is holding a competition to come up with a new doghouse design. Specifically, the company is looking for a doghouse that will keep a dog comfortably warm outdoors during the winter and cool during the summer.

To enter the competition, you must build a prototype (scale model) of a doghouse. The prototype will be tested in hot and cold conditions to see how long the inside of the doghouse will stay at a comfortable temperature. The K-9 Doghouse Company would like the designers to present the prototype to its Board of Directors. The designers need to point out the pros and cons of their design, and convince the Board that the prototype deserves to be mass-produced.

Unit Task By the end of the Heat in the Environment unit, you will be able to demonstrate your learning by completing this Unit Task. As you work through the unit, continue to think about how you might meet this challenge. Read the detailed description of the Unit Task on page 254, and look for the Unit Task icon at the end of selected sections for hints related to the task.

Assessment

You will be assessed on how well you

- identify several possible designs
- develop a plan for building a prototype based on one of your possible designs
- build a prototype based on one of your designs
- test your prototype and make modifications that improve its effectiveness
- use the concepts and terminology of the unit to communicate the development and testing of your prototype

Heating and Cooling

▶ **KEY QUESTION: How does heat affect matter?**

Looking Ahead

● Heating and cooling are important in everyday natural and artificial processes.

● The particle theory explains heating and cooling.

● Heat is the transfer of energy from warmer substances to cooler substances.

● Most materials expand when they are heated and contract when they are cooled.

● Investigation skills can be used to learn about expansion and contraction of different materials.

VOCABULARY

particle theory of matter

heat

kinetic energy

temperature

thermal energy

thermal expansion

thermal contraction

180 Chapter 7 • Heating and Cooling

NEL

Warm and Cold

It is a freezing cold winter morning and I am waiting for a bus at a crowded bus stop. Although I am wearing thick wool gloves, my hands feel cold.

As I look around, I notice that people are pacing. I realize that everyone is breathing out puffs of white mist. Why does this happen in the winter, but not in the summer? As the bus arrives, I notice that the windows are frosted and white smoke is coming out of the bus' exhaust pipe. I wonder what the white smoke is made of, and what it could be doing to the environment.

I start to feel warm as soon as I get on the bus. I notice that I can no longer see everyone's breath. As the bus pulls away from the stop, I look out the window and see a bright yellow sign on the side of the road that says "Danger Bridge Ices." Soon, the bus goes over a bridge, and I feel several bumps and hear some thumping noises. Why are bridges always bumpy? And why are there special signs warning motorists about ice on bridges? It is cold enough outside for ice to form on all roads, whether the roads go over bridges or not. I wonder…

Cold hands, cloudy breath, icy bridges, and frosty windows are some of the signs of cold weather that I have noticed all my life. I have often wondered why certain things happen in cold weather but not in warm weather.

LINKING TO LITERACY

Verifying Understanding

After reading, effective readers verify their understanding by reflecting on the ideas presented and discussing what they have read. They may even research some aspect of the topic.

1. The story you read introduced some of the ideas that will be discussed in Chapter 7. Create and complete a 3-2-1 table (Table 1). In the table, record three things that you discovered by reading the story, two interesting things, and one question that you have after reading the story. Discuss your table with a partner.

Table 1

Three things I discovered	Two interesting things	One question I'd like answered

7.1 Warmth and Coldness

Living things are sensitive to warmth and coldness. They need a certain amount of warmth to survive. Humans keep warm by wearing clothes, performing physical activities, and burning various fuels in fireplaces and furnaces. Many birds fly south when it gets cold in northern regions (Figure 1(a)). Snakes and lizards bask in the sun to keep their bodies warm (Figure 1(b)).

Figure 1 Animals such as geese (a) and lizards (b) need warmth in order to survive.

Figure 2 A dog pants to cool down.

However, living things avoid excessive warmth because it is dangerous for their health. Animals that overheat can suffer damage to their internal organs and can even die. Different types of living things have developed different ways of dealing with excessive warmth. For example, dogs cool off by panting (Figure 2). Honeybees flap their wings to cool their hives in hot weather. People use electric fans and air conditioners to cool their homes and other buildings when the weather is too warm.

Heating and Cooling Our Buildings

Homes and buildings are designed to keep their interiors warm in winter and cool in summer. In fact, heating, ventilation, and air conditioning (HVAC) is a $12 billion industry in North America. About 250 000 people have jobs in the HVAC industry. It is not easy to keep homes and other buildings comfortable during the hot, humid summers and cold winters of Ontario (Table 1).

Table 1 Average Monthly Temperatures for Ottawa, Ontario

	Jan	Feb	Mar	Apr	May	Jun	Jul	Aug	Sep	Oct	Nov	Dec
Average temp (°C)	−10	−9	−2	6	14	18	21	20	15	6	1	−7

For thousands of years, people have warmed their homes in winter by burning wood in fireplaces. They have cooled their homes in the summer by placing blinds on windows and planting shade trees in their gardens. In ancient Rome, some buildings were sometimes cooled by running cold river water through the walls. Other buildings were cooled by installing a shallow indoor pool. In ancient China, some palaces had raised floors. This design permitted servants to tend fires beneath the floors during the winter. In the early 1800s, a few wealthy people began to install central heating systems in their homes. These systems consisted of furnaces that moved warm air or water to the rooms of a building. Modern electric air conditioners were first used in North America in the early 1900s (Figure 3). 🌐

Today, most Ontario homes are built with central heating systems. Some also contain central air conditioners (Figure 4). The furnaces in these systems typically burn fuels like oil (petroleum) or natural gas. Oil and natural gas are found in limited supplies deep within Earth's crust. If we continue to use these fuels at our current rate, scientists estimate that we will run out of them within a few decades. In some cases, buildings are heated with electric heaters, which use electricity to produce warmth. Electric heaters may consume fuels indirectly, depending on the electricity source.

Figure 3 Air conditioners are often fitted into building windows, where they draw in outside air, cool it, and blow it back into the building.

To learn more about the history of air conditioning,
Go to Nelson Science 🌐

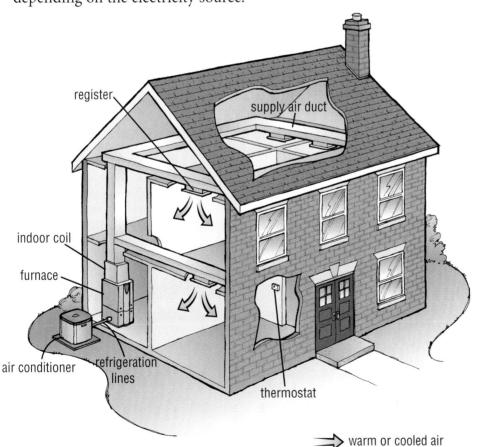

register
supply air duct
indoor coil
furnace
air conditioner
refrigeration lines
thermostat

⟹ warm or cooled air

Figure 4 A typical home central heating and cooling system. The furnace heats the home in the winter; the air conditioner cools it in the summer. The same air ducts are used for both heating and cooling.

LINKING TO LITERACY

Cause-and-Effect Text Pattern
Science text is often written in a cause-effect order. It explains events that have occurred (cause) and what happens as a result of these events (effect). As you read this page, consider the effects or drawbacks of the way we heat or cool buildings.

Figure 5 Many buildings have chimneys on their roofs to allow toxic waste gases to escape.

Wood, coal, oil, and natural gas release energy and gases as waste when they burn. Some of these waste gases are toxic and must be removed from the building. Chimneys are vents that carry these gases to the air outside (Figure 5).

In the summer, buildings can be cooled by fans, window air conditioners, or central air conditioners. These devices do not normally produce toxic fumes during their use, but they do consume electricity. Air conditioners use much more energy than fans do.

Keeping interiors comfortable all year long is important to consider in the construction and maintenance of all buildings. Heating and cooling are expensive processes. They are also harmful to the environment. We should use them as little as possible. Imagine if we only had to turn on the air conditioner for a few minutes once a day to cool a building. The building would then stay at a comfortable temperature for the rest of the day. Think how much electricity we could save! Understanding more about heating and cooling may help people keep buildings comfortably warm or cool, while minimizing negative effects on the environment.

TRY THIS: Conduct a Heating and Cooling Survey

SKILLS MENU: questioning, planning, analyzing, evaluating, communicating

SKILLS HANDBOOK
3.K.2., 6.D.2.

In this activity, you will survey people to find out how they keep their homes, or businesses, warm in the winter and cool in the summer. You may ask about the heating and cooling methods they currently use, or have used in the past. You may also ask about methods they may have used in other parts of the world.

Equipment and Materials: writing instruments (pencils, pens); paper

1. Think of 6 to 10 questions that ask participants how they keep (or kept) their homes or businesses warm in cold weather and cool in hot weather. Your questions may ask about the types of devices used, the sources of energy used to run the devices, the effectiveness of the methods used, or effects on the environment.

2. Organize your questions into a questionnaire.

3. Ask at least six people to answer your questionnaire. Collect their responses.

A. Analyze the answers. Write a brief report describing your findings. You may organize your findings using tables and graphs if appropriate.

B. Exchange reports with a classmate. Read your classmate's report and note any differences and similarities in your findings. Together with your classmate, write a brief expository paragraph that summarizes your joint findings. Your paragraph should answer the following questions:

- What methods do people use to heat and cool the buildings in which they live?

- How effective are the methods that people use to heat and cool their buildings?

- How do the heating and cooling methods employed affect the environment?

CHECK YOUR LEARNING

1. **(a)** Give two examples of ways in which animals keep themselves warm or cool.

   (b) Give one example each of ways in which people keep themselves warm and cool.

2. Describe how home heating and cooling has changed over time, and how it has remained the same.

3. Why do buildings have chimneys?

4. List two costs, or drawbacks, of using an electric air conditioner, and two benefits.

5. Why should we try to use less oil, natural gas, and electricity?

Explaining Hot and Cold

We use the word "heat" to describe something that produces warmth. But what is heat? How does heat affect matter? Scientists have tried to understand the causes of warmth and coldness for a long time. Eventually, they developed several explanations for these ideas. Today, scientists explain heat using a theory called the particle theory of matter.

The Particle Theory of Matter

In the early 1800s, scientists suggested that warmth is caused by the motion of the small particles that make up matter (Figure 1). The faster the particles move, the warmer the material feels. The slower the particles move, the colder the material feels. This explanation of warmth and coldness eventually became part of the **particle theory of matter** (also shortened to "the particle theory"). The main points of the particle theory are listed below:

- All matter is made up of tiny particles.
- Particles have spaces between them.
- Particles are moving all the time.
- Particles move faster when they are heated.
- Particles attract each other.

particle theory of matter: a theory that explains what matter is made of, and how it behaves

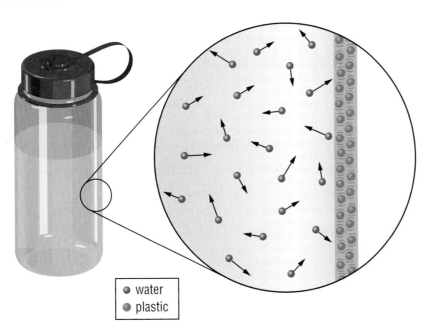

- water
- plastic

Figure 1 The particle theory applies to all matter, including the water in this bottle and the bottle itself.

Heat

The particle theory helps us explain many characteristics of matter, including how matter warms up and cools down. When an object is heated, its particles move faster. When an object is cooled, its particles move slower.

When a warm object comes into contact with a cold object, the faster-moving particles of the warm object bump into the slower-moving particles of the cold object. As a result, energy is transferred. This causes particles of the cold object to speed up and the particles of the warm object to slow down. If you watch a game of billiards being played, you will see a similar transfer of energy. When a fast-moving billiard ball (the white cue ball in Figure 2(a)) collides with a stationary ball, some energy is transferred. The stationary ball starts to move and the white ball slows down (Figure 2(b)).

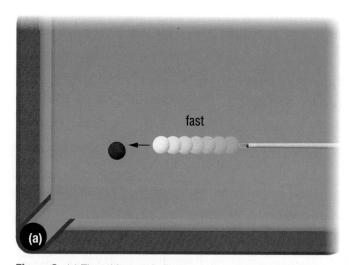 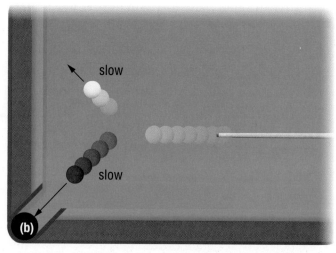

Figure 2 (a) The white cue ball causes the red ball to move by transferring energy to it. (b) When the cue ball hits the red ball, the cue ball slows down and the red ball speeds up.

heat: the transfer of energy from the particles of a warmer object to the particles of a cooler object

To heat an object means to transfer energy to the particles of that object. Heat is not a thing or substance that an object can contain. Instead, **heat** is the transfer of energy from warmer things to cooler things.

You should be careful about how you use the word "heat." In an investigation, you may be instructed to "Heat the water in the beaker by placing it on a hot plate." You should not, however, say, "Water absorbs heat when it is placed on a hot plate." A substance cannot absorb heat. When water is heated, it absorbs energy, not heat.

CHECK YOUR LEARNING

1. **(a)** Describe a key idea about heat that you understood from this section.
   (b) How does the scientific definition of heat compare to the use of the word "heat" in conversational English?
   (c) Discuss this idea of heat with a classmate or with your teacher. Write an explanation of heat in your own words. If you like, you may use diagrams or pictures.

2. Summarize the key ideas of the particle theory in your own words or with labelled diagrams.

3. How does the particle theory help to explain the difference between a drop of cold water and a drop of hot water?

4. Explain what is wrong with the statement: "A mug of hot chocolate contains more heat than a glass of cold water."

Kinetic Energy, Heat, and Temperature

Warmth and coldness involve the motion of the particles of matter. Since they are always moving, the particles of matter possess a form of energy called **kinetic energy**. All moving objects, large and small, possess kinetic energy (Figure 1). Flying airplanes, the flapping wings of a bird, and invisible vibrating particles all possess kinetic energy.

kinetic energy: energy that all moving objects possess; a particle has more kinetic energy when moving faster and less kinetic energy when moving slower

  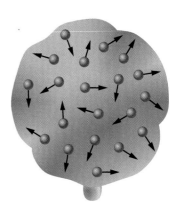

Figure 1 All objects that move have kinetic energy. There are even moving particles inside of a balloon.

All of the particles in a substance are attracted to each other. So, why do the particles not stick together and stop moving? Particles have a lot of kinetic energy, which keeps them moving. When the environment gets colder, they slow down and come closer together. They never slow down enough to come to a complete standstill.

If you could see the particles of an object, you would notice that they are not all moving at the same speed. Particles of matter collide with each other much like bumper boats in an amusement park ride. Bumper boats collide randomly as they move from place to place (Figure 2). Sometimes, several boats collide in such a way that some slow down and some speed up. Particles of matter also move and collide randomly, some speeding up and some slowing down. Particles do not all possess the same amount of kinetic energy at any given time. Some particles have more kinetic energy than others.

Figure 2 Bumper boats move and collide with each other randomly. The particles of matter do the same thing.

Temperature

If you could see the particles of a hot object and the particles of a cold object, you would see that *most* of the particles of the hot object move faster than *most* of the particles of the cold object. Thus, the average kinetic energy of the particles of a hot object is higher than the average kinetic energy of the particles of a cold object.

Temperature is a measure of the average kinetic energy of particles. If most of the particles of air in your kitchen are moving faster than most of the particles of air in your bedroom, then the temperature of the air in your kitchen is higher than that of the air in your bedroom.

temperature: a measure of the average kinetic energy of the particles of a substance

Particle Theory and the States of Matter

Matter exists in three common states: solid, liquid, or gas (Table 1). The particle theory can be used to explain the characteristics of solids, liquids, and gases.

Table 1 States of Matter

State of matter	Description	
solid	The shapes and volumes of solids do not change because the particles of a solid vibrate. They cannot move past each other. The kinetic energy of the particles is too low to overcome the forces holding the particles together. The particles are packed close together, and are difficult to squeeze into a smaller space.	
liquid	Liquids take the shape of their containers and have fairly constant volumes. The particles of a liquid move faster than the particles in a solid of the same substance. The particles vibrate, rotate, and move past one another. The speeds of the particles prevent the forces of attraction from holding them in one place. However, there is still enough attraction between the particles to keep them from separating completely. The particles of a liquid are slightly more spread out than the particles of a solid. The particles of liquids strongly resist being squeezed closer together.	
gas	Gases expand to fill an empty container. This means that both their volume and shape can change. The particles of a gas vibrate, rotate, and move past one another much more than the particles of solids and liquids. The fast motions of the particles prevent their forces of attraction from holding them close together. Gas particles have very large spaces between them. Their movement is only limited by the size of the container. Gases are relatively easy to compress.	

Particle Theory and Changes of State

According to the particle theory, particles of matter are constantly moving and are attracted to each other. The motions of the particles of a substance (their kinetic energies), and their attraction for each other, determine whether the particles form a solid, a liquid, or a gas. The kinetic energy of the particles *and* the energy of attraction between them are called **thermal energy**. We can increase the thermal energy of a substance by heating it, and we can decrease the thermal energy by cooling the substance. Changes in thermal energy can also cause a substance to change state (Figure 3 on the next page). For example, increasing the thermal energy of a solid may cause it to melt, becoming a liquid.

thermal energy: the total kinetic energy and energy of attraction of all the particles of a material

To review the particle theory and the states of matter,

Go to Nelson Science

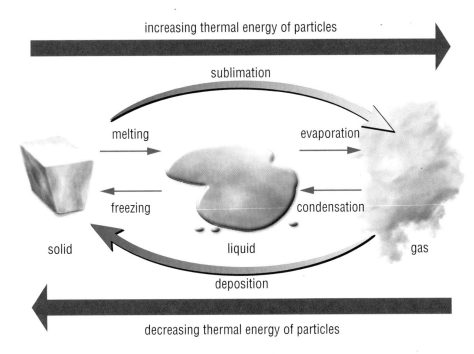

increasing thermal energy of particles

sublimation

melting → ← evaporation

freezing ← condensation

solid   liquid   gas

deposition

decreasing thermal energy of particles

Figure 3 Changes of state involve changes in thermal energy.

LINKING TO LITERACY

Skimming
Good readers realize that they may not have understood all of the ideas presented when reading. They verify understanding by skimming through the section to locate important information to reread. Skim the text to recall the meanings of thermal energy, thermal expansion, and thermal contraction.

thermal expansion: an increase in the volume of a substance caused by heating

thermal contraction: a decrease in the volume of a substance caused by cooling

Thermal Expansion and Contraction

When solids, liquids, and gases are heated, their volumes usually increase. This process is called **thermal expansion** (Figure 4). Heating a substance speeds up its particles, so they have more kinetic energy. The faster-moving particles travel greater distances, so they occupy more space.

When solids, liquids, and gases are cooled, their volumes usually decrease. This process is called **thermal contraction**. Cooling a substance slows down its particles, so that they have less kinetic energy. The slower-moving particles travel shorter distances, so they occupy less space.

During thermal expansion and contraction, the mass of the object stays the same. The change in volume is not due to an addition or removal of particles, or to a change in the size of the particles. The change in volume is due to an increase or decrease in the spaces between particles. In general, for a given change in temperature, gases expand and contract more than liquids and solids, and liquids expand and contract more than solids.

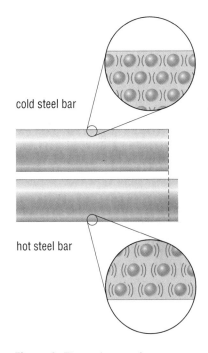

cold steel bar

hot steel bar

Figure 4 Thermal expansion occurs when particles move farther apart.

✓ CHECK YOUR LEARNING

1. Name and briefly describe the two kinds of energy that all particles possess.

2. Describe the relationship between temperature and energy.

3. List the three states of matter in order of decreasing kinetic energy.

4. **(a)** Which state of matter is most easily compressed to take up a smaller volume?
   (b) Write a sentence explaining this observation.

5. When a substance is cooled, what happens to its particles? How does cooling affect the volume of the substance?

Expanding and Contracting

All forms of matter change when they are heated or cooled. In this investigation, you will study the effect of heat on the volume of a liquid (water), a gas (air), and a solid (brass).

Testable Questions

SKILLS HANDBOOK 2.B.1.

Part A: Read Part A of the Experimental Design and the Procedure, then write a testable question for Part A.

Part B: Read Part B of the Experimental Design and the Procedure, then write a testable question for Part B.

Part C: Read Part C of the Experimental Design and the Procedure, then write a testable question for Part C.

Hypothesis/Prediction

SKILLS HANDBOOK 2.B.3.

Part A: Make a hypothesis regarding your testable question for Part A. Your hypothesis should include a prediction and reasons for it.

Part B: Make a hypothesis regarding your testable question for Part B. Your hypothesis should include a prediction and reasons for it.

Part C: Make a hypothesis regarding your testable question for Part C. Your hypothesis should include a prediction and reasons for it.

Experimental Design

Part A: Coloured water in a test tube fitted with a narrow plastic tube is warmed up, and then cooled down. Any change to the water level in the tube is measured and recorded.

Part B: A glass bottle with an empty rubber balloon stretched over its mouth is warmed up, and then cooled down. Any changes to the balloon are observed and recorded.

Part C: A brass ball that barely passes through a brass ring is warmed up, and then cooled down. Any changes to the ball are observed by attempting to stick the ball through the ring.

Equipment and Materials

- eye protection
- apron
- test tube
- rubber stopper with plastic tubing
- glass marking pen
- 2 large beakers
- glass bottle with narrow neck
- empty rubber balloon
- brass ball and ring
- water
- food colouring
- ice

eye protection

apron

test tube

rubber stopper with plastic tubing

glass marking pen

2 large beakers

glass bottle with narrow neck

empty rubber balloon

brass ball and ring

water

food colouring

ice

Be careful when handling glass. Report any breakages to your teacher immediately.

Procedure

Part A: Heating a Liquid

1. Put on your apron and eye protection.

2. Add room temperature water to a beaker. Add a few drops of food colouring and swirl the water to mix the colour in. Fill a test tube with the coloured water and then rinse the beaker.

3. Insert a stopper with plastic tubing into the test tube. Ensure that there is no air trapped in the test tube. The coloured water should move up the tube. Use the glass marking pen to mark the water level.

4. Add 300 mL of hot tap water to a beaker.

 Be careful not to scald yourself with the hot water.

5. Add 200 mL of cold tap water to a second beaker. Add ice to the water, bringing its volume to 300 mL.

6. Place the test tube in the hot water bath. After 3 min, mark the water level on the plastic tubing and record your observations.

7. Transfer the test tube to the cold water bath. After 3 min, mark the water level on the plastic tubing and record your observations.

8. Remove the test tube from the cold water.

Part B: Heating a Gas

9. Add new hot water and ice to the water baths.

10. Stretch the opening of an empty rubber balloon over the mouth of a glass bottle.

11. Place the glass bottle in a hot water bath for 5 min. Observe any changes in the balloon, and record your observations.

12. Remove the bottle from the hot water bath and place it in a cold water bath for 5 min. Observe any changes in the balloon, and record your observations.

Part C: Heating a Solid (Demonstration)

13. Your teacher will show you a brass ball and ring apparatus.

14. Your teacher will attempt to pass a brass ball through a brass ring when both are at room temperature. Record your observations.

15. Your teacher will heat the brass ball, and attempt to pass it through the cooler brass ring. Record your observations.

16. Your teacher will cool the brass ball to room temperature, and attempt to pass it through the brass ring. Record your observations.

Analyze and Evaluate

(a) Did the evidence you obtained in Part A support your hypothesis? Explain.

(b) Did the evidence you obtained in Part B support your hypothesis? Explain.

(c) Did the evidence you obtained in Part C support your hypothesis? Explain.

(d) Answer your Testable Questions.

(e) How confident are you about your answers to your Testable Questions? Explain.

(f) In Part B, what happened to the air in the glass bottle when it was placed in the cold water bath? Provide evidence and explain the results using the particle theory.

(g) In Part C, what happened to the brass ball when it was heated? What happened when it was cooled? Provide evidence and explain the results using the particle theory.

Apply and Extend

(h) State an everyday example in which you observe
   (i) a gas expanding when heated
   (ii) a solid contracting when cooled

(i) Materials do not expand by the same amount when heated. What problems might this cause when designing products? Give an example.

Living with Thermal Expansion and Contraction

Materials in our world are exposed to changing temperatures. Computer chips warm up when a computer is turned on and cool down when it is turned off. Buildings and bridges warm up during the day, and then cool down again at night. Buildings also have to withstand the changes that occur between the seasons. Materials expand and contract, sometimes dramatically, during temperature changes. When different materials are used to build a structure, designers must understand how the materials behave when they are heated or cooled.

Expansion and Contraction of Solids

It is important to choose the right materials when designing structures that are exposed to changing temperatures. Imagine that designers choose to use two solids that expand or contract differently when heated or cooled. The structure could be damaged by the different amounts of expansion and contraction. For example, the concrete used to build bridges and buildings is reinforced by steel rods (Figure 1). The steel used to make the rods is designed to expand at the same rate as the concrete. If the rods expanded at a different rate, the concrete would crack. The structure could, over time, crumble and fail. In the same way, when a dentist fills a decayed tooth, the filling material must change its volume to the same degree as the tooth itself. Some scientists specialize in the development of dental filling materials that expand and contract just like real teeth.

Bridges and sidewalks are built in segments. They have spaces called expansion joints between them. The expansion joints allow the concrete and steel to expand without buckling and cracking (Figure 2). The thumping sound you hear when you drive over a bridge in a car or bus is the sound of the tires going over the expansion joints.

Figure 1 The steel rods (at the worker's feet) used to reinforce concrete are designed to expand and contract in the same way the concrete expands and contracts.

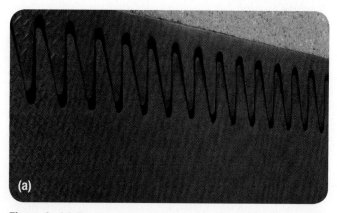

Figure 2 (a) The expansion joints narrow when bridge segments expand in hot weather. (b) Expansion joints in a bridge separate when the side-by-side segments of a bridge contract in cold weather.

Expansion and Contraction of Gases

When a gas in a container is heated, the kinetic energy of the gas particles increases. The particles of the warmer gas hit the walls of the container more often and with greater force. If the walls of the container are flexible, as in a balloon, the more frequent and faster collisions may cause the walls of the container to expand (Figure 3).

(a)

(b)

Figure 3 The helium gas in a Mylar balloon expands a great deal when the balloon is taken from the cold outdoors into a warm room.
(a)   At a low temperature, the average kinetic energy of the particles in the balloon is low, so the frequency and force of collisions on the inside walls of the balloon are low.
(b)   As the temperature of the gas inside the balloon rises, the particles collide more often with the walls of the balloon. They are also travelling faster. These stronger collisions cause the balloon to expand.

Thermal expansion and contraction affect the volume and pressure of tires, volleyballs, and basketballs. When cars are moving quickly, the rubbing between the tires and the road increases the temperature of the air in the tires. This causes the tires to expand. Tires must be inflated according to manufacturers' recommendations. If they are overinflated when cool, they can burst when they warm up. Volleyballs and basketballs left out in the cold become smaller and softer because of the thermal contraction of the air inside.

TRY THIS: Hot and Cold Balloons

SKILLS MENU: hypothesizing, observing, analyzing

In this activity, you will observe the thermal expansion and contraction of the air in rubber balloons.

Equipment and Materials: 3 rubber balloons (same type and same size); black marker; flexible tape measure; refrigerator/ freezer

1. Read the procedure, and then write a hypothesis about how the volume of an air-filled rubber balloon may change when it is (a) placed at room temperature for 10 min, (b) placed in a cold freezer for 10 min, and (c) immersed in hot tap water for 10 min. Your hypotheses should include both a prediction and an explanation.

2. Number the balloons 1, 2, and 3.

3. Blow up the balloons to the same volume. Tie the openings to seal the balloons.

4. Using a flexible tape measure, measure and record the circumference at the widest point of each balloon.

5. Expose the balloons to the conditions described in step 1.

6. After 10 min, measure and record the circumference at the widest point of each balloon. (Quickly measure the balloon in the freezer without removing it from the freezer compartment.)

A. Compare the volumes of balloons 1, 2, and 3 before and after the treatments in step 5.

B. Evaluate your hypotheses by comparing them to the evidence you gathered in steps 4 to 6.

Expansion and Contraction of Liquids

Thermal expansion and contraction affect the volumes of liquids that are used every day. Cars provide a good example of this. Cold gasoline in a car's gas tank expands in hot weather. If the tank is filled to the brim, the gas may overflow. Also, if a car engine is filled with cold liquid coolant, the coolant will warm up and expand when the car is running, and may overflow.

Studies over the past 100 years show that the average temperature of Earth's oceans has been steadily increasing. As the ocean water warms up, its volume increases due to thermal expansion. The greater volume leads to rises in sea levels. This could lead to floods in coastal cities.

Unit Task How can you apply what you have learned about thermal expansion and contraction of solids to the design of your doghouse?

✓ CHECK YOUR LEARNING

1. Carefully read the following statements and decide if they are true or false. If the statement is false, then rewrite the statement to make it true. (Do not simply restate the statement in the negative.)
   (a) The particles of a material get bigger when heated.
   (b) The particles of a material move faster when heated.
   (c) Of the three states of matter, gases expand the least.
   (d) The particles of a solid vibrate.

2. A metal entrance door swings freely in the winter, but when the weather turns warm, the door sticks and seems too big for the doorframe. Using your knowledge of particle theory, explain what is happening.

3. When building a device or structure, engineers must carefully consider how the materials they choose will change when heated and cooled. List four situations where thermal expansion and contraction could be a problem.

4. List three unique examples of situations in your daily life where expansion and contraction occur.

5. You want to inflate an air mattress to use in a swimming pool on a hot summer day. Should you fill the mattress with as much air as possible? Why or why not?

Tech CONNECT

Sun Kinks, Breather Switches, and Train Disasters

Travelling by train is popular. Passenger trains carry people between towns and cities every day. Freight trains transport products over long distances.

Train cars glide on long parallel steel rails. Train tracks are manufactured in 20 m lengths that are welded together. This ensures a smooth, quiet ride. The continuous welded rail can be several kilometres long.

Railway tracks in Canada are exposed to extreme changes in temperature. These changes can cause a lot of thermal expansion of the rails in summer, as well as contraction in winter. To avoid these changes, the tracks are heated before being put together. Nevertheless, sudden bouts of extremely hot weather can cause a rail to buckle. This forms a twist in the rail that some people call a "sun kink." Sun kinks are extremely dangerous and have been linked to some serious train disasters.

On July 4, 2005, a train carrying 51 empty fuel cars derailed near Ottawa (Figure 1). It is believed that sun kinks were the cause. Luckily, there were no injuries or deaths in this accident. However, the derailment disrupted normal passenger service between Montreal and Toronto for several days. Passenger train derailments involving sun kinks have caused many injuries and deaths. Scientists and engineers are working to develop rail technology that minimizes the possibility of sun kinks.

One method used to avoid sun kinks is to cut the rails at sharp angles. This leaves a small gap between the cut surfaces. These gaps are called "breather switches" (Figure 2). Engineers continue to work on methods that will improve train transportation safety.

To learn more about sun kinks and breather switches,

Go to Nelson Science

Figure 1 If the cars had been filled with fuel, the derailment would have caused serious damage to wildlife and the surrounding environment.

Figure 2 A breather switch. The sharp angle at which rails are cut ensures a relatively smooth and quiet ride for passengers.

Heating and Cooling

BIG Ideas

- ☑ Heat is a form of energy that can be transformed and transferred. These processes can be explained using the particle theory of matter.

- ☐ There are many sources of heat.

- ☐ Heat has both positive and negative effects on the environment.

Looking Back

Heating and cooling are important in everyday natural and artificial processes.

- All living things are most comfortable within a certain temperature range.
- Many animals adapt their behaviour to keep their bodies at a comfortable temperature.
- Humans adapt to their surroundings by using heating and cooling technologies.

The particle theory explains heating and cooling.

- All matter is made of invisible particles. Particles have spaces between them. Particles are moving all the time. Particles move faster when they are heated. Particles attract each other.
- Heating and cooling a substance affects the motion of its particles.
- Solids, liquids, and gases can be described in terms of the arrangement and motion of their particles.
- Moving particles possess kinetic energy. A faster-moving particle possesses more kinetic energy than a slower-moving particle.
- Thermal energy includes the kinetic energy of all the particles in a substance and the energy associated with the attractive forces between the particles in the substance.

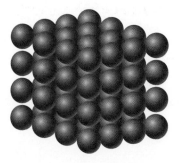

Heat is the transfer of energy from warmer substances to cooler substances.

- Temperature is a measure of the average kinetic energy of the particles in a substance.
- The faster the particles of a substance move, the hotter the substance is; the slower the particles of a substance move, the colder the substance is.
- When a hot object comes into contact with a cold one, the fast-moving particles of the hot object bump into the slow-moving particles of the cold object. The fast-moving particles slow down as they transfer energy to the slow-moving particles.

Most materials expand when they are heated and contract when they are cooled.

- When a material is heated or cooled, the motion of its particles is affected. When heated, the particles move faster and farther apart. When cooled, the particles move slower and come closer together.
- The expansion and contraction of solids, liquids, and gases must be considered when designing structures or devices that are subjected to changes in temperatures.
- When the temperature changes, solids expand and contract the least, while gases expand and contract the most.

VOCABULARY

particle theory of matter, p. 185

heat, p. 186

kinetic energy, p. 187

temperature, p. 187

thermal energy, p. 188

thermal expansion, p. 189

thermal contraction, p. 189

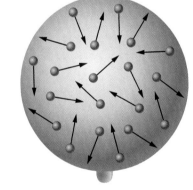

Investigation skills can be used to learn about expansion and contraction of different materials.

- Expansion and contraction of solids, liquids, and gases can be observed and analyzed.
- The particle theory can be used to explain observations made about expansion and contraction.

CHAPTER

7 REVIEW

The following icons indicate the
Achievement Chart categories:

K/U Knowledge/Understanding   **T/I** Thinking/Investigation
C Communication   **A** Application

What Do You Remember?

1. (a) Describe two things that humans do to warm up.

   (b) Describe two things that animals other than humans do to warm up. **K/U**

2. Briefly summarize the particle theory in your own words. **K/U**

3. Copy Table 1 into your notebook and complete it. **K/U**

Table 1 Descriptions of Three States of Matter

	Solid	Liquid	Gas
volume			
shape			
type of particle motion			
spaces between particles			

4. Use the particle theory to explain why gases expand more than liquids or solids when they are heated. **K/U**

5. Write a definition of "heat," using your own words. **K/U**

6. From what you have seen or read, list two examples each of

   (a) thermal expansion in solids

   (b) thermal expansion in liquids

   (c) thermal expansion in gases **K/U** **A**

What Do You Understand?

7. (a) List five situations where heat plays a role in your daily life (for example, cooking an egg). **T/I** **A**

   (b) Give three examples of state changes that you see happening in your daily life. **A**

8. Solids expand slightly when heated. For this reason, bridges and railway tracks are built with expansion joints. Use the particle theory to explain what might happen on a hot day if expansion joints were not used. **K/U** **A**

9. Use diagrams and words to explain what happens to the particles of matter in each of the following situations (Figure 1(a) to 1(c)). Consider these questions: Are the particles moving faster or slower? Are the particles getting closer or farther apart? What change of state is occurring?

   (a) Droplets of water form on the outside surface of a glass of water.

   (b) Butter melts in a hot skillet.

   (c) The red line in a liquid thermometer gets shorter as the temperature drops. **K/U** **C**

(a)   (b)   (c)

Figure 1

10. Perspiration (sweat) helps a person cool down. What change of state is involved in sweating? **K/U** **A**

11. You are boiling vegetables on the stove and notice the lid of the pot moving up and down. Use the particle theory to explain what is happening. **K/U**

12. Thermal expansion can be useful or it can be a problem. Research the effects and uses of thermal expansion. Choose one example of thermal expansion and write a summary paragraph about it. **K/U** **A**

Go to Nelson Science

Solve a Problem!

13. (a) Many containers that hold food are made of glass sealed with a metal lid. These lids can be difficult to remove. Holding the lid of the jar under hot water for a short time makes the lid easier to remove. Explain why this works.

(b) An auto mechanic is having difficulty loosening the nut on a bolt using only a wrench and a pair of pliers. How can the mechanic use the ideas in this chapter to solve this problem? K/U A

14. (a) Some people hang wet clothing out to dry on warm, sunny days. Why does wet clothing dry in this weather?

(b) Some people hang wet clothing out to dry even on freezing cold days. Will wet clothes dry in this weather?

(c) What would happen to juicy vegetables left on a plate in a freezer for a long time? How can this be prevented? K/U A

15. A bimetallic strip is made of one type of metal on one side and a different metal on the other side (Figure 2). The strip bends one way when heated.

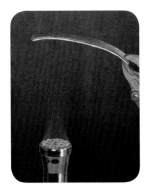

Figure 2

(a) Explain why the strip bends when heated.

(b) Conduct library or Internet research to determine how bimetallic strips are useful.

(c) How could a bimetallic strip be used to help you perform a practical task in everyday life? K/U A

Create and Evaluate!

16. An amount of ice is lighter than an equal amount of liquid water. Use the library or the Internet to research and explain what this statement means. Write a short script, story, or poem describing the implications of this effect for life on Earth. T/I A C

17. Using the Internet, research the thermoscope. Write a short description of this instrument, indicating how it worked and what it was made of. Compare the thermoscope with thermometers used today. How useful would the thermoscope be in everyday tasks? T/I A

Go to Nelson Science

Reflect on Your Learning

18. Think back to the Key Question on the first page of this chapter.

(a) In a brief paragraph, answer the Key Question. You may use diagrams.

(b) Write one or two more questions about the topic of this unit that you would like to explore.

19. Think about a new idea regarding heat that you have learned in this chapter. How may this idea change some of the things you do on a daily basis?

20. Which concept presented in this chapter did you find the most interesting? What new questions do you have about this concept?

8 Energy Transfer and Conservation

KEY QUESTION: How does the transfer of energy affect natural and human-built environments?

Looking Ahead

- Energy may be transferred by conduction, convection, and radiation.

- The transfer of energy may be studied through the skills of experimentation.

- The transfer of energy drives natural processes.

- We can conserve energy by effectively controlling energy transfer.

- New methods of controlling energy transfer may be explored by applying the skills of technological problem solving.

VOCABULARY

conduction	convection
geothermal energy	radiant energy
igneous rock	radiation
metamorphic rock	

A SUMMER DAY AT THE BEACH

LINKING TO LITERACY

Getting Ready to Read

When good readers start to read about a subject that is new to them, they use a number of strategies to get ready to read. They make connections to their prior knowledge of the subject, they use pictures, layout, and titles to make predictions, and they identify the questions they might already have.

1 Look carefully at the beach scene on this page. What does the title make you think of? How many different sources and effects of heat can you identify? What questions do you have? When you make a list, work with a partner to compare your findings and questions.

Thermal Energy Transfer

TRY THIS: Make a Mini Windmill

SKILLS MENU: questioning, predicting, planning, observing, analyzing, evaluating, communicating

In this activity, you will create a simple device similar to a windmill. You will make this windmill turn without touching it.

Equipment and Materials: scissors; large paper clip; 5 cm × 5 cm piece of paper

1. Bend a large paper clip so that it forms a stand (Figure 1).

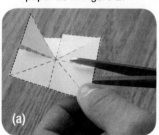

Figure 1 Bend the paper clip to form a stand.

2. Prepare a paper windmill by cutting and folding the piece of paper as in Figure 2.

Figure 2 (a) Make eight cuts, but do not cut all the way to the centre. (b) Fold each triangle the same way to make angled fan blades.

3. Choose a place in your home or classroom where the air is still. Place the paper clip stand on a tabletop, and balance the paper windmill on top of the paper clip (Figure 3).

Figure 3 It may take a few tries to get the paper balanced on the paper clip.

4. Keep your hands away from the windmill apparatus and stay very still until the paper part stops moving.

5. Gently cup your hands around the paper clip stand as in Figure 4. Watch what happens. Record your observations in your notebook.

Figure 4 Do not touch the stand or the paper.

6. Predict what happens to the fan when you change the positions of your hands. Test your predictions and record your observations.

7. Analyze your observations. Can you identify any patterns in the results of your tests? Provide a possible explanation for your observations.

8. Write a testable question about this phenomenon that you could explore further.

9. Make a prediction related to your testable question. Your prediction should involve new variables that are different from those that you have already tested.

10. Plan a procedure for testing your prediction. Ask your teacher to approve your procedure, and then perform your procedure. Record and analyze your observations. Compare your prediction to your observations.

A. What do you think is responsible for your observations in step 5?

B. Explain your results using the particle theory.

Humans have invented many technologies that transfer energy from one object to another, or from one place to another. We commonly use central heating furnaces to warm the air throughout our homes during the winter. We use refrigerators and freezers to keep foods cold for long periods of time (Figure 5). How would your life be affected if your home had no furnace or refrigerator?

Figure 5 Refrigerators keep food cool in our homes.

Thermal energy naturally moves from a substance with a higher temperature to a substance with a lower temperature. This energy will continue to move until the temperatures of the two substances are the same. When you put a frozen juice box into your lunch bag, it eventually melts as energy is transmitted from less cold items in your lunch to the drink. Technology allows us to control the rate of heating and cooling. If you want the drink to melt faster, you could put it near a hot radiator in your classroom. If you want it to melt more slowly, you could put it into a refrigerator. What other devices allow you to control the processes of heating and cooling?

Thermal energy can be transmitted in several ways. When you understand each of these ways, you will be able to understand, and even control, the transfer of thermal energy more effectively.

✔ CHECK YOUR LEARNING

1. In what direction does thermal energy flow naturally?
2. Give an example of thermal energy being transferred from one material to another.

3. Suggest one way to slow down the transfer of thermal energy into or out of a substance with the aid of technology.

The Transfer of Energy through a Substance

Imagine that your first few steps in bare feet in the morning are on a rug. Then, you walk onto a wooden floor. Which do you think would feel cooler, the rug or the wooden floor? The wooden floor feels cooler. Can you suggest a reason? When your feet first touch the floor, they are warmer than the floor. Thermal energy is transferred from your feet to the floor. The area of floor under your feet gets warmer, and your feet get cooler. Some substances transfer energy more effectively than other substances. The wooden floor feels cooler than the rug even though both are at the same temperature. This is because wood has a better ability than a rug to transfer energy away from your body. You can notice a similar effect when you touch objects in your environment. For example, a metal doorknob transfers energy away from your fingers more quickly than does a book. That is why doorknobs often feel cold.

SKILLS MENU
- ☐ Questioning
- ☐ Hypothesizing
- ☐ Predicting
- ☐ Planning
- ☐ Controlling Variables
- ☐ Performing
- ☐ Observing
- ☐ Analyzing
- ☐ Evaluating
- ☐ Communicating

Testable Question

What kind of material transmits thermal energy most effectively: glass, metal, wood, or plastic?

Hypothesis/Prediction

SKILLS HANDBOOK 2.B.3.

Read the Experimental Design and Procedure. Then, hold the four rods provided in your hands, one at a time. Note the sensation of each rod. Write a hypothesis based on the Testable Question. Your hypothesis should include both a prediction and reasons for your prediction. Base your reasons on the sensations you felt when you held the rods in your hands.

Experimental Design

You will compare the effectiveness of heating rods of various materials in transmitting thermal energy along their lengths. You will use drops of wax to indicate the transfer of thermal energy. The rods will be heated equally, two at a time.

Equipment and Materials

- eye protection
- apron
- glass rod, metal rod, wooden rod, plastic rod (of equal length and diameter)
- 2 support stands
- 2 clamps
- hot plate
- timing device
- candle
- matches

eye protection

apron

glass rod, metal rod, wooden rod, and plastic rod (of equal length and diameter)

2 support stands

2 clamps

hot plate

timing device

candle

matches

Procedure

SKILLS HANDBOOK 5.B.

1. Clamp the metal rod and the wooden rod to separate support stands so that the rods are horizontal.

2. Use a lit candle to drip small beads of wax, equally spaced, along the rods.

 Use care with an open flame. Do not touch wax while it is liquid. Hot wax can burn you. Do not allow the glass or metal rod to touch the hot plate.

3. When the wax on the rods has solidified, arrange the rods so that each rod has one end above the hot plate (Figure 1).

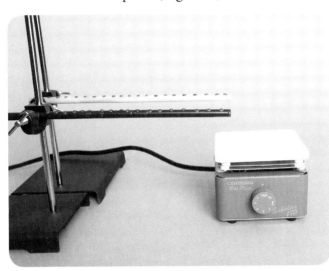

Figure 1 Step 3

4. Turn on the hot plate and time how long it takes each wax bead to melt. Record your observations.

5. Turn off the hot plate after it appears that melting has come to a stop.

6. Test the glass and plastic rods the same way you tested the metal and wood rods. Compare them with each other, and with the metal and wood rods. Record your observations.

Be careful when using a hot plate. Do not touch the top of the hot plate at any time. When unplugging the hot plate, pull the plug, not the cord.

Analyze and Evaluate

SKILLS HANDBOOK 2.B.2., 2.B.7.

(a) Did the evidence you obtained in this experiment support your hypothesis? Explain.

(b) Answer the Testable Question.

(c) Rank the materials in order, from slowest to fastest transmission of thermal energy.

(d) Is there an additional test that you could carry out to help you answer the Testable Question? Explain.

(e) When conducting the test in (d), what would the independent and dependent variables be? List the controls that you would use.

Apply and Extend

(f) The particle theory can be used to explain many of the behaviours of substances. Which part(s) of the particle theory may apply to your observations in this investigation? Explain your findings using the particle theory.

(g) Imagine that you have the job of selecting materials for making cookware (pots and pans) (Figure 2). Which materials would you choose for the base of a pot or pan? Which materials would you choose for the handles? Explain why.

Figure 2 What kinds of materials should you use when making cookware?

Unit Task How can you apply what you have learned about energy transfer through different materials to your doghouse design?

Conduction

When you cook an egg sunny side up in a pan on a hot stove, there is a transfer of thermal energy. The thermal energy transfers from the hot stove burner and through the pan. The energy then moves from the pan and into the cold egg (Figure 1).

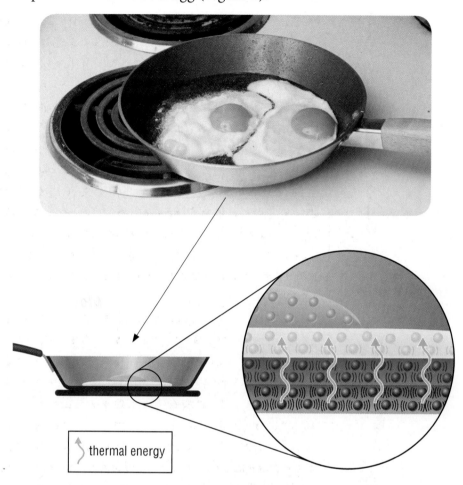

thermal energy

Figure 1 Energy from the burner travels through the pan and into the egg. The particles of the pan collide with the particles of the egg, causing the egg's particles to move faster. This faster motion causes the temperature of the egg to rise.

The particles in the hot stove burner vibrate quickly. When the pan comes into contact with the burner, the fast-moving particles of the burner collide and transfer energy to the slow-moving particles of the cold pan. This energy transfer raises the temperature of the pan.

The same process occurs between the hot pan and the cold, raw egg. The egg is in direct contact with the pan, so the fast-moving particles of the hot pan collide and transfer energy to the particles of the cold egg. The temperature of the egg rises, and the egg begins to cook.

Cooking an egg in a pan on a stove is an example of conduction. **Conduction** is the transfer of thermal energy through a substance, or between substances in contact. This energy transfer is caused by the collision of particles.

Some devices we use are designed to conduct energy quickly. The pots and pans we use for cooking conduct energy quickly from a hot burner to cold food. Metals, such as copper and aluminum, are called "conductors" because they transfer energy easily (Figure 2). Other devices are designed to prevent conduction. The boots we wear in the winter are designed to prevent energy transfer from our warm feet to the cold snow. The foam, fleece, or felt that lines the boots is called an "insulator" because it reduces the conduction of thermal energy (Figure 3). A chef usually stirs hot soup with a wooden or plastic spoon instead of a metal spoon. Thermal energy is transferred less easily through wood and plastic than through metal. This means that there is less chance of the chef burning his or her hand.

conduction: the transfer of thermal energy through a substance, or between substances in contact, by the collision of particles

Figure 2 Metals are good conductors of energy and are used in many useful products.

Figure 3 Insulators are used in products to prevent the transfer of energy.

Unit Task How can you apply what you have learned about conductors and insulators when selecting materials for your doghouse?

✔ CHECK YOUR LEARNING

1. How has your understanding of the word "conductor" changed since you read this section?

2. In your own words, explain how thermal energy is transferred by conduction.

3. List one material that is a good conductor and one that is a good insulator. Suggest one use for each material.

4. Sketch a diagram that shows how thermal energy is transferred from a pot of hot soup to a chef's hand, if the chef uses a metal spoon to stir the soup. What advice could you give the chef to help her avoid a painful burn?

Conduction and Geological Processes

Figure 1 Exposed rock of the Canadian Shield can be seen along many highways in Ontario.

geothermal energy: energy contained below Earth's surface

Have you ever seen rock formations like those in Figure 1? The wavy dark and light lines in the rock indicate that the rock may not always have been completely solid. Were these solid rocks once softer and flexible a long time ago? If so, where did the energy that softened the rock come from? Have you ever wondered why the rocks in this area look the way they do?

The Sun is a major source of thermal energy on Earth's surface. Another large hidden source of thermal energy is **geothermal energy** within Earth. We can see the effects of this energy directly during volcanic eruptions (Figure 2). We also see geothermal energy where hot springs bring boiling liquid to the surface of Earth (Figure 3).

Earth's interior is composed of four layers. The first is a thin layer of solid rock called the crust. The second is a hot, flexible layer of rock called the mantle. Then there is a molten outer core and a solid inner core of iron and nickel (Figure 4). The temperature of Earth's core is estimated to be close to 7000 °C. Although it is not obvious, even Earth's cooler outer crust contains a significant amount of geothermal energy.

Thermal energy from deep within Earth is conducted through the matter in the upper layers. This energy helps form rocks and minerals.

Figure 2 Volcanic eruptions provide evidence of geothermal energy.

igneous rock: rock formed from magma that has cooled and solidified

Figure 3 Geothermal energy heats the liquid in hot springs.

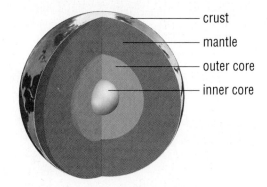

crust
mantle
outer core
inner core

Figure 4 This cross-section shows the four layers that make up Earth's interior.

Heat and Rock Formation

Rocks inside Earth are constantly melting and solidifying. When rock is heated to high temperatures (between 625 °C and 1200 °C), it melts into magma. When hot magma is pushed to the surface in a volcanic eruption, it cools and solidifies into new rock. This new rock is called **igneous rock** (Figure 5). Common igneous rocks include pumice, obsidian, and granite.

Figure 5 Pumice is an igneous rock.

Earth's crust, which consists of the continents and ocean floors, is constantly moving very slowly. Movements of Earth's crust have significantly changed our planet. Sometimes two pieces of Earth's crust push against each other. This collision pushes existing rocks deep into Earth, toward the hot core. When the rock is exposed to high pressure and temperatures above 200 °C, the particles of the rock absorb the geothermal energy. The particles are rearranged, resulting in the formation of a new type of rock, called **metamorphic rock** (Figure 6).

The Canadian Shield is made mostly of metamorphic rock, and contains some of the oldest rock on Earth (about 4 billion years old). You can see examples of the Canadian Shield through much of Northern Ontario, especially in the Sudbury area. The Canadian Shield covers about two-thirds of Ontario.

metamorphic rock: rock that is formed when heat and pressure change existing rock

Figure 6 Gneiss (pronounced "nice") is an example of metamorphic rock.

Diamond

Diamond is a mineral composed of pure carbon and is the hardest natural material found on Earth (Figure 7(a)). Diamonds form deep in Earth's crust (about 150 km below the surface). At these depths, heat and pressure may change graphite (another form of carbon) into diamond. Therefore, diamonds are a type of metamorphic rock.

Diamonds are often found near the sites of old volcanoes, where magma from ancient eruptions carried rocks containing diamonds closer to Earth's surface. Diamonds are crystals that can be cut, polished, and used in jewellery (Figure 7(b)). Since they are very hard, diamonds are also used on the tips of saw blades and drill bits to cut through rock and steel (Figure 7(c)).

To learn more about diamonds,

Go to Nelson Science

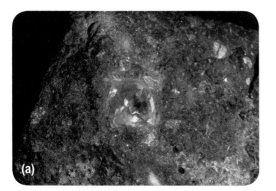

Figure 7 (a) A rough diamond found in a mine, (b) a cut and polished diamond set in a ring, and (c) an industrial diamond in a saw blade

✔ CHECK YOUR LEARNING

1. Describe the formation of rocks due to conduction of geothermal energy within Earth.

2. Name two types of rocks and one mineral formed by conduction of energy.

3. What are some relationships between moving continents, geothermal energy from within Earth, and metamorphic rock?

4. Why can diamond be considered a type of metamorphic rock?

8.5 Convection

In substances such as water and air, thermal energy can be transferred from one area to another. This transfer of energy relies on the fluid characteristics of such materials. For example, think about a pot of soup cooking on a stove. When the soup is heated, the water particles near the bottom of the pot start to move faster and farther apart. This makes the particles near the bottom less dense (and lighter) than those near the top. Therefore, the colder, denser soup near the top sinks to the bottom of the pot. This causes the less dense soup to move upward and replace the cold soup. This movement creates a current in which colder soup near the top of the pot moves to the bottom and warms up. Then, warmer soup near the bottom of the pot moves to the top and cools down (Figure 1).

LINKING TO LITERACY

Finding the Main Idea
Finding the main idea involves being able to summarize what you read into one or two ideas that tell the most important facts or messages from a long passage of text. The main ideas are usually found at the beginning of paragraphs or sections of text. Can you find a main idea about convection on this page?

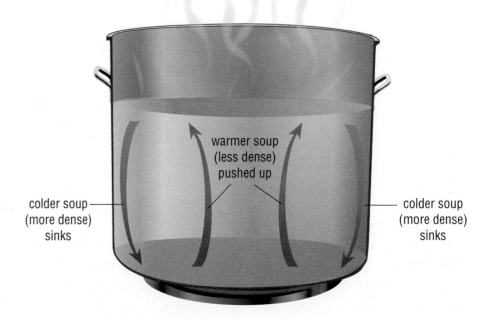

colder soup (more dense) sinks

warmer soup (less dense) pushed up

colder soup (more dense) sinks

Figure 1 Soup is heated by convection.

The continuous movement of warmer and colder soup in a pot is an example of convection. This process transfers energy from one part of a fluid to another. Thus, **convection** is the transfer of thermal energy caused by the flow of a fluid's particles (a gas or liquid). Convection does not occur in solids because the particles of a solid only vibrate; they cannot flow.

convection: the transfer of thermal energy from one part of a fluid to another by a circulating current of faster-moving and slower-moving particles

SKILLS MENU: observing, analyzing, communicating

In this activity, you will actually see convection currents in action.

Part A: Convection in a Liquid

Equipment and Materials: 100 mL beaker; retort stand and ring clamp; hot plate; water; food colouring

1. Set up the beaker, stand, and clamp so that only half of the beaker is on the hot plate. This way, one side of the beaker will be heated more than the other side (Figure 2).

   🤚 Be careful when using a hot plate. Do not touch the top of the hot plate at any time. When unplugging the hot plate, pull the plug, not the cord.

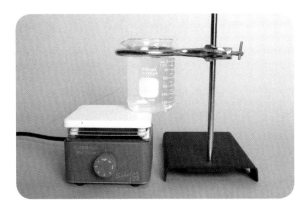

Figure 2   Setup of the beaker on the hot plate

2. Fill the beaker with cold water. Now, add a single drop of food colouring to the beaker on the side over the hot plate.

3. Heat the beaker and observe the motion of the food colouring. Record your observations.

A. Draw a diagram of the motion of the food colouring. Show where you think the water would be warmer and where it would be cooler.

B. What caused the motion of the food colouring? Describe the motion of the water and the food colouring using the particle theory.

Part B: Convection in a Gas—Demonstration

1. Look at the gas convection apparatus shown in Figure 3. Predict what will happen when smoking paper is held above the chimney. Record your prediction.

Figure 3   The burning candle is placed beneath one chimney; the smoking paper is held above the other one.

2. Your teacher will set up the apparatus, and hold the smoking paper over one chimney. Record your observations.

A. Draw a diagram of the motion of the smoke. Show where you think the air particles would be moving faster and where they would be moving more slowly.

The circular flow of water particles in a warming pot of soup is called a convection current. Convection currents do not only form in pots of soup. Convection currents also form in lakes, oceans, aquariums, and in the air around you.

Unit Task   How can you apply what you have learned about convection to the design of your doghouse?

 CHECK YOUR LEARNING

1. Explain how thermal energy is transferred through convection.

2. Use the particle theory to explain how a convection current starts in a fluid.

3. Give two examples of convection currents that you might encounter in everyday life.

4. If you wanted to warm your room using a portable heater, where would you place the heater? Why?

8.6

Convection in the Environment

Uneven heating of liquid on a stove can produce convection currents. Similarly, uneven heating of air at Earth's surface can produce convection currents in the air. Large convection currents in air are called "wind."

The air feels cooler near lakes and oceans in the summer because the energy from the Sun does not heat the air over land and water evenly. Near a lake, the air above the water is colder than the air above the land because land requires much less of the Sun's energy to warm up than does water. The warm air particles above the land are more strongly heated by the warm land surface below. They move faster and spread apart. This makes the air above the land less dense (lighter) than the air over the water. The cool, dense (heavy) air above the water moves down and toward the land. This pushes the warm air over the land upwards (Figure 1). We feel this movement of cool air off the water and toward the land as a cool sea breeze. The warm air that rises high into the atmosphere over the land eventually moves over the water, cools down, sinks, and then moves toward the land again. This daytime movement of air near a body of water is caused by convection.

LINKING TO LITERACY

Synthesizing Information
When you read text that presents new information or ideas, you compare it with what you have read or already know, or compare it with other sources. Use both the text and the diagram on this page, together with what you already know, to help you understand convection in the environment.

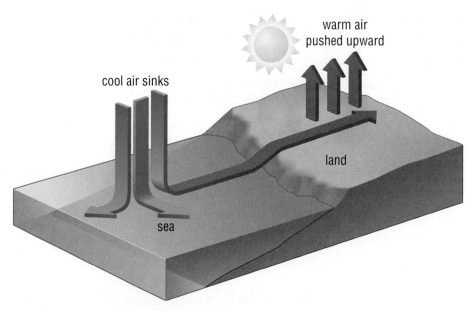

Figure 1 The uneven heating of Earth's surface creates warm and cool air, similar to the convection current in a pot of heated water or soup.

When the Sun goes down in the evening, the land cools more quickly than the water. The warm water heats the air above it, making the air less dense. The cool, dense (heavy) air over the land moves down and out toward the water. This pushes the less dense (lighter) air over the water higher into the atmosphere. A "land breeze" then moves from the land toward the water.

Thunderstorms

Thunderstorms produce lightning and thunder, and are usually associated with strong winds and heavy rains (Figure 2). Thunderstorms create severe weather such as hail, tornadoes, and hurricanes.

Thunderstorms often form on hot, humid days. Earth's surface is warmed by energy from the Sun. The energy is then transferred to the air above the surface of the ground by conduction. This warmed air is less dense than the surrounding cooler air. The warm air is rapidly pushed up higher into the atmosphere by convection, carrying water vapour along with it. As convection pushes the air higher, the water vapour cools and condenses into microscopic droplets of water that appear as large puffy clouds (Figure 3). Large amounts of thermal energy are released as the water vapour condenses. This energy warms the air, so it is pushed even higher into the atmosphere. As the warm, moist air rises higher, it spreads out and the remaining water vapour condenses, forming large clouds called thunderheads (Figure 4). The water droplets in thunderheads eventually become heavy enough to fall as rain.

Convection and Geological Processes

The temperature of Earth's mantle increases as you go deeper. So, the top of the mantle is cooler than the bottom. Over millions of years, cooler mantle rock sinks as warmer mantle rock rises closer to Earth's crust. This creates very slow convection currents (Figure 5). These convection currents transfer energy and may cause volcanic eruptions.

Figure 2 Lightning is a common sight during thunderstorms.

Figure 3 These puffy white clouds form because of convection currents.

Figure 4 Thunderheads result as air in clouds warms and rises higher.

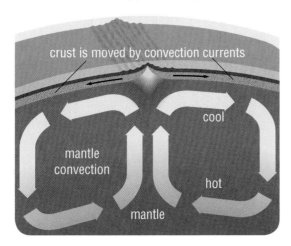

crust is moved by convection currents

cool

mantle convection

hot

mantle

Figure 5 Convection currents below Earth's crust

✔ CHECK YOUR LEARNING

1. List three natural processes that depend on convection.
2. **(a)** Draw two diagrams to explain land and sea breezes.
   (b) Label each diagram "day" or "night," as appropriate.
3. What geological events occur because of convection currents in Earth's mantle?

4. **(a)** For thunderstorms to occur, the air must have two characteristics. What are they?
   (b) Are thunderstorms more likely to form over land or over water? Why?

Radiation

When you look out into space, you see stars and planets. Did you know that there are almost no particles in the space between Earth and the Sun? How, then, does energy travel from the Sun to Earth? Conduction and convection both require particles to transfer energy. We know that energy reaches Earth from the Sun because our bodies are warmed by the Sun on a sunny day (Figure 1). Without this energy, there would be no life on Earth.

Figure 1 How is the Sun's energy transferred to Earth?

There is a way in which energy can be transferred without the use of particles. A form of energy called **radiant energy** travels outward from the Sun through empty space. Radiant energy travels in the form of electromagnetic waves, or rays. Radiant energy from the Sun includes visible rays (light) and invisible rays (ultraviolet (UV) rays and infrared rays). We use the term **radiation** to describe the transfer of radiant energy in the form of electromagnetic rays. The Sun emits electromagnetic rays in all directions, but only a small portion of them reach Earth.

Matter can both absorb and emit (give off) radiant energy. Benches at a baseball field get quite hot when the radiant energy from the Sun shines on them (Figure 2). This is because the radiant energy is absorbed by the particles of the benches and converted to thermal energy. When this occurs, the particles of the material move faster. This raises the temperature of the benches. The seats that are in the shade are usually much cooler to the touch.

radiant energy: energy that travels in the form of electromagnetic waves through empty space; includes visible light, ultraviolet rays, and infrared rays

radiation: the transfer of radiant energy by means of electromagnetic waves

LINKING TO LITERACY

Asking Questions
Good readers are always questioning before, during, and after they read. Sometimes they find the answers in the text; other times, they do more research. As you read about radiation, think about the different questions you have:
- questions about words or ideas in the text that you do not understand
- questions about something that interests you

Figure 2 Radiant energy from the Sun makes the benches hot.

There are also sources of radiant energy on Earth. For example, candle flames and incandescent light bulbs glow and feel hot. They glow because they give off visible light. They feel hot because they emit infrared rays. Infrared rays are also emitted by hot objects that do not glow, such as curling irons and hot plates. If you place your hand near (but not on) a curling iron or a hot plate, you can feel that they are giving off a form of energy. The energy given off by objects that emit infrared rays is converted to thermal energy in your skin, which is why they feel hot.

Absorption and Reflection of Radiation from the Sun

Most of the radiant energy from the Sun (also called solar energy) that reaches Earth's surface is in the form of visible light and infrared rays (Figure 3). Other forms of radiant energy from the Sun, including UV rays, X rays, and gamma rays, are mostly absorbed by Earth's atmosphere. Only a small amount of these rays reach the surface of the planet. The amount of UV rays that reaches Earth's surface depends on a number of factors, such as the level of ozone in the atmosphere, the time of day, the season, and the weather. The remaining radiant energy passes through the upper atmosphere and is absorbed or reflected by clouds, water, land, buildings, our bodies, and all other living things.

To learn more about what happens to solar radiation that reaches Earth,
Go to Nelson Science

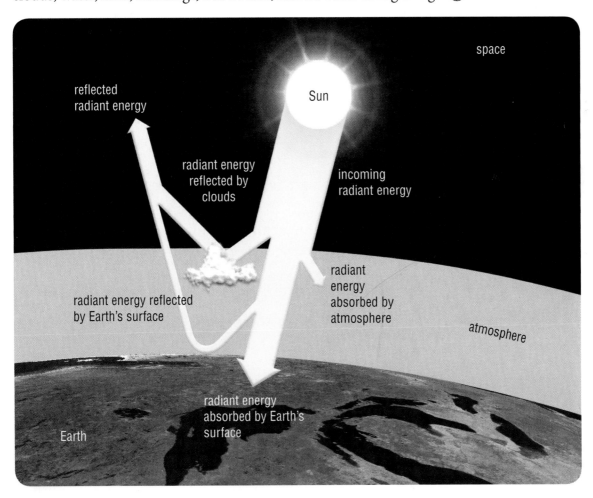

Figure 3 Earth and Earth's atmosphere both absorb and reflect radiant energy from the Sun.

Figure 4 Rock exposed as glaciers melt absorbs more energy than it reflects.

During the day, when radiant energy from the Sun strikes an object, the energy may be reflected or absorbed. Energy that is absorbed warms the object. The colour and texture of objects affect how much energy is absorbed. For example, snow and ice reflect much of the Sun's radiant energy back into space. They do so because they are white and smooth. However, when snow melts, it uncovers the darker rock below. When sea ice melts, it exposes the ocean water. The rocks and water are less able to reflect the visible light of the Sun. The exposed rock and water absorb more of the radiant energy (Figure 4). Cities also absorb a lot of radiant energy because many roads and buildings are dark. Darker colours tend to absorb radiant energy better than lighter colours or shiny surfaces.

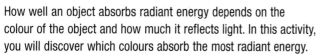

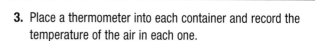

TRY THIS: Radiant Energy and Colour

SKILLS MENU: predicting, observing

SKILLS HANDBOOK
2.B.3., 6.A.4.

How well an object absorbs radiant energy depends on the colour of the object and how much it reflects light. In this activity, you will discover which colours absorb the most radiant energy.

Equipment and Materials: paint brush; 4 thermometers; source of radiant energy (for example, the Sun); 4 containers (small coffee cups with lids or pop cans); 4 different colours of paint

 Do not touch the hot lamp. To unplug the lamp, pull the plug and not the cord.

1. Look at the four colours of paint. Using what you have learned about the absorption of radiant energy, write a hypothesis relating the colour of the containers and their relative temperatures after they have been exposed to radiant energy for 20 min.

2. Paint each container a different colour.

3. Place a thermometer into each container and record the temperature of the air in each one.

4. Place all four containers in a source of radiant energy for 20 min. Make sure that each container is receiving the same amount of radiant energy, and that no containers are touching.

5. After 20 min, measure and record the temperature of the air in each container.

A. Compare the temperatures of the containers.

B. Evaluate your hypothesis based on your observations and temperature measurements.

C. Make a conclusion about radiant energy, temperature of an object, and its colour.

Scientists are concerned that the average temperature of Earth's surface is steadily increasing. This problem may get worse as Arctic ice melts and water and rock below are exposed.

Unit Task How can you apply what you have learned about radiation as you design your doghouse?

CHECK YOUR LEARNING

1. List two objects that absorb radiant energy from the Sun.

2. List two objects here on Earth that are sources of radiant energy. How can you tell that they emit radiant energy?

3. Distinguish between the effects of solar radiation on a snow-covered asphalt driveway and a shovelled asphalt driveway.

4. Why do you suppose bee keepers use white paint and use shiny aluminum lids on their bee hives?

5. What form of energy do you think microwave ovens use? Explain your reasoning.

Managing the Transfer of Thermal Energy

We are all stewards of Earth and its resources. It is every person's responsibility to be less wasteful and to conserve Earth's resources. Using energy efficiently and managing it well are important parts of reducing society's impact on Earth. A major way to conserve energy is to manage the transfer of energy into and out of buildings. By understanding what affects the transfer of energy, a building designer is able to make sure that the building's occupants are comfortable. A designer can also ensure that the building wastes as little energy as possible. Poor materials and planning can result in a building that wastes energy (Figure 1). This makes poor use of Earth's resources.

> **LINKING TO LITERACY**
>
> **Making a Connection**
> Good readers often interact with the text by making text-to-self connections. They relate what they read to personal experiences. Think about a time when you directly experienced the loss of energy in a building. How could this energy transfer have been prevented?

Figure 1 The red, yellow, and white areas in this infrared photo of a house show energy loss. From this photo, can you identify the parts of the house that lose the most energy?

Insulators are materials designed to reduce the flow of energy by limiting conduction, convection, or both. Radiant barriers reduce the loss of energy by radiation. These materials help warm spaces remain warm and cold spaces remain cold.

Architects want to design a house that wastes as little energy as possible. They have to think about everything that separates the house from the outside environment. This is the building's "thermal envelope." The thermal envelope includes walls, the building's roof, insulation, windows, doors, finishes, weather stripping, and air/vapour barriers. The thoughtful design of these parts of the building can reduce conduction, convection, and radiation.

Figure 2 Insulation is put into the walls and roof of a house to prevent the transfer of energy.

Table 1 R-Values for Common Insulation Materials

Insulation material (2.5 cm thick)	R-value
wood	0.71–1.41
fibreglass batt	3.2–3.6
cellulose	3.1–3.7
polystyrene foam board	3.6–5.0

Figure 3 Tiny pockets of trapped air prevent energy from being transferred.

Preventing Conduction

Using insulating materials is the best way to prevent heat transfer by conduction and convection. Insulating materials are poor conductors of thermal energy and also limit the movement of air in spaces, reducing convection. Insulation slows the rate at which unwanted energy enters the home in the summer. It also slows the escape of energy in the winter (Figure 2). Thermal energy moves slowly through the insulation and does not readily escape to the outside air.

Insulating materials are tested and given a Thermal Resistance Value (R-value). The higher the R-value, the more difficult it is for energy to move through the material by conduction, convection, or radiation (Table 1). To reduce energy loss, builders should increase the amount of insulation in basement walls, the roof, and exterior walls. Recall that polystyrene blocks are being used to build and insulate the Narangs' new home (Unit Opener, page 176).

Air—An Excellent Insulator

Fur, wool, and down keep animals warm. How do animal fibres keep animals and people warm? They all contain many small air-filled spaces (Figure 3). Air is a gas. Its particles are far apart. Air is not very good at transferring energy by conduction or convection. Relatively thick materials containing small air pockets are good insulators.

Green Roofs

A recent innovation in building design is the green roof (Figure 4(a)). A green roof system has a waterproof barrier, drainage, a lightweight growth medium that acts like soil, and vegetation (Figure 4(b)).

A study in Ottawa in 2001 found that green roofs reduced energy transfer year-round. There was a 10 % reduction in heating costs during the winter. There was also a 25 % saving in air conditioning costs in the summer. Green roofs last a long time, improve air quality, and even provide recreational opportunities.

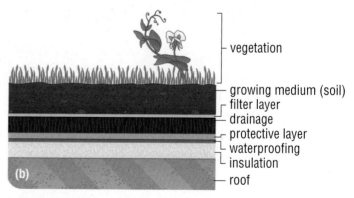

- vegetation
- growing medium (soil)
- filter layer
- drainage
- protective layer
- waterproofing
- insulation
- roof

Figure 4 (a) This green roof on the University of Toronto Scarborough campus is one of over 600 that have been installed in Toronto. (b) A typical green roof system

Reducing Energy Transfer by Convection

Energy moves through every house by convection. The second floor of a house is often warmer than the ground floor and basement. Air currents in a house move energy just like winds do outside. Convection also allows energy to escape through gaps around doors and windows.

To prevent energy loss by convection, any gaps in the thermal envelope of a house should be sealed. This stops the flow of air into or out of the house. Moving air is a serious cause of energy loss in a home. In winter, warm indoor air escapes through leaks and is replaced by cold outdoor air. Weather stripping around doors and windows helps keep warm air trapped inside the house (Figure 5). Switches and electrical sockets on outside walls are also common sites of energy loss. Insulating switch plate covers reduces drafts that transfer energy to the outside environment.

Some homes are tightly sealed to greatly reduce the loss of moisture and energy through the walls. This has both a positive and a negative outcome. On the positive side, moisture from outside cannot get into the house. On the negative side, any moisture inside the house—from people breathing, cooking, and taking showers—is trapped. Here, it may help mould grow and wood rot. Sealing all of the cracks in a home can also trap unhealthy gases produced by certain types of furniture and carpeting. To avoid these problems, all homes need a way to exchange stale indoor air with a good supply of fresh outdoor air. Is there a way to reduce the loss of thermal energy and still bring fresh air in from the outside?

The problem of reducing thermal energy loss and providing proper ventilation has been solved by the air-to-air heat exchanger. This device allows some of the thermal energy in the outgoing warm air to be transferred to the incoming fresh cold air (Figure 6).

Figure 5 Weather stripping reduces drafts and energy loss.

LINKING TO LITERACY

Reading a Diagram
Diagrams often illustrate text. Read the legend and scan the diagram. Take a moment to think about how the air-to-air heat exchanger allows thermal energy to be transferred.

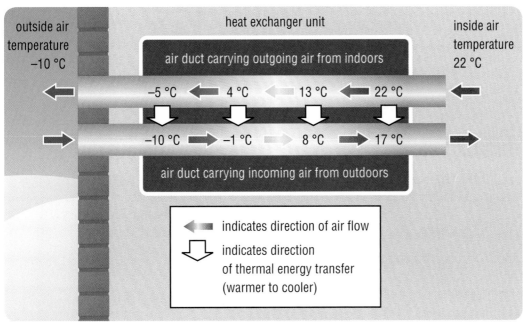

Figure 6 An air-to-air heat exchanger

In a heat exchanger, the air ducts carrying the stale indoor air are in close contact with the ducts carrying the fresh outside air. This allows a continuous transfer of thermal energy from the outgoing warm air to the incoming cool air. By the time the old indoor air leaves the heat exchanger, much of its thermal energy has been transferred to the incoming air. As a result, the fresh air entering the home is already warm.

Reducing Energy Transfer by Radiation

Radiation is the transfer of energy by means of electromagnetic waves. In the winter, if your home is warm, it will radiate energy to the colder outside. In the summer, the strong sunlight warms your house. To prevent this unwanted energy transfer, homebuilders sometimes install a shiny radiant barrier in the attic (Figure 7). The shiny surface reflects radiant energy, preventing it from warming the home. The barrier should be installed with the reflective surface facing up toward the roof. The radiant barrier can then reflect up to 97 % of radiant energy.

Radiant barriers are not used in attics only. Radiant barriers can also be applied to air ducts and water pipes to prevent energy loss as warm air and hot water travel throughout the house.

A lot of radiant energy is lost through windows. Today, most builders install windows that have low-E (low-emissivity) glass. Low-E glass has a special ultra-thin surface layer that reduces the transfer of radiant energy. Like radiant barriers, low-E glass helps keep radiant energy inside during the winter and outside during the summer. One way to reduce heating and cooling costs is to replace older windows with low-E windows.

Controlling the transfer of energy in buildings is important. It helps us to conserve energy resources for future generations.

Figure 7 Radiant barriers are generally installed in the attic of a house to minimize energy transfer into the home.

To learn more about controlling the transfer of energy in homes and buildings,

Go to Nelson Science

Unit Task There are several ideas in this section that you might be able to apply to the design of your doghouse. Make a list of those that you think will be useful.

CHECK YOUR LEARNING

1. Describe an idea in the reading that is new to you. How does this idea add to your understanding of how we can manage energy transfer?

2. Why is it important to consider the transfer of energy when building a house?

3. Explain why the walls and doors of refrigerators and freezers contain thick slabs of polystyrene foam.

4. High-quality modern homes are very well sealed.
   (a) How does this help conserve energy?
   (b) What problem may this create?
   (c) How does an air-to-air heat exchanger overcome this problem and still help conserve energy?

5. Describe one way that builders can reduce each of the types of heat transfer in a building.

Tough Decisions

There is a famous story about three little pigs. The first pig built a straw house because it was cheap and easy; the second pig used sticks because sticks were stronger than straw. The third little pig built a house out of bricks, which took more effort and probably cost a lot more, but it was worth it. The big bad wolf huffed and puffed and blew down the houses made of straw and sticks, but he could not blow down the brick house (Figure 1).

Figure 1 Clearly, the third little pig thoroughly researched building materials!

The moral of the story, of course, is that you should make wise decisions in everything you do, especially when it comes to important things like building a house. The wiser the choices we make, the healthier we will keep the planet for ourselves and future generations.

The Issue

Imagine that your family has decided to buy a brand new home. You offer to help out by researching on the Internet, and then reporting your findings back to your family. Your research reveals that some homebuilders' advertisements focus on the location of the house, others focus on the quality of the building materials (Figure 2), and still others focus on energy conservation. All of these qualities affect the price of the home. Which home will you recommend?

Figure 2 Do the building materials used in new homes help conserve energy?

Goal

Explain to your parents the energy-conserving features of the home you recommend, and try to convince them that the home is worth the price. When everyone in the class has found the home that they would recommend, they will present their choices in a class discussion.

Gather Information

1. Look at information provided by a number of homebuilders on the Internet. Consider the advantages and disadvantages of each home. List any topics that you think need more information.

   Go to Nelson Science

2. Learn as much as you can about the different energy-conserving strategies of various homes. What are the advantages and disadvantages of the homes you are considering? The price of the home is important, as is the cost of upkeep.

3. Be sure to consider factors other than the house itself. How long will it take your parents to commute to work? Is there access to public transit? Does the house have a big backyard? Are there any natural areas, such as forests, near the home? These factors also affect how we use Earth's resources and conserve energy.

4. Speak to your friends, relatives, and parents about buying a new home. What would they look for? Ask them about energy conservation.

Identify Solutions

Organize your information into tables and graphs. Select the home that you will recommend, highlighting the energy-conserving features.

Make a Decision

Decide which home you would recommend. Be sure to have support for your decision.

Communicate

Present your recommendation to your teacher (who will act as your parents). Prepare a short presentation to the class that includes the three or four main reasons for your selection. Be prepared to justify why you did not choose the other homes.

8.10

The Amazing Coffee Keeper

Whether you are designing a building, a winter jacket, or a lunch bag, the choice of materials and their arrangement affect the final function of the product. Understanding how energy transfer works allows you to design a product that efficiently manages the transfer of energy.

SKILLS MENU

- ☐ Identify a Problem/Need
- ☑ Planning
- ☑ Selecting Materials and Equipment
- ☑ Designing
- ☑ Testing
- ☑ Modifying
- ☐ Communicating

Scenario

Every Saturday morning, your dad pours himself a cup of coffee, and then he gets busy around the house. By the time he has a chance to drink his coffee, it is cold. Your dad has asked you to design a device that will keep his coffee warm until he has time to drink it.

Design Brief

You are to build a device that will prevent 300 mL of hot water from cooling more than 10 °C in 30 min. The device must fit on a kitchen table, cannot include any form of heater, and must allow water to be easily poured in and out. Use materials efficiently to keep costs low. All materials must be safe for use in the classroom and home.

Research and Consider

Research similar devices, such as a thermos. Find out how a thermos is constructed. How does each component help to prevent energy transfer?

 Go to Nelson Science

With your team, brainstorm possible solutions to this problem, following the design brief. Draw sketches for three different designs.

Plan and Construct

SKILLS HANDBOOK 4.B.3., 4.B.4.

1. Select the best design. Complete a scale drawing of the selected device.

2. Write a list of materials and tools that you will need. (Reduce, reuse, recycle!)

3. Write a step-by-step plan for creating the device. Ask your teacher to approve both the list of materials and the plan.

✋ Use care when cutting materials and when handling hot substances.

4. Once you have approval, build your device.

Test and Modify

 SKILLS HANDBOOK 4.B.5., 4.B.6.

Test how well your device keeps just-boiled water hot for 30 min. How much did the temperature of the water change during that time? Note any problems, and then modify your design to correct these problems. Continue correcting your design until it meets the design criteria.

Evaluate

(a) Describe how your device prevented energy loss by (i) conduction, (ii) convection, and/or (iii) radiation.

(b) What were some of the design challenges that you encountered? How did you overcome them?

(c) If you were to do this project again, what would you do differently? Explain.

Communicate

Prepare a short presentation to a potential investor to explain how your device works. Your presentation should demonstrate how your device is used, explain how it prevents heat transfer, and include the results of the testing.

Energy Transfer and Conservation

BIG Ideas

☑ Heat is a form of energy that can be transformed and transferred. These processes can be explained using the particle theory of matter.

☑ There are many sources of heat.

☑ Heat has both positive and negative effects on the environment.

Looking Back

Energy may be transferred by conduction, convection, and radiation.

- Conduction involves the transfer of energy through a material, or from one material to another by direct contact. It involves only the vibration of the particles of the material. Conduction explains why objects feel hot or cold to the touch.
- Convection involves the transfer of energy within liquids and gases. It involves the movement of the particles in convection currents.
- Radiation involves the transfer of energy by electromagnetic waves. Particles are not involved in the transfer of radiant energy, so radiant energy may travel through empty space.

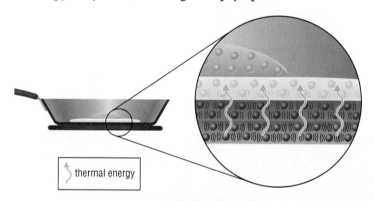

thermal energy

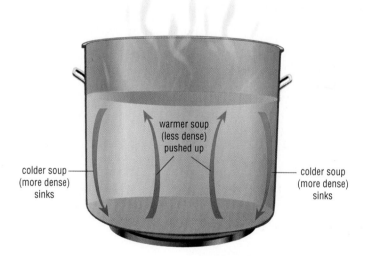

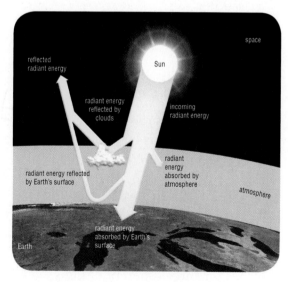

The transfer of energy may be studied through the skills of experimentation.

- The transfer of energy by conduction, convection, and radiation may be analyzed by conducting fair tests.

The transfer of energy drives natural processes.

- The formation of igneous and metamorphic rock and diamonds results from conduction.
- Winds, thunderstorms, and the movement of Earth's crust all result from convection.
- Energy reaches Earth from the Sun as a result of radiation. Without this radiant energy there would be no life on Earth.

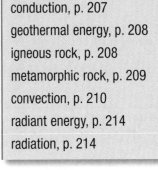

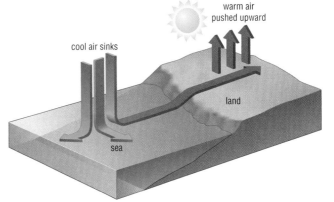

warm air pushed upward

cool air sinks

land

sea

We can conserve energy by effectively controlling energy transfer.

- Designers can select materials (such as thermal insulators and radiation barriers) that reduce unwanted transfers of energy.
- Limiting unwanted energy transfer conserves energy and reduces the costs (both financial and environmental) of heating and cooling our buildings.

New methods of controlling energy transfer may be explored by applying the skills of technological problem solving.

- Technological problem solving skills may be used to design and construct devices that control the transfer of thermal energy.
- Research skills may be used to explore the technologies that scientists and engineers have devised to control energy transfer.

CHAPTER

8 REVIEW

The following icons indicate the Achievement Chart categories:

K/U Knowledge/Understanding
C Communication
T/I Thinking/Investigation
A Application

What Do You Remember?

1. List the three ways in which energy can be transferred. Briefly describe each way. You may want to use diagrams in your descriptions. K/U

2. Write a paragraph describing the transfer of energy from the Sun to Earth. Use the following terms in your paragraph: "electromagnetic radiation," "space," "light," "infrared radiation," "thermal energy," "absorbed," and "transmitted." K/U C

What Do You Understand?

3. What is unique about the way energy reaches Earth from the Sun? K/U

4. We use a variety of different methods to cook food (Figure 1). For the methods below, list the form(s) of energy transfer involved in the cooking method. Be sure to explain your answer.

(a) grilling hamburgers on a barbecue

(b) baking cookies in an oven

(c) making pancakes in a frying pan K/U A

Figure 1

5. Copy Table 1 into your notebook. In each column, list at least three ways that energy transfer affects the natural environment. K/U

Table 1 Methods of Energy Transfer

Conduction	Convection	Radiation

6. How does reducing energy loss from homes demonstrate environmental stewardship? A

7. Explain why a down-filled jacket loses its insulating ability when it gets wet. K/U A

8. Using the Internet and other sources, research what a "thermal" in the atmosphere is. Describe one way in which organisms use thermals to their advantage. A

Go to Nelson Science

9. Using the Internet and other sources, find out what a temperature inversion is. Why do temperature inversions occur? What type of energy transfer do they prevent? What are some of the effects of a temperature inversion? A

Go to Nelson Science

10. Look back at Figure 1 in Section 8.8. This picture is called a "thermogram." What type of energy transfer is important to thermography? Research other uses of thermograms on the Internet. A

Go to Nelson Science

11. Specialized clothing, such as space suits and wet suits, has special properties to keep people warm. Research one type of specialized clothing and explain how energy transfer is taken into account when designing and making the clothing. A

Go to Nelson Science

Solve a Problem!

12. A well-insulated home is more comfortable and costs less to heat.

(a) What are some areas of your home where energy might be lost?

(b) What can be done to reduce this loss?

(c) What are the benefits of reducing energy loss? K/U A

13. Insulated clothing protects our bodies and increases our ability to enjoy outdoor activities in winter. What concepts from this chapter might clothing designers consider when they design cold-weather coats? T/I A

14. Spoons made of different materials sat partially submerged in a container of very hot water for 5 min. The temperatures of the parts sticking out of the water were measured (Table 2). What conclusions can you draw from these findings? T/I

Table 2 Spoon Temperatures

Spoon material	Temperature after 5 min (°C)
stainless steel	80
wood	25
plastic	50
silver	95

15. Name five things that you and your family can do to reduce thermal energy transfer around your home. T/I A

Create and Evaluate!

16. (a) What might be some deterrents to having a green roof?

(b) Suggest how these deterrents might be overcome.

(c) Would you suggest to the government that all government building roofs be converted to green roofs? Why or why not? T/I A

17. (a) What are some of the disadvantages to having airtight buildings?

(b) How can these problems be solved?

(c) How effective are your solutions? T/I A

18. Some older homes and buildings use hot water heating systems (Figure 2). Research what a hot water heating system is (include a diagram). Do you think that hot water heating systems are efficient? Explain your answer. K/U A

Figure 2

Go to Nelson Science

Reflect on Your Learning

19. Think back to the Key Question on the first page of this chapter.

(a) In a brief paragraph, answer the Key Question. You may use diagrams.

(b) Write one or two more questions about the topic of this unit that you would like to explore.

20. Think back to an idea in this chapter that has changed the way you think about thermal energy transfer. Write a brief paragraph describing how your understanding has changed and how this new understanding may affect activities in your everyday life.

9 Heat Sources in the Environment

▶ **KEY QUESTION: What are the relationships between heat, energy sources, and the environment?**

Looking Ahead

- There are different types of energy and different sources of energy.

- Technological devices allow us to transform one type of energy into another.

- The human production of greenhouse gases is causing changes in global climate.

- There are significant advantages and disadvantages to using conventional and alternative energy sources.

- The choices we make in everyday life significantly affect the environment.

- The skills of scientific inquiry can be used to investigate conventional and alternative energy sources.

VOCABULARY

solar energy

friction

conventional energy source

renewable energy resource

non-renewable energy resource

fossil fuels

Earth's energy balance

greenhouse effect

greenhouse gases

global warming

alternative energy source

passive solar heating

active solar energy system

biofuel

The Energy Blues

Energy...
Sometimes I think I'm runnin' out
Seems like we use an awful lot
For heatin' and lightin' and drivin'
Readin' and writin' and jivin'
Energy... You'd think we'd be savin' it up.

Energy... You can get it by dammin' up a river
Energy... A windmill can make the breeze deliver
But even with millin' and dammin'
Our needs are so much more demanding
For energy... We have to use some kind of fuel.

Chop, chop, chop, the cavemen used wood to
    start their fires.
Chop, chop, chop, they made all the tools that
    they required.
Chop, chop, chop, inventions got more and
    more inspired.
The fires got higher and higher,
And clearings got wider and wider.
Energy... They were burnin' 'bout all their
    wood up.

Then one day men discovered that coal would
    do it better
Miners dug, and it looked like it might just
    last forever.
It seemed like the final solution.
It started the Industrial Revolution.
Energy... We could just keep on diggin' it up.

Now in 1859— way out in western
    Pennsylvania—
A man had built a rig that got some laughs from
    folks who came there
But suddenly, a mighty roar came up from under
    the ground.
And soon a gusher, gushin' oil, soaked all who
    stood around.
Now no one knew, when that gusher blew,
The petroleum years were on us,
Or that so many cars and trucks would come to
    cause a crisis.

Energy... We're looking to try and find some
    new kinds.
Energy... Exploring to try and make a new find.
Nuclear and thermal and solar,
If we miss we'll get colder and colder.
Energy... We've gotta stop usin' you up.

So don't be cross when momma says turn
    that extra light out.
Just turn it off 'til we find us a
    fuel that never runs out.
If everyone tries a bit harder,
Our fuel will go farther and
    farther.
Energy... We're gonna be
    stretchin' you out.

LINKING TO LITERACY

Synthesizing
Effective readers collect pieces of information as they read. They combine new information with what they already know, and what they are learning, to gain deeper understanding.

1. Read the title. What do you predict the song will be about? As you read the song, identify new information or phrases that express the key ideas. Reflect on the new ideas presented and how they fit with the other ideas you have gathered.

2. After reading, summarize the text. You may consider questions like: What does the songwriter mean by: "Energy... A windmill can make the breeze deliver"? How does the title convey the meaning of the song?

9.1 Energy Sources

Heat is very important in our daily lives. We heat our homes and wear insulating clothes to keep warm in the winter. We heat water for showering and for cooking. Each of these processes involves the transfer of thermal energy. What are the sources of thermal energy?

Solar Energy and Geothermal Energy

The most obvious direct source of energy on Earth is the Sun (Figure 1). The Sun provides over 90 % of the energy that warms Earth's surface and atmosphere. The Sun's energy comes from deep within its core. This is where nuclear reactions release huge amounts of energy. Most of this energy, called **solar energy** or radiant energy, moves away from the Sun in all directions as visible light and infrared radiation.

solar energy: radiant energy (mostly visible light and infrared radiation) produced at the Sun's outer surface and radiated out into space

LINKING TO LITERACY

Summarizing
Informational text often asks a question (main idea) that will be answered in the text that follows (supporting details). Use sticky notes to keep a record of the information that answers the question, "What are the sources of energy?" What textbook features help you identify the sources of energy?

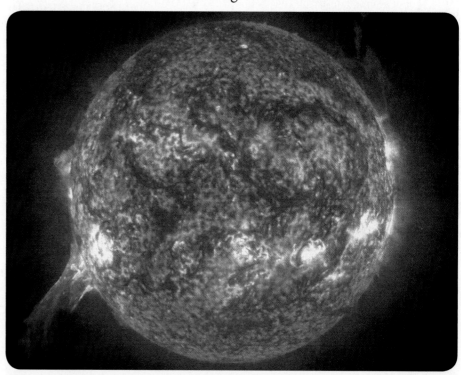

Figure 1 The Sun is the source of most of our energy, even though Earth only captures a tiny portion of the energy emitted by the Sun.

A tiny fraction of solar energy eventually reaches Earth. Here, some of it is absorbed and transformed into thermal energy. It is this energy that heats the land and air, evaporates water, and produces winds, clouds, and precipitation. Earth would quickly become a lifeless deep freezer without the continuous supply of energy from the Sun!

Earth also possesses a large store of geothermal energy. Recall that geothermal energy is the thermal energy contained in the hot core and mantle of Earth. Engineers have developed ways of harnessing this thermal energy for our use.

Solar energy and geothermal energy are large continuous sources of thermal energy. However, they are not the only sources.

Energy Transformations

Many forms of energy, such as chemical energy, can be transformed into thermal energy. Wood and other fuels, such as oil and natural gas, contain large quantities of chemical energy. The chemical energy in wood is transformed into thermal energy when wood is burned (Figure 2). Natural fires, such as forest fires, can be harmful for wildlife. Controlled fires, such as the burning of fuels in furnaces, car engines, and thermal-electric power stations, are useful for humans (Figure 3).

Figure 2 The chemical energy stored in wood is sometimes released in forest fires. Huge quantities of thermal energy are released to the atmosphere, along with gases and ash.

Figure 3 In home furnaces, the chemical energy stored in natural gas is released in a very controlled fashion. This energy is then used to warm your home.

On a smaller scale, you can produce thermal energy by **friction**: the force produced when objects rub together. Just rubbing your hands together produces thermal energy. The motion of your hands (mechanical energy) increases the kinetic energy of the particles in your skin. This results in warmer skin. Friction can transform mechanical energy into thermal energy and radiant energy (light). This occurs when a hard, rough, fast-moving surface rubs against another surface (Figure 4).

friction: a force produced when objects rub against each other

Thermal energy is extremely useful for heating. However, we also need energy for cooling, lighting, communication, transportation, and manufacturing. Our modern lifestyle and high standard of living depend on having energy available to meet our wants and needs.

Figure 4 The sparks tell us that both radiant energy and thermal energy are released when metal is being cut.

Many everyday technological devices use electricity as their direct energy source. The devices transform the electricity into other forms of energy. Where does the electricity come from in the first place?

Sources of Electrical Energy

There is no ready-made usable source of electricity anywhere in the world. Electricity is produced naturally—by lightning in thunderstorms—but not in a form that we can use (Figure 5).

So far, scientists and engineers have not developed an effective method for harnessing the energy in lightning. We need to generate electrical energy from other sources. Scientists and engineers have invented devices that transform almost all other forms of energy into electricity. For example, hydro-electric generating stations transform the mechanical energy of falling water into electrical energy. Nuclear power plants (nuclear reactors) transform nuclear energy into electricity. Thermal-electric power stations transform the chemical energy in certain fuels into electricity. Other forms of energy that can be transformed into electrical energy include radiant energy from the Sun (solar energy), mechanical energy of wind (wind energy), and geothermal energy.

The production and consumption of useful energy have significantly improved our standard of living. This use of energy, however, is also responsible for many serious impacts on the environment, including air and water pollution and climate change. In the remainder of this chapter, we will examine the different ways in which useful energy is produced. We will also consider the advantages and disadvantages of energy production and use, and environmental impacts of energy use and production. We will suggest some ways to minimize the negative impacts.

Figure 5 Lightning contains a lot of electrical energy that scientists have not yet been able to harness effectively.

CHECK YOUR LEARNING

1. Compare the thermal energy of the Sun to geothermal energy in the interior of Earth by answering the following questions:
   (a) How does the Sun's energy reach Earth's surface?
   (b) How does geothermal energy reach Earth's surface?

2. Which naturally occurring source of energy are we not yet able to harness and use? Can you think of any others?

3. Which two forms of energy are most widely used in Canada? Give an example of how each form of energy is used.

AWESOME SCIENCE

Cooling Downtown Toronto with Deep Lake Water

In the middle of the day in summer, temperatures in Toronto (Figure 1) can reach 40 °C. As a result, air conditioners run all day to provide a comfortable environment for people who live and work downtown in tall buildings. Most of these buildings do not have windows that open. Air conditioning systems are expensive and require lots of electricity to operate. The City of Toronto has recently installed a new air conditioning system called Enwave. Enwave is a Deep Lake Water Cooling System that uses cool water from Lake Ontario to remove thermal energy from some buildings in the downtown core.

Figure 1 Downtown Toronto

Cold water is more dense than warm water. During the winter months, cold, dense water on the surface of Lake Ontario sinks. Warmer, less dense water from below the cold water moves toward the surface to take its place. As a result of this, there is a layer of cold water deep in the lake in the spring and summer months, when city temperatures become very warm.

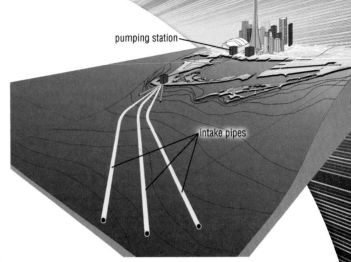

Figure 2 The three intake pipes of Enwave collect water from far and deep in Lake Ontario.

Enwave has three large intake pipes that extend 5 km off the shore of Lake Ontario and 83 m below the surface (Figure 2). Here, the temperature of the lake water is 4 °C all summer long.

The cool water is transported through the pipes to a pumping station that uses some of the cold lake water to cool buildings. The rest of the water is used for normal distribution in the city's water supply.

In 2007, 27 buildings, including the Air Canada Centre, the Metro Toronto Convention Centre, and the TD Centre, were already using the Enwave system. Eventually, Enwave will cool up to 100 large buildings in downtown Toronto.

The Enwave system uses 90 % less electricity than the air conditioning systems that it replaces. This results in millions of dollars in financial savings. The Enwave system also produces far lower greenhouse gas emissions due to reduced electricity consumption.

To learn more about Enwave,
Go to Nelson Science

Conventional Energy Sources

Thermal-electric power plants, hydro-electric power plants, and nuclear power plants supply most of the electrical energy used in Ontario. These three methods of producing electricity are often referred to as **conventional energy sources**. This means that they are the more traditional or more commonly used sources of electrical energy. Why are these conventional energy sources so widely used? What advantages and disadvantages do they have compared to other energy sources? Think about these questions in this section.

conventional energy source:
a source of energy that has been widely used for many years

Hydro-Electric Energy

Electrical energy is produced in hydro-electric power plants from the energy stored in water behind a dam (Figure 1). As this water falls through the penstock, the water's energy of motion spins the turbines. The spinning turbines turn the electrical generator that transforms the water's mechanical energy into electrical energy.

renewable energy resource:
a source of energy that can be used indefinitely, without running out

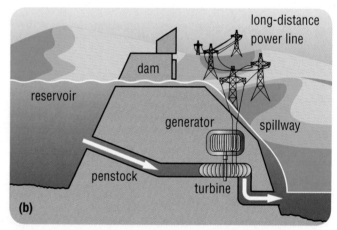

Figure 1 (a) A hydro-electric power plant on the Niagara River (b) Cross-section of a hydro-electric power plant

Hydro-electricity is a **renewable energy resource**. The water above the dam is replaced continually by natural processes (rain). We can obtain energy from a hydro-electric power plant almost indefinitely.

Hydro-electricity is often thought of as a "clean energy" source because hydro-electric power plants produce little to no pollution. This does not mean that they have no impact on the environment. The construction of a major hydro dam often results in the flooding of a large area of land (Figure 2). The dam also stops fish and other animals from moving up and down the river. Water in reservoirs above hydro-electric power plants may also get warmer and become lower in oxygen content than free-flowing river water. This also negatively affects the water's ecosystem.

May 15, 2006

July 17, 2000

Figure 2 The top photo shows water flooding the land above the Three Gorges Dam (China).

Another disadvantage of hydro-electricity is that the dams can only be built on certain sites. For example, although Ontario has many rivers and streams, there are few suitable sites for more large hydro-electric power plants.

Nuclear Energy

Nuclear energy is produced from the nucleus of the tiny particles that make up matter. The nucleus of a particle stores large quantities of nuclear energy. Canadian nuclear power plants use the nucleus of a substance called uranium as fuel. The nuclear energy in the uranium nucleus is transformed into thermal energy. This thermal energy is used to boil water to produce very hot, high-pressure steam. Then, the steam is used to turn the turbines of an electricity generator (Figure 3).

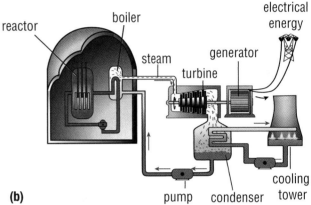

Figure 3 Nuclear power accounts for approximately 52 % of Ontario's electrical energy supply. (a) A nuclear power plant in Pickering, Ontario (b) Cross-section of a nuclear power plant

Like other sources of energy, nuclear energy has significant advantages and disadvantages. Nuclear energy is the most highly concentrated form of energy. Just 1 kg of uranium has more energy than 2000 kg of coal!

Nuclear power plants have some major disadvantages. They are complex and expensive to build and maintain. Nuclear fuel is highly radioactive. The radiation that it gives off can damage or kill living cells. Some forms of nuclear fuel are used in atomic weapons. This means that uranium mines and nuclear power plants must be designed and monitored to ensure safety. A number of serious accidents have occurred at nuclear power plants around the world. These accidents released large amounts of radioactive materials into the atmosphere and into nearby bodies of water. Unlike hydro-electricity, uranium is a **non-renewable energy resource**. This means that it is a resource that is in limited supply and could eventually be completely used up.

non-renewable energy resource: a source of energy that could eventually be used up

Another important disadvantage of nuclear power is that uranium remains dangerous for a very long time. Used nuclear fuel (called spent or depleted fuel) must be safely stored, and not allowed to escape into the environment. Radioactive substances break down into less harmful materials, but this process can take hundreds or thousands of years. We have to be willing to safely store nuclear waste. This is a very long and expensive commitment. The advantages and disadvantages of nuclear power are quite dramatic. Nuclear energy is one of the most controversial of all energy sources.

Thermal-Electric Energy and Fossil Fuels

In thermal-electric power plants, electrical energy is produced by burning coal, oil, or natural gas. In this process, the thermal energy released when these fuels are burned is used to boil water. This produces steam. The steam is used to spin the turbines of generators that produce the electricity (Figure 4).

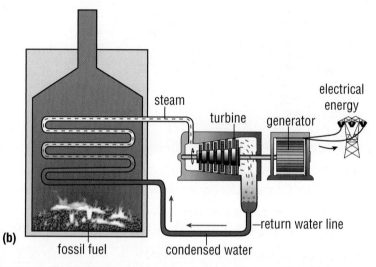

Figure 4 (a) The Lambton coal-fired thermal-electric generating station near Sarnia, Ontario (b) Cross-section of a coal-fired thermal-electric generating station

fossil fuels: concentrated sources of chemical energy such as coal, oil (petroleum), and natural gas that were formed deep in Earth's structure over millions of years from decayed and compressed plant and animal material

To learn more about fossil fuels,

 Go to Nelson Science

Coal, oil, and natural gas are concentrated sources of chemical energy called **fossil fuels**. Fossil fuels are formed from decayed and compressed plant and animal material from millions of years ago. Fossil fuels are extremely valuable in modern society. They are easy to transport and can be obtained at a relatively low cost. However, although fossil fuels are used around the world, they are only mined in certain areas, including parts of Canada. Because fossil fuels are so valuable and they are not found everywhere, international politics is very much involved in producing and distributing fossil fuels.

Fossil fuels are used to generate electricity. They are also used for heating. Natural gas and oil are burned in furnaces to heat many homes, schools, and commercial buildings. Fossil fuels also provide the energy for virtually all of our transportation needs. Without gasoline, diesel, and jet fuels, our economy would come to a grinding halt (Figure 5).

In Ontario, fossil fuels provide almost all of the energy used for transportation. Fossil fuels also provide one-quarter of the energy used to produce electricity, and about two-thirds of the energy used to heat residential and commercial buildings.

Figure 5 Oil refineries use crude oil as a raw material to produce gasoline, motor oil, diesel fuel, and jet fuel.

The Fossil Fuel Dilemma

At present, fossil fuels account for more than 80 % of global energy production. Fossil fuels are extremely valuable, but they have two major disadvantages.

First, fossil fuels are non-renewable. We are consuming them far faster than they can be replaced. This poses a big problem for society and the economy. Some scientists think that we will run out of oil and natural gas within the next few decades. We will need to find other sources of energy to take their place as our fossil fuel supplies run out. Alternative forms of energy are available, but not without problems.

Second, burning fossil fuels produces air pollution. This pollution contributes to acid rain and smog. Burning fossil fuels also causes an increase in the concentration of carbon dioxide. This results in climate change and global warming.

✔ CHECK YOUR LEARNING

1. Describe an idea in this section that is new to you. How does this idea add to your understanding of heat in the environment?

2. List three conventional sources of energy.

3. Briefly describe the difference between renewable and non-renewable energy sources, with examples.

4. Construct a chart to compare the advantages and disadvantages of fossil fuels, hydro-electricity, and nuclear power.

5. How might concern for the environment affect your choice of the best energy source to use?

6. Some conventional energy sources are non-renewable. Why is this important?

Global Warming

Recent studies show that Earth's average temperature is increasing. This increase in temperature will likely have a serious effect on Earth's climate (Figure 1). What are these effects? Why is the temperature increase happening now?

The Greenhouse Effect

Earth's atmosphere has been warmed mainly by radiant energy from the Sun for millions of years. Earth's temperature depends on how much energy is absorbed by the atmosphere, and on how much energy radiates into space. This is known as **Earth's energy balance**. This energy balance is influenced by the amount of incoming solar radiation as well as by the amount of energy that radiates from Earth back into space. If Earth's atmosphere is altered, this energy balance may tip in either direction.

The **greenhouse effect** is a process in which the Sun's radiant energy becomes temporarily trapped by Earth's atmosphere. Much of the Sun's high-energy visible light passes easily through the atmosphere to reach Earth's surface. The waves of light are absorbed by rocks, soil, plants, and oceans. Most of this absorbed energy is then radiated back into the atmosphere as low-energy infrared (IR) radiation. However, some of this IR radiation is absorbed by certain gases. These gases are called **greenhouse gases** because they trap thermal energy near the surface of Earth (Figure 2). This effect is like the glass of a greenhouse causing the temperature inside to rise. The most important greenhouse gases are water vapour, carbon dioxide, methane, and nitrous oxides.

Figure 1 Scientists have evidence that global warming is causing environmental changes around the world.

Earth's energy balance: the balance between the energy lost by Earth into space and the energy gained by solar radiation trapped by Earth's atmosphere

greenhouse effect: a rise in temperature resulting from certain gases in the lower atmosphere trapping radiant energy and warming Earth's surface

greenhouse gases: gases such as water vapour, carbon dioxide, methane, and nitrous oxides that trap energy in Earth's atmosphere

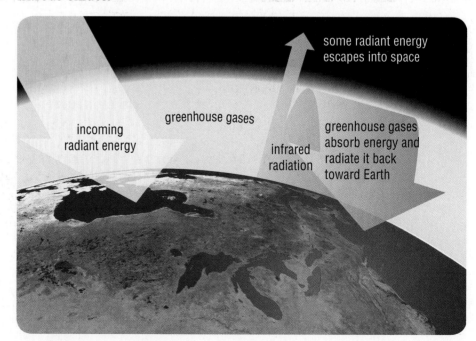

some radiant energy escapes into space

greenhouse gases

incoming radiant energy

infrared radiation

greenhouse gases absorb energy and radiate it back toward Earth

Figure 2 Certain gases create a greenhouse effect in Earth's atmosphere.

Sources of Greenhouse Gases

Greenhouse gases occur naturally and are a necessary part of our atmosphere. Without these gases, much more energy would be released into space. Earth would be too cold to support life. However, human activity is causing increases to the levels of some greenhouse gases in the atmosphere.

In the last two centuries, humans have burned large quantities of fossil fuels for power, transportation, and heating. Burning these fuels always produces carbon dioxide. Carbon dioxide is also released when humans burn forests to clear land for farming.

Mining fossil fuels causes methane (natural gas) to leak into the atmosphere from deep inside Earth. Cattle produce methane gas in their intestines and release it when they breathe. Worldwide, more than 1 billion cattle are raised by humans. This huge number of cattle means that methane is produced in large enough amounts to be a problem. Large garbage dumps (landfills) and some agricultural crops (such as rice) also produce and release methane gas.

Most nitrous oxides are produced during the breakdown of artificial fertilizers and animal manure, and by the burning of fossil fuels.

Table 1 summarizes the major greenhouse gases, their sources, and how their production is increasing. What do you think the effect of increasing levels of greenhouse gases might be on the environment?

LINKING TO LITERACY

Summarizing
Table 1 summarizes the information presented in the text. Read the table to review key information. Ask yourself, "How has the production of each gas changed over time? What is its contribution to global warming?"

Table 1 Major Greenhouse Gases Associated with Human Activity

	Carbon dioxide	Methane (natural gas)	Nitrous oxides
major sources related to human activity	• burning of fossil fuels for power generation, transportation, and heating • intentional burning of forest to clear land for farming	• agricultural practice—livestock emissions • fossil fuel processing and natural gas leaks • landfills	• agricultural practice—fertilizers • burning of fossil fuels
global trend in production			

The Link to Global Warming and Its Effects on Society and the Environment

global warming: an increase in Earth's global temperature due to changes in the atmosphere that enhance the greenhouse effect

Recent measurements show that the average temperature of Earth's oceans is increasing. The temperature of the air near Earth's surface is also increasing. This trend of increasing average global temperature is called **global warming**. Scientists believe that our increased production of greenhouse gases has affected Earth's energy balance and is causing a bigger greenhouse effect. This appears to be causing global warming. Scientists predict that during the 21st century, the average global surface temperature may increase by several degrees Celsius. This increase will almost certainly have many effects on Earth (Table 2).

Table 2 Effects of Global Warming

Effect	Details	
ecological disturbances	The world's habitats depend on the balance of rainfall and temperature. Less rainfall in some forests increases the chance of forest fires. Fires disrupt all of the organisms in that habitat. Changes to many habitats are expected to cause the extinction of many plants and animals. Some diseases and pests, once common only in the south, are moving north as the climate warms.	
rising sea levels	The melting of glaciers and polar ice and an increase in the volume of ocean water due to thermal expansion are causing ocean levels to rise. These factors will result in flooding of coastal areas, as seen in the photo on the right. This will impact shoreline ecosystems and disrupt many human populations. The economic cost of damage to buildings will be huge.	
crops and food supply	Some areas may become warmer and allow new crops to grow, while some areas where we now grow crops could experience drought. Overall, global warming is expected to reduce our ability to grow food.	

Taking Action on Climate Change

We choose to do many things that result in greenhouse gases being produced. Burning fuels to warm our homes or drive our cars is an obvious source of greenhouse gases. Less obvious is the use of electricity to light rooms and buildings, and to run computers. Some electricity is produced by burning fossil fuels in thermal-electric power plants. Even the choice of foods you eat for lunch can affect greenhouse gas production and global warming.

To learn more about how our food choices affect global warming,
Go to Nelson Science

We all need to make lifestyle changes that reduce our production of greenhouse gases. One way to do this is to consume less of Earth's resources, especially non-renewable energy resources. Switching to renewable energy sources will reduce our greenhouse gas emissions.

You can reduce your energy consumption every day. You can walk to school or take public transit instead of asking your parents for a ride in a car (Figure 3). You can use less hot water and turn off electrical devices when you are not using them. You can choose to eat foods that are grown locally rather than transported great distances by airplanes or trucks.

Figure 3 What steps can you take to reduce your energy consumption?

TRY THIS: The Green Team Action Challenge

SKILLS MENU: questioning, planning, observing, analyzing, evaluating, communicating

The Green Team Action Challenge gets you to track your daily actions to reduce greenhouse gas emissions. At the end of the week, you will tally your individual and team scores and see which Green Team has been most successful in reducing its environmental impact.

1. In your class Green Team, list as many Green Actions as you can think of. Focus on actions that you could take to reduce the production of greenhouse gases. Ask your teacher to approve the actions.

2. In the following week, take as many of the Green Actions as you can. At the end of each day, place a check mark for that day next to each Green Action that you have taken.

3. At the end of the week, add up the total number of check marks that you have entered for the seven days. Add up your team's total score.

A. Which Green Actions were the easiest to perform, and which were the most difficult? Explain.

B. Which Green Actions do you think had the biggest impact on reducing greenhouse gas emissions?

C. Why do you think more people are not already doing these actions every day?

D. Which of the Green Actions will you continue doing and why?

Scientists, researchers, and concerned citizens think that global warming and climate change are the most serious issues facing us today. There are problems associated with climate change and the looming shortage of fossil fuels. It makes sense for us to find ways to reduce our reliance on fossil fuels and to obtain the energy we need in other ways.

To learn more about global warming and climate change,
Go to Nelson Science

CHECK YOUR LEARNING

1. Draw a simple diagram to explain how the atmosphere and incoming solar radiation create a greenhouse effect.

2. (a) What is the main factor that affects Earth's average temperature?
   (b) What do scientists believe is causing the temperature of Earth's atmosphere to increase?

3. List at least three possible effects of an increase in the global temperature.

4. How might thermal expansion affect future sea levels?

5. (a) List at least three activities you perform that contribute to global warming by producing greenhouse gases.
   (b) List at least three changes that you could make in your behaviour to reduce your contribution to global warming.

9.4 Alternative Energy Sources: Wind and Wave Energy

alternative energy source: a source of energy that is not as common as conventional sources; alternative energy sources tend to be renewable and have few negative impacts on the environment

Conventional sources of energy have been used because they have been relatively inexpensive and easy to obtain until now. It would be difficult to imagine a cheaper fuel than coal. In many parts of the world, coal can simply be scooped out of Earth's surface and burned!

Alternative energy sources include wind, waves, solar energy, geothermal energy, and biofuel. These sources are not always as common or cheap as conventional sources of energy. Many alternative energy sources are renewable and have very few negative impacts on the environment.

Wind energy and wave energy are very promising alternative energy sources. Both are non-polluting and renewable. Winds are produced by convection currents. The currents are formed by the uneven heating of the land and water by the Sun. Water waves are often produced by the action of strong winds on the surfaces of lakes and oceans. Therefore, wind energy and wave energy are really products of solar energy.

Wind is a very old source of energy. Winds have pushed sailing ships all over the world for thousands of years. Windmills have ground grain for centuries. Today, engineers have developed devices called wind turbines that can transform the mechanical energy of wind into electrical energy (Figure 1).

Figure 1 Wind turbines can be set up on land or in shallow water—wherever they will get strong wind.

Modern wind turbines are efficient, economical, and environmentally friendly. They are initially expensive to install, but they require little upkeep and produce electricity at very low cost. Wind power is the fastest growing alternative energy source.

There are some drawbacks to wind power. Some people do not like the appearance of large wind turbines. Also, wind turbines can produce some noise pollution. Concerns have also been raised about the number of birds that may be killed by the moving blades. Recent studies suggest that this is not a significant problem as long as the turbines are not placed near bird migration flight paths.

Of course, to be useful, wind turbines must be installed where it is windy! In Ontario, the best places for wind energy are over and along the Great Lakes. In June 2006, Canada-based Trillium Power Energy Corporation announced plans for a wind power project called *Trillium Power Wind 1*. This project is to be located in shallow water approximately 15 km off the shores of Lake Ontario (Figure 2).

Moving water, in the form of waves and tides, is another source of energy. Engineers are working on harnessing this energy. They plan to use underwater turbines to transform mechanical energy into electrical energy (Figure 3). Capturing the energy from large waves and tidal flows is difficult. There are a few coastal locations around the world, including some Canadian locations, that are collecting energy from waves and tides.

Figure 2 The *Trillium Power Wind I* project will have over 140 wind turbines in Lake Ontario. When completed, the turbines will look similar to these turbines off the coast of Denmark.

To learn more about wind and water energy,

Go to Nelson Science

Figure 3 Underwater turbines may capture both tidal and flowing river energy and convert it into electricity.

✔ CHECK YOUR LEARNING

1. Describe an idea in this section that is new to you. What connections have you made between this idea and your understanding of heat in the environment?

2. Wind and water energy are renewable energy sources. Why is this so important?

3. Wind and wave energy may be used to generate electrical energy. What is the ultimate source of energy for both wind and water waves?

4. **(a)** What is the best geographic location for wind turbines?
   (b) What is the best geographic location for water turbines?

9.4 Alternative Energy Sources: Wind and Wave Energy

Alternative Energy Sources: Solar Energy

Solar energy is used as a source of energy in a number of ways. Buildings may use **passive solar heating** if there are large windows on the south-facing side (Figure 1). (Of course, homes in the southern hemisphere would need their large windows on the north side!) These windows allow sunlight to enter the building. Once inside, the radiant energy is absorbed by the floor and walls, where it is transformed into thermal energy. Passive solar heating helps reduce the need for other sources of thermal energy.

passive solar heating: heating caused by the passage of radiant energy through the windows of a building

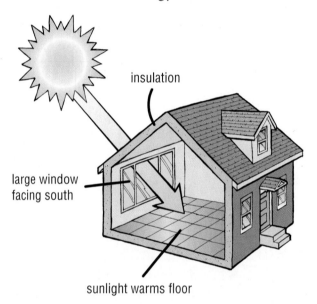

Figure 1 Buildings with large south-facing windows benefit from passive solar heating.

active solar energy system: a device that harnesses radiant energy from the Sun and converts it into a more useful form of energy

Active solar energy systems need equipment to trap the Sun's energy. There are two main types of active solar energy systems. In the first type, solar energy heats water running through panels placed on roofs. (Figure 2(a)). In the second type, photovoltaic panels or "solar cells" convert radiant energy directly into electrical energy (Figure 2(b)). Photovoltaic panels are an alternative form of electricity generation.

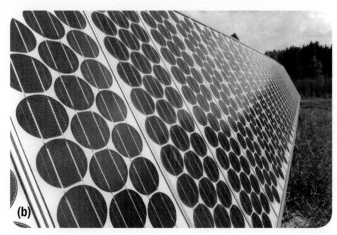

Figure 2 (a) A solar hot water system (b) A solar photovoltaic panel

There are a number of reasons why people are interested in solar energy. Conventional energy sources are getting more expensive. People are also getting more involved in conserving resources. Recent advances in technology have made large-scale solar energy projects cheaper. Some projects use large arrays of photovoltaic panels to generate electricity. In other cases, mirrors can be arranged to concentrate sunlight on a central tower. The tower produces steam for electricity generation. The Ontario government has recently approved a plan by OptiSolar Farms Canada Inc. to build what would be the largest solar photovoltaic plant in North America (Figure 3).

Solar energy has many advantages over other energy sources. It is renewable, there is a lot of it, and it is non-polluting. Compared with conventional energy sources, solar power is expensive. However, recent advances in the design and production of photovoltaic panels are reducing the cost of this very environmentally friendly source of energy.

Figure 3 OptiSolar Farms Canada Inc. plans to install more than 1 million solar panels at four farms near Sarnia, Ontario, by 2010. The project will produce enough electrical energy to power 6000 homes.

TRY THIS: Make a Solar Oven

SKILLS MENU: planning, observing, analyzing, evaluating, communicating

SKILLS HANDBOOK 4.C., 7.C.

In this activity, you will design and build a miniature "solar oven" to test how well sunlight heats a confined space. The solar oven is a box with a clear window to allow sunlight to enter (Figure 4). Large reflectors are often added to direct the sunlight into the cooking chamber. Painting the inside of the chamber black increases its ability to absorb energy.

Figure 4 A solar oven

1. Working with a partner or a small group, choose a simple solar oven design that you have found on the Internet. Or, you could design your own solar oven! It should use only materials that are easy to find and to work with.

Go to Nelson Science

2. Gather the materials you will need, and work as a team to build your solar oven. When it is done, have it checked by your teacher.

3. When all student groups have made their solar ovens, organize a class competition. On a sunny day, see how quickly each oven can melt an ice cube or heat a container of water to a specific temperature.

A. Submit a drawing or photograph of your solar oven.

B. Explain how each part of the oven helps to increase the temperature of the cooking chamber.

C. What are some of the advantages and disadvantages of using a solar oven to cook food? Use the knowledge you gained about conduction, convection, and radiation in the last chapter in your explanation.

CHECK YOUR LEARNING

1. Describe two differences between passive solar heating and active solar heating systems.

2. In Canada, which side of a building receives the most radiant energy from the Sun?

3. What type of energy is produced from radiant energy in photovoltaic panels?

9.6 Alternative Energy Sources: Geothermal Energy

Geothermal energy is the energy contained deep within Earth. Although the quantity of geothermal energy is virtually unlimited, it is not easily accessible everywhere. Few places on Earth are located near highly concentrated sources of geothermal energy. Volcanoes, geysers, and hot springs are sources of geothermal energy.

Geothermal energy is a non-polluting renewable energy source. Over 20 countries in the world use geothermal energy to generate electricity. These include the United States, Iceland, and New Zealand (Figure 1). In Canada, we have an experimental geothermal-electrical site in British Columbia, in the Meager Mountain–Pebble Creek area.

Figure 1 Iceland gets a lot of its electricity from geothermal energy.

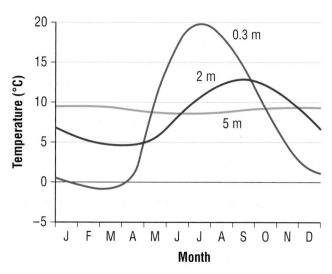

Figure 2 The ground temperature at different depths throughout the year in Ottawa, Ontario

Geothermal Energy and Heat Pumps

You do not need a power plant to take advantage of geothermal energy. The ground outside and around your house contains a huge amount of thermal energy. Around most of Ontario, the temperature of the ground several metres below the surface remains relatively constant throughout the year. It never freezes, even in the coldest winter months. For example, in the Ottawa area, the ground temperature at a depth of 5 m remains close to 9 °C throughout the year (Figure 2).

There is a relatively easy way to transfer thermal energy from the ground below a house into the house. You are already very familiar with this technology. It is the same device used in refrigerators, freezers, and air conditioners—a heat pump. A heat pump is a device that moves thermal energy from one location to another. Look at the functions performed by the different heat pumps listed in Table 1.

Table 1 Uses of Heat Pumps

Type of heat pump	Function
air conditioner	transfers, or removes, thermal energy from the air inside a building (or car) to the air outside the building (or car)
refrigerator or freezer	transfers, or removes, thermal energy from the air inside a refrigerator or freezer to the air outside the refrigerator or freezer
geothermal heat pump	transfers thermal energy from deep in the ground to the air inside a building

Many houses are now being built with geothermal heat pumps, rather than natural gas furnaces, for heating. A geothermal heat pump system consists of water-filled pipes that are buried underground near a building (Figure 3). A pump circulates the water through the pipes. In the winter, the water removes thermal energy from the ground and brings it into the building. Here, it is concentrated by the heat pump, and then circulated by an air delivery system. In the summer, the heat pump can be operated in reverse, so the water transfers thermal energy from the building back into the ground.

(a) (b)

Figure 3 A geothermal heat pump transfers energy to and from the ground to keep a house (a) cool in summer and (b) warm in winter.

Geothermal heat pumps are very efficient. They only use a small amount of electrical energy to transfer a very large amount of thermal energy. Heat pumps are better for the environment than the more common furnaces. They also cost much less to operate. Using a geothermal heat pump to heat a home can cost 80 % less than using a natural gas–fired furnace. The disadvantage is that installing heat pumps can be very expensive. 🌐

To learn more about geothermal energy and geothermal heat pumps,

Go to Nelson Science

✔ **CHECK YOUR LEARNING**

1. Describe an idea in this section that has added to your understanding of heat and the environment. Share your new ideas with a classmate.

2. What are two technologies that use geothermal energy?

3. Describe three different uses for a heat pump.

4. Describe the relationship between soil temperature and depth.

5. Describe two advantages and two disadvantages of using a geothermal heat pump to heat and cool a home.

Alternative Energy Sources: Biofuels

There is growing interest in producing fuels that can replace fossil fuels like gasoline. One possible option is the production of biofuels. **Biofuels** are fuels produced from virtually any kind of plant or animal material. Grain crops, such as corn, can be grown and then processed to make ethanol (Figure 1). When ethanol is burned, it releases carbon dioxide into the air. Carbon dioxide contributes to global warming. However, this release of carbon dioxide is partially balanced by the carbon dioxide that is removed from the air when the corn plants are growing. (All plants absorb carbon dioxide from the air during the process of photosynthesis.) Plants can be grown and harvested year after year. Therefore, biofuels are a renewable source of energy. Biofuels can even be made from waste plant or animal materials, such as wood chips or used frying oil from fast-food restaurants.

biofuel: a liquid fuel, such as ethanol, produced from plant or animal material

Biofuels offer several advantages over many other energy sources. Plants can be grown wherever there is adequate soil and water, and suitable weather conditions. Biofuels are also fairly inexpensive to produce. The technology that converts the plant material to clean, purified fuels is not as expensive as other energy sources (for equivalent energy production).

Unfortunately, crops such as corn often require large quantities of pesticides, chemical fertilizers, and fuel for farm equipment. It can actually take more fossil fuel energy to grow, harvest, and process the crops than is obtained when the biofuels are burned! Biofuel crops also require agricultural land. A large demand for biofuels could take up farmland needed to grow food crops. The price of food could rise because fewer food crops are grown.

Figure 1 Ethanol is a biofuel that can be used in vehicles powered by a fossil fuel.

CHECK YOUR LEARNING

1. What raw materials can be used to produce biofuels?

2. Why are biofuels becoming a popular alternative source of energy?

3. List two possible disadvantages of using biofuels.

More Nuclear Power?

The demand for electricity in Ontario is increasing much faster than the supply. The Government of Ontario has pledged to provide Ontario with "a safe, clean, reliable, secure, and affordable supply of electricity."

SKILLS MENU

☐ Defining the Issue
☑ Researching
☑ Identifying Alternatives
☑ Analyzing the Issue
☑ Defending a Decision
☑ Communicating
☑ Evaluating

The Issue

To meet Ontario's growing demand for electricity, the provincial government plans to spend about $45 billion to build several new nuclear power generating stations (Figure 1).

Goal

Review and evaluate the Ontario government's plans for providing energy to the people of Ontario, including its plans for taking advantage of conventional and alternative forms of energy production.

Gather Information

SKILLS HANDBOOK
3., 7.C.

Work in a small group to learn more about the provincial government's plans for supplying electrical energy. Learn more about the reactions of a variety of stakeholders to the government's proposals.

Go to Nelson Science

Figure 1 Darlington Nuclear Generating Station is located in Durham Region, 70 km east of Toronto.

Identify Solutions

SKILLS HANDBOOK
3.J.6., 3.K.

Consider the following strategies to help you identify solutions:
• Conduct a cost-benefit analysis to assess the social, environmental, and economic costs and benefits of the Ontario government's plans.
• Conduct library or Internet research to compare Ontario's energy supply plans with the plans of other provinces.
• Survey your classmates and family to determine their opinions on these issues.

Make a Decision

Review and evaluate the provincial government's energy plans. Which programs should it continue with? Which should it abandon? Which new strategies should it adopt? What criteria will you use to decide on your recommendations?

Communicate

Write an article to send to a school or community newspaper. Your article should summarize the information and opinions that you have researched, evaluate the government's current energy program plans, and recommend the best solution for Ontario's energy future.

Heat Sources in the Environment

BIG Ideas

☐ Heat is a form of energy that can be transformed and transferred. These processes can be explained using the particle theory of matter.

☑ There are many sources of heat.

☑ Heat has both positive and negative effects on the environment.

Looking Back

There are different types of energy and different sources of energy.

- We classify energy sources as conventional or alternative, and as renewable or non-renewable.
- Energy sources include the Sun (solar energy); Earth's interior (geothermal energy); fossil fuels and biofuels (chemical energy); particles (nuclear energy); and wind energy, wave energy, and waterfalls (mechanical energy).

Technological devices allow us to transform one type of energy into another.

- Energy from a variety of sources is transformed into electricity in electricity generators.
- Electricity can be transformed into many useful forms of energy, including radiant energy, thermal energy, and mechanical energy.

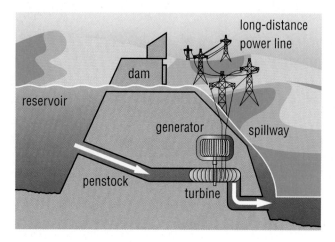 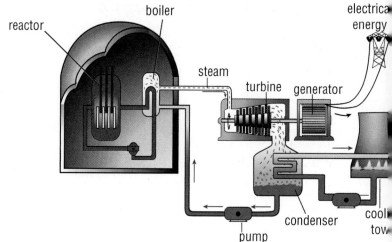

The human production of greenhouse gases is causing changes in global climate.

- The major greenhouse gases are water vapour, carbon dioxide, methane, and nitrous oxides.
- Greenhouse gases are produced by mining and burning fossil fuels, raising cattle, and growing certain crops (for example, rice).
- The increase in greenhouse gases in the atmosphere is altering Earth's energy balance, leading to global warming.
- Global warming has significant impacts on society and the environment.

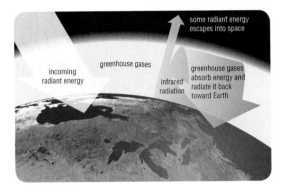

VOCABULARY

solar energy, p. 230

friction, p. 231

conventional energy source, p. 234

renewable energy resource, p. 234

non-renewable energy resource, p. 235

fossil fuels, p. 236

Earth's energy balance, p. 238

greenhouse effect, p. 238

greenhouse gases, p. 238

global warming, p. 240

alternative energy source, p. 242

passive solar heating, p. 244

active solar energy system, p. 244

biofuel, p. 248

There are significant advantages and disadvantages to using conventional and alternative energy sources.

- Advantages of conventional energy sources are that they are well established and relatively inexpensive, and there are well-developed technologies for their production and use. Disadvantages include pollution (greenhouse gases from fossil fuels), lack of suitable rivers (for hydro-electricity), and long-term storage (for nuclear energy).
- Advantages of alternative energy sources are that many of them are non-polluting, produce no dangerous products that need special storage, and are renewable. Disadvantages include a lack of established technologies for production and use, and high initial costs.

The choices we make in everyday life significantly affect the environment.

- Our everyday activities affect the quantity of greenhouse gases that enter the atmosphere. This affects global warming, which in turn affects society and the environment.
- We can choose activities that reduce our impact on the environment.

The skills of scientific inquiry can be used to investigate conventional and alternative energy sources.

- Analysis skills can be used to determine the impacts of using conventional and alternative sources of energy

What Do You Remember?

1. (a) List four fossil fuels.

   (b) Why are these fuels called fossil fuels?

   (c) What form of energy do fossil fuels contain?

   (d) What forms of energy are produced when fossil fuels burn? K/U

2. (a) Why is hydro-electric power considered a "clean" source of energy (Figure 1)?

   (b) Why is hydro-electric power considered a renewable source of energy?

   (c) Why do hydro-electric power plants produce only about 3 % of the electrical energy in the world today? K/U

Figure 1

3. Describe how the energy in uranium is used to produce electrical energy in a nuclear power plant. K/U

4. How is the greenhouse effect affecting Earth's energy balance? Explain. K/U

5. Identify four greenhouse gases and one common source for each gas. K/U

6. How may global warming lead to the flooding of coastal areas around the world? K/U T/I

7. Describe two ways in which home builders may take advantage of passive solar heating. T/I

8. (a) Name a heat pump that you use every day at home.

   (b) What is a geothermal heat pump, and how does it work? K/U T/I A

What Do You Understand?

9. Why are fossil fuels the most common source of energy for heating and transportation today? K/U A

10. What are some possible effects of an increase in the global temperature? Can you think of other effects not mentioned in the chapter? If so, what are they? K/U T/I

11. How might your choice of the best energy source depend on your geographic location? K/U T/I

12. A family is deciding whether to install a geothermal heat pump to warm and cool their home. State and explain two financial considerations that they need to take into account when making this decision. T/I A

13. Describe the role of radiant energy in heating and cooling Earth. Explain how greenhouse gases affect the transmission of radiated heat through the atmosphere. K/U

14. Imagine that you are planning to plant a row of tall trees alongside your house to help keep your house warmer in winter.

    (a) Would you plant deciduous trees or evergreens? Why?

    (b) Would you plant the trees on the north or south side of the building? Why? K/U T/I A

15. You are planning to install solar hot water panels on the roof of your home.

    (a) Would you install the panels on the side of the roof that faces south or on the side of the roof that faces north? Explain.

    (b) What type of energy transformation will occur in the panels?

    (c) How will this help reduce the greenhouse effect and global warming? K/U T/I A

16. Large solar energy or wind energy projects may involve hundreds of photovoltaic panels or wind turbines in one area. Currently, both options are relatively expensive methods for generating electrical energy. Describe two benefits and one additional drawback for each of these methods of producing electrical energy. K/U T/I A

17. (a) What is a biofuel? Provide one example.

   (b) State one similarity and one difference between biofuels and fossil fuels.

   (c) State one advantage and one disadvantage of using biofuels as an energy source. T/I

18. (a) In what ways does your choice of foods contribute to global warming?

   (b) What can you do to reduce your contribution to global warming, yet still get enough to eat? T/I A

Solve a Problem!

19. Research the types of plants that are good candidates for biofuel production in Canada. T/I

Create and Evaluate!

20. We use incandescent light bulbs as a source of radiant energy (light), but they primarily produce thermal energy instead. Describe an alternative to incandescent light bulbs and explain why it is a better or worse alternative. K/U A

21. Your family is building a new home. Present a case for installing a geothermal heat pump. In your discussion, be sure to include the benefits and costs from both an environmental perspective and an economic perspective. K/U A

22. Make a case for (or against) using rural land or marginal land-use areas for wind turbine farms. K/U A

23. (a) Some people feel quite strongly about nuclear energy. Why do you think the people in Figure 2 are protesting?

   (b) Do you promote this type of action? Why or why not? A

Figure 2

Reflect on Your Learning

24. (a) How do you feel about the issue of climate change? Discuss your feelings about climate change with a classmate. Identify similarities and differences in your feelings.

   (b) How do your feelings about climate change affect your ability to learn about climate change?

   (c) How do you think climate change will affect your future? How concerned are you? Discuss your concerns with a classmate or teacher.

25. Think back to the Key Question on the first page of this chapter.

   (a) In a brief paragraph, answer the Key Question. You may use diagrams.

   (b) Write one or two more questions about the topic of this unit that you would like to explore.

Designing an Energy-Efficient Doghouse

Background

Choosing the best materials is important when you are planning a building project. Insulation can slow down the transfer of thermal energy through the walls of a building. If the designer wants to keep the building cool, she or he might choose to paint the building a light colour, or use a material on the outside walls that is shiny. The designer must consider form and function.

Scenario

The K-9 Doghouse Company is holding a design competition to develop a new doghouse. The company is looking for a doghouse that will keep a dog comfortably warm during the winter months and cool during the summer.

Design Brief

Designers must build a prototype of a doghouse that is designed to keep a dog warm during the winter and cool during the summer. The prototype must not exceed 15 cm × 15 cm in floor area, and 15 cm in height, inside. There must be a doorway. Designers are encouraged to use materials efficiently, to keep the doghouse affordable, and to minimize negative effects on the environment (Figure 1). All materials must be safe for use in the classroom and home.

Research and Consider

SKILLS HANDBOOK
4.B.3., 4.C.

Before designing your doghouse, research different types of materials. Remember that energy can be transferred by conduction, convection, and radiation.

Figure 1 Your doghouse must be affordable, with minimal effects on the environment.

Draw sketches of designs for your doghouse. Your sketches should show the structure, dimensions, and types of materials to be used. Keep in mind the comfort and safety of the dog when designing and choosing materials.

Plan and Construct

SKILLS HANDBOOK
4.B.4.

Choose one of your designs and build a prototype doghouse for the design competition. Before building, you should do the following:

- Complete a scale drawing of the doghouse.
- Produce a list of equipment and materials to be used during construction.
- Create a step-by-step plan for building the prototype.

- Produce a list of job responsibilities for each team member (if you are working in a team).
- Ask your teacher to approve the list of materials and the building plan before you begin.

Test and Modify

SKILLS HANDBOOK
4.B.5., 4.B.6.

Test the doghouse prototypes using the procedures in Table 1:

Table 1   Cold Weather and Warm Weather Tests

Cold weather test	Warm weather test
1. Measure the temperature inside the doghouse at room temperature and record it as the initial (comfortable) temperature. Leave a thermometer inside the doghouse.	Repeat the procedure for the cold weather test, except put the doghouse in direct sunlight for 10 min.
2. Put the doghouse prototype into a freezer for 10 min.	
3. Remove the doghouse prototype from the freezer and quickly read the thermometer inside the doghouse. Record this temperature as the final doghouse temperature.	
4. If the temperature of your doghouse changed to an uncomfortable temperature during the trial, work with your team to make modifications to the design.	
5. Build your redesigned prototype and retest it.	

Evaluate

Answer the following questions:
1. Which elements of the doghouse design prevented the inside temperature from dropping too quickly when the prototype was placed in the freezer?
2. Which elements of the doghouse design kept the inside temperature comfortable when the prototype was placed in direct sunlight?
3. Compare the test results from your doghouse with those of other prototypes. Give reasons for the outcome.

Communicate

SKILLS HANDBOOK
8.A.7., 8.B.

Make an oral presentation to the "Board of Directors" of K-9 Doghouse Company that points out the pros and cons of your design. You need to convince the Board that the prototype deserves to be mass-produced. Create a poster that features a scale drawing of your doghouse design, highlights the ways in which the doghouse prevents heat loss and overheating, and displays the results of the cold weather and warm weather tests.

Assessment

You will be assessed on how well you

- state the design problem or challenge
- identify several possible design solutions
- make sketches of several possible designs
- develop a plan for building a prototype, based on one of your possible designs
- build a prototype based on one of your designs

- test your prototype and record observations, make modifications, or identify modifications that could be made to improve the effectiveness and efficiency of the prototype
- evaluate your prototype according to your observations and the criteria
- use the concepts and terminology of the unit to communicate the development and testing of your prototype

Heat in the Environment

Make a Summary

During this unit, you have learned many new concepts about heat and its effects on the environment. The Chapter Review for each chapter lists the new words and terms that you learned. In this activity, you will use those words to complete a series of activities.

Equipment and Materials

- markers
- sticky tape or glue
- sticky notes or small pieces of paper
- chart paper

SKILLS HANDBOOK
7.C.

Procedure

1. Form a team of three or four people.

2. Work together to write each of the vocabulary words on the sticky notes. Write one word (or one term) only on each note.

3. Place a piece of chart paper in the centre of your team. Share the vocabulary words equally among team members.

4. Organize the words into two to five logical groupings on the chart paper. You can use any criteria you like to put the words into groups.

5. Once your team agrees on how the words are grouped, stick the words in place on the chart paper.

6. Write a title above each group that describes why the words are in that particular group.

7. Below each list of words, write one sentence that describes an important idea from the unit that is associated with that group of words.

8. Use these sentences as the basis of a paragraph or two, summarizing your learning in this unit.

Unit C Review Questions

The following icons indicate the Achievement Chart categories:	K/U Knowledge/Understanding	T/I Thinking/Investigation
	C Communication	A Application

What Do You Remember?

1. Which of the following types of energy is most commonly used for home heating?

   (a) chemical energy
   (b) mechanical energy
   (c) friction
   (d) solar energy K/U

2. Which form of energy transfer is primarily responsible for thunderstorms?

   (a) convection
   (b) conduction
   (c) friction
   (d) radiation K/U

3. Which type of rock is formed as molten lava cools?

   (a) metamorphic
   (b) sedimentary
   (c) igneous
   (d) all of the above K/U

4. The radiant energy of the Sun is directly transformed into electrical energy in a

   (a) wind turbine
   (b) photovoltaic panel
   (c) geothermal heat pump
   (d) nuclear reactor K/U

5. Decide whether each of the following statements is true or false. If the statement is false, rewrite the statement to make it true.

   (a) Heat is energy that is transferred from a cooler object to a warmer object.

   (b) Heated liquids expand much more than heated solids.

   (c) Visible light is a form of chemical energy.

   (d) Wind is caused by the transfer of energy through conduction. K/U

6. When a substance's particles absorb energy, what happens to the motion of the particles? K/U

7. A cup of hot chocolate is set on a table before you drink it (Figure 1). Suggest two different ways in which energy is transferred away from the hot chocolate, allowing it to cool. K/U

Figure 1

8. What invisible form of electromagnetic radiation is emitted by low-temperature objects like the human body? K/U

9. Matter can exist as a solid, a liquid, or a gas. Which state(s) of matter

   (a) has particles that are free to move long distances in all directions?

   (b) has the most effective forces of attraction between the particles?

   (c) efficiently transfers energy by conduction?

   (d) has a fixed volume, but takes the shape of its container? K/U

10. What causes lightning to form in a thunderstorm? K/U

11. Rearrange the following phrases into an order that describes the production of energy by a hydro-electric power plant:

    (a) Water flows into a river.

    (b) A generator turns.

    (c) Water is held in a reservoir.

    (d) Electricity is produced.

    (e) Water flows through a penstock.

    (f) A turbine turns. K/U C

12. Radiant energy from the Sun can pass through the atmosphere to reach the surface of Earth, and some of the radiant energy from Earth passes back through the atmosphere toward space. How is some of the radiant energy from Earth prevented from escaping through the atmosphere? K/U

What Do You Understand?

13. Explain how thermal energy is involved in each of the following situations:

    (a) A cool breeze blows from a lake onto a beach on a sunny summer day.

    (b) You clutch a cup of hot chocolate with your hands on a cold winter night.

    (c) A large thundercloud rolls with thunder on a springtime afternoon. K/U A

14. The thermal expansion of materials can be an advantage or a drawback. Provide an example of each. K/U A

15. How can you prevent the unwanted transfer of thermal energy in your home by

    (a) radiation?

    (b) convection?

    (c) conduction? K/U A

16. Scientists studying glaciers have found that the snow is contaminated with tiny specks of black soot released from factory smoke stacks.

(a) How could this observation help explain why glaciers are melting faster than predicted?

(b) Is the melting of glaciers an environmental concern? Explain. K/U A

17. When engineers design a device or structure composed of different materials, they consider how materials expand and contract. Why is this an important consideration? Provide an example. K/U A

18. On a particularly cold winter day, you hear a neighbour exclaim, "So much for global warming!"

(a) What does your neighbour mean by this statement?

(b) Is your neighbour's exclamation reasonable? Explain. K/U A

Solve a Problem!

19. You have just been selected to join a field trip to the Arctic in January. What type of clothing will you pack? Describe the properties of the clothing that you will choose. Explain your choices. T/I A

20. An adventure company wants to design a new camp stove to be used by backpackers to boil water while out on the trail. Using a small candle as a source of thermal energy, suggest a design that will transfer the greatest amount of energy from the burning candle into the water in a kettle. Draw a detailed sketch of your camp stove design. T/I A

21. To help keep pizza hot during delivery, restaurants put the pizza boxes in a delivery bag (Figure 2).

(a) How does the design of the pizza bag help to keep the pizza hot? K/U

(b) How could the delivery bag in Figure 2 be improved? A

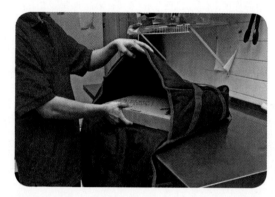

Figure 2

22. The Space Shuttle has a "Thermal Protection System" mainly consisting of thick dark tiles that line the bottom surface. These tiles protect the Shuttle and its occupants when it re-enters Earth's atmosphere prior to landing.

(a) Why would the bottom surface of the Space Shuttle warm up as it descends through Earth's atmosphere? K/U

(b) What form of energy transfer do you think the tiles are designed to prevent? K/U

(c) If you were a NASA engineer assigned the task of designing these tiles, what material would you use? What would influence your choice? T/I A

23. Methane is one of the greenhouse gases you read about in Section 9.3. Methane has a much higher global warming potential than carbon dioxide. One kilogram of methane warms Earth 25 times as much as 1 kg of carbon dioxide. Research the main sources of methane. How can you reduce the amount of methane released into the atmosphere as a result of your actions? T/I A

Create and Evaluate!

24. Most scientists believe that global warming is mainly caused by an increase of greenhouse gases, like carbon dioxide, in the atmosphere. Create a plan to make one change in your life that will reduce your greenhouse gas emissions. Evaluate your plan, and explain why it will have the desired effect. T/I A

25. Which devices in your home use the most energy? What can you do to reduce the amount of energy they use? Research more about the energy consumption of home devices by using the Internet or going to the library. Based on your research, evaluate which devices in your home would be best to replace or upgrade so that you can reduce your family's energy consumption. T/I A

 Go to Nelson Science

26. A scientist claims that "it takes more energy to make ethanol biofuel than you get out of it." Evaluate this claim by researching and comparing the amount of energy needed to make a litre of ethanol from corn and the energy we can get from the litre of ethanol. T/I

Go to Nelson Science

Reflect on Your Learning

27. Thermal energy has both positive and negative effects on the environment. Draw a table similar to Table 1 in your notebook. Complete the table by listing the positive and negative effects of thermal energy that you have learned. In the third column, list facts that you may have found particularly interesting or meaningful.

Table 1 Effects of Thermal Energy on the Environment

Positive	Negative	Interesting/ meaningful

28. Reread Section 9.3. Think about the issues presented in this section. Write a brief expository paragraph, a poem, or a lyric that expresses your feelings about these issues. If you prefer, you may draw a cartoon, compose a poster, or write a slogan. Share your composition with a classmate and discuss common interests and concerns.

29. The particle theory is a model that helps us visualize an idea.

(a) How did using a model (the particle theory) help you as you learned about how energy affects matter?

(b) What are the disadvantages of using a model like the particle theory?

(c) How have you used this model to help make sense of the things you see in the world around you?

UNIT D

FORM AND FUNCTION

Look around you. You might see a desk, a chair, or a TV. Look out the window and you might see a building, a car, or a bird's nest. Each of these objects has a particular shape and accomplishes a particular task. A chair must be comfortable and support the person who sits in it. A car must safely carry passengers and cargo in all weather conditions. A bird's nest must hold eggs and chicks far from the reach of predators. A waterslide has to be fun and exciting, but must also be safe for riders. Buildings are designed to keep bad weather out and to be strong and stable, but they may also be interesting to look at.

How are structures built to perform tasks? How can structures be built to be safe, comfortable, long lasting, and attractive? What should we do with structures when they are no longer useful?

In this unit, you will learn about both the form and the function of structures and how they are related. You will also learn about how structures withstand forces and support loads. Finally, you will learn about the importance of considering many factors when designing and building structures.

BIG Ideas

☐ Structures have a purpose.

☐ The form of a structure is dependent on its function.

☐ The interaction between structures and forces is predictable.

RIDING THE BEHEMOTH!

I have been looking forward to this for months. I read on the Canada's Wonderland website last year that something big was coming. Well, it's finally here—the Behemoth.

On the day we finally go to Canada's Wonderland, I am so excited that I can hardly stand it. Seeing the Behemoth from the parking lot, I realize that everything about the roller coaster is true. Once we get into the park, my brother and I run to the Behemoth. Hundreds of eager thrill-riders are waiting for their 3 min and 10 s of airborne excitement. We join the line to wait with them.

While I wait, I wonder about how roller coaster designers come up with their ideas. How do they know what will be exciting, yet safe? The first drop of the Behemoth is about 70 m high and is a very steep 75°, but the only restraint on the ride is a lap restraint—there are no shoulder restraints at all! How does this work? Why won't I fall out when I go down that first hill?

We're now at the front of the line. As we sit in the very front of other Behemoth passengers, the roller coaster operator checks our restraints. My brother and I plan to keep our arms up the entire ride. As soon as we start up that first hill, I change my mind. I dig my nails into that lap bar and hold on for dear life! Click, click, click. We approach the peak of the first drop. Suddenly, we are speeding downward! I try to scream, but find that I can't! Tears stream from the corners of my eyes. We bolt up, down, round and round, and after eight deep plunges we come to a halt. As I try to figure out what I just experienced, my brother laughs at my new hairdo. It is out of control!

Build a Textbook Holder

Your chair is a structure that supports you when you are sitting. Your desk is a structure that supports your notebooks and your upper body when you lean on it. In this activity, you and a partner will use building rods to construct a structure that will support a textbook without falling over.

1. Your task is to build a structure, using "building rods," that supports a textbook at a height of at least 20 cm above your desk. Your structure should be able to stand on its own without tipping over. Think back to what you learned in previous grades about structures.

2. To make a building rod, roll a piece of scrap paper, 216 × 279 mm (8½ × 11 in.), tightly into a cylinder and secure it with tape. (Figure 1). You can attach building rods to each other with tape.

Figure 1 A building rod constructed out of scrap paper

3. Each building rod costs 10¢ and each metre of tape costs 50¢. Working in pairs, build your textbook holder for as low a cost as possible.

4. After completion, you and your partner will present your textbook holder and total building cost to the rest of the class. Explain

   (a) why you built your textbook holder the way you did

   (b) why it cost what it did to build it

Answer the following questions on your own:

A. How expensive was your textbook holder? How did you try to keep the cost to a minimum?

B. How did the total cost of construction of your textbook holder compare with that of other groups?

C. What parts of your textbook holder worked well? If you had the chance to build it again, what would you do differently to improve its performance? Why would these changes be effective?

D. Predict how you would change your textbook holder if:

   (a) the height of the textbook holder had to be greater than 20 cm

   (b) you had to support two textbooks at the 20 cm level

   (c) part of the textbook had to extend beyond the edges of the textbook holder

E. Test your predictions by building new textbook holders. Get permission from your teacher. Make sure you have enough time and materials.

Play Time Is the Best Time

All structures are designed and built for specific uses. Think about a playground. Each piece of equipment is designed to do something different. Slides are used for one kind of play, while swings are used for another.

Your task is to work with a partner to construct, test, and promote a piece of playground equipment. This task will consist of three parts:

1. **Design and Construction** Research how playgrounds are designed and built, and the factors that are considered when building a safe and interesting play area. Then, design and construct a model of a piece of playground equipment. Your model must be constructed to scale, be structurally sound, apply ideas you learn in this unit, and be safe for all potential users.

2. **Promotion and Advertising** Prepare an audiovisual advertisement for your playground equipment. Your ad must include audio (verbal) and visual components, such as a poster, a product brochure, or a radio broadcast or video clip. Your goal is to convince community organizations that are planning to build new playgrounds to use your design.

3. **Presentation** Present your multimedia advertisement to a group of your classmates. In your presentation, convince your audience that your playground equipment is
   - safe
   - environmentally friendly
   - structurally sound
   - fun for as many users as possible

Unit Task By the end of the Form and Function unit, you will be able to demonstrate your learning by completing this Unit Task. As you work through the unit, continue to think about how you might meet this challenge. Read the detailed description of the Unit Task on page 340, and look for the Unit Task icon at the end of selected sections for hints related to the task.

Assessment

You will be assessed on how well you

- meet the established criteria
- demonstrate an understanding of concepts, principles, and terminology
- carry out the plan using technical skills and procedures when necessary
- relate your finished product to society and how it could affect the lives of people

10 Structures in the World

▶ **KEY QUESTION: How do structures resist forces?**

Looking Ahead

- A structure is anything made of parts that are put together in a specific way for a specific purpose (or purposes).

- A force is either a push or pull on an object.

- Structures can be classified as solid, frame, shell, or a combination of these.

- Forces acting on structures have certain characteristics.

- The skills of scientific inquiry can be used to investigate the effects of forces on structures.

VOCABULARY

structure	solid structure
function	frame structure
form	shell structure
force	external force
gravity	internal force
mass	point of application
weight	plane of application
load	tension
dead load	compression
live load	torsion
dynamic load	shear

Inbox

New   Reply   Forward   Print   Send & Receive

From: Gordon

To: Dad

Subject: Three Gorges Dam—We finally made it!

Hi Dad,

When Mom first told me I would be able to come with her and the rest of the Canadian engineering team to the Three Gorges Dam in China, I thought I would be bored. When we first arrived at the dam, all I could do was stare—it's so huge! Even the engineers who know all about the dam are astonished at just how big it is. I definitely will not be bored on this trip!

First, we met with the chief engineer of the dam. He explained that the Three Gorges Dam on the Yangtze River was built to provide hydro-electric power for the people of China. It now provides almost 10 times more power than the generating stations in Niagara Falls. The power is clean and better for the environment than burning coal or using nuclear power.

Later, Mom explained that China had asked for help to assess the dam and all the problems it was causing. Over a million people had been moved from their homes. Thousand-year-old villages and temples were now underwater from when the river valley was flooded. One of the environmental specialists said the damage to the environment was really bad and was going to get worse. The fish and animals that depended on the Yangtze River were dying and algae were starting to bloom downriver. Rockslides and flooding could mean that even more people would have to be moved and lose their homes—maybe as many as 4 million people!

Seeing the dam was really thrilling, Dad. The dam is probably one of the most amazing engineering feats of this century (Mom said that part). Now that I've seen the problems with the environment and the people losing their homes, I'm wondering if the power from the dam is worth it.

Gordon

LINKING TO LITERACY

Share Your Thoughts: Point of View
Take a few moments to reflect on the following questions. Then, share your thoughts with a partner.

1 How might points of view be the same or different for the engineers, the villagers, environmentalists, and Gordon?

2 What information does the text give you to support each of these points of view?

3 What can you infer to support each of these points of view? Use the information in the text and your background knowledge to make an inference.

4 Make a connection. How does this situation remind you of other environmental situations that have occurred in Canada?

5 Write two questions that you have after reading this e-mail. How will you find the answer to your questions?

Structures All Around Us

When you think of structures, you probably think of buildings, such as your home, your school, or the movie theatre. However, structures are more than just buildings. A telephone pole, a railway car, a cup, a pencil, and an umbrella are all examples of structures. A **structure** is something made of parts that are put together for a particular purpose. These objects can be as large and complicated as a car parking lot (Figure 1), or as small and simple as a saltshaker.

structure: anything made of parts put together for a particular purpose (or purposes)

Figure 1 The VW Autostadt structure in Wolfsburg, Germany, stores cars until the automated system retrieves them.

Structures can be human-made or found in nature. A coral reef, a spiderweb, and an anthill are examples of structures in nature. The bird's nest and beehive seen in Figures 2 and 3 are also structures in nature. What are some other examples of structures in nature you would recognize?

All structures have at least one main **function**, which is the task or purpose that the structure is designed to perform. However, function is only one feature of a structure. Another feature is the structure's **form**, which is the physical appearance of a structure. A structure's shape and appearance can be related to its function.

Figure 2 This Vitelline Masked-weaver's nest in Samburu National Reserve, Kenya, is an example of a structure.

function: the task or purpose of a structure

form: the shape and physical appearance of a structure

Figure 3 A beehive is an example of a structure found in nature.

Function

The main function of the roof of a house is to protect the house from weather conditions. The shape of a roof in an area of high snowfall is usually steep (Figure 4). The shape of the roof in a desert area might be flat because there is little rain and no snow to damage the roof (Figure 5).

Natural structures perform useful functions as well. What is the main function of a spiderweb? How many functions are performed by an elephant's trunk?

Figure 4 The steep shape of this chalet roof allows heavy snowfalls to slide off.

Form

Function is often the main purpose of a structure, but humans usually want their structures to look good, too (Figure 6).

Figure 5 The flat roofs on these adobe homes work well in areas with very little rainfall.

Figure 6 This distinctive building in Prague, Czech Republic, is known as the Dancing House. Does its form make you think of dancers?

Companies and organizations sometimes want people to pay attention to their structures. As with any structure, the form must be both safe and functional. The Burj Dubai in Dubai, United Arab Emirates (Figure 7) is an example of a very noticeable form.

Figure 7 On May 12, 2008, the Burj Dubai reached 629.18 m, making it the tallest human-made object on Earth.

Unit Task How will you take form and function into account when designing your playground equipment for the Unit Task?

✔ CHECK YOUR LEARNING

1. **(a)** What is a structure?
   (b) Name three examples of structures.
   (c) Describe one function for each structure in (b).

2. Why do humans consider the form of structures in their designs?

3. Describe the form and main function of
   (a) a baseball bat
   (b) an umbrella
   (c) a STOP sign

Forces

How would you move a stool? You could push the stool away from you (Figure 1(a)), pull the stool toward you (Figure 1(b)), or lift the stool upward (Figure 1(c)). Each case involves the application of a **force**, which is a push or a pull.

force: a push or a pull

gravity: the force of attraction between all objects; it is noticeable when at least one of the objects has a large mass; it is a non-contact force

Figure 1 The application of a force on a stool

To lift the stool, you must overcome the downward pull of Earth. This pull is known as gravitational force, or gravity. **Gravity** is a force of attraction that exists between all objects. Gravity acts differently on objects with different masses. The gravity that pulls objects of small mass together is very weak. Any movement of the objects toward each other is not visible. However, the gravity of objects with very large mass, such as Earth, is able to move an object with a small mass, such as an eraser, a large distance. This is why an eraser falls to the ground when it is released.

In most cases, a force can only be applied when objects come in contact with each other. For example, your hand must contact a ball to push it (Figure 2). However, gravity pulls a ball down to the ground without Earth and the ball coming into contact (Figure 3). Forces that push or pull things without contact include gravity, magnetic force (the force that pulls two magnets together), and electrostatic force (the force that causes static cling).

Figure 2 You must be in contact with a ball to apply force to it.

Figure 3 Earth and this basketball do not have to come into contact for gravity to act on the ball.

Forces that push or pull objects when the objects come in contact are called applied forces. The following are common examples of applied forces:

- your feet applying a downward force on a bicycle's pedals
- an oar of a boat applying a force on water (Figure 4)
- a hailstone striking a window
- a tennis racket hitting a tennis ball (Figure 5)
- your heart pushing blood through your blood vessels

Figure 4 The oar of a rower applies a force to water to move the boat.

Figure 5 When you hit a tennis ball with a racket, you apply a force to the ball. This makes the ball move.

Forces Have Magnitude and Direction

Every force has a strength and a direction. Common directions include up, down, left, right, and sideways. In diagrams, forces are represented by arrows. The thickness of the arrow indicates the magnitude, or strength, of the force. The arrow's point shows the direction of the force. Figure 6 illustrates three forces of different magnitudes and directions.

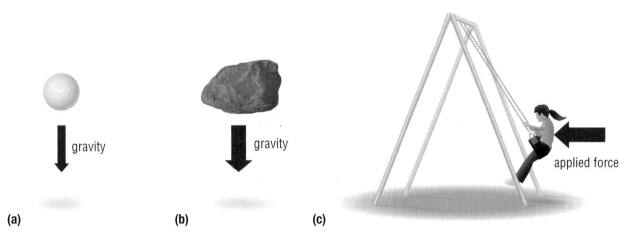

(a)   **(b)**   **(c)**

Figure 6 The direction of force in (a) and (b) is the same, but the magnitude is different. The magnitude of the force of gravity on a rock (b) is greater than that on a tennis ball (a). When someone pushes another person on a swing (c), the force applied is in a different direction than the force of gravity.

Distinguishing between Mass and Weight

In everyday speech, the words "mass" and "weight" are often used to mean the same thing. For example, a grocery store package might say that a hamburger patty weighs 200 g. In science, however, mass and weight have different meanings and different units of measurement. **Mass** is the quantity of matter in an object. Mass can be measured using a balance or a scale. Common units of mass are grams (g) and kilograms (kg). **Weight** is the force of Earth's gravity acting on an object. It is measured in newtons (N). The newton is named after Sir Isaac Newton, a famous scientist who lived in England from 1642 to 1727. A spring scale, like the one shown in Figure 7, can be used to measure weight. Some spring scales can also measure mass. Weight is the measure of a force, so it has magnitude and direction. A mass of 1 kg has a weight of nearly 10 N downward (toward Earth's centre).

mass: the quantity of matter in an object, commonly measured in grams (g) or kilograms (kg)

weight: the force of gravity acting downward on an object, measured in newtons (N)

To learn more about Sir Isaac Newton,

Go to Nelson Science

LINKING TO LITERACY

Questioning the Text

To maintain your reading focus and get more meaning from a text, ask questions as you read.

Begin by scanning the page and reading the title and headings. What questions come to mind?

Read the first paragraph. Stop and reflect on what you have read. What questions do you have? What more do you want to learn about this topic? What words do you find confusing?

Move to the next paragraph, and again, stop to ask questions. As you read and question, you will create a conversation in your head. Your conversation will help you to make connections and think more deeply about your reading.

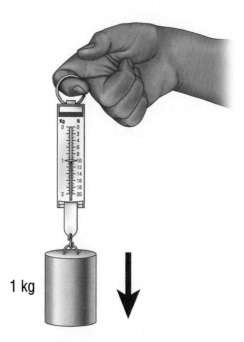

1 kg

Figure 7 A 1 kg mass has a weight of about 10 N. Weight is commonly measured with a spring scale.

The mass of an object remains the same anywhere in the universe, but its weight can change depending on its location. The weight of an object on Earth is very different from the weight of the same object on the Moon. For example, an astronaut with a weight of 900 N downward on Earth would weigh only one-sixth as much (150 N downward) on the Moon. This occurs because the Moon has a smaller force of gravity than Earth. Imagine how different high jumping or playing baseball would be on the Moon!

Loads

Structural designers have to consider all the forces that will act on a structure. For example, a bridge designer has to consider what will travel on top of a bridge and what forces will affect the sides and the underside of the bridge. A stable structure must be able to withstand all of the forces that act on it. The force acting on a structure is called the **load**.

Figure 8 illustrates how loads can be classified. Static loads result from gravity, which always acts downward. Static loads are further classified as "dead" or "live." **Dead load** is the weight of the structure itself. **Live load** is the weight of the objects that a structure supports. The bridge in Figure 8 is strong enough to support its own weight plus the weight of whatever crosses the bridge.

load: a force acting on a structure

dead load: a type of static load caused by the weight of the structure itself

live load: a type of static load caused by the weight of the objects it supports

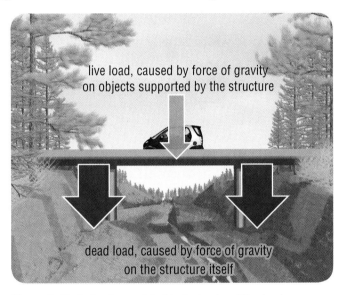

live load, caused by force of gravity on objects supported by the structure

dead load, caused by force of gravity on the structure itself

Figure 8 Static loads consist of both dead and live loads.

dynamic load: any load on a structure that is not caused by gravity; for example, wind or rushing water

In addition to static loads, a structure may be affected by dynamic loads. A **dynamic load** is a load caused by forces other than the force of gravity. Moving water and high winds are examples of dynamic loads that must be considered when designing structures. In Figure 9, the dynamic load is the rushing water in the flooded river pushing against the bridge. Other examples include a car that strikes a guardrail (think of both the guardrail and the car!) and the forces that occur when a baseball bat strikes a ball.

Figure 9 Rushing water striking a bridge is an example of a dynamic load.

✔ CHECK YOUR LEARNING

1. Provide four examples of forces that you have experienced today. Classify each force as either non-contact or applied.

2. Earth's gravity pulls down on a skydiver with 845 N of force.
   (a) What is the magnitude of the force of gravity on the skydiver?
   (b) In what direction is the force of gravity acting?

3. Distinguish between mass and weight. Include the definitions, units of measurement, how they are measured, and what they depend on.

4. For a playground swing, identify at least one example of
   (a) a dead load   (c) a dynamic load
   (b) a live load

Classifying Structures

What makes some structures similar and others different? We can group structures based on their function. Bridges serve one function (connecting two areas separated by a gap), while houses serve another (keeping people warm and comfortable).

Structures can also be classified using three basic forms: solid, frame, or shell. More complex structures are often combinations of these three forms. Each one of these forms can withstand different loads. Designers must consider the loads that the structures will experience before they can decide which forms to use.

Solid Structures

solid structure: an object that uses solid construction to support loads

A concrete dam, a wooden telephone pole, and a marble statue are all solid structures. A **solid structure** is strong, relying on solid construction materials to support loads. Large, strong structures have a large mass. The dam in Figure 1 is made of concrete that is very thick at the bottom where the load forces of the water are huge. A well-made solid structure can last for a very long time.

Figure 1 A dam is made of poured concrete, which is a mixture of sand, cement, and water that hardens to become very strong, solid concrete.

frame structure: a network of parts that supports loads

Frame Structures

Frame structures use a network, or skeleton, of materials that support each other (Figure 2). Your body's skeleton is a frame structure. Other examples are a goalie's net, a spiderweb, and the network of steel or wood beams supporting a bridge or a building (Figure 3). Frame structures can be very strong if their parts support each other and help resist forces. A single part of a frame structure cannot support the mass of the structure by itself.

Figure 2 A glass sponge has a skeleton composed of silica (glass).

Figure 3 The St. Mary Axe building in London, England, shows its frame structure.

The individual parts of a frame structure are connected to one another. These connections require special support so that they do not bend and collapse. A frame structure may have a membrane stretched over it (for example, a tent), but the membrane does not help support loads. Frame structures are widely used and can be very sturdy. They have the advantage of being lighter than solid structures.

Shell Structures

A **shell structure** is a structure with a hollow, curved shape. A bird's beak, a pop can, and a bike helmet (Figure 4) are all shell structures. Shell structures can be very light, and yet have a great deal of strength and rigidity (Figure 5).

shell structure: a hollow structure with a curved shape providing high strength and rigidity

Figure 4 A helmet is an example of a shell structure.

Figure 5 An egg is a shell structure too!

Combination Structures

The human skeleton is a framework of bones that hold muscles, tendons, and ligaments (Figure 6). The skull is curved, hard, and hollow like a shell structure. The femur, located in the thigh, can be considered a solid structure. The human body is a combination structure containing various solid, frame, and shell components.

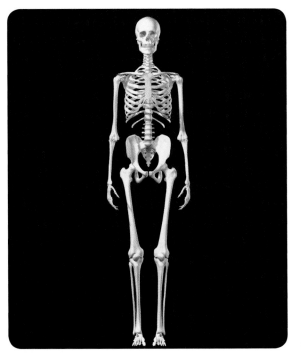

Figure 6 The human skeleton is a combination structure.

LINKING TO LITERACY

Summarize Your Understanding

Work with a partner to complete this activity. In your own words, briefly retell what you have learned about solid, frame, shell, and combination structures. Refer to the photos to support your understanding. Then, have your partner take a turn to share his or her understanding. Compare your summaries to make sure you included all the main ideas.

To learn more about classifying structures,
Go to Nelson Science

SKILLS MENU: observing, analyzing, communicating

In this activity, you will work with a partner to analyze the photographs of structures that appear in this textbook and classify them as solid, frame, shell, or combination structures.

1. Copy Table 1 into your notebook.

Table 1

Photograph	Classification (solid, frame, shell, or combination)	Justification
CN Tower		
Three Gorges Dam		
beehive honeycomb		
bird's nest		
Dancing House		
Burj Dubai		

2. With your partner, analyze the structure in each photograph. Does it match the definition of a solid, frame, or shell structure? Is it a combination structure? Record your observations in your table.

3. Choose three familiar objects from your classroom and add them to your table. Analyze their structure and classify the objects as solid, frame, shell, or combination. Remember to justify your classification.

4. Share your results with the class.

A. Did any of the classifications surprise you?

B. Did all the groups classify the structures the same way? How would you resolve any conflicting classifications?

Figure 7 This automobile chassis is a combination structure with both shell and frame components.

Most structures are combination structures. Houses, and most other buildings, have a solid foundation. They also have a frame of wood or metal that supports a shell of brick, concrete, wood, or metal. Other combination structures include cars (metal frame and a shell of plastic or metal) (Figure 7), some bridges (solid piers and steel frame girders), and domed stadiums (solid concrete walls and frame and shell roof).

Unit Task Which shape—solid, frame, shell, or combination—will be best suited for the design of your playground equipment?

✔ CHECK YOUR LEARNING

1. Classify each of these structures as solid, frame, shell, or combination: garbage can, airplane, hydro tower, pebble, basket, bicycle.

2. List the advantages and disadvantages of the three basic forms of structures (solid, frame, or shell).

3. The Cinesphere was the world's first Imax theatre (Figure 8). Classify the Cinesphere's structure. Justify your answer.

4. A turtle shell, the canopy of an umbrella, and the roof of a domed stadium are all curved. Classify each of these structures as solid, frame, shell, or combination.

Figure 8

External and Internal Forces

Designers must consider all forces that can act on a structure. For example, when architects are designing buildings in an area that experiences earthquakes, they must design the buildings carefully. They must use the right types of materials to withstand an earthquake and any aftershocks that may occur. If the area is also close to a coastline, then designers must also consider problems related to water acting on structures as well. If all possible forces are not considered, then buildings can collapse (Figure 1).

Figure 1 This building was destroyed by the earthquakes in Sichuan Province, China, in 2008.

There are two types of forces that designers have to consider. **External forces** are forces that act on a structure from the outside. Forces that act between two different parts of a structure are called **internal forces**.

External Forces

The most obvious external force acting on structures is gravity. On Earth, gravity always acts downward. Gravity is a non-contact force. Non-contact forces are those applied to an object by another object not in contact with it. Applied forces, or contact forces, also act on an object from the outside. You apply external forces when you push a swing, pull an elastic, or throw a ball. External forces on buildings include wind, earthquakes, the weight of people on the floors of the building, and the weight of the building itself. A structure is designed so that external forces will not cause it to break or fall over.

external force: a force acting on an object or structure from the outside

internal force: a force acting between two parts of a body

point of application: the location on an object where an external force is applied or concentrated

plane of application: an imaginary flat surface through which an applied force passes

To move a filing cabinet across the floor, you can apply an external force on one of its sides. Examine Figure 2. The **point of application** is the location on an object where an external force is applied. The **plane of application** is an imaginary flat surface through which the applied force passes.

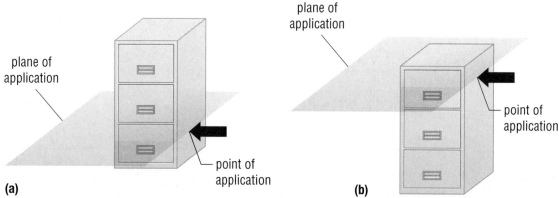

plane of application

plane of application

point of application

point of application

(a)

(b)

Figure 2 Illustrating point of application and plane of application of force applied to a filing cabinet

In Figure 2, the magnitude and direction of the applied force are the same. However, the point of application and the plane of application are different. If you push low on the cabinet, it will slide sideways (Figure 2(a)). If you push high on the cabinet, it is likely to tip over (Figure 2(b)). The point and plane of application make a difference in how an applied force affects a structure.

Another important external force is the force in the direction opposite to gravity. Think of the forces on you when you are sitting on a stool. You know that the force of gravity on you (your weight) is an external force that pulls you downward. However, if the force is pulling you toward the centre of Earth, why are you not moving toward Earth's centre? The reason is that the stool is also applying a force on you, pushing upward. The magnitude of the downward force (gravity) equals the magnitude of the upward force (stool on you) (Figure 3). This means that you are able to sit still.

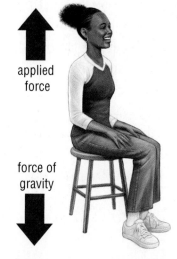

applied force

force of gravity

Figure 3 The upward applied force of the stool on the student is equal in magnitude to the downward force of gravity.

Internal Forces

Internal forces act between different parts of the same structure. There are four types of internal forces: tension, compression, torsion, and shear.

Tension

When you pull on an elastic band, the force of your finger pulling on the elastic band is an external force. This force creates an internal force called **tension**, which causes all of the particles of the elastic band to pull apart. Tension can act on a variety of objects, for example, a stretched skipping rope, a trampoline, an electrical power line, guitar strings, and the cables of a suspension bridge (Figure 4). You know that if an elastic band is stretched too far, it breaks. The particles of an elastic material can move apart only up to a maximum distance. This point is called the breaking point. If stretched to this point, the particles in an object break apart and can no longer pull the material back together.

tension: an internal force pulling the particles of an object apart

Figure 4 The main cables in a suspension bridge, like the Capilano Bridge in British Columbia, have tension forces acting on them.

Compression

An object that is pressed or squeezed experiences compression. **Compression** is an internal force that presses the particles of an object together. The springs inside a mattress undergo compression when you lie down on the mattress (Figure 5). Compression also occurs when you kick a soccer ball, step on the sole of your shoe, or lay your head on a foam cushion. Compressed objects usually return to their original shape after the external force is removed.

compression: an internal force that presses or squeezes the particles of an object together

Figure 5 These mattress springs have compression forces acting on them.

Torsion

Torsion acts in an object when the object is twisted (Figure 6). Torsion is evident when a skater twists in a jump, a washcloth is wrung out, and a doorknob is turned. Torsion can be created when both ends of a structure are twisted. Torsion can also be created when only one end of a structure is twisted while the other end remains stationary.

Shear

Shear forces occur when forces push or pull in opposite directions within an object. Shear forces usually result in an object being bent, torn apart, or cut. A strong wind that is blowing horizontally against a tree anchored to the ground causes shear forces inside the tree. These forces can cause it to bend or break (Figure 7). Scissors use shear force to cut paper in half. The blades of the scissors move in opposite directions and create two pushing forces against the paper, which result in the paper being cut.

torsion: internal twisting forces created in an object as a result of a twisting motion being applied to the object

Figure 6 This figure skater is experiencing torsion force as she twists her body in a spin.

shear: forces acting in an object as a result of pushes and/or pulls in opposite directions; usually results in rips or tears in an object

To learn more about internal forces,

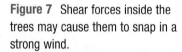
Go to Nelson Science

Figure 7 Shear forces inside the trees may cause them to snap in a strong wind.

✔ CHECK YOUR LEARNING

1. Classify these forces as external or internal:
   (a) shear
   (b) gravity
   (c) torsion
   (d) the force of the floor on your feet when you are standing

2. You are lying in bed.
   (a) List the internal forces that are acting on the mattress.
   (b) What is the external force acting on the mattress?

3. Explain the difference between the direction of force and the plane of application of force. Use a diagram to help you.

4. Figure 8 shows a solid block-shaped structure in four different situations involving applied forces (the arrows). Name the internal forces in each diagram.

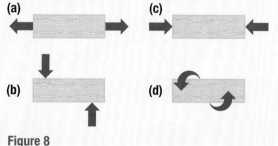

Figure 8

AWESOME SCIENCE

Tacoma Narrows Bridge: When Structures Fail

The Tacoma Narrows Bridge in Tacoma, Washington, was the third-largest suspension bridge in the United States when it opened on July 1, 1940. Its graceful, curved design was very attractive. However, this design also had the flaw of swaying and rippling in the wind. Residents dubbed the bridge "Galloping Gertie." People from hundreds of kilometres away would come to drive on the bridge to watch the cars in front of them disappear, and then reappear as the road structure rippled in the wind.

On November 7, 1940, a windstorm hit the Tacoma area. Winds of 67 km/h caused Gertie to twist in a torsional way (Figure 1). The left side of the bridge would rise and the right would fall, and then vice versa. Eventually, the bridge collapsed (Figure 2). Although there was no human life lost, there was one fatality—a dog named Tubby.

Figure 2 The collapse of the Tacoma Narrows Bridge

The Tacoma Narrows Bridge was rebuilt, starting in 1948. This time, however, engineers built a small scale model of the new bridge and tested it in a wind tunnel— a long, tunnel-like building in which models can be tested under conditions of high wind. The research showed engineers exactly why the first Tacoma Narrows Bridge collapsed. It also allowed engineers to determine how to avoid another such collapse.

As a result of the collapse of the Tacoma Narrows Bridge, all major structures today undergo a test in a wind tunnel. The wind tunnel demonstrates any problems with the design before the structure is actually built.

Figure 1 Blowing wind resulted in the torsional twisting of the Tacoma Narrows Bridge, photographed shortly before its collapse.

To learn more about the collapse of the Tacoma Narrows Bridge,
Go to Nelson Science

Modelling Internal Forces

If the internal forces in structures are too great, then the structure may fail or collapse (Figure 1). In this activity, you will model some internal forces that can affect the ability of structures to maintain their forms.

SKILLS MENU

- ☐ Questioning
- ☐ Hypothesizing
- ☐ Predicting
- ☐ Planning
- ☐ Controlling Variables
- ■ Performing
- ■ Observing
- ■ Analyzing
- ■ Evaluating
- ■ Communicating

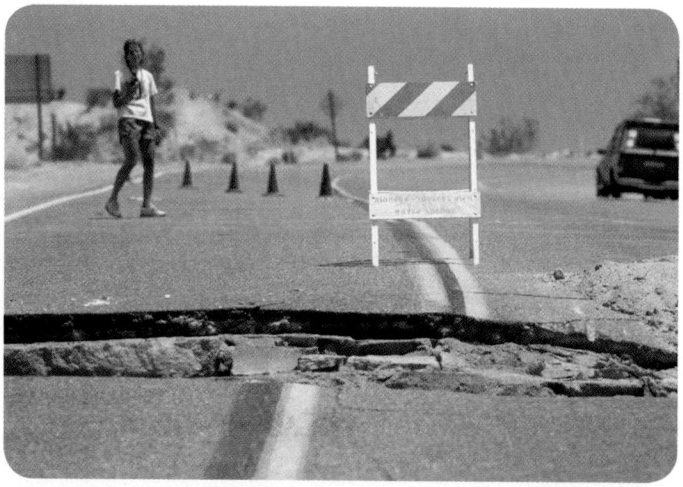

Figure 1 This road failed because of shear forces. An earthquake caused the two sides of the road to slide in opposite directions.

Purpose

To create models of the internal forces that act on structures.

Equipment and Materials

- permanent marker
- scissors (optional)
- 2–3 cellulose or synthetic sponges

permanent marker   scissors   2–3 cellulose or synthetic sponges

Procedure

Part A

1. Copy Table 1 into your notebook. Make sure to create enough room for your sketches.

Table 1

Internal force	Diagram of shape of the lines before force applied	Diagram of the shape of the lines as force is applied	Description of the effect of force on the lines of the sponge
compression			
tension			

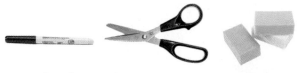

2. Use a marker to make a series of parallel, horizontal lines on the side of the sponge (Figure 2).

Figure 2 The horizontal markings on your sponge

3. Use your hands to squeeze the sponge from top and bottom. This creates compression forces inside the sponge. Observe any effects on the shape of the lines on the sponge. Record your observations, including a sketch of the sponge, in your table.

4. Using step 3 as a guide, design a method to determine the effect of tension on a sponge. Record your procedure.

5. Construct your model and test for the effect of tension using the same sponge as in step 2, or a new sponge. Record your observations in your table.

6. Using the sponge from step 5, apply a force on the sponge that creates torsion. Observe any effects on the spacing of the lines on the sponge after the application of this force. Record your observations.

Part B: Teacher Demonstration

7. Make observations as your teacher creates shear forces in a sponge. Observe any effects on the spacing of the lines on the sponge as it is being torn apart. Record your observations, including a sketch of the lines on the sponge, in your table.

Analyze and Evaluate

(a) Describe what happened to the spaces between the lines as you created each of the internal forces in the sponge.

(b) In which case(s) was the sponge able to return to its original form?

(c) In which case(s) was the sponge not able to return to its original form? Explain.

(d) Exchange your procedure for modelling tension with a classmate. Using a Venn diagram, compare the two procedures. Which procedure models tension more accurately? Justify your answer.

Apply and Extend

(e) Would your answers to (b) and (c) have changed if you had created the four forces in a rigid foam cup? Explain.

(f) Find an example of each of the four forces acting within structures in your home.

(g) Identify which internal forces are at work in each of the following:

    i)   the beams of a roof (Figure 3)
    ii) the support cables of a suspension bridge
    iii) a twisted plastic ruler
    iv) the pin that holds scissors together

Figure 3 What force is at work in roof beams?

Unit Task When designing your playground equipment, be sure to consider the internal forces that can act on a structure.

Structures in the World

Looking Back

A structure is anything made of parts that are put together in a specific way for a specific purpose (or purposes).

- Every structure has a function or task that it is meant to perform.
- Form is the physical appearance and shape of a structure.
- Humans often want structures to be attractive.

A force is either a push or pull on an object.

- Gravity is a force that pulls two objects together.
- The magnitude of force refers to the size or strength of a force.
- The direction of force is the direction in which a force is applied.
- The point of application of force is the point of contact between a force and a structure.
- The plane of application of force is the flat, imaginary, two-dimensional surface in line with an applied force.

Structures can be classified as solid, frame, shell, or a combination of these.

- Solid structures rely on solid construction materials to support and transfer loads to the ground (for example, a dam).
- Frame structures use a network of materials to support loads. Frame structures sometimes have sheets of materials stretched over them (for example, a tent).
- Shell structures have curved shapes that enclose a hollow space and provide support (for example, an egg).
- Combination structures contain a combination of solid, frame, and shell components (for example, the human body).

 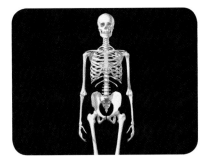

Forces acting on structures have certain characteristics.

- External forces act on a structure from the outside.
- Internal forces act between parts of the same object.
- The internal forces that act within structures are compression, tension, torsion, and shear.
  - Compression forces are created when an object is squeezed.
  - Tension forces are created when an object is pulled or stretched.
  - Torsion forces are created when an object is twisted.
  - Shear forces are created when an object is pushed or pulled in opposite directions, and the object bends, rips, tears, or snaps.

The skills of scientific inquiry can be used to investigate the effects of forces on structures.

- The four internal forces can be modelled using everyday materials.
- The effect of internal forces on structures can be observed using models.

VOCABULARY

structure, p. 268
function, p. 268
form, p. 268
force, p. 270
gravity, p. 270
mass, p. 272
weight, p. 272
load, p. 273
dead load, p. 273
live load, p. 273
dynamic load, p. 273
solid structure, p. 274
frame structure, p. 274
shell structure, p. 275
external force, p. 277
internal force, p. 277
point of application, p. 278
plane of application, p. 278
tension, p. 279
compression, p. 279
torsion, p. 280
shear, p. 280

Chapter 10 Summary **285**

CHAPTER 10 REVIEW

The following icons indicate the Achievement Chart categories: **K/U** Knowledge/Understanding **C** Communication **T/I** Thinking/Investigation **A** Application

What Do You Remember?

1. What is a structure? **K/U**

2. What is the main function of the following structures? **K/U**

   (a) an airport

   (b) an apartment building

   (c) a bicycle

   (d) a dam

3. Clearly distinguish between function and form. **K/U**

4. In your notebook, complete the following sentences by filling in the most appropriate word(s): **K/U**

torsion	dead	pull	magnitude
internal	matter	push	gravity

   (a) Force is defined as either a _____ or a _____.

   (b) Mass is the amount of _____ inside an object.

   (c) Your weight is due to the force of _____ acting on you.

   (d) _____ forces act between different parts of the same structure.

   (e) The strength of a force refers to its _____.

   (f) A twisting force produces _____.

   (g) The actual weight of a structure is known as the _____ load.

5. Would your mass or weight change if you went to the Moon? Explain. **K/U**

6. What type of internal force is created in a wet dishcloth when you wring it out? **K/U**

7. Classify each structure in Figure 1 as solid, frame, shell, or combination. Justify your choice. **K/U**

   (a)
   (b)
   (c)

Figure 1

What Do You Understand?

8. Choose a building in your community. Which factor appears to have been more important in its design: function, form, or both? Explain. **A** **C**

9. Describe how tension and torsion are different from one another. **K/U**

10. Which of the internal forces is represented in each of the examples listed below? Provide a second example of your own for each example listed. **K/U**

    (a) ripping a piece of paper towel off the paper towel roll

    (b) pulling on ropes to set up a tent

    (c) twisting the lid off of a container

    (d) squeezing the tire on a bicycle to check its pressure

11. You are being pushed on a swing. Use the terms "point of application" and "plane of application" to describe this activity. **K/U** **C**

12. Pick a structure and identify parts that perform a function and parts that provide form. You may want to use a diagram to organize your answer. **T/I** **A**

13. Which do you feel is more important, form or function? Explain how this applies to some of the products that you have purchased in your own life. **T/I**

Solve a Problem!

14. (a) Freezing rain has caused the electrical wires to sag in your neighbourhood (Figure 2). Clearly distinguish between dead load and live load in this situation.

(b) What can electric companies do to help prevent wires from breaking when ice accumulates on them? K/U A

Figure 2

Create and Evaluate!

15. Think of how you would design a science lab, the function of which is to allow students to perform investigations (Figure 3).

(a) In a small group, brainstorm advantages and disadvantages of each design. Summarize your main arguments.

(b) Compose a letter to the Director of Education to persuade her or him that your design should be considered in any renovation or new construction. T/I C

(a) Perimeter lab with outside benches

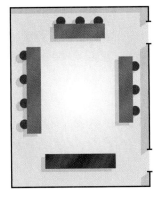

(b) Desk/Lab classroom

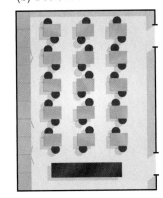

Figure 3

16. Reread the chapter narrative about the Three Gorges Dam. Pretend you are a member of the Canadian engineering team. Using your learning from this chapter, evaluate the dam in terms of form and function. K/U A

17. In the library or on the Internet, read the story of the Three Little Pigs.

(a) Explain how the Big Bad Wolf applies a force on the little pigs' homes. In a paragraph, use the vocabulary in this chapter to describe the force and the factor(s) that may have led to the collapse of each pig's home.

(b) What is the moral of the story in terms of the form and function of the structures commonly used in the construction of homes?

(c) Write your own brief children's story that describes forces acting on structures, and the effects of those forces on the structures. K/U A C

Go to Nelson Science

Reflect on Your Learning

18. Look at structures in your home and list examples of the four internal forces. Are you surprised at how relevant this is to your home? Explain.

19. Think back to the Key Question on the first page of this chapter.

(a) In a brief paragraph, answer the Key Question. You may use diagrams.

(b) Write one or two more questions about the topic of this unit that you would like to explore.

Structural Strength and Stability

> **KEY QUESTION:** What factors make structures strong and stable?

Looking Ahead

- A stable structure maintains its shape and position over an extended period of time.

- Beams, trusses, arches, and domes are used to help structures support loads.

- The skills of scientific inquiry can be used to investigate the factors that affect the ability of a structure to support a load.

- The skills of technological problem solving can be used to determine the most efficient way for a structure to support a load.

- Structural failure occurs when all or part of a structure loses its ability to support a load.

- The skills of scientific inquiry can be used to investigate methods used to ensure that structures are safe.

VOCABULARY

stability	cantilever
centre of gravity	truss
beam	arch
I-beam	dome
corrugation	structural failure

The Ritual of the Calling of an Engineer

In 1922, Canadian Herbert Haultain created a ceremony for new engineers. New engineers are asked to recite an Obligation to their profession. They also are given an iron ring to wear on their little finger. The ring is a symbol to new engineers. It reminds engineers of their pride in their profession and their responsibility to safety.

The idea that engineers needed to be more responsible may have come from the Quebec Bridge disaster. The Quebec Bridge collapsed in 1907, killing 75 workers. The cause was an engineering error. In 1917, the rebuilt bridge collapsed. This time, 11 people were killed.

Haultain wrote to author and poet Rudyard Kipling for help with creating the ceremony. Kipling responded with *The Ritual of the Calling of the Engineer*. The first ceremony was held in 1925. The yearly ceremony continues to this day.

The words of the Obligation of *The Ritual of the Calling of the Engineer* are secret. However, Kipling is well known for his poetry on engineering and building subjects. This example was written in 1911:

Modern Machinery

We were taken from the ore-bed and the mine,
We were melted in the furnace and the pit—
We were cast and wrought and hammered to design,
We were cut and filed and tooled and gauged to fit.
Some water, coal, and oil is all we ask,
And a thousandth of an inch to give us play:
And now, if you will set us to our task,
We will serve you four and twenty hours a day!
(*"The Secret of the Machines," verse 1*)

LINKING TO LITERACY

Making Inferences
Texts can have "literal" meanings or "inferred" meanings. "Literal" means that the text means exactly what it says. "Inferred" means that a text says something, but really means something more.

Readers make inferences by thinking about what they have read in a text. Then, they make a connection to what they already know to make an informed guess about what a text really means. See if you can infer the meaning of the text for each situation.

1 In 1922, Herbert Haultain created a ceremony for new engineers. What inference does this text suggest for why he created this ceremony?

2 The words of the Obligation are secret. Kipling wrote this example of a poem about something that engineers would build. What can you infer about the words in the real Obligation?

3 The poem that is included in this text is from *The Secret of the Machines*. This is verse 1. What can you infer about the actual length of this poem?

11.1 Stability of Structures

Imagine you are standing on a public bus (Figure 1). The bus is speeding up and slowing down. You probably would feel more stable with your feet flat on the floor and spread apart. Why is this so?

LINKING TO LITERACY

Reading for Meaning
When reading science texts, look for explanations or definitions of difficult or scientific words as you read. Sometimes, explanations are in the main text; sometimes they will be given in a sidebar or caption under a picture. Locate two definitions that are given on this page. How do these help you to better understand your reading?

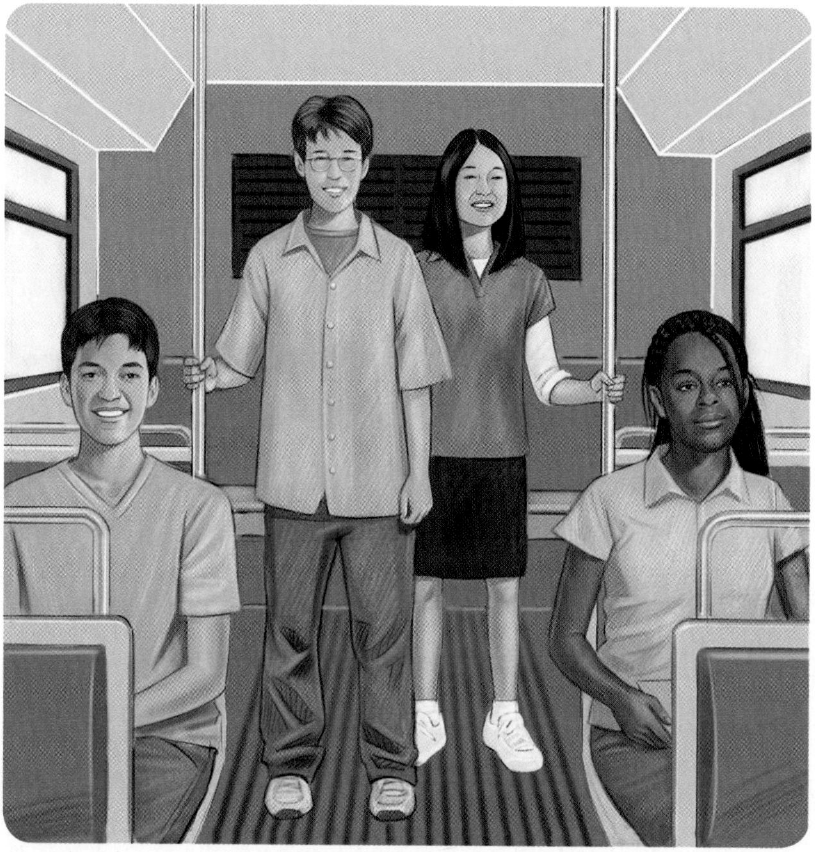

Figure 1 How do you keep from falling when you are standing on a moving bus?

Your body is a structure that is able to maintain its position when external forces try to push or pull it out of balance. **Stability** is the ability of a structure to maintain, or regain, a stable (balanced) position when external forces act on it. When engineers design structures, they must make sure that the structures are stable. Stable structures are safer because they do not easily topple over or fall down. Almost all structures, from small toys to huge buildings, are designed to be stable. Some toys and rides at amusement parks are designed to appear to be unstable to make them seem exciting and unpredictable.

stability: the ability of a structure to remain in or return to a stable, balanced position when forces act on it

An important characteristic of any structure is its centre of gravity. Finding a structure's centre of gravity helps designers determine its stability. **Centre of gravity** is the point around which a structure's mass is equally balanced in all directions. The centre of gravity is also the point at which the entire mass of an object seems to be concentrated.

centre of gravity: the point around which an object's mass is equally balanced in all directions; the point where the mass seems to be concentrated

SKILLS MENU: predicting, analyzing, evaluating, communicating

Locating the centre of gravity in an object is complicated. However, it is possible to find the horizontal balance point of long, thin objects. The horizontal balance point is very close to an object's centre of gravity. In this activity, you will predict, locate, and test the horizontal balance point of various objects.

Equipment and Materials: metre stick; tape; large rubber stopper; various long, thin, rigid objects; scissors; cardboard; pencil; 216 × 279 mm (8½ × 11 in.) piece of scrap paper; tape; pin; metal washer; string

Part A

1. Hold a metre stick by placing your index fingers near the two ends of the stick (Figure 2). *Slowly* slide your fingers toward each other until they meet. The location where they meet is the horizontal balance point of the metre stick. Record your observations.

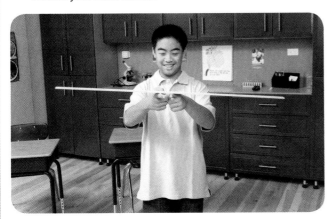

Figure 2 Step 1

2. Tape a large rubber stopper at one end of a metre stick. With one hand, hold the metre stick with the rubber stopper to get a sense of how the metre stick's mass is distributed. Predict the location of the horizontal balance point of the metre stick with the stopper attached. Record your prediction. Test your prediction: repeat step 1 with the metre stick–stopper combination. Record your observations.

3. Predict and then find the horizontal balance point of other long, thin, rigid objects. Record your observations.

Part B

4. Work with a partner for Part B. Carefully cut a piece of cardboard into an L-shape. Tape a piece of scrap paper onto the shape so that the paper covers the shape, and also covers the space where the cardboard was cut out (Figure 3). Predict the location of the horizontal balance point of the shape, and mark it with a pencil.

 Be very careful when using sharp objects.

Figure 3 Step 4

5. With a pin, make a hole near the edge of the shape. Make the hole slightly larger than the pin so that when the object is held up by the pin, the shape can rotate.

6. Make a plumb line by tying a washer to the end of a piece of string. Hold the shape by the pin, and hang the plumb line from the pin (Figure 4). Using a pencil, trace the line made by the hanging plumb line on the shape. Label this line AB.

Figure 4 Step 6

7. Make a second hole in the shape. Repeat step 6, but this time, label the new plumb line CD (Figure 5).

Figure 5 Step 7

8. Identify the point where line CD crosses line AB. Label this point X. Point X is very close to the shape's centre of gravity. Try to balance the shape horizontally by placing the blunt end of a pencil on point X. Will the shape balance on point X? Record your observations.

9. Repeat steps 4 to 8 with other unusual shapes cut out of cardboard. Record your observations.

A. Evaluate each of the predictions you made in the activity.

B. Write your own definition for "horizontal balance point."

C. Can the horizontal balance point of an object be outside the object itself? How do you know?

The Centre of Gravity of Common Structures

All structures have a centre of gravity. In the previous Try This activity, you used several different methods for locating an object's horizontal balance point. (Remember, the horizontal balance point is close to the centre of gravity.) An object's centre of gravity is usually located deep inside the object, not on its surface. For example, when you are standing upright, your centre of gravity is located deep inside your body, just below your belly button (Figure 6).

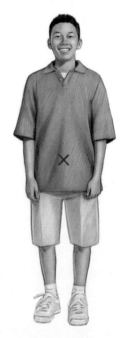

Figure 6 Centre of gravity of the human body when standing

However, your body's centre of gravity changes every time you move or bend your body into different shapes. The centre of gravity of an object depends on the shape of the object and how its mass is distributed. In some cases, the centre of gravity is outside the object itself (Figure 7).

(a)

(b)

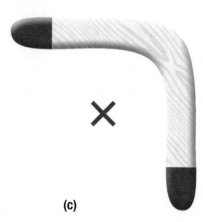

(c)

Figure 7 The centre of gravity of various objects
(a) middle of a solid ball
(b) middle of a hollow ball
(c) outside of a boomerang

SKILLS MENU: predicting, analyzing, evaluating, communicating

If you bend forward and let your arms hang in front of you, you may feel as though you are going to fall forward. Your body feels less stable in this position because its centre of gravity has moved in front of the centre of its base (your feet). In this activity, you will learn how a structure's (your body's) stability relates to its centre of gravity and its support base.

Equipment and Materials: object that can be lifted with one hand (for example, a dumbbell or textbook)

 If you have any problems in lifting objects or bending over, be careful in deciding which steps to follow. These activities should be performed with a partner, with one partner acting as a spotter. Work on a gym mat.

1. Refer to Figure 8. The region enclosed by the footprints is shaded and represents the support base of a person standing upright.

   (a) Stand upright with your arms at your sides and your feet about 50 cm apart. Have your partner look at you from a place in front of position F. Above which point, A to G, does your body's centre of gravity feel like it is positioned?

   (b) Slowly raise your right foot off the floor. Above which point, A to G, does your body's centre of gravity feel like it is positioned now?

   (c) Stand erect with your feet together. Hold a heavy (but not too heavy) object in one hand near your stomach. With your partner still in front of position F, determine what happens to your body, especially to your hips, as you move the object out to one side (toward either A or E). Where does your centre of gravity appear to lie now?

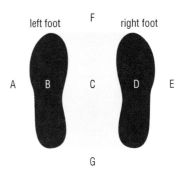

Figure 8

2. **(a)** Stand sideways against a wall with the side of one foot pressed against the wall. *Slowly* raise the other foot off the floor. Describe what happens. Where is your body's centre of gravity relative to your support base?

   (b) Stand with your back to the wall and your heels pressed against the wall. *Slowly* bend over to try to touch your toes. Describe what happens. Where is your body's centre of gravity relative to your support base?

A. Which provides greater stability, a high centre of gravity or a low one? Support your answer with an example.

B. Which provides greater stability, a small support base or a large one? What evidence supports your answer?

C. Explain the observations you made in step 2. (Hint: Think of how your centre of gravity moved with each position that you attempted.)

Conditions for Greatest Stability

Consider the sports car and the truck in Figure 9. The truck is more likely to tip over. The car has greater stability because of two features: it has a low centre of gravity, and it has a wide support base (when compared to its height). Objects with a low centre of gravity and a wide support base tend to be stable.

Figure 9 Which vehicle is more stable?

To maintain stability, the centre of gravity must lie directly over the support base. Stability decreases as the centre of gravity rises. If the centre of gravity rises higher and is no longer above the support base, the object will fall over. This is shown in Figure 10 for a truck going around a banked curve with different-sized loads. The truck on the far right will tip because its centre of gravity (the red X) lies outside of the two wheels.

LINKING TO LITERACY

Compare and Contrast
Good readers gain meaning from texts by analyzing the information they read. One way to analyze is to look for ways that information is the same or different. On this page, the author gives four examples of how stability works: trucks, boats, a bird, and an acrobat.

After you read this page, take a moment to reflect and analyze what you have read. How are these examples the same? How are they different?

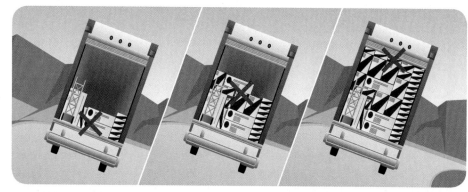

Figure 10 The truck is unstable when its centre of gravity does not lie above its support base.

Stability is also important for ships, boats, and canoes. Canoeists know how important it is to maintain a low centre of gravity. Standing in a canoe is dangerous. It raises the centre of gravity, and the canoe could easily tip over.

Examples of stability are also found in nature. The loon is a bird that is well adapted to water. The loon's feet help it to dive and swim quickly. However, on land, the loon is very awkward. Its centre of gravity lies ahead of its feet. The loon has to lean backward as it walks forward.

Thinking about how your own body reacts to external forces helps you to understand other structures. When you carry a backpack on your back, hold a suitcase by your side, or stand on your toes, your body has to adjust to help you keep stable. An acrobat walking on a tightrope applies a similar principle. The acrobat carries a downward curving pole that is heavy at both ends (Figure 11). The pole helps to lower the centre of gravity, and that means greater stability.

Figure 11 The long pole helps lower the acrobat's centre of gravity.

Unit Task How will you use what you learned about centre of gravity and stability when designing your playground equipment?

✔ CHECK YOUR LEARNING

1. Describe how you would find the approximate centre of gravity of
   - **(a)** a golf club
   - **(b)** a framed painting
   - **(c)** a coat hanger
   - **(d)** a tennis racquet

2. State the location of the centre of gravity of
   - **(a)** a golf ball
   - **(b)** a bagel

3. What two features of an object provide good stability?

4. State the conditions needed for stability.

5. Which is more stable? Explain why in each case.
   - **(a)** a turtle or a giraffe
   - **(b)** the CN Tower or your school building

Making Structures Strong: The Beam

Many structures have similar features. You may have seen many bridges that look similar. You may also have seen many buildings being constructed that use similar features—most house frames look very similar, even if the finished house looks very different. One of the features common to many structures is the beam.

A **beam** is any reasonably level structure that is designed to support a load. The frame of a typical doorway consists of a horizontal upper beam and two vertical supports (Figure 1). One of the oldest beam structures was probably a log lying across the banks of a river—a log bridge. In this case, the log is a beam that is supported by the banks of the river.

beam: a horizontal structure designed to support a load

LINKING TO LITERACY

Making Predictions
Prepare for reading by making a prediction about the information that will be explained or described on this page. Start by scanning the page for the most visible information: the title, subtitles, pictures, and margin information. Then, skim the first sentence of the first one or two paragraphs of the text.

What do these tell you about this text? What kind of information will be described or explained on this page?

Make a prediction about the text. As you read, confirm or change your prediction. Make new predictions about what will come next.

Making predictions will help to make reading informational text easier.

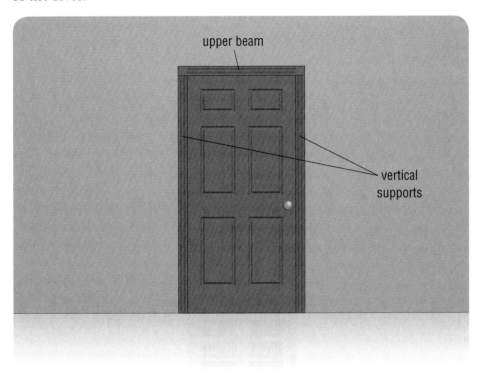

Figure 1 A typical doorframe is a beam structure.

Strengthening the Beam

On its own, a beam may not be able to support a large load. Some beams can bend or break if the load on them is too great. Beams can be strengthened in several ways. One way is to change the material that a beam is made of. A beam made of balsa wood is not as strong as one made of steel. Beams can be made out of many different materials, such as wood, stone, concrete, or steel, depending on the load requirements of the structure. Choosing the right material is an important factor in building a strong and stable structure. Steel is stronger than wood, but steel is also heavier. An engineer needs to consider both strength and mass when selecting the material for any structure.

I-Beams

I-beam: a beam that is in the shape of the letter "I" when seen from the end

Another way to strengthen a beam is to change its form. A stronger beam shape is the **I-beam**. When you look at the end of an I-beam, it looks like the letter "I." I-beams are commonly used in the construction of buildings, including houses (Figure 2). Wooden I-beams, sometimes called I-joists, are now being used as the structural support for ceilings and floors in homes. These beams are much lighter than steel beams, but they can still support very heavy loads. They also make use of wood chips, rather than solid wood. This means that they could reduce the amount of trees needed in construction.

Corrugation

corrugation: multiple folds in a material that provide additional strength

Folding the beam also adds strength. Placing triangular ridges, grooves, or folds in a structure is called **corrugation** (Figure 3). Corrugation is common in cardboard boxes. Corrugation is applied to plastic and metal, particularly for roofing, to provide additional strength.

Figure 2 A steel I-beam is used to provide structural strength.

Figure 3 The corrugation in a steel roof provides added strength.

LINKING TO LITERACY

Reading for Meaning
Scientific words are defined or explained on this page: I-beam, corrugation, and rebar. What do these mean? How do these explanations help you to better understand your reading?

Rebar

Concrete beams are often strengthened with steel reinforcing rods. A beam experiences compression on top and tension on the bottom. Concrete can withstand a great deal of compression, but it is very weak when it experiences tension. Steel reinforcing bars called rebar are placed in the concrete to help it resist the forces of tension. Concrete that contains rebar is known as "reinforced concrete" and is able to resist both compression and tension (Figure 4).

Figure 4 Steel reinforcing bars (rebar) serve to strengthen concrete by allowing it to resist both tension and compression.

The Cantilever

Beams are not always supported at both ends. A **cantilever** is a beam that is supported, or fixed, at only one end (Figure 5). A branch on a tree and a diving board are examples of simple cantilevers. Cantilevers are very common. Canopies over entrances to buildings and apartment balconies are also examples of cantilevers.

Cantilevers are useful in spanning great distances without the use of a central support. Cantilevers are used in areas where a central supporting structure would be unrealistic, such as over a deep gorge. Look at Figure 5. This cantilever is on the Observation Tower over the American Falls at Niagara Falls. Can you imagine trying to build a supporting structure at both ends of the cantilever at this location?

Figure 5 A cantilever is a beam that is supported at only one end.

cantilever: a beam supported at only one end

Supporting the Beam

Adding structural support also strengthens a beam (Figure 6). A tie is a structural support that is part of a framework and is designed to resist tension forces. A tie is usually set at an angle between a beam and its support base (the wall in this example). A strut is similar to a tie, but it is placed below a beam where it provides resistance to the forces of compression. A gusset is a flat, plate-like device, often triangular, that supports a beam by reinforcing the connection between the beam and its support base.

tie

strut

gusset

Figure 6 The tie, strut, and gusset add support to the beam.

Unit Task How will you use what you learned about the beam in the design of the playground equipment for the Unit Task?

✓ CHECK YOUR LEARNING

1. Briefly describe four ways that a beam can be strengthened.

2. How is a cantilever different from a fully supported beam?

3. Provide two examples of cantilevers that you have seen in your neighbourhood.

Factors Affecting a Structure's Ability to Support a Load

SKILLS MENU

☐ Questioning   ☑ Performing
☑ Hypothesizing   ☑ Observing
☑ Predicting   ☑ Analyzing
☐ Planning   ☑ Evaluating
☑ Controlling   ☑ Communicating
   Variables

Imagine that you have to design a bridge to span a stream. What design provides enough strength but the least mass of materials? How can you perform a fair test to discover how factors affect the strength of a beam? In this investigation, you will develop answers to these and other questions.

Testable Question

How do the mass, shape, and form of a beam affect the beam's ability to support a load?

Hypothesis/Prediction

SKILLS HANDBOOK 2.B.3.

Read the Experimental Design and Procedure, and examine the figures to see the different beam designs you will be testing. Make and record a hypothesis about which design will be the strongest and which will be the weakest. Your hypothesis should include a prediction and reasons for your prediction.

Experimental Design

Your group will build six different beam "bridges." Four have the same mass, while the remaining two have twice as much mass. You will test each beam's strength by pulling down on its centre with a spring scale. Use as little masking tape as possible, and recycle the cardboard after completing the investigation.

Equipment and Materials

- ruler or metre stick
- scissors
- spring scale
- 2 stools or movable desks
- 8 pieces of file-folder cardboard
- masking tape
- string

ruler or metre stick   scissors   spring scale

stools or movable desks   pieces of file-folder cardboard   masking tape

string

 Be very careful when using sharp objects.

Procedure

SKILLS HANDBOOK 6.A.3., 6.D.1.

1. Mark and cut out eight pieces of cardboard, 24 cm long × 12 cm wide. Draw lines on five of the pieces of cardboard, and fold the cardboard as shown in Figure 1 on the next page. Tape the edges together to close the beam. Make three flat beams, one triangular beam, one cylindrical beam, and two rectangular beams.

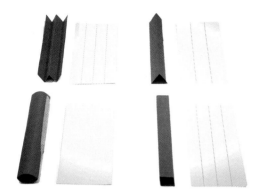

Figure 1 The four beam designs

2. Design a table to record the measurements taken during the tests you will be performing.

3. Set up a single flat beam as a bridge supported at the ends by two stools or desks separated by 18 cm. The overlap at the ends of the beam should be equal. Tie a loose loop of string around the middle of the beam. Suspend the spring scale from it. As you read the force on the scale, very gently pull straight down until the beam fails (Figure 2). Record the force that caused the failure.

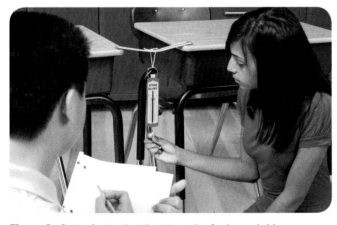

Figure 2 Setup for testing the strength of a beam bridge

4. Tape two flat beams together to double the mass. Repeat the test in step 3.

5. Repeat step 3 for the triangular beam, the cylindrical beam, and a rectangular beam.

6. Mark and cut the last piece of cardboard into four equal strips 24 cm long and 3 cm wide. Fold these strips width-wise. Tape them together to form a corrugated row about 24 cm long. Place this row into the second rectangular beam (Figure 3). Use tape to secure it to the ends of the beam. Close the sides of the beam, and tape the edges that meet. Test this beam as you did in step 3.

Figure 3 Reinforcing a rectangular beam

Analyze and Evaluate

(a) Rank the beams in order of weakest to strongest.

(b) Describe three independent variables you tested in this investigation. State how each variable affected the beam's ability to support a load.

(c) Answer the Testable Question.

(d) About how many flat (or solid) beams would be needed to provide the same strength as a single reinforced rectangular beam? How would the masses compare?

Apply and Extend

(e) If you were allowed four 24 cm × 12 cm pieces of cardboard, what design would you use to maximize a beam's strength? Draw a sketch of your design.

(f) Metal support beams are made in the shape of a capital L or a capital I. Describe the advantages of this design.

Making Structures Strong: The Truss, Arch, and Dome

Designers sometimes want to use shapes other than beams to make structures stronger and more interesting looking. They can do this by adding triangles (trusses) or curves (arches and domes).

The Truss

truss: a network of beams arranged in triangles

A **truss** is a network of beams that form triangles. A truss can be used as a bridge or a cantilever, and for many other applications. In the following Try This activity, you will learn how trusses can be strengthened and how their mass can be reduced.

TRY THIS: Building and Testing Trusses

SKILLS MENU: performing, observing, analyzing, communicating

SKILLS HANDBOOK
4.C.1.

In this activity, you will learn how to build trusses and reduce their mass while maintaining their strength. You will test for strength, not for failure, by gently pushing on your structures. In each step, record your observations.

Equipment and Materials: 11–15 equal-sized strips of stiff cardboard or large craft sticks with a small hole drilled near each end; paper fasteners (brads); string

1. Construct a four-piece structure using cardboard and fasteners (Figure 1(a)). With the structure resting upright, determine how sturdy it is.

2. Add a fifth component to create a bridge truss made of two triangles (Figure 1(b)). Place the truss to span a small space between two textbooks. Gently test how sturdy this truss is, but *do not* break it.

3. Make a larger truss using the triangular design (Figure 1(c)).

   (a) Test the sturdiness of the truss as a bridge spanning a space.

   (b) Test the sturdiness of the truss when used as a cantilever (over the edge of a book).

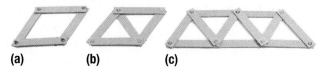

(a)   **(b)**   **(c)**

Figure 1   Structures used in steps 1 to 3

4. Reduce the mass of your truss bridge by replacing beams with pieces of string (Figure 2). Start by replacing one beam, and then two beams, and so on. Draw a diagram of your final design. Gently test its strength.

Figure 2   Reduce the mass of a suspended truss

5. Turn over the truss you made in step 4. Describe what happens to its sturdiness.

6. Put the long truss back together and support it at one end only (as a cantilever). Discover how to reduce the mass of the cantilever by replacing at least one beam with string (Figure 3). Draw a diagram of the cantilever truss with the least mass.

A. What basic form provides a truss with strength?

B. How can a spanning truss be reduced in mass while maintaining strength?

Figure 3   Reduce the mass of the cantilever

Most people are familiar with the trusses used in the roofs of home construction (Figure 4). You can see examples of trusses in many places. Construction cranes, communication and hydro towers, bridges, and the International Space Station all contain trusses.

Trusses can be bent or curved and still retain their strength (Figure 5). Trusses take advantage of the strength of triangles to make structures strong. In a truss, forces are distributed between the points of the triangles that make up the truss. The triangles help the structure support more weight. Notice the complex truss structure that makes up the circle of the Ferris wheel. A beam used in this application could be too heavy. Remember that the structure needs to support its own weight as well as the weight of the passengers. Using trusses allows for different structural designs. Trusses can be used for applications that other types of supports, such as beams, cannot be used for.

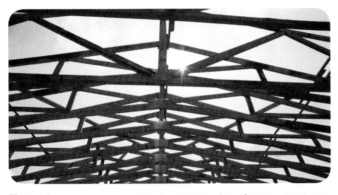

Figure 4 Trusses are used in the construction of many structures.

Figure 5 Trusses provide strength to this Ferris wheel.

The Arch

An **arch** is a curved structure often used to support loads. Arches are used in spaces where supporting beams are not practical. Such spaces include doorways or windows, bridges, or places of worship. An arch's curved design transfers compression force downward (Figure 6). Like the beam and the truss, the arch is one of the basic components of structures.

Many early civilizations, such as the Romans, used the arch when building structures. Some of the arches that the Romans built over 2000 years ago are still standing. Today, arches are still used to span long distances (Figure 7).

arch: a curved structure used to span a space while supporting a load

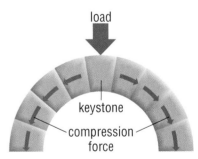

Figure 6 The arch transfers compression force downward from each stone to the next.

Figure 7 Arches can be used to make bridges stronger.

11.4 Making Structures Strong: The Truss, Arch, and Dome **301**

The Dome

dome: a shell structure that looks like the top half of a sphere

A **dome** is a structure that looks like the top half of a sphere or an egg. Like an arch, a dome directs compression force downward. In an arch, the compression force occurs in only one plane of application (Figure 8). However, in a dome, the compression force is directed downward in many planes at once (Figure 9). You could consider a dome to be a series of arches that have been connected at a centre point.

Figure 8 The compression force on this arch is directed downward in a single plane.

Figure 9 The compression force on this dome is directed downward in many planes at once.

Domes are popular structures because they are strong and can still enclose a large volume of space. Planetariums, churches, mosques, and many stadiums use domes in their design (Figure 10).

Figure 10 The Pantheon in Rome, Italy, is an example of a dome.

Unit Task Will you be able to use trusses, arches, or domes in your playground design for the Unit Task?

✓ CHECK YOUR LEARNING

1. What are some advantages of using trusses?

2. List four examples of structures that use trusses.

3. Describe the similarities and differences between arches and domes.

4. Explain how compression forces are different in arches and domes.

Carbon Nanotubes

Carbon nanotubes are made of a single layer of carbon atoms. The atoms are arranged in a hexagonal (six-sided) shape (Figure 1). They are 10 000 times thinner than human hair but stronger than steel! Their light weight and extreme strength make them ideal for structures that will face extreme conditions.

Figure 1 This diagram of a carbon nanotube shows its hexagonal structure.

Carbon nanotubes (Figure 2) have great potential in many areas, from designing sports gear to fighting infection in medicine. Carbon nanotubes can be used to build better and smaller electrical circuits. These circuits operate on the level of the individual particles of matter. Nanotube technology has even been developed to make solar power more efficient. Microscopic solar cells can be applied to flexible plastic sheets and stuck on windows, skylights, and car windshields. Someday, even house paint may contain energy-collecting nanotubes!

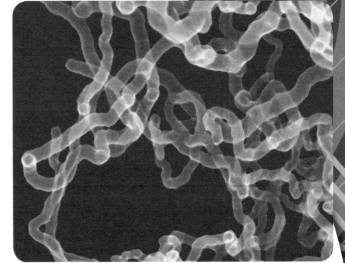

Figure 2 Actual carbon nanotubes that have been magnified 40 000 times in an electron microscope

Fibres made of carbon nanotubes may be the first commercial application of nanotube technology. These super-strong fibres could be used in vehicle armour for Formula 1 racecars and bodysuits for racecar drivers. Nanotubes could be used in other woven fabrics and textiles that would face extreme conditions, such as protective equipment for sports.

To learn more about carbon nanotubes,
Go to Nelson Science

LINKING TO LITERACY

Synthesize

Readers synthesize information by summarizing what they have read and making connections, or thinking creatively to draw a conclusion, come up with a new idea, or think about information in a new way.

Summarize your reading about carbon nanotubes. Make a connection to a similar science text you have read. What conclusions can you draw? How else might nanotubes be used? How might nanotubes be similar to or different from other technology?

Design a Scaffold

In this activity, you will consider as many of the ideas you have learned as possible as you design, build, and test a structure that is efficient and useful at supporting a load. To be efficient, a structure must be low in mass but high in strength. To be useful, a structure must be both stable and safe.

SKILLS MENU
- ☐ Identify a Problem/Need
- ☐ Planning
- ☐ Selecting Materials and Equipment
- ☐ Designing
- ☐ Testing
- ☐ Modifying
- ☐ Communicating

Scenario

At summer camp, your group has been assigned the task of painting the outside of your cabin. To make the painting easier and safer, you decide to design a scaffold. The scaffold must be strong and stable, yet light enough to move from one location to another (Figure 1). It should also have steps at one end to allow you to safely climb up to the main platform. Your group will design, build, and test a scale model of a scaffold that is 3 m long × 1.5 m high × 0.75 m wide.

Figure 1 How will the features of your scaffold compare to the features of the scaffold shown here?

Design Brief

In this activity, you will work in a small group to build a scale model of the scaffold described in the Scenario. The model will be free-standing and will have a set of steps at one end. Using a scale of 1 cm to 10 cm, your model will be 30 cm long × 15 cm high × 7.5 cm wide. As a class, you will decide on the types of materials allowed.

You will try to apply as many of the ideas as possible from earlier in Chapters 10 and 11 to design a scaffold with a low mass. Then, you will test the steps at the end of the scaffold, one at a time, to see if each one can hold a 500 g mass without breaking or becoming unstable. You will also test the scaffold to see if it can safely hold a 4 kg mass in the middle without breaking or falling over. You will then determine the efficiency of the model by dividing the live load mass (4000 g) by the dead load mass. (As an example, a 100 g scaffold that supports a 4000 g load before breaking is quite efficient, but a 500 g scaffold that supports the same load is inefficient.)

Equipment and Materials

- eye protection
- apron
- scissors
- hand drill
- screwdriver
- 4 kg mass
- 500 g mass
- spring scale
- ruler
- construction materials
- fastening materials

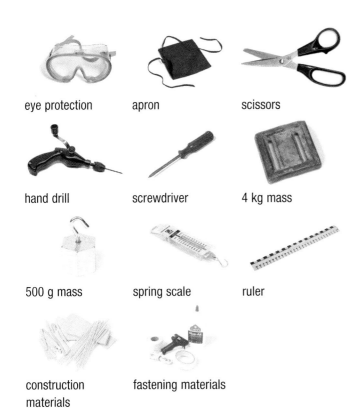

eye protection   apron   scissors

hand drill   screwdriver   4 kg mass

500 g mass   spring scale   ruler

construction   fastening materials
materials

Research and Consider

Review what you have learned in this unit.

- What type of structure (solid, frame, shell, or combination) would be best for an efficient scaffold made of simple materials?
- How can a span (the top of a scaffold) be reinforced without adding too much extra mass?
- What design will ensure that the scaffold remains stable even if a person walks up the steps at one end of the scaffold?

Use these notes, research, and brainstorm with others to generate ideas. You may wish to use the Internet to see designs of different scaffolds. Make sketches of different designs that you might use.

Go to Nelson Science

Plan and Construct

SKILLS HANDBOOK
4.B.2., 4.B.4.

1. In your group, choose the model that you will use from your brainstorming sessions. Make a working drawing of your best choice.
2. Create a step-by-step plan for building your scaffold. Include a list of materials you will use and equipment you will need.
3. Finalize your plan and have your teacher check it.
4. Construct your model.
5. Determine the model's mass in grams by hanging it from a spring scale.

Test and Modify

SKILLS HANDBOOK
4.B.5., 4.B.6.

Test your scaffold to see if each step can hold a 500 g mass without breaking and without causing the scaffold to tip. Then, test the main part of the scaffold to see if it can hold the 4 kg mass in the middle without breaking. If necessary, modify the design, and find its new mass. Perform the same tests for strength and stability. Keep a written record of the modifications you make and the results of these modifications.

Evaluate

Compare the performance of your scaffold with the criteria in the Design Brief. Answer the following questions:

1. How strong and stable was your scaffold when you first tested it?
2. What modifications did you make or would you make next time to create a stronger and more stable structure?
3. How did the efficiency of your scaffold compare to the efficiencies of the other scaffolds in class?

Communicate

Prepare a report to describe the final design of your scaffold. Include a detailed diagram and any calculations you made.

Structural Failure

An umbrella bends out of shape in a wind gust (Figure 1). A suitcase handle breaks. A bridge collapses. A drinking glass cracks (Figure 2). These are examples of structures that have failed. **Structural failure** occurs when a structure, or part of a structure, loses the ability to support a load. Once the structure loses its load-carrying ability, it cracks, deforms, or even collapses completely. There are many reasons why a structure can fail.

structural failure: the failure of a structure as a result of the structure, or part of the structure, losing the ability to support a load

Figure 1 Structural failure of an umbrella from a gust of wind

Figure 2 Structural failure of a drinking glass

Bad Design

Approximately 40 % to 60 % of all structural failures are due to bad design. Bad designs can be caused by design errors such as failure to account for load, specifying incorrect materials, or not considering important factors and stresses.

On January 28, 1986, just 73 s after takeoff, the space shuttle *Challenger* exploded (Figure 3). All seven crew members were killed. The explosion was caused by a gas leak when an O-ring failed. An O-ring is a circular piece of plastic or rubber that stops water or gases from escaping. An O-ring is usually in a connection between two pipes (Figure 4). In the case of the *Challenger*, the weather in Florida was unusually cold. The cold O-ring failed and caused the gas leak that led to the explosion. 🌐

To learn about *Challenger* Learning Centers,
Go to Nelson Science 🌐

Figure 3 The explosion of the *Challenger* as a result of the failure of an O-ring

Figure 4 Inside the end of a garden hose is a round washer. This flexible washer works in a similar way to an O-ring.

SKILLS MENU: observing, communicating, analyzing

Different materials change at different temperatures. Materials can become more brittle at some temperatures and more flexible at other temperatures. In this activity, you will observe the effect of temperature on elastic bands.

Equipment and Materials: 2 bulldog paper clips; 2 identical elastic bands; 2 small bowls or glasses; 250 mL warm water; 250 mL ice water

1. Fold each elastic band in half and clamp it with a bulldog clip.

2. Place one elastic band and clip in the cup of ice water. Place the other elastic band and clip in the cup of warm water (Figure 5).

3. After 5 min, remove the elastic bands and bulldog clips from the water.

4. Remove the clips from the elastic bands. Examine the elastic bands. Using a graphic organizer of your choice, compare the size, shape, and texture of the two elastic bands.

Figure 5

A. What did you observe about the elastic bands? Write a brief report of your observations.

B. In small groups, discuss how the results of this activity may relate to the O-ring failure in the space shuttle *Challenger* disaster.

Faulty Construction

Faulty construction is the second most common cause of structural failure. Construction errors can result from the use of poor quality materials, poor installation from either sloppiness or lack of expertise, or a combination of these. For example, homeowners are aware of how easily shingles are blown off a roof in windy conditions. This is a bigger problem if the shingles were poorly installed by not securing them correctly with the right type of nail (Figures 6 and 7). Using the wrong nail for the job can mean the difference between a roof that lasts for 20 years and one that fails on the first windy day.

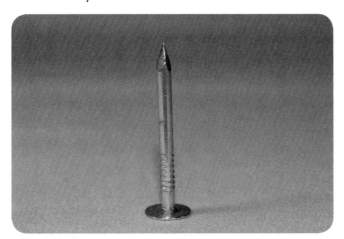

Figure 6 A roofing nail is rustproof and has a large head and a notched shank to hold down the shingles in windy conditions.

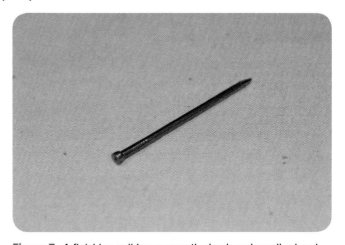

Figure 7 A finishing nail has a smooth shank and smaller head that is less visible on wood trim around doorways or cabinets. What would happen if a worker used finishing nails for roof shingles?

Faulty construction can have tragic consequences. The Sampoong Department Store (Figure 8) in Seoul, South Korea, collapsed on June 29, 1995. The collapse killed 501 people. An investigation of the disaster showed that the construction materials were inadequate, and that the installation and building methods were poor. The government allowed the structure to pass inspections that it should have failed. The chairman of the building was charged with negligence for his disregard for public safety. Several government officials were also charged with accepting bribes to conceal the building's flaws.

To learn more about the Sampoong Department Store collapse,

Go to Nelson Science

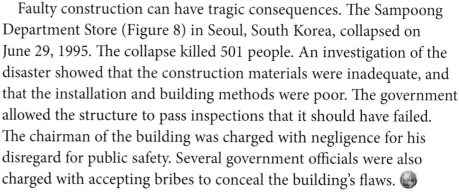

Figure 8 The remains of the Sampoong Department Store after its collapse

Extraordinary Loads

Extreme conditions can also result in structural failure. Often these failures are not the result of poor design, but the result of unexpected events that create extraordinary loads on structures.

In January 1998, North America experienced a massive ice storm. For days, parts of Ontario, Québec, Nova Scotia, New York, and Maine were drenched with freezing rain. The rain coated everything with a 120 mm–thick layer of ice. About 130 transmission towers were crushed under the weight of the ice (Figure 9). More than 4 million people in Québec, Ontario, and New Brunswick had no electricity. Some people had no electricity for more than a month. At least 25 people died, many of them from the cold.

To learn more about the 1998 ice storm,

Go to Nelson Science

Figure 9 Transmission towers toppled from the weight of the ice. Previously, the worst ice storm on record was in 1961. In that case, only 60 mm of ice accumulated and lasted only a day or two.

Foundation Failure

Failure of a structure's base, or foundation, is less common than bad design and faulty construction. However, it can also lead to significant structural problems. Foundation failure can be caused by poor soil conditions, poor installation, a foundation that is not large enough for the load of the structure, or earthquakes.

A well-known example of foundation failure is the Leaning Tower of Pisa in Italy (Figure 10). The tower was built in 1178 on sandy, unstable soil with an inadequate foundation. The soil shifted and the tower began to lean almost right after construction began. Over the centuries, the tower leaned more and more. Modern construction methods have finally slowed down the movement of the tower and returned it to the angle at which it was leaning in 1870.

To learn more about the Leaning Tower of Pisa,

Figure 10 The Leaning Tower of Pisa

Foundation failure is more common in smaller buildings. Cracks in the walls of a house or misaligned doors are often the result of a house's foundation shifting due to poor soil conditions. However, any structure can shift as a result of a poor foundation.

Unit Task How can you use what you have learned about structural failure in your Unit Task?

✔ CHECK YOUR LEARNING

1. **(a)** List four possible causes of structural failure.
   (b) Identify a structural failure that occurred on account of each of the four causes.
   (c) Suggest one way in which each of the structural failures in (b) could have been prevented.

2. A 12-year-old student sits on a child's tricycle and one of the rear wheels breaks off.
   (a) What was the most likely cause of the structural failure?
   (b) How could this failure have been prevented?

Preventing Structural Failure

SKILLS MENU

☐ Identify a Problem/Need
☐ Planning
☐ Selecting Materials and Equipment
☐ Designing
☐ Testing
☐ Modifying
☐ Communicating

Structures are designed to certain specifications to fulfill their purpose. Safety is an important component in the design and use of structures. Engineers use several methods to ensure structural safety so that the design serves its purpose.

Scenario

You are the chief designer for Design Construction Ltd. The company relies on you to make sure that the structures they build meet their design requirements and are also safe. Your firm has entered a design competition for a new building. Your team will build and test a model of a structure that incorporates features that help prevent structural failure.

Design Brief

In this activity, you will work with a partner to build the tallest, most stable structure possible. Use only three sheets of newspaper and 75 cm of masking tape to build a model. You must anchor the structure to the ground. Your structure must be able to withstand the force of the wind from a fan on high power that is placed 1 m from the tower without falling over or irreversibly buckling. If the structure topples over then it has failed the test. Your structure may buckle a little bit, but if it buckles so much that the form of the structure changes permanently, then your structure has failed.

Use several techniques to ensure the safety of your design. Create a sensor using a party streamer to determine where your structure might fail.

Equipment and Materials

- electric fan
- calculator
- scissors
- 3 sheets of newspaper
- masking tape
- party streamers

electric fan

calculator

scissors

3 sheets of newspaper

masking tape

party streamers

 Be very careful when using sharp objects.

Research and Consider

Use the Internet and other resources to investigate how

- wind tunnel testing is used to check a structure's integrity (The fan at 1 m will be acting as your wind tunnel.)
- structures are over-engineered with a factor of safety so that they can withstand greater forces than anticipated
- sensors can be used to detect early warnings of failure

Go to Nelson Science

Plan and Construct

SKILLS HANDBOOK 4.B.4., 4.C.

1. Using what you have learned in this unit and from your research, design a few different structures. Remember the design requirements in the Design Brief.

2. Choose the sketch that you think will be the most stable.

3. Write a step-by-step plan for creating your design. Be sure to include a scale drawing of your structure.

4. Use party streamers to act as sensors (Figure 1). Cut the streamer with a narrow centre so that it will fail with very little force.

Figure 1 Use party streamers with narrow centres in your design.

5. Finalize your plan and have your teacher check it.

6. Construct your design.

Test and Modify

Test your structure to see if it is successful. Make any necessary modifications, and then retest your structure. Continue to improve your design. Now, test how well your design exceeds its engineering requirements by measuring the exact point of failure of the structure. Slowly slide the fan from its 1 m test position toward your structure until your structure fails. Measure this distance in centimetres. You may want to modify your structure again to improve the over-engineering in its design.

Evaluate

1. If your first structure failed the wind tunnel test, explain what design flaw may have led to that failure.

2. What design modifications did you make as a result of your tests?

3. Why were you asked to use sensors in your tests? How did you incorporate the sensors to create a good indicator of early failure?

4. Your tower has a design requirement to be stable in a wind at a distance of 1 m. Determine how much over-engineering was built into your tower by calculating the factor of safety for your final tower:

   Factor of safety = 1 m ÷ (distance in centimetres between fan and tower at failure)

   Hint: Convert 1 m to 100 cm before calculating the factor of safety.

5. Do you think your factor of safety was large enough for a safe design? Explain.

6. Would a tower with a factor of safety less than 1 be considered a safe structure? Explain.

7. Compare the factors of safety for all the towers in the class. Did the tower with the highest factor of safety also have the greatest height? Why or why not?

8. Can you think of other materials or designs that you could use to make your sensor more effective?

Communicate

SKILLS HANDBOOK 4.B.7.

Prepare a one-page report that describes the final version of your model, and how successfully it meets the design requirements. Include your factor of safety calculation, how you used the sensors to detect early failure, the height of your tower, and an accurate diagram of the final version of the model that you used.

Structural Strength and Stability

BIG Ideas

- ☐ Structures have a purpose.
- ☑ The form of a structure is dependent on its function.
- ☑ The interaction between structures and forces is predictable.

Looking Back

A stable structure maintains its shape and position over an extended period of time.

- A structure's centre of gravity affects its stability.
- Objects with a low centre of gravity and a wide support base tend to be stable.

 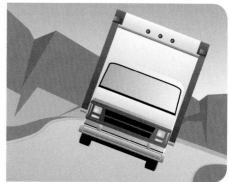

Beams, trusses, arches, and domes are used to help structures support loads.

- The beam can be strengthened by changing its shape or composition (for example, I-beam, corrugation, rebar) or by adding supports (for example, tie, strut, gusset).
- The cantilever is a beam supported at only one end.
- In a truss, force is distributed through the structure at the points of contact of the triangles.
- An arch's curved design transfers compression force downward into the ground.
- A dome is a structural element that looks like the top part of a sphere. Like an arch, a dome also transfers compression forces to the ground.

The skills of scientific inquiry can be used to investigate the factors that affect the ability of a structure to support a load.

- Models can be used to determine how well structures support a load.
- The shape, mass, and form of a structure affect how much force a structure can support.

The skills of technological problem solving can be used to determine the most efficient way for a structure to support a load.

- Using structural supports and different construction materials can make a structure more efficient.
- The efficiency of a structure can be calculated by dividing the live load mass by the dead load mass.

Structural failure occurs when all or part of a structure loses its ability to support a load.

- Structures can fail due to factors such as bad design, faulty construction, extraordinary loads, and foundation failure.
- Many structural failures can be linked to human error.

The skills of scientific inquiry can be used to investigate methods used to ensure that structures are safe.

- Research skills can be used to learn more about the methods that engineers use to ensure that structures are safe.
- Technological problem-solving skills can be used to model safety tests that engineers use when designing and building structures.

CHAPTER 11 REVIEW

The following icons indicate the Achievement Chart categories: **K/U** Knowledge/Understanding **C** Communication **T/I** Thinking/Investigation **A** Application

What Do You Remember?

1. In your notebook, match each definition in the left-hand column of Table 1 with the most appropriate word from the right-hand column. **K/U**

Table 1

Definition	Term
(a) a beam supported at only one end	arch
(b) folding a material repeatedly to provide additional strength	rebar
(c) steel rod used to reinforce concrete	truss
(d) looks like the top part of a sphere	cantilever
(e) a curved structure used to support a load, or make an opening in a bigger structure	dome
(f) a network of beams that form triangles	corrugation

2. Distinguish between a simple beam and a cantilever. Provide two examples of each. **K/U**

What Do You Understand?

3. (a) Why are trusses so useful in structures?

   (b) List three structures that make use of trusses. **K/U**

4. (a) Use a Venn diagram to compare the arch and the dome.

   (b) Provide two examples of each from your home, your school, or your community. **K/U** **A**

5. (a) Why is regular maintenance important for the safety of structures?

   (b) Provide an example of regular maintenance of a structure that helps ensure safety. **K/U** **A**

6. "Human factors are the most common cause of structural failure." After reading this chapter, what do you think is meant by this statement? **K/U**

7. A student is leaning back in a chair. Eventually, the student falls over backward. Explain what happened using the terms "force," "centre of gravity," and "stability." **K/U** **T/I**

8. What are three factors that can affect a structure's ability to support a load? Provide an example of structural success and structural failure for each of these three factors. **K/U**

9. "Corrugation is just a series of connected arches." Do you agree with this statement? Explain. **K/U**

10. Consider the picture of the Eiffel Tower in Figure 1. What basic form is the Eiffel Tower? What structures can you identify in the tower? **K/U** **A**

Figure 1

11. Research in the library or on the Internet the shapes of traffic and subway tunnels. What is the most common shape of tunnels? Why do you think this is so? **K/U** **T/I** **A**

Go to Nelson Science

12. Why is rebar so common in the construction of structures using concrete? **K/U**

Solve a Problem!

13. Study the picture of the car in Figure 2.

(a) Identify what structural form the cabin of the car most resembles. Why did engineers use this form?

(b) Is this the best form to use for the cabin of a car? Why or why not?

(c) Suggest an alternative form for the cabin of a car. Why did you choose this alternative? K/U T/I A

Figure 2

14. In the library or on the Internet, research the Quebec Bridge disaster in 1907 (Figure 3). What was the cause of its collapse? Suggest design changes that could have prevented the collapse. T/I A

Figure 3

Create and Evaluate!

15. Most countries have building codes. These are laws that determine how certain structures should be built to withstand forces. Should building codes differ from country to country or from region to region within a particular country? Why or why not? T/I A

16. In 1999, an apartment building in Foggia, Italy, collapsed, killing 67 people.

(a) Why might this collapse have occurred?

(b) Tenants had complained for years about cracks in the walls. What kind of internal forces were probably acting on this building that ultimately led to its collapse?

(c) Use the Internet and other sources to find out what caused the apartment to collapse. Could this catastrophe have been prevented? Explain.

(d) Write your findings in a brief letter addressed to the mayor of Foggia. K/U T/I

Reflect on Your Learning

17. (a) Which concepts in this chapter did you find easy to understand? Explain.

(b) Which concepts in this chapter did you find difficult to understand? Explain.

(c) Name two things you could do to help you understand these concepts better.

18. The beam and the arch are two basic building components used to construct structures.

(a) Were you surprised to learn that these components have been used for thousands of years? Explain.

(b) Look at the structures around you and examine them for either the beam or the arch. Does this knowledge change how you view familiar structures? Explain your thinking on this.

19. Think back to the Key Question on the first page of this chapter.

(a) In a brief paragraph, answer the Key Question. You may use diagrams.

(b) Write one or two more questions about the topic of this unit that you would like to explore.

12 Form, Function, and Beauty

KEY QUESTION: What factors make a structure useful and attractive?

Looking Ahead

- The product development process considers human wants and needs, and also societal and environmental factors.

- Structures that are symmetrical are usually more stable and more aesthetically pleasing than those that are asymmetrical.

- Structures intended for human use need to be designed for human characteristics.

- The skills of scientific inquiry can be used to study the ergonomics of everyday tools.

VOCABULARY

symmetry	ergonomics
line of symmetry	repetitive strain injury
aesthetics	universal design

The Michael Lee-Chin Crystal

The Michael Lee-Chin Crystal is the official name of the Royal Ontario Museum's (ROM) recent addition. It is named after Michael Lee-Chin, who donated $30 million to its construction. The addition was designed by architect Daniel Libeskind, who was inspired by the museum's gem and mineral collection and sketched his initial concept on a napkin. The original design called for stunning glass walls, a triumph of form over function.

However, it was impossible to build the Crystal as planned. The glass walls were not strong enough to support the weight of ice and snow. There were also fire and safety concerns. All of this resulted in significant changes to the outside structure. The 3000 steel beams making up the skeletal framework are now mostly covered by aluminum siding rather than glass. Only a few small slits were left for windows and light. Libeskind's original design shape, however, remains intact.

The Michael Lee-Chin Crystal opened on June 1, 2007, to a very mixed reception. Some people thought it was a striking architectural gem. Other people saw it as an ugly structure that did not match the classical design of the ROM. Many people said that it resembled a spaceship that had crashed into the ROM.

The interior design makes installing exhibits difficult. Most visitors agree that the dinosaur galleries seem to make effective use of space. However, even here, unusual angles and unused spaces are everywhere.

LINKING TO LITERACY

Process for Determining the Main Idea

To determine the main idea of a text, look for key information in the topic sentences. Often, the first sentence of a paragraph will be the topic sentence. For example, the sentence that begins with "The Michael Lee-Chin Crystal is the official…" is the topic sentence.

Here is a process you can follow to help you formulate the main idea for this text:

1. Locate the topic sentence for each paragraph.

2. Write each topic sentence in your journal or notebook. Then, cross out any unnecessary information. (You may need to change or add a few words to connect the remaining information into sentences.)

3. Now, state the general or "big picture" idea from these sentences in your own words. This will be the main idea of the text.

The Product Development Process

Companies consider three important sets of factors before they build a new product or redesign an existing product—design, manufacturing, and sales. To discuss the factors involved in these processes, we will focus on the design, manufacture, and sale of a specific product that you use regularly: backpacks (Figure 1).

Figure 1 Many Canadian students use backpacks for school every day.

Design Factors

A company wants to sell backpacks to students. Designers and managers hold a brainstorming session to decide what factors to consider before they begin designing and manufacturing new backbacks. Each factor listed below is followed by questions that designers and managers ask. Think of questions you would add in each category.

- **Individual users:** Should we create a one-size-fits-all backpack, or a backpack with adjustable features? Should the backpack have an outer frame, an inner frame, or no frame at all? Should we use detachable components for storage? Is a backpack the best design, or should we consider front packs or side packs?
- **Society:** Do consumers care if we transport raw materials and finished products all over the world, using valuable resources for shipping?
- **The economy:** Should the backpack components be made in Canada, or should we reduce costs by using overseas manufacturers?
- **The environment:** Should we make as many components as possible recyclable (Figure 2)?
- **Safety and health:** How can we make sure that the packs are the best size and weight to prevent back and shoulder problems? The static load should be no more than 15 % of the user's weight.
- **Legal aspects:** Do we need to worry about lawsuits? What if, without our knowledge, our suppliers have dangerous levels of toxins, such as lead, in the materials they provide?

  After discussing these questions, the company begins market research to determine what features customers want in a backpack. Then, the company can decide what improvements are needed.

To learn more about the City of Toronto's garbage and its plans for recycling and composting,
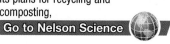
Go to Nelson Science

Figure 2 From April to August 2007, the City of Toronto trucked nearly 12 000 tonnes of garbage to the Green Lane landfill near London, Ontario, almost 200 km away.

Manufacturing Factors

Companies consider factors related to the manufacturing process before the process begins. Each factor is followed by some brainstorming questions:

- **Suitability of materials:** Should the materials be waterproof? Which, if any, parts should be made of metal, hard plastic, flexible plastic, fabric, or Velcro? Will the fabric deteriorate in sunlight? How strong should the thread be? Will the materials be attractive to consumers (Figure 3)?
- **Availability and cost of materials:** Are the required materials and labour force for manufacturing available in Canada at a reasonable cost? If manufacturing is located elsewhere, are there concerns about worker rights and safety, and environmental conditions (Figure 4)?
- **Shipping costs:** How can shipping costs be kept as low as possible?
- **Disposal:** Should we make the backpacks to last, or should they break down so that we can make money selling replacements?

Following the brainstorming sessions, the company develops the new designs and manufacturing procedures for producing the new product.

Figure 3 Companies try to choose colours and styles that appeal to as many people as possible.

Figure 4 Companies using overseas manufacturers must consider worker rights and safety.

⏱ TRY THIS: Market Research for Backpacks

SKILLS HANDBOOK
3.K.2.

SKILLS MENU: planning, analyzing, evaluating, communicating

In this activity, you will use backpacks as the focus to analyze the needs and wants of the intended customers.

1. In a group, brainstorm what you think are the most important design and manufacturing factors to consider in creating backpacks. Use the factors that are described above and add more ideas of your own.

2. Choose three design factors and three manufacturing factors that your group agrees are most important. Create six to twelve survey questions for those six factors. (You can refer to the questions mentioned above, but you must add questions of your own.) Make your questions easy to answer and evaluate.

3. Discuss and record the answers to your own questions.

4. Trade survey questions with another group, and answer each other's questions.

A. Summarize the answers to your group's survey questions.

B. Analyze the answers to your survey questions and draw conclusions about each of the design and manufacturing factors your group considered.

C. How will the results of the survey help your group design and manufacture a better backpack?

D. What are some limitations of market research surveys? How can we overcome these limitations?

Sales Factors

Once a product has been manufactured, it is made available to potential customers. To sell a product, the company must consider the following:

• **Packaging design, displays, and labelling:** Packaging is designed to protect the product in transport and storage. Packaging may also be used to attract customers (Figure 5). Labels provide product information and the company's identity. What packaging and displays make backpacks more attractive to customers? What packaging is environmentally friendly? What should be on the labels?

• **Sale price:** The price of a product determines who can afford to buy it (Figure 6). The price reflects the cost of production and the profit a company makes in selling the product. What is a reasonable price for a backpack? How might the price be related to quality?

• **Advertising:** Advertising informs potential customers of the availability of products. It allows customers to compare different products. How should backpack companies advertise?

• **Customer Support:** After a product is sold, customers may need more information on the product, especially if something goes wrong. What form of customer support should companies provide? Should the support be free?

Figure 5 Displays help attract customers to a product.

Figure 6 Price determines who can afford a product.

Design, manufacturing, and sales factors are all important considerations for companies when they decide to create a new product. Companies need to ensure that what they create will be desirable to the market, but they must also consider the impact that building the product will have on society and the environment.

To learn more about the manufacturing and sales process,

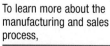 Go to Nelson Science

✓ CHECK YOUR LEARNING

1. What do you think is the most important set of factors for a company to consider—design, manufacturing, or sales? Explain your reasoning.

2. What three factors do companies consider before they build a new product?

3. Consider a company that would like to start designing, building, and selling new bicycles.

   (a) Describe one economic, one environmental, and one health and safety factor the company could consider.

   (b) Describe one packaging, one advertising, and one customer support factor the company could consider.

A Megatron in Townsville

SKILLS MENU
☐ Defining the Issue
☑ Researching
☑ Identifying Alternatives
☑ Analyzing the Issue
☑ Defending a Decision
☑ Communicating
☑ Evaluating

Townsville is a community in Central Ontario. Many businesses in its downtown area are closing. Consumers are being drawn to the large shopping mall on the outskirts of town.

The Chamber of Commerce of Townsville wants to install a large high-definition television (HDTV) billboard at the main intersection of town. The proposed HDTV Megatron would be larger than the Videoboard at the Rogers Centre in downtown Toronto (Figure 1). The Chamber is hoping that having "the largest HDTV panel in Canada" will attract visitors, businesses, and investment downtown. The Megatron is very expensive. The Chamber claims that the HDTV Megatron will eventually pay for itself by attracting businesses and by selling advertising time on its screen.

Figure 1 The Videoboard at the Rogers Centre measures 34 m × 10 m and is capable of displaying 4.3 trillion colours.

The Issue

The Townsville Heritage Society is concerned about how the Megatron will look in their small, Victorian town (Figure 2). The Society thinks the new billboard will drive away tourists. The local Friends of the Environment group is worried about the amount of power the new screen will use. They are also worried about the added light pollution that may disrupt the flight of migratory birds. The townspeople are concerned about extra noise and accidents caused by drivers who are distracted by the giant screen.

Should Townsville install the Megatron? You are being asked to participate in a town hall meeting to discuss this important issue.

Figure 2 How will a Megatron look in a small, Victorian town, such as Goderich, Ontario?

Goal

To evaluate the Townsville Chamber of Commerce's plans for installing a Megatron at the main intersection of Townsville.

Gather Information

How will you prepare for the town hall meeting? You might investigate the purchase costs, the power cost, and how long the TV would last before needing replacement. You could research how many birds die from striking buildings and other human-made structures. What are the causes and effects of driver distraction? Where could you find more information about small town renewal projects in Ontario?

Go to Nelson Science

Identify Solutions

You may want to consider the following to help you identify solutions:
- Can the Megatron be designed and constructed in a way that minimizes its negative effects on the environment and still attracts people and businesses to Townsville's downtown?
- Are there more structural ways to revitalize Townsville's downtown area that still fit with its Victorian style?

Table 1 offers some different points of view about the new Megatron.

Table 1 The Megatron: Points of View

Role	Points of View
Chamber of Commerce	Local businesses are failing. The Megatron will show businesses and investors that Townsville is a good place to do business.
Townsville Heritage Society	Townsville's Victorian architecture should be preserved. The Megatron will look terrible. Tourists who are looking for small-town atmosphere will be driven away.
Friends of the Environment	Migratory birds will be killed due to the light pollution of the new sign. The Megatron wastes energy.
Townsperson #1	All that extra noise and distraction will ruin our town. There will be more car accidents.
Townsperson #2	We had to close down our business this year; everyone is shopping at the new mall. Townsville needs something to bring business back to the downtown core.

Make a Decision

Choose a point of view and make a clear decision about whether to install the Megatron or not. What criteria did you use in coming to your decision?

Communicate

Participate in the town hall meeting. When the meeting is over, write a brief report on the outcome. Explain what the final decision was and how it was made.

Symmetry in Form and Function

We immediately notice a structure's shape and size when we look at it. The shape of an object helps us identify it. The shape also helps us distinguish it from other objects. One aspect of shape is symmetry. A structure displays **symmetry** (is symmetrical) if it can be divided in half, creating two pieces that are mirror images of each other. A **line of symmetry** is an imaginary line that divides a symmetrical object into two mirror image halves (Figure 1).

symmetry: an exact reflection on opposite sides of a line dividing an object in half

line of symmetry: a line that divides an object in half; helps display symmetry

(a)

(b)

(c)

(d)

Figure 1 The CN Tower (a), jet aircraft (b), table lamp (c), and butterfly (d) all display symmetry.

Symmetry in Nature

Symmetry is an important principle in nature. Look at yourself in the mirror. Pretend that there is a line going down from your forehead, over the tip of your nose, through the middle of your chin, and then straight down the centre of your body. You will notice that the two halves of your body on each side of this imaginary line are nearly mirror images of each other. (No one is perfectly symmetrical.) The entire human body is nearly symmetrical when a line of symmetry is drawn in this way (Figure 2). Humans usually have two kidneys, two lungs, two symmetrical rib cages—even the human brain is divided into two symmetrical lobes. Is the human body symmetrical if viewed above and below the waistline?

Humans exhibit symmetry. Dogs, cats, butterflies, flowers, leaves, and sea stars all exhibit symmetry. Symmetrical structures are all around us.

Figure 2 In 1492, Leonardo da Vinci illustrated the symmetry in the human body in one of his most famous drawings, the *Vitruvian Man*.

The Role of Symmetry

Symmetry is an important idea when considering the aesthetics of a structure. **Aesthetics** determine how visually appealing something is. Many people consider objects that are symmetrical to be more appealing than objects that are asymmetrical (not symmetrical) (Figure 3).

aesthetics: the concept of how visually attractive or beautiful something is

Asymmetrical Design

Would you like to live in a building where the walls were not straight, the floor was uneven, and none of the windows were the same size? These designs were all used in structures designed by Austrian artist Friedensreich Hundertwasser (1928–2000). Hundertwasser is famous among modern artists for rejecting symmetry as a design principle. Most of Hundertwasser's structures (Figure 4) and designs are controversial. Today, people find Hundertwasser's designs to be interesting because they are unique. It remains to be seen whether his structures will still be appreciated years from now.

To learn more about Friedensreich Hundertwasser and his designs,

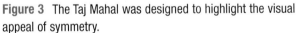

Figure 3 The Taj Mahal was designed to highlight the visual appeal of symmetry.

Figure 4 Hundertwasser rejects symmetry in his designs, but do they still have aesthetic appeal?

TRY THIS: Choosing an Apartment

SKILLS HANDBOOK
8.B.2.

SKILLS MENU: performing, evaluating, communicating

In this activity, you will role-play a real estate agent and an apartment hunter, and explore the benefits of symmetry and asymmetry in an apartment.

1. Work with a partner for this activity. Choose one of you to role-play the real estate agent and one the apartment hunter.

2. The real estate agent will prepare a convincing argument on why an asymmetrical apartment is better than an apartment in a more symmetrical building.

3. The apartment hunter will evaluate the argument and decide whether it would convince him or her to live there.

4. Now, switch roles. This time, have the new real estate agent prepare a persuasive argument on the benefits of a symmetrical apartment. The new client will evaluate the argument.

A. Were your partner's arguments convincing? Why or why not?

B. Now that you have completed this activity, which apartment would you prefer? Explain.

Symmetry, Centre of Gravity, and Stability

Symmetry is usually considered attractive. It is also useful in the design of stable structures. The dead load of a symmetrical structure is usually spread more evenly along the length of the structure. This makes the structure more stable.

A designer constructs a more stable structure by considering the location of the centre of gravity in a structure's design. The location of the line of symmetry can sometimes help to locate a structure's centre of gravity. In Figure 5, the pyramid is completely symmetrical. A line of symmetry could be drawn through any of the four triangular faces of the pyramid. In this case, the centre of gravity is located directly below where the lines of symmetry would meet, deep in the very centre of the pyramid. Pyramids like this are very stable.

While lines of symmetry sometimes help to locate a structure's centre of gravity, this is not always true. A structure's centre of gravity is only located on its line of symmetry when the mass of the structure is evenly spread out. A line of symmetry is only visual. It does not account for the mass of a structure and how that mass is arranged. Consider Figure 6. The pyramid is still symmetrical. However, the centre of gravity is no longer on any line of symmetry because the mass of the pyramid is no longer evenly spread out. One side has more mass than the other side.

Figure 5 El Castillo, located in Chichen Itza, Yucatan, Mexico, was built by the Mayans between the eleventh and thirteenth centuries CE.

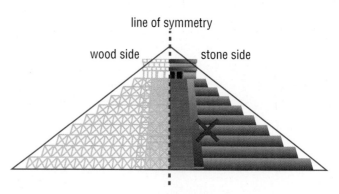

Figure 6 The left side of this pyramid has been built out of wood. The centre of gravity is no longer on the line of symmetry.

Unit Task How can you apply your understanding of symmetry to the Unit Task?

✔ CHECK YOUR LEARNING

1. Draw three symmetrical geometrical figures. Clearly mark the line of symmetry on each figure.

2. Why is symmetry considered to be an important principle in the design of structures? Give two reasons in your explanation.

3. **(a)** Give two examples of symmetrical objects from nature, and two that have been built by humans.

   (b) Find an example of an asymmetrical structure, either human-made or from nature. Evaluate the structure in terms of stability and aesthetics.

Ergonomics: Designing for Human Comfort and Safety

You use tools every day. You may use a knife, shovel, or toothbrush (Figure 1) in your everyday life. Does the tool fit comfortably into your hand? When you type an e-mail message or open a car door, is the task completed quickly and easily? The science of designing structures and systems that help people do tasks comfortably and safely is called **ergonomics**.

Small design changes can make a big difference in a structure's ergonomics. For example, using a snow shovel can mean getting a backache from all the bending and lifting. The ergonomic snow shovel in Figure 2 has a bent handle. This type of handle reduces the amount of bending a person has to do when shovelling. The design reduces back strain and helps prevent back injuries.

ergonomics: the science of using knowledge of human characteristics to design structures and systems that are comfortable, safe, and efficient

Figure 1 Ergonomic designs can be applied to many everyday structures.

Figure 2 The bent handle of this ergonomic snow shovel means less stress on the spine and reduced risk of back injuries.

LINKING TO LITERACY

Word Origin
Sometimes knowing where a word comes from helps us to understand its meaning. The word "ergonomics" comes from the Greek words *ergon*, meaning "work," and *nomos*, meaning "natural law."

In the 1600s, doctors knew that people who worked in awkward positions for long periods of time would develop illnesses and injuries. Today, ergonomics is often used in the design of workplace tools. Workers can complete tasks faster, more accurately, and with fewer injuries using ergonomic tools and workstations. Sitting at a computer for long periods of time can cause strain to your neck, wrists, lower back, and your eyes if your workstation is organized poorly. Now imagine a factory with heavy machinery. The risk of injury increases if the tools and workstations in a factory are not ergonomically designed.

Designers can create tools, workstations, and systems that are easier, more comfortable, and safer for workers using these principles of ergonomic design:
- Tools and workstations should allow workers to change their position regularly to other equally comfortable positions. Workers could stand at a workbench or sit on a stool to complete a task.
- Tools and workstations should reduce the amount of force or effort that a task requires. Workers should never strain at an activity. They could use power tools rather than hand tools.
- Tools and workstations should promote good posture for the body. A worker's back, neck, and wrists should remain straight. His or her arms should remain close to the body when working. Equipment should be positioned within easy and comfortable reach.

TRY THIS: Analyze Your Computer Workstation

SKILLS MENU: observing, analyzing, evaluating

Computers are a part of our daily lives. If computer workstations are not ergonomic, then they can lead to injuries. In this activity, you will work with a partner to examine your computer workstation for correct ergonomics.

Equipment and Materials: computer workstation

1. Examine Figure 3. Note how the student's eye level is about 5 cm from the centre of the top of the monitor screen. The monitor and keyboard are centred in front of her. The student's feet are flat on the footrest and her wrists are flat (not bent).

2. Have your partner sit at a computer workstation as he or she normally would do. Observe your partner's sitting position and the arrangement of the computer workstation. Make notes and a sketch of your partner's sitting position.

3. Now switch roles and complete step 2 again.

A. According to your observations, is your computer workstation designed ergonomically?

B. What, if any, recommendations would you make to improve your computer workstation?

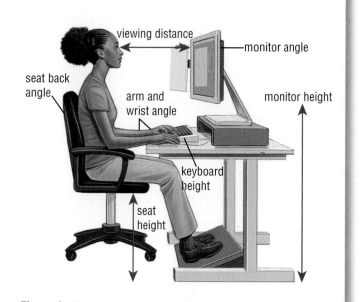

Figure 3 An ergonomic workstation

The knife, like the snow shovel, is another common tool that has been improved with the application of ergonomics. Humans have used knives for millennia. The first knife was probably as simple as a stone with a sharp edge, or a sharp piece of seashell (Figure 4). Today, knives are designed for specific needs (Figure 5). The ergonomic knife is designed to keep your wrist in a comfortable, straight position. Keeping the wrist straight decreases the risk of repetitive strain injuries. **Repetitive strain injuries** are sprains or strains of the small muscles of the hands or wrists that come from constant and repeated activities. Using ergonomically designed tools correctly reduces the risk of these injuries. Using any knife correctly can reduce the risk of accidental cuts.

repetitive strain injury: damage, usually to the small muscles of the wrists or hands, from repeated activities over a long period of time

Figure 4 This knife was carved from obsidian sometime between 300 BCE and 500 CE.

Figure 5 With this ergonomic chef's knife, your wrist is kept straight and your fingers are kept far away from the blade.

Unit Task How could you apply your understanding of ergonomics to your plans for the Unit Task?

✔ CHECK YOUR LEARNING

1. In your own words, define "ergonomics."

2. Choose a device that you use often (for example, cell phone, MP3 music player, computer, television remote control). Suggest some improvements to make this device more ergonomic, using the principles of ergonomics listed in this section.

3. The *ulu* (rocking knife), invented by Inuit (Figure 6), uses an efficient rocking motion that requires less strength to use. Discuss the benefits of this design.

4. What is a repetitive strain injury? How can people avoid getting such injuries?

Figure 6 An *ulu*

12.4 Ergonomics: Designing for Human Comfort and Safety **329**

Applying Ergonomics— Making a Better Keyboard

In a mechanical typewriter, pressing down a letter key caused a metal arm with a raised form of the letter to lift up. The letter form would strike the piece of paper, leaving an imprint of that letter. Christopher Latham Sholes originally used alphabetical order for the keys. In this design, the metal arms would cross on their way to striking the paper, and frequently jam. He rearranged the keys with the most frequently typed letters spread out. This layout slowed the typist down and ensured that keys did not jam as often. Sholes's layout is called the QWERTY keyboard (Figure 1), named after the order of the first six characters in the upper row. In this activity, you will attempt to design a keyboard that is more ergonomic than the QWERTY keyboard.

SKILLS MENU

- ☐ Questioning
- ☐ Hypothesizing
- ☐ Predicting
- ☐ Planning
- ☐ Controlling Variables
- ☑ Performing
- ☑ Observing
- ☑ Analyzing
- ☑ Evaluating
- ☑ Communicating

Figure 1 The QWERTY keyboard

Purpose

To redesign a standard computer keyboard to make it more ergonomic.

Equipment and Materials

- one 200-word section of prose for each group; each piece of prose should be different
- 279 mm × 432 mm (11 in. × 17 in.) sheet of paper

200-word section of prose

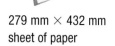
279 mm × 432 mm sheet of paper

Procedure

1. Copy Table 1 into your notebook. Tally the number of times (the frequency) each letter of the alphabet appears in your group's section of prose. Record this number on your table.

Table 1

Alphabet	Tally
A	
B	
C	
D	

2. Draw another table, and reorder the letters from most frequent to least frequent. This is your frequency table.

3. Use your frequency table to redesign the order of letters on the keyboard. Consider these ergonomic tips in your keyboard design:

   - It is more comfortable to type when the typing alternates between the left and right hands. Typing too many letters with only one hand is tiring. Spread the most frequently used letters from your frequency table evenly between the left and the right sides of the keyboard.

   - Place the most frequently used letters from your frequency table in the middle row of your keyboard. This means that fingers will have to move the least distance.

   - The most difficult row for fingers to reach is the bottom row. Place the least frequently used letters on your frequency table on the bottom row.

   - The ring fingers and little fingers are less strong than the middle and index fingers of the hand. Use the ring finger and little finger for the less frequently used letters on your frequency table.

4. Draw a blank keyboard on a large piece of paper. Place your new arrangement of letters on the keyboard.

5. If time permits and if a computer keyboard is available, compare your typing efficiency using the QWERTY keyboard and your redesigned keyboard.

Analyze and Evaluate

(a) Justify your keyboard arrangement. Why would your arrangement be more comfortable to use, and would it reduce stress injuries from repeated motions?

(b) Compare your keyboard layout with the keyboard designs of your classmates. Identify similarities and differences.

(c) Compare your list of the most frequently appearing letters with your classmates' lists. Look at the top 10 most frequently appearing letters. Why are there differences in the frequency lists?

(d) Conduct research on the DVORAK keyboard, a keyboard designed according to the ergonomic principles similar to those in this activity. Compare your final keyboard design to the DVORAK keyboard. Identify similarities and differences. Consider some reasons why the QWERTY keyboard is still widely used, despite the DVORAK keyboard being a better ergonomic design.

Apply and Extend

(e) Combine all of the original frequency charts from all the groups in the class to create a new master list. Working as a class, redesign the keyboard using the new master list. Compare your class's keyboard to your group's original keyboard. Why are there some differences?

(f) Compare the class's keyboard to the DVORAK keyboard. Why are there differences?

Universal Design

How easily could you move around your school or community in a wheelchair (Figure 1)? People who use wheelchairs have special needs. People with vision or hearing difficulties, and people who are elderly, also have special needs. Children need help with many tasks that adults find easy. Many people have many different kinds of physical challenges. Buildings that are "accessible" are designed for people with special needs (Figure 2).

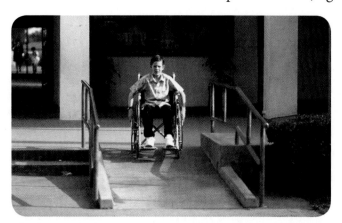

Figure 1 Accessible design allows everyone to have access to buildings.

Figure 2 Icons or symbols indicate accessible features of buildings.

People with special needs have had a long struggle to get their needs addressed in structural designs. Designers began to pay attention to special needs after World War II. Many war veterans returned home with injuries. Ramps to homes and office buildings were built. Elevators were designed to indicate the floor through buttons with Braille lettering and numbering, as well as through sight and sound.

Buildings need to be accessible for everyone. Buildings and parts of buildings are designed so that simple tasks are convenient for everybody. Everyone should be able to open a door (Figure 3), turn on a tap, or reach items on a shelf. A design that combines everyday usage with special needs usage is more universal. **Universal design** is an arrangement of the parts of a structure or device that creates a user-friendly product.

universal design: an arrangement of the components of a structure or device resulting in the most user-friendly product possible

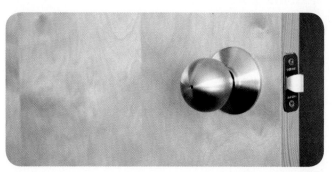

Figure 3 Imagine that your hands are damp as you try to turn each doorknob. Which doorknob design do you think would be easier to use?

Main Principles of Universal Design

There are specific principles of good universal design (Figure 4). Universal design means that structures should be

- *equal* (as equal as possible) for all users
- *flexible* (useful for a wide range of abilities and choices)
- *simple* to use and *informative* (easy to use, whatever the user's experience, knowledge, language skills, or physical abilities)
- *safe and tolerant of errors* (provides warnings and safety features in case of errors by the users)
- *ergonomic* (provides enough space and reduces the need for excess force or repeated actions)

Universal design is more functional than basic accessible design. Universal design considers special needs due to injury, illness, or old age to be a normal part of the human range. It is a way of saying, "We are all in this together."

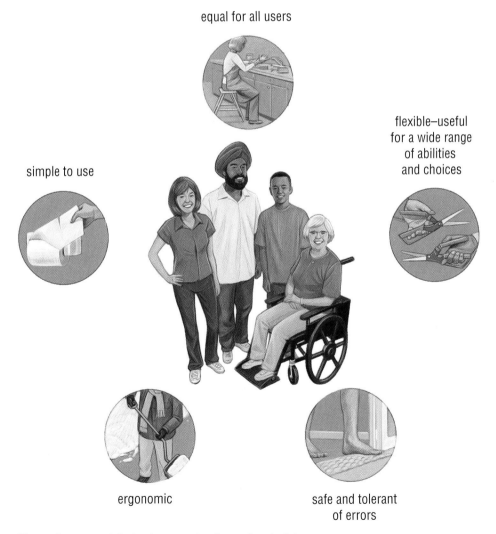

equal for all users

flexible–useful for a wide range of abilities and choices

simple to use

ergonomic

safe and tolerant of errors

Figure 4 Universal design incorporates five main principles.

Universal designs are comfortable and convenient for anyone using the tool, not just those with special needs. Universal design is also better for the environment. Today's houses are built with wide hallways and doorways. This way, houses do not have to be renovated to accommodate someone in a wheelchair. That means less construction waste in landfills. Universal design is efficient design because it lasts longer.

TRY THIS: Using the Principles of Universal Design

SKILLS MENU: planning, analyzing, evaluating, communicating

SKILLS HANDBOOK 4.B.

Choose one of the items listed below. You may choose to work in partners or groups. On paper, create a universal design that would be appropriate for the greatest variety of people. As you plan and alter your diagrams, be sure to consider the five main principles of universal design.

1. Design a bedroom closet that can be arranged for three generations of users: a 5-year-old child, someone your age, and an older person, such as a grandparent.

2. A compost collection bin with two wheels is short and awkward to pull (Figure 5). Redesign a similar bin that is more universal. Consider both the homeowner and the workers who collect the waste.

Figure 5 How can the design of this bin be made more universal?

3. A city wants to improve the way bicycles can be placed onto a public bus to promote the use of bicycles. The design must be safe, secure, and fast to use.

4. Choose a school spectator sport, either indoor or outdoor. Create a set of bleachers and communication methods so that every fan in the bleachers is able to follow the minute-by-minute action and know such details as the score and time remaining.

A. Is your design attractive and appealing enough for people to actually want to use it? Explain.

B. Could your design be used by all people, no matter what their size or abilities? Who would not be able to use your design easily?

C. How is your design environmentally responsible?

D. Self-evaluate your design by giving it a mark out of 10 for each of the items described below, and then add the marks and express your evaluation as a percentage.
   • visual appeal
   • environmental responsibility
   • each of the five principles of universal design

E. Describe two ways you could improve your design.

Unit Task   How could you apply your understanding of universal design to your plans for the Unit Task?

CHECK YOUR LEARNING

1. In your own words, define "universal design."

2. When did designers start to pay attention to people with special needs? Explain why.

3. List the five principles of universal design.

4. State two examples of non-universal design based on your own observations and experience.

5. For each of the following examples, state at least one principle of universal design that is *not* followed:
   (a) A stove has control knobs at the front of the burners.
   (b) A study lamp has a small-diameter switch that the user must rotate.
   (c) A backpack digs into your back and shoulders.
   (d) An umbrella flips inside out in the wind.
   (e) The support cables of a playground swing are made of strong but small-diameter metal wire.

SCIENCE WORKS

The Golden Ratio

Sculptors, builders, and engineers have known for a long time that a particular height-to-width ratio is pleasing to the eye. This is known as the golden ratio. The golden ratio is also sometimes known as "phi" and is represented by the Greek symbol ϕ. The actual value of the golden ratio is approximately 1.618. Like the number pi (π), the numbers of phi go on forever without repeating. Ancient Greek mathematicians studied the golden ratio because it often appears in geometry. Discovery of this ratio is often attributed to Pythagoras.

The golden ratio was used in the design of the Great Pyramid of Giza. If you compare the height of the Great Pyramid to half its length, the result is the golden ratio. Artists also make use of the golden ratio. The dimensions of the height to the width of the face of Leonardo da Vinci's *Mona Lisa*, one of the most famous paintings in the world, are in the golden ratio.

Most people find a rectangle with a width-to-height ratio of 1:1.6 (rounded to one decimal place) to be more pleasing to the eye than any other dimensions. A rectangle with these dimensions is known as a golden rectangle. The Parthenon in Greece exhibits many golden rectangles in its design (Figure 1).

Figure 1 Built over 2500 years ago, the Parthenon has many golden rectangles throughout its structure.

Many objects in nature also exhibit the golden ratio. Examine the image of the tiger in Figure 2. Measure the length of the tiger's body, and the length of its head. Divide these numbers by one another. What do you get? Try this with more animal pictures and check the validity of your first result.

To learn more about the golden ratio,

Go to Nelson Science

Figure 2 Discover the golden ratio in nature.

LINKING TO LITERACY

Making Inferences

Texts can have "literal" meanings or "inferred" meanings. "Literal" means that the text means exactly what it says. "Inferred" means that a text says something, but really means something more.

Readers make inferences by thinking about what they have read in a text. Then, they make a connection to what they already know, to make an informed guess about what the text really means.

See if you can infer the meaning of the following:

- If the tiger calculation equals the golden ratio, what "inference" can you make about calculations for other animals?

Form, Function, and Beauty

BIG Ideas

- ☑ Structures have a purpose.
- ☑ The form of a structure is dependent on its function.
- ☐ The interaction between structures and forces is predictable.

Looking Back

The product development process considers human wants and needs, and also societal and environmental factors.

- Design factors relate to designing the product.
- Manufacturing factors relate to manufacturing the product.
- Sales factors consider the places where a product will be sold, the price of the product, and support for the purchaser.
- Companies try to ensure that products will be successful by conducting market research.

Structures that are symmetrical are usually more stable and more aesthetically pleasing than those that are asymmetrical.

- Symmetry is present in nature and in the human-made world.
- Many people consider objects that are symmetrical to be more appealing than those that are asymmetrical.
- The line of symmetry can help to locate a structure's centre of gravity.

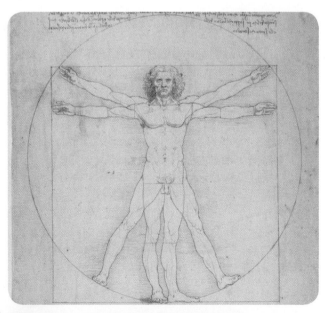

Structures intended for human use need to be designed for human characteristics.

- Ergonomics is an important consideration in the design, construction, and use of a product.
- Ergonomically designed structures are safer and prevent injuries.
- Different groups of people have different needs and require products that are designed for them.
- The principles of universal design help make structures accessible to all people of all abilities.

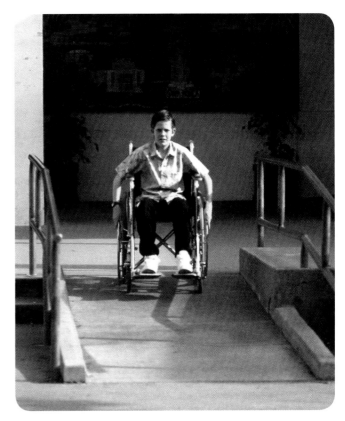

The skills of scientific inquiry can be used to study the ergonomics of everyday tools.

- The QWERTY keyboard is a tool used by many people every day. The science of ergonomics can be used to redesign the keyboard to make it more efficient and easier to use.

CHAPTER 12 REVIEW

The following icons indicate the Achievement Chart categories:　K/U Knowledge/Understanding　T/I Thinking/Investigation　C Communication　A Application

What Do You Remember?

1. (a) List the four design factors.

   (b) List two questions that you would ask for each of these factors when designing a product such as a running shoe. K/U T/I

2. (a) What is market research?

   (b) Why is market research important to companies?

   (c) Why might market research be important to consumers? K/U

3. In your own words, define "ergonomics." K/U

4. How are ergonomics and universal design related? K/U

What Do You Understand?

5. (a) When thinking about a purchase, do you consider the product's life cycle and disposal? Why or why not?

   (b) What benefits would be gained if everyone considered a product's life cycle before making a purchase? Explain. T/I

6. The Royal Bank Plaza towers in Toronto have over 70 000 g of real gold coating on their windows (Figure 1). One reason is to provide thermal insulation. What other reasons did the bank consider when they decided to use gold-coated glass? K/U T/I

Figure 1

7. (a) What is meant by the term "symmetry"?

   (b) List three structures that you have seen today that clearly exhibit symmetry. K/U A

8. (a) How does market research benefit society? How does it cause harm to society?

   (b) How does market research benefit the environment? How does it cause harm to the environment? K/U A

9. (a) Why is symmetry important in the natural world?

   (b) Is the importance of symmetry in human-made structures the same or different as in the natural world? Explain. K/U

10. Did universal design lead to accessibility, or did accessibility lead to universal design? Explain. K/U

11. (a) The amount of energy it takes to produce a product is an important factor for manufacturers to consider in the development of a new product. Why?

    (b) What other factors do manufacturers need to consider in a product's development? K/U

12. Why do some manufacturers want to build products that wear out quickly? K/U

Solve a Problem!

13. (a) Why is ergonomics an important part of the design process?

    (b) Pick an item from your everyday life, such as your computer desk, a light switch, or a remote control, that you think could have a more ergonomic design. What would you do to improve its design?

    (c) Would you pay more for an ergonomically designed product? Why or why not? K/U A

Create and Evaluate!

14. (a) Using library resources and the Internet, research the Aeron chair.

(b) Is your classroom chair as ergonomic as the Aeron chair? Explain. In your notebook, copy and complete Table 1 to help you organize your thinking. T/I A

Table 1

Alike	Different

15. Municipalities often spend public tax dollars on the aesthetics of civic buildings.

(a) How do governments justify spending large amounts of public money on aesthetics?

(b) In your opinion, how reasonable is this point of view? A C

16. Manufacturers often use computer simulations when designing new products. What are the advantages and disadvantages of designing with computer simulations? Use a t-chart to organize your thinking. A C

17. Environmentalists often say that true conservation will only arrive when consumers pay the true cost of a product.

(a) What do you think is meant by this statement?

(b) Analyze some of the hidden costs in the manufacture of a backpack.

(c) Do you believe that paying the true cost would result in real conservation? Justify your opinion.

(d) Many products today advertise themselves as "green." Why do they do this? Examine the claims of one such product, and evaluate the validity of the claims. A

18. Your parents are thinking of moving into a Hundertwasser design–inspired structure.

(a) Compare the positives and negatives of such a move. Use a t-chart to help organize your thinking.

(b) Would you like to live in such a building? Why or why not? A C

19. Examine the image in Figure 2. The BCE Place Galleria won a major architectural award. Assess the design styles used in the Galleria. Why was this structure found to be so outstanding? Do you find this design to be unique and interesting? Is it beautiful? If yes, explain why. If no, clearly outline your areas of criticism. K/U T/I A C

Figure 2

Reflect on Your Learning

20. In this chapter, you have learned that ergonomics is important to design.

(a) What did you understand about ergonomics before reading about it in this chapter?

(b) How has your understanding of ergonomics changed?

21. Think back to the Key Question on the first page of this chapter.

(a) In a brief paragraph, answer the Key Question. You may use diagrams.

(b) Write one or two more questions about the topic of this unit that you would like to explore.

Play Time Is the Best Time

Background

The modern playground is designed to be innovative, challenging, safe, and fun. New materials allow designers to come up with designs that would have been unlikely just a short time ago. Many playgrounds are designed to be accessible to children with disabilities.

Scenario

You work for an engineering firm that makes playground equipment. Your design team has been chosen to create a new piece of playground equipment. You and your team have three challenges:

1. **Design and construct a model of a new piece of playground equipment.** Your model should include a scale diagram for construction, including a front, side, and top view. Your diagrams should include an explanation of why you selected the design that you used. Be sure to include the ages of the children who will be using the equipment and whether your equipment will be accessible to children with disabilities (Figure 1).

Figure 1 Will your new playground equipment be accessible to children with disabilities?

2. **Promote your new equipment.** You will prepare an advertisement for your playground equipment. Your advertisement must include audio (verbal) and visual parts. It must be designed to inform and persuade communities that are building new playgrounds to use your design. They must see the advantages of your piece of playground equipment. Remember to write in a persuasive but truthful way.

3. **Prepare your presentation.** You will prepare a multimedia presentation for your board of directors. The presentation will explain how your team met the challenge of designing an exciting and safe piece of playground equipment, and created a way to promote the equipment to the community.

Design Brief

In your design brief, clearly describe your piece of playground equipment and why you have selected this particular piece to build. You should also include a description of your design and how you intend to build your model. Include a description of who will use the equipment.

Equipment and Materials

SKILLS HANDBOOK
4.B.3.

Make a list of all the equipment and materials your team will need to complete your challenge. Use as many found materials as possible. Remember to consider whether your materials can be reused or recycled. Make sure to include the materials you will need for parts 2 and 3 of your challenge, as well as those you will need for your model.

Research and Consider

Research what kinds of playground equipment already exist, what equipment is popular, and what needs the popular equipment meets.

 Go to Nelson Science

Plan and Construct

Write step-by-step instructions of how you will build your model and assign tasks to your team members. Make sure that everyone contributes equally. Try to be innovative in your design. Remember that the playground must be both fun and safe. You may decide that you want your equipment to be accessible to children of all ages and abilities. If so, then this will be a major factor in your design process.

Test and Modify

 SKILLS HANDBOOK 4.B.5., 4.B.6.

Make sure you leave enough time to test your model and make changes, if necessary. Use jot notes to keep track of ideas for your promotion and your presentation.

Evaluate

Does your equipment model meet its design criteria? Is it to scale, strong enough to support loads, stable, and fun for the children who will use it? Use the Assessment box to help you.

Communicate

 SKILLS HANDBOOK 8.

Your promotional material should stress safety design factors, innovation, creativity, and how much fun can be had on the playground. Universal design, including accessibility for children with disabilities, should also be highlighted if these were major design factors for your equipment. Make sure that there are both audio and visual parts to your promotional material (poster, brochure, and script or storyboard).

You will also prepare a multimedia presentation for your board of directors on your design. Be sure to make your equipment sound exciting, yet safe. Your presentation should also describe your advertisement.

Assessment

You will be assessed on how well you

- meet the established criteria
- demonstrate an understanding of concepts, principles, and terminology
- show effective and safe use of materials
- understand the specific challenges
- make a plan to solve the problem
- carry out the plan, applying technical skills and procedures when necessary

- use critical/creative thinking processes to analyze the results
- prepare an appropriate presentation of the task that includes a clear expression and organization of ideas and information
- relate your finished product to society and how it could affect the lives of people
- assess the practical problems relating to the challenge and how they could affect the environment

Form and Function

Make a Summary

Word Summary

Review the vocabulary terms from this unit with a small group of classmates. Choose one vocabulary term from each chapter. Your teacher will keep a master list to make sure each group chooses different terms. For each vocabulary term, have each group member copy and complete the Vocabulary Terms Chart (Figure 1). Then, compare your charts. Were any of the other definitions different from yours? Update your Vocabulary Terms Charts with the new information.

Review the Vocabulary Terms Chart as a class. Create a Vocabulary Terms class book for the whole class to use as a reference.

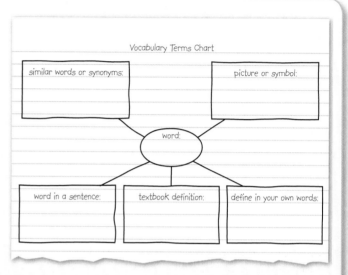

Figure 1

Unit Review Questions

What Do You Remember?

The following icons indicate the Achievement Chart categories:

K/U Knowledge/Understanding   T/I Thinking/Investigation
C Communication   A Application

1. In your notebook, complete each sentence by filling in the most appropriate word(s): K/U

truss	arch	stable	magnitude
rebar	centre of gravity	shape	form

(a) An object is _____ if it maintains its shape and position over an extended period of time.

(b) The horizontal balance point of an object is very close to its _____.

(c) A network of beams that form triangles is known as a(n) _____.

(d) The strength of a beam can be changed by changing its _____.

(e) The shape and outer physical appearance of a structure is known as its _____.

(f) A(n) _____ supports a load by directing force downward along a curve.

(g) Reinforcing steel rods in concrete are called _____.

(h) The term _____ refers to the size of a force.

2. (a) Clearly distinguish between external and internal forces.

(b) List the four internal forces, and give a brief description of each. K/U

3. Identify and describe

(a) three factors that could determine the ability of a structure to support a load

(b) four factors that can cause a structure to fail K/U

4. Briefly list four ways that a beam can be strengthened. K/U

5. What is the main function of market research? K/U

6. Concrete is one of the basic materials used in modern structures.

(a) How does concrete react to compression and tension forces?

(b) How do engineers strengthen concrete? K/U

What Do You Understand?

7. Classify each of the structures in Figure 2 (a) to (d) as solid, frame, shell, or combination. Justify your choices. K/U

(a)

(c)

(b)

(d)

Figure 2

8. Why is symmetry such an important concept in how we design and build structures? K/U

9. Classify each of these examples as applications of the four internal forces:

(a) sitting on a cushion

(b) ripping a piece of paper in two

(c) stretching an elastic band

(d) a sweater twisted in a clothes dryer K/U A

10. (a) The International Space Station uses the truss as a framework for the entire station (Figure 3). Why is a truss such a useful structure in this situation?

Figure 3

(b) Provide three examples of trusses in structures in your community. K/U A

11. You are seated at your desk in school writing in your notebook.

(a) Describe an external force that is acting on the desk.

(b) Describe some of the internal forces acting on the desk, and where these forces are located.

(c) What would happen to the desk if the internal forces acting on it became too large for the desk to support?

K/U A T/I

12. Apply the terms "point of application" and "plane of application" to

   (a) pushing on a car that is stuck in the snow

   (b) pulling with both hands on a heavy garbage can to drag it out to the curb for pickup K/U A T/I

13. What is the relationship between an arch and a dome? Provide an example of an arch and an example of a dome. K/U A

14. Describe a dead load and a live load that acts on each of the following structures:

   (a) a set of stairs at school

   (b) bleachers in the school gymnasium K/U A

15. Clearly state the difference between a fully supported beam and a cantilever, and provide two examples of each. K/U A

16. Identify the structures in Figure 4 (a) to (d) as cantilever, truss, fully supported beam, or arch. K/U A

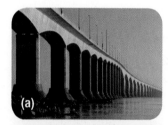
(a)

(c)

(b)

(d)

Figure 4

17. With a partner, brainstorm ergonomic reasons why a calculator and a computer numeric keypad have a different number placement than a telephone keypad. T/I

18. (a) What forces are acting on the diver in Figure 5?

   (b) What kind of force is acting on the top of the diving board? On the bottom?

   (c) What kind of beam is a diving board? K/U

Figure 5

19. (a) Research the Quebec Bridge collapse. Using a Venn diagram, compare the reasons for the collapse of the Quebec Bridge and the Tacoma Narrows Bridge.

   (b) Could these collapses have been prevented with the knowledge available at the time they were built? Explain. K/U T/I

Go to Nelson Science

20. Why is ergonomics important in the design of products? K/U

Solve a Problem!

21. Ergonomics has had a major impact on the design of objects. Think of a structure that you use regularly (for example, TV remote, iPod, backpack).

   (a) Describe ergonomic features that make this device comfortable to use.

   (b) Suggest a change in the structure or appearance of the device that may improve how comfortable it is to use. K/U A T/I

Create and Evaluate!

22. Evaluate the following structures under the categories of function and form:

    (a) your home

    (b) your school building

    (c) a mall T/I A

23. (a) How would you classify the ancient structures in Figures 6 and 7? Why do you think they have lasted hundreds of years?

    (b) Are there any modern structures that you think will last hundreds of years? Explain.
    K/U A

Figure 6   Figure 7

24. (a) Identify two disposable products, and suggest an alternative for each that people could use instead.

    (b) Why might some people prefer the disposable product compared to your suggested alternative?

    (c) What can you do to convince others to use your alternative product rather than the disposable product? T/I

25. (a) Large modern structures have deep foundations that are often drilled right into the rock that underlies the soil. Why is this done?

    (b) Would the Leaning Tower of Pisa have benefited from this construction method when it was being built? Explain. Why do you think they did not do this? A T/I

26. You have been asked to create a new reading lamp that cannot be easily tipped over. What design factors would you use to make a stable lamp? T/I A

Reflect on Your Learning

27. Think about a structure in your community.

    (a) Reflect on how important function and form are for this structure.

    (b) Do you like the structure? Explain.

    (c) Is the structure well built? Explain.

    (d) Describe one improvement that could be made to the structure. Why would this change improve the structure?

28. Science classifies structures on the basis of how they are put together as solid, frame, shell, or combination structures. In everyday life, however, we usually do not classify structures in this way. How might people classify structures in everyday life?

29. (a) In what way has what you learned in this unit made you look at everyday structures differently?

    (b) What was the most surprising idea you learned about in this unit? Explain.

SKILLS
HANDBOOK

Contents

1. The Nature of Science and Technology

1.A. Science Is About Understanding Nature

As you observe the world around you, you encounter objects and events that you want to know more about. Observations are evidence gained by the five senses: touch, smell, taste, hearing, and seeing. If you take time to reflect on your observations, ask questions about what you observe, and carefully search for answers, you will think and act more like a scientist.

One of the most important things you can do in science is ask questions. For example, suppose you observe that the leaves of a plant in your school suddenly turn yellow and begin to fall off their stems. You want to find out what has happened. First, you recall what you already know about plants. You remember that plants are living things that require water, light, and soil. You may also remember that adding fertilizer to soil helps plants stay healthy. As you compare what you already know about plants with your observations, you will likely ask questions and suggest possible reasons for the plant's poor health.

- Did the plant receive enough water?
- Was the plant exposed to the right amount of light?
- Did someone use the wrong fertilizer?
- Has an insect used the plant as food or given the plant a disease?

Observations and questions start the scientific thinking process by providing a topic to study and a reason to study it further.

Once you have asked some critical questions, you set out to answer those questions by making more detailed observations. You may examine the plant for marks on its stems and leaves, and look for unusual insects crawling in the soil.

You may take a picture of the plant and use library books or the Internet to identify it, determine its needs, and see if others have experienced the same problem. You are conducting an investigation. Eventually, you will find answers to your questions that increase your knowledge and understanding. You can then share your knowledge with others so that together you may solve new problems and prevent similar problems from happening again.

This is what science is all about: exploring the world, asking questions, and searching for answers that increase our understanding. We call this process **scientific inquiry**. Albert Einstein was only four or five years old when he started inquiring about the world around him. He was fascinated at how a magnetic compass works, and why the planets continuously move around the Sun. He asked questions like "How does the force of gravity keep the planets in place as they travel around the Sun?" Eventually, Einstein proposed an explanation for the force of gravity (Figure 1).

Figure 1 Albert Einstein

Dr. Dorothy Crowfoot Hodgkin was only ten years old when she first fell in love with crystals. She asked questions such as, "Why do crystals have a regular structure?" and "What do crystals look like under a microscope?" A family friend, Dr. A. J. Joseph, who lived next door to her in Sudan, encouraged her to study science. Many years later, Dr. Hodgkin won a Nobel Prize by using X-ray crystallography to discover the structure of the antibiotic called penicillin (Figure 2). If you have ever taken penicillin to clear up an infection, you are probably very thankful for Dr. Hodgkin's early interest in science.

Now, it is your turn. Look around and start asking questions about the world around you. Try experimenting. Use simple equipment like a tape measure, a thermometer, or a magnifying glass to observe and measure things. Then, use the library or the Internet to obtain more information, and discuss your findings with your teacher, friends, and family. Remember to write down what you learn!

1.A.1. Goals and Beliefs of Science

Some people think that science is mainly about facts and theories. But, this is only partly true. In addition to defining a large body of knowledge, science also involves a particular *way of learning* about the world by observing, asking questions, proposing answers, testing proposed answers, and sharing results with others.

A primary goal of science is to understand the natural and human-made world. This goal leads to the development of new knowledge and understanding. Laws and theories express our knowledge and understanding of nature, and they allow us to make and test predictions, which lead to new knowledge. For example, when Galileo first used a telescope to observe objects in the sky, he discovered several small moons around Jupiter. Galileo carefully recorded all of his observations so he could make sense of what he observed. When his findings were published, this information became available for other scientists to read and study.

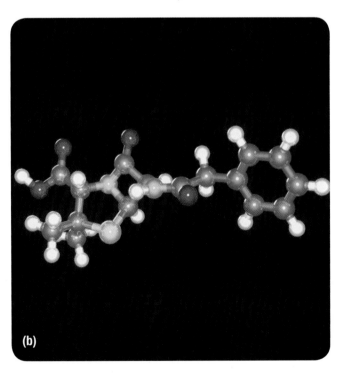

Figure 2 (a) Penicillin capsules (b) The chemical structure of penicillin

Sir Isaac Newton read about Galileo's discoveries. Newton used these and other observations to formulate the law of gravity to accurately describe the movements of Jupiter's moons, as well as the movements of the six planets known at that time. Other scientists later used the law of gravity to predict the existence of other planets in the solar system, outside of Jupiter and Saturn. This led to the identification of Uranus and Neptune. Sharing knowledge is important in helping scientists increase their understanding of the world (Figure 3).

Scientists begin with some basic beliefs about science:

- The natural world functions in consistent ways that can be studied, described, and understood.
- Scientific inquiry is one of the best ways to study the natural world.

- Scientific knowledge is limited. Scientists cannot always make accurate observations, measurements, and predictions.
- Scientific knowledge is never complete. Someone may develop a new idea that changes or adds to what we already know. However, much of our scientific knowledge is well founded. Some fundamentals, such as the laws of energy, the particle theory of matter, and the cellular basis of life, are unlikely to change.
- The components of the natural world are interconnected. Environments, ecosystems, living organisms, chemicals, fluids, oceans, and structures interact with each other in complex ways (Figure 4).
- The results of science can be helpful or harmful to society and the environment depending on how the knowledge is used.

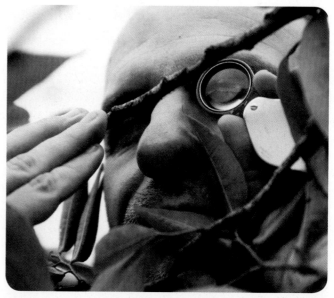

Figure 4 This botanist is studying the effect of pollution on trees.

Figure 3 Galileo's observations led to other important discoveries.

1.A.2. Scientific Laws and Theories

Laws What happens when a hot object comes into contact with a cold object? You hold a glass of cold water in your warm hand. Your hand cools down while the water slowly warms up. Your hand loses energy and the water gains energy. This is an example of a scientific law: Energy always flows from a warmer object to a colder object until both objects have the same temperature.

A **law** is a general statement that describes a commonly occurring natural event. It does not explain why or how a natural event occurs; it just describes what happens in detail. Scientific laws are very important and potentially useful ideas. Hundreds of years ago, Blaise Pascal discovered an important law about fluids. Pascal's Law states that when pressure is applied to a fluid at rest, the pressure is transmitted to all parts of the fluid equally. Hydraulic hoists are commonly used in automobile repair shops (Figure 5).

In a hydraulic hoist, the pressure that is applied to one part of the fluid moves through the fluid to the cylinders, which lift the car up.

Theories Scientific laws provide detailed descriptions of our observations of nature. Scientific theories, however, provide explanations of our observations. For example, a law of heat states that energy always flows from hot objects to cold objects. But, why does energy always flow from hot objects to cold objects? A theory is developed to answer this question. A **theory** provides an explanation. According to the particle theory of matter, particles in hot substances are moving with more energy than particles in cold substances, and when they come in contact with each other, the more energetic particles in the hotter substance collide with the less energetic particles in the colder substance and transfer some of their energy (Figure 6).

Figure 5 A hydraulic hoist, shown in this historical photograph of the early Goodrich car plant, uses Pascal's Law to lift a car above the ground so that the technicians can work underneath.

Figure 6 The particle theory explains how energy travels up the spoon to the hand from the hot coffee.

1.B. Technology Is About Solving Problems

Technology does not just refer to computers. It refers to all sorts of devices and processes that help solve problems, make life easier, or meet human needs and desires. An electric wheelchair is technology, as are the processes for designing and building these wheelchairs. The stove in your kitchen is technology, as are the pots, pans, and recipes you use to prepare your food. Refrigerators, televisions, hammers, iPods, windows, soap, and clothing are all forms of technology, and so are all of the processes used in the design, production, and use of these convenient things.

You use technology every day, and you have probably already designed and produced some technology. Have you ever noticed a problem with something at home and tried to solve it? If so, then you have engaged in the process of technological problem solving. Perhaps you have used a paper clip as an emergency replacement for a broken zipper (Figure 7). This is technology in practice.

Technology usually arises from problems. Below is a list of some everyday problems that require a technological solution:

- a bird feeder that attracts squirrels and chipmunks
- a door that needs to stay open
- a drafty window
- a poster that needs to be seen in the dark

When the first computers were made, people found it difficult and time-consuming to use a keyboard to move the cursor around the computer screen. Douglas Engelbart noticed the problem, and in 1963, he decided to do something about it. He invented the first computer mouse (Figure 8). The handheld mouse navigates the cursor around the computer screen. When someone recently asked Dr. Engelbart where the name "mouse" came from for his invention, he laughed and said that someone in the lab must have looked at the small wooden box with a long electrical cord sticking out of it and started calling it a mouse.

Figure 7 A paper clip can be used to solve a number of technological problems.

Figure 8 The first mouse had wheels or dials on it that moved in two different directions.

Although Engelbart's invention was modified from its original form (**Figure 9**), he still has the satisfaction of seeing hundreds of millions of people all over the world use a computer with ease.

Figure 9 The modern computer mouse is quite different from Engelbart's original design.

1.B.1. Goals and Beliefs of Technology

The main goal of technology is to help people live better by developing products and processes that solve problems and meet human needs. However, if the environment is negatively affected by our efforts to make living easier, then life will be more difficult for all living things over time. An increasingly important goal of technology, in addition to meeting human needs, is to protect the environment (Figure 10).

When designing and building a structure such as a chair or bridge, a problem is being solved and a need is being met. When a system to filter water for drinking is designed and tested, a goal of technology is being met. When you figure out how to protect the ecosystem around your school from the effects of acid rain, a goal of technology is being met.

The basic beliefs underlying the practice of technology include the following:

- Every person has a right to meet his or her basic needs.
- Technological problem-solving skills are transferable and will help people solve problems in a wide variety of areas.
- Technology and its products should be used to serve others, not just oneself.
- The production and use of technology should not affect the environment in ways that will prevent future generations from enjoying and benefiting from Earth as much as we have.
- If a technology can reduce human problems such as disease, ignorance, poverty, or war, then it is a technology worth pursuing (Figure 11).

Figure 10 Students working on a schoolyard greening project

Figure 11 Canadian organizations help build wells in Africa.

1. The Nature of Science and Technology **353**

1.B.2. The Costs, Risks, and Benefits of Technology

Almost everything associated with technology has costs, risks, and benefits. Technology usually involves making a product out of materials and tools that need to be purchased. And then there is the cost of lost time and space. For example, a deck that you and your family build in your backyard may take more time to construct than originally planned. It will mean less garden space for you to grow vegetables. There are also risks involved. If the support posts are not designed and constructed properly, the deck may collapse after a few years. But think of the benefits! On warm days, you can sit outside with your friends and enjoy the fresh air. Your family can enjoy summer barbecues on the deck. You must take extra care with the design of the deck so that the risks and costs do not outweigh the benefits of the technology.

Look over the following list of suggestions and, for each one, decide which are greater—the costs, the risks, or the benefits in planning and building your deck:

- You decide to use untreated wood because the price of treated lumber is twice the price of untreated lumber (some lumber is treated with chemicals to prevent rotting).
- You give up a couple of days of your holidays to read "how-to" books and search the Internet for deck-building instructions.
- You decide to make a very small deck to save money on lumber.

1.C. Science and Technology Work Together

Science is about asking questions and conducting investigations to understand the natural world. Technology is about solving problems and creating products to meet human needs and wants. Even though they are different in many ways, science and technology actually work together quite closely. Throughout history, technology has had a huge impact on society, from the arrowheads of the Stone Age, to the great wall of the Qin Dynasty in China, to the cellphones of today (Figure 12). However, technology has often relied on scientific knowledge to make inventions possible. What kind of steel is best for supporting heavy loads? How can information travel through empty space? The scientific answers to these questions have helped in the development of technologies such as bridge building and radio communications. Science, in turn, has often relied on technology to give it the tools and equipment needed to conduct scientific investigations, including microscopes, telescopes, and sensitive weighing balances.

Figure 12 When visitors see the ancient technology of the Great Wall of China for the first time, many use the modern technology of cellphones to call and tell their families how amazing it is!

The scanning electron microscope (SEM) is one example of how science and technology work together. Scientific knowledge about the nature of light and electrons led to the development of highly advanced microscopes like the SEM. This microscope allows scientists to examine very small specimens in fine detail. For example, Figure 13 shows an SEM image of the compound eye of a fly. Technology like the SEM allows scientists to make important observations and discoveries.

Both science and technology have a tremendous influence on society and the environment. Science has changed our understanding of matter, space, energy, and the interactions between living things and the environment. Technology has changed the way people communicate, prepare food, and treat sickness and disease. Table 1 lists some of the relationships between science and technology.

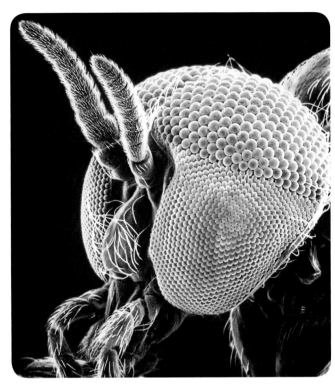

Figure 13 Scanning electron microscope images have a 3-D appearance. This allows scientists to study the surface of a specimen in incredible detail.

Table 1 Science and Technology Work Side by Side

Science	Technology
• begins by asking questions about the natural world	• begins by noticing unsolved problems or human needs and wants
• involves the process of scientific inquiry	• involves the process of technological problem solving
• looks for answers to questions or explanations about things	• looks for solutions to problems or devices to meet human needs and wants
• shares new knowledge as well as social and environmental connections	• shares products and solutions as well as their environmental and social implications

2. Scientific Inquiry and Experiments

2.A. Thinking as a Scientist

Imagine that you are planning to buy an MP3 player. First, you write a list of questions. Then, you visit stores, check print and Internet sources, and talk to your friends to find out which is the best purchase. When you try to solve problems in this way, you are conducting an investigation and thinking like a scientist.

- *Scientists investigate the natural world to describe it.* For example, earth scientists study rocks to find out what their properties are, how they were formed, and how they change (Figure 1).

Figure 1 Using the "streak test" to study minerals

- *Scientists investigate objects to classify them.* For example, chemists examine substances and classify them as pure substances or mixtures (Figure 2).

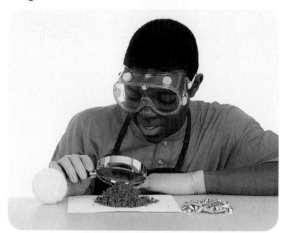

Figure 2 Using a magnifier to examine mixtures

- *Scientists investigate the natural world to test their ideas about it.* For example, botanists ask cause-and-effect questions about the growth of plants and trees. They propose hypotheses to answer their questions. Then, they design investigations to test their hypotheses. This process leads scientists to come up with new ideas to be tested and more questions that need answers.

2.B. Scientific Inquiry

You need to use a variety of skills when you do scientific inquiry and design or carry out an experiment (Figure 3). Refer to this section when you have questions about how to use any of the following skills and processes:

- questioning
- controlling variables
- predicting
- hypothesizing
- planning
- performing
- observing
- analyzing
- evaluating
- communicating

Figure 3 You need a variety of skills to carry out experiments successfully.

2.B.1. Questioning

Scientific investigations start with good questions. To write a good question, you must decide what you want to know. This will help you think of, or formulate, a question that will lead you to the information you want. Remember, good scientific questions should not lead to simple "yes" and "no" answers. Your question must be *testable* for it to lead to an investigation.

Sometimes, an investigation starts with a special type of question, called a cause-and-effect question. A **cause-and-effect question** asks whether something is causing something else. It might start in one of the following ways: What causes…? How does…affect…? What would happen if…? When an investigation starts with a cause-and-effect question, it also has a hypothesis.

PRACTICE: Think About Cause and Effect

Think of some everyday examples of cause and effect, and write statements about them. Here is one example: "When I stay up too late, I'm tired the next day." Then turn your statements into cause-and-effect questions: for example, "If I stay up late tonight, how tired will I feel tomorrow?"

2.B.2. Controlling Variables

When you plan an investigation, you need to make sure that you conduct a fair test. To make sure that an investigation involves a fair test, scientists identify all the variables that might affect their results. **Variables** are any conditions that could affect the outcome of an investigation. Scientists then make sure that they change only one variable at a time. This way, they may assume that their results are caused by the variable they changed and not by any of the other variables they identified.

There are three kinds of variables in an investigation (Figure 4):

- The variable that is changed is called the **independent variable**, or cause variable.
- The variable that is affected by a change is called the **dependent variable**, or effect variable. This is the variable you measure to see how it was affected by the independent variable.
- All the other conditions that remain unchanged in an investigation, so that you know they did not have any effect on the outcome, are called the **controlled variables**.

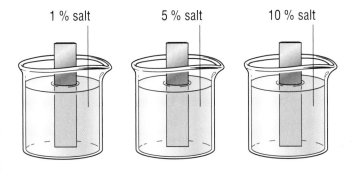

Figure 4 This investigation was designed to find out if the amount of salt in a solution has an effect on the rusting of metal.
- The amount of salt in each solution is the independent variable.
- The amount of rust that developed on each piece of metal is the dependent variable.
- The amount of water in each beaker and the amount of time the metal strips stay in the water are two of the controlled variables.

PRACTICE: Design a Fair Test

Suppose that you notice mould growing on an orange. You want to know what is causing the mould. What variables will you have to consider in order to design a fair test? Which variable will you try changing in your test? What is this variable called? What will your dependent variable be? What will your controlled variables be?

2.B.3. Predicting and Hypothesizing

A **prediction** states what is likely to happen as the result of a controlled experiment. Scientists base predictions on their observations and knowledge. They look for patterns in the data they gather to help them understand what might happen next or in a similar situation. A prediction may be written as an "if…then…" statement. For example, in an experiment on static electricity, your prediction might be, "If the number of times a balloon is rubbed in hair (the cause or independent variable) is increased, then the length of time it sticks to a wall (the effect or dependent variable) will also increase."

Remember, however, that predictions are not guesses. They are suggestions based on prior knowledge and logical reasoning (Figure 5). To show that a prediction is based on knowledge and reasoning, a hypothesis is stated.

A **hypothesis** is a prediction about the outcome of a controlled experiment along with an explanation for the outcome. A hypothesis may be written in the form of an "if…then… because…" statement. *If* the cause variable is changed in a particular way, *then* the effect variable will change in a particular way, and this change occurs *because* of certain reasons. For example, "If the number of times a balloon is rubbed against hair is increased, then the length of time it sticks to a wall will also increase because additional rubbing increases the amount of static charge on the balloon."

If your observations confirm your prediction, then they support your hypothesis. You can create more than one hypothesis from the same question or prediction. Another student might test the hypothesis, "If the number of times you rub a balloon on your hair is increased, then the length of time it sticks to a wall will be unchanged because rubbing a balloon on your hair has no effect on the balloon." Of course, both of you cannot be correct. When you conduct an investigation, your observations do not always confirm your prediction. Sometimes, you show that your hypothesis is incorrect. An investigation that does not support your hypothesis is not a bad investigation or a waste of time. It has contributed to your scientific knowledge. You can re-evaluate your hypothesis and design a new investigation.

Figure 5 You may have noticed that a charged balloon sticks to surfaces. You can use this information to make predictions.

PRACTICE: Write a Hypothesis

Write hypotheses for questions or predictions about rubbing a balloon on your hair and sticking it on a wall. For example, suppose that your question is "Does a balloon stick better if you rub it more times?" Your hypothesis might be, "If the number of times you rub a balloon on your hair is increased, then the length of time it sticks to a wall will also increase because your hair makes the balloon sticky."

2.B.4. Planning

You have been asked to design and carry out your own investigation. You have a question: How much water do plants need to grow well when they are young? First, you make a hypothesis. Your hypothesis states that seeds grow best when they receive a small amount of water every day, because you know from experience that some plants do not grow well when they are given water too infrequently. Your hypothesis suggests a fair test. Then, you have to decide which species of plant to test. You choose a house plant that grows rapidly. To make a fair test, you decide to change only one variable: the frequency with which you water the plant. This is your independent variable. You will plant four seeds of the same plant, and water each of the seeds at a different frequency (for example, you water one seed every day, another seed once every two days, and so on). You are careful to keep the amount of water you give them constant—each plant will receive 25 mL of water. You put the seeds into the same type of soil, and into the same-sized containers with equal amounts of soil. You also place them in a location where they receive the same amount of light each day. These are the controlled variables. When the plants appear above the surface of the soil, you start measuring their heights (Figure 6). This is the dependent variable.

Figure 6 Plant height is the dependent variable.

Now consider the equipment and materials you need. Be sure to include any safety equipment, such as an apron or eye protection, in your equipment and materials list. Will you use hot or cold water each time you water the plant? Will you use natural or artificial light? Will you just test one seed for each frequency of watering, or will you test two or three seeds? Why? How long will your investigation last? Will you measure the height of the plants each day? How will you measure the heights? How will you record your data?

You need to write a **procedure**—a step-by-step description of how you will perform your investigation. A procedure should be written as a series of numbered steps, with only one instruction per step. It should be written in past tense in passive voice. Your procedure must be clear enough for someone else to follow, and it must explain how you will deal with each of the variables in your investigation. The first step in a procedure usually refers to any safety precautions that need to be addressed, and the last step relates to any cleanup that needs to be done. Your teacher must approve your procedure and list of equipment and materials before you begin.

PRACTICE: Plan an Investigation

Suppose your question is whether salt or sugar is more soluble in water. First, make a hypothesis. Then, brainstorm different ways that you might test your hypothesis. Choose the method that causes the least waste, gives the clearest result, and uses equipment and materials that you have in your kitchen at home.

Now, write out a procedure for this investigation. Include the equipment and materials that you will need. Have you controlled all the variables? How will you organize the data that you collect from this experiment, without losing any important information?

2.B.5. Performing

As you carry out an investigation, be sure to follow the steps in the procedure carefully and thoroughly. Use all equipment and materials safely, accurately, and with precision. (To learn more about safety, refer to "Safety, Tools, and Equipment.") Be sure to take detailed, careful notes, and to record all of your observations. Record your numerical data in a table.

2.B.6. Observing

When you observe something, you use your senses to learn about it. You can also use tools, such as a balance, metre stick, or microscope. Some observations are measurable. They can be expressed in numbers. Observations of time, temperature, volume, and distance can all be measured. These types of observations are called **quantitative observations**.

Other observations are not measurable. They describe characteristics that cannot be expressed in numbers. The smell of a fungus, the shape of a flower petal, and the texture of soil are all characteristics that cannot be measured. These are called **qualitative observations**. Qualitative observations also include colour, taste, clarity, and state of matter. Qualitative observations can be recorded using words, pictures, or labelled diagrams.

Measuring Measuring is an important part of observation (Figure 7). When you measure an object, you describe it precisely and keep track of any changes. To learn about using measuring tools, turn to "Using Mathematics in Science and Technology."

Making a Labelled Diagram You use labelled diagrams to record accurate observations. You also use them in your Lab Report to communicate to others. Here are some tips for making scientific diagrams.

Getting Started The following materials and ideas will help you get started:

- Use blank paper. (For technical drawings, use graph paper. See "Technical Drawings.")
- Use a sharp pencil rather than a pen or marker, as you will probably need to erase parts of your drawing and do them over again.
- Your drawings should be large enough to show details. For example, if you are drawing a cell, you may want to use a quarter of a page. For a complex drawing, you may need to use a complete page.
- Scientific diagrams should always have labels and a title. When you are planning the space for your diagram, leave enough space for these labels. They are usually placed on the right of the diagram.
- Observe and study your specimen or device carefully, noting details and proportions, before you begin the diagram.

Figure 7 Measuring accurately requires care.

Drawing Techniques

- For scientific drawings, you usually present a two-dimensional drawing. (For three-dimensional drawings, see "Technical Drawings.")
- Do not put anything in your drawing that you cannot see, even if you know it is there.
- Use clear, carefully drawn lines to indicate the important details of what you observe.
- Instead of using colours or shading, you can place a collection of dots inside a figure to indicate something that looks darker than the parts around it (Figure 8). This technique is called stippling.

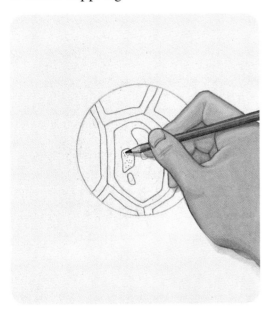

Figure 8 When making scientific drawings, use stippling instead of colour or shading.

Labelling the Drawing

- Always label your scientific drawings, using lines and labels on the side rather than directly on the drawing.
- Rulers or straight edges should be used to create horizontal label lines (Figure 9).
- Labels should be in singular form. For example, use the label "chloroplast," not "chloroplasts," and make sure your label line points to only one chloroplast.

- Write your labels on the right, so that they line up vertically on the page (Figure 10).
- Place a title at the top of your drawing (Figure 10). The title should describe the object you are drawing.
- If you are using a microscope to magnify the object, write the total magnification at the bottom of the drawing (Figure 10).

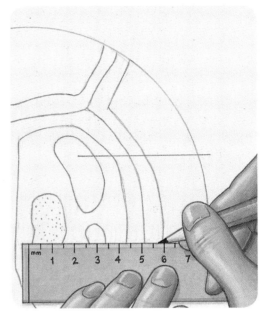

Figure 9 Use a ruler to create straight label lines.

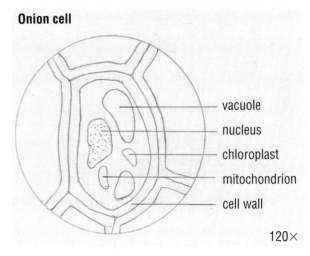

Onion cell

- vacuole
- nucleus
- chloroplast
- mitochondrion
- cell wall

120×

Figure 10 A properly labelled scientific drawing

Scale Ratio You may want to indicate the actual size of your object on your diagram. To do this, you use a ratio called the scale ratio.

- If your diagram is 10 times larger than the real object (for example, a tiny organism), your scale ratio is 10✕. Figure 10 on the previous page, for example, shows a cell drawing with scale ratio 120✕.

- If your diagram is 20 times smaller than the real object (for example, a hydraulic system), your scale ratio is 1/20 or 0.05.

- In general, scale ratio = $\dfrac{\text{size of drawing}}{\text{actual size of object}}$

You can also show the actual size of the object on your diagram (Figure 11).

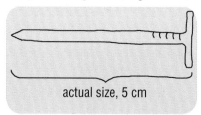

actual size, 5 cm

Figure 11 A scientific drawing indicating the actual size of the object

Checklist for Scientific Drawing

✓ Use blank paper and a sharp, hard pencil.

✓ Draw as large as necessary to show details clearly.

✓ Do not shade or colour.

✓ Draw label lines that are straight and parallel, and run outside your drawing. Use a ruler!

✓ Include labels, a title, and the magnification of the microscope you are using.

As you work on an investigation, be sure to record all of your observations, both qualitative and quantitative, clearly and carefully. If a data table is appropriate for your investigation, use it to organize your observations and measurements. Include all observations and measurements in your final lab report or presentation.

2.B.7. Analyzing

When you analyze data from an investigation, you make sense of it. You examine and compare the measurements you have made. You look for patterns and relationships that will help you explain your results and give you new information about the question you are investigating.

Often, making tables or graphs of your data will help you see patterns and relationships more easily. Turn to the section "Using Mathematics in Science and Technology" to learn more about creating data tables and graphing your results.

Once you have analyzed your data, you can tell whether your prediction or hypothesis is correct. You can also write a conclusion that indicates whether or not the results support your hypothesis. You may even come up with a new hypothesis that can be tested in a new investigation.

Inferring You can also make an inference based on your observations or by analyzing a graph. An **inference** is a possible explanation of something you observe—it is an educated guess based on your experience, knowledge, and observations. If you observe on your water bill that your family's water consumption goes down significantly in the winter compared to the fall, you might infer that people in your family have fewer showers in the winter. Of course, there may very well be another reason for this observation.

PRACTICE: Inference or Observation?

Decide whether each statement below is an observation or an inference:

- You see a wasp crawling on the ground instead of flying. You conclude that it must be sick.
- You notice that you are thirsty after playing soccer.
- You see a bottle filled with clear liquid. You conclude that it must be water.

Classifying You classify things when you sort them into groups based on their similarities and differences. When you sort clothes, sporting equipment, or books, you are using a classification system. To be helpful to other people, a classification system must make sense to them. If, for example, your local supermarket sorted all the products by price, so that expensive items were all together on the same shelf, no one would be able to find anything! Classification is an important skill in science. Scientists group objects, organisms, and events to understand the nature of life (Figure 12).

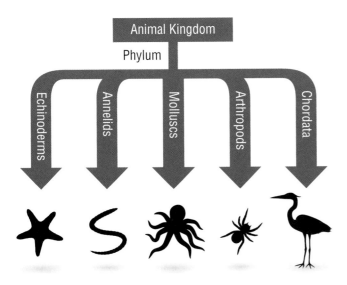

Figure 12 Scientists divide the animal kingdom into five smaller groups called "phyla" (singular is *phylum*).

PRACTICE: Create a Classification System

Classify photos of 15 to 20 different insects, seashells, or flowers. Try to include as much variety as possible. How are all your samples alike? How are they different?

2.B.8. Evaluating

How useful is the evidence from an investigation? The answer to this question is important because we need quality evidence before we can evaluate our prediction or hypothesis. If the evidence is poor or unreliable, you can still identify areas of improvement for when the investigation is repeated.

Here are some things to consider when evaluating an investigation:

- *Plan*: Were there any problems with the way you planned your experiment or your procedure? Did you control for all the variables, except the independent variable?
- *Equipment and Materials:* Could better equipment have been used? Was something used incorrectly? Did you have difficulty with a piece of equipment?
- *Observations:* Did you record all the observations that you could have? Or did you ignore some observations that might have been important?
- *Skills:* Did you have the appropriate skills for the investigation? Did you have to use a skill that you were just learning about?

Once you have identified areas in which errors could have been made, you can judge the quality of your evidence.

2.B.9. Communicating

When you plan and carry out your own investigation, it is important to share both your process and your findings. Other people may want to repeat your investigation, or they may want to use or apply your findings in another situation. Your write-up, or report, should reflect the process of scientific inquiry that you used in your investigation.

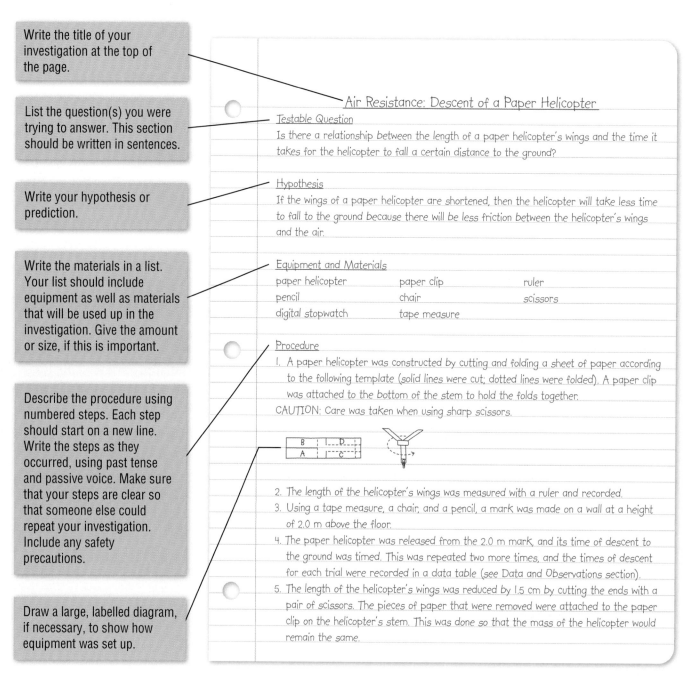

Write the title of your investigation at the top of the page.

List the question(s) you were trying to answer. This section should be written in sentences.

Write your hypothesis or prediction.

Write the materials in a list. Your list should include equipment as well as materials that will be used up in the investigation. Give the amount or size, if this is important.

Describe the procedure using numbered steps. Each step should start on a new line. Write the steps as they occurred, using past tense and passive voice. Make sure that your steps are clear so that someone else could repeat your investigation. Include any safety precautions.

Draw a large, labelled diagram, if necessary, to show how equipment was set up.

Air Resistance: Descent of a Paper Helicopter

Testable Question

Is there a relationship between the length of a paper helicopter's wings and the time it takes for the helicopter to fall a certain distance to the ground?

Hypothesis

If the wings of a paper helicopter are shortened, then the helicopter will take less time to fall to the ground because there will be less friction between the helicopter's wings and the air.

Equipment and Materials

paper helicopter	paper clip	ruler
pencil	chair	scissors
digital stopwatch	tape measure	

Procedure

1. A paper helicopter was constructed by cutting and folding a sheet of paper according to the following template (solid lines were cut; dotted lines were folded). A paper clip was attached to the bottom of the stem to hold the folds together.
CAUTION: Care was taken when using sharp scissors.

2. The length of the helicopter's wings was measured with a ruler and recorded.
3. Using a tape measure, a chair, and a pencil, a mark was made on a wall at a height of 2.0 m above the floor.
4. The paper helicopter was released from the 2.0 m mark, and its time of descent to the ground was timed. This was repeated two more times, and the times of descent for each trial were recorded in a data table (see Data and Observations section).
5. The length of the helicopter's wings was reduced by 1.5 cm by cutting the ends with a pair of scissors. The pieces of paper that were removed were attached to the paper clip on the helicopter's stem. This was done so that the mass of the helicopter would remain the same.

6. The helicopter with shorter wings was released from the 2.0 m mark, and its time of descent was measured and recorded. This was repeated two more times.

7. Steps 5 and 6 were repeated.

Data and Observations

Wing length (cm)	Descent time (s)			
	Trial 1	Trial 2	Trial 3	Average
9.0	2.28	2.22	2.26	2.53
7.5	1.93	1.98	1.95	1.95
6.0	1.50	1.59	1.53	1.54

Analysis and Evaluation

The average descent time decreased as the helicopter's wing length decreased. This result supports my hypothesis. See the graph on page 3. We did our best to always line up the bottom of the helicopter to the 2.0 m mark on the wall before releasing it, but we might not have been completely accurate. This error could be reduced by having a horizontal bar sticking out of the wall at the correct height. Another possible source of error is the air currents caused by people walking around the room. This could be reduced by conducting the experiment in a place where students are not walking around.

Answer to Analyze and Evaluate Question

(a) The helicopter's wing length was the independent variable since we changed this variable by cutting pieces off of the wing. The descent time was the dependent variable because we did not know ahead of time what it would be, but we measured it after releasing the helicopter in each of the trials. The mass of the helicopter, the helicopter design, and the distance it was released from were controlled variables.

Applications and Extensions

The results of this experiment show that the descent of a falling object is faster when there is less friction with the air. This knowledge is important to the engineers who design real helicopters since they have to determine best length for a helicopter's blades. This knowledge may also be used by parachute designers who need to know how large a parachute should be for it to safely land a skydiver.

Present your observations in a form that is easily understood. Data should be recorded in one or more tables, with units included.

Qualitative observations can be recorded in words or drawings. Observations in words can be in point form.

Analyze your results and evaluate your procedure. If you have used graphs, refer to them here, and include them on a separate piece of graph paper. Write a conclusion indicating whether or not your results support your hypothesis or prediction. Answer any Analyze and Evaluate questions here.

Describe how the knowledge you gained from your investigation relates to real-life situations. How can this knowledge be used? Answer any Apply and Extend questions here.

3. Scientific Research

In our modern society, there is a tremendous amount of "scientific" information available to us. However, not all the information out there is truly scientific. Here are some tips to help you conduct scientific research.

3.A. Ask Questions About the World Around You

You can begin by asking questions about the world around you. Look at Figures 1 and 2. What questions can you think of that could lead to an investigation? A question might come to mind from your experience or something you have observed. For example, you might have heard that North America is in danger of running out of fresh water. You come up with a question: How much fresh water does Canada have compared to the United States and Mexico?

3.B. Identify a Research Topic and Develop a Research Question

After coming up with some questions, you can identify your research topic. What is the purpose of your research? What do you, or your group, already know about your topic? What are some things that you do not know? A graphic organizer can help you organize your thoughts. (See "Study Skills for Science and Technology.") Develop a list of key questions that you need to answer. If possible, narrow this down to one key research question.

3.C. Identify Sources of Information

Identify places where you could look for information about your topic. These places might include programs on television, people in your community, print sources, and electronic sources (refer to the section "Using the Internet").

Figure 1 Snow hides a world of life underneath.

Figure 2 First Canadian Place is Canada's tallest skyscraper.

Remember, getting information from a variety of sources will improve the quality of your research.

3.D. Evaluate the Sources of Information

Preview your sources of information and decide whether they are useful and reliable. Here are five things to consider:

- *Authority:* Who wrote or developed the information, or who sponsors the website? What are the qualifications of this person or group?
- *Accuracy:* Are there any obvious errors or inconsistencies in the information? Does the information agree with other reliable sources?
- *Currency:* Is the information up to date? Has recent scientific information been included?
- *Suitability:* Does the information make sense to someone your age? Do you understand it? Is it well organized?
- *Bias:* Are facts reported fairly? Are there reasons why your sources might express some bias? Are facts deliberately left out?

3.E. Record and Organize the Information

Once you have gathered and evaluated your sources of information, you can start organizing your research. Identify categories or headings for note taking. Use point-form notes to record information in your own words, under each category or heading. You must be careful not to copy information directly from your sources. If you quote a source, use quotation marks. Record the title, author, publisher, page number, and date for each of your sources. For websites, record the URL (website address). Keeping track of these details will help you when you create your bibliography. If necessary, add to your list of questions as you find new information. To help you organize the information further, you may want to use pictures, graphic organizers, and diagrams (see the "Study Skills" section).

3.F. Make a Conclusion

Look at your original research question. What did you learn from the information you gathered? Can you state and explain a conclusion based on that information? Do you need further information? Do you have an informed opinion on the research topic that you did not have before you started?

Connect your conclusion or opinion with a similar topic. For example, perhaps you found out that Canada has more fresh water than Mexico or the United States (Figure 3). Is Canada selling large amounts of its water to the United States (Figure 4)? Will this affect our future water supplies?

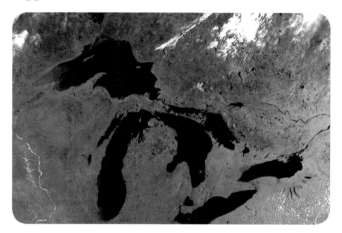

Figure 3 Canada's abundant fresh water supplies include the Great Lakes.

Figure 4 Is Canada selling too much of its fresh water?

3.G. Evaluate Your Research

Now that your research is complete, reflect on how you gathered and organized the information. Can you think of ways to improve the research process for next time? How valuable were the sources of information you selected?

3.H. Communicate Your Conclusions

Choose a format for communication that suits your audience, your purpose, and the information you gathered. Should you use any labelled diagrams, graphs, or charts?

3.I. Using the Internet

The Internet is a vast and constantly growing network of information. You can use search engines like Google to help you search the Web, but keep in mind that not everything you find will be useful. It is so easy to put information on the Internet that anyone can post almost anything without proof that it is true or accurate. Because of this, it is very important for you to evaluate the information that you find online.

3.I.1. Search Results

Once you have done a search, you will be provided with a list of web pages and the number of matches for your search. If your keywords are general, you are likely to get a high number of matches and you may need to refine your search. Most search engines provide online help and search tips. You can look at these to find ideas for better searching.

3.I.2. Evaluating Internet Resources

Use the following questions to determine the quality of an Internet resource. The greater the number of questions answered "yes," the more likely it is that the source is of high quality.

- Is it clear who is sponsoring the page? Does the site seem to be permanent or sponsored by a permanent organization?
- Is there information about the sponsoring organization? For example, is a phone number or address given to contact for more information?
- Is it clear who developed and wrote the information? Are the author's qualifications provided?
- Are the sources for factual information given so that they can be checked?
- Are there dates to indicate when the page was written, placed online, or last revised?

3.I.3. Using School Library Resources

Many schools and school boards have access to online encyclopedias with science sections in them. Find out if your school or board has a website where you can access these resources. You may need a password.

3.I.4. Using the Nelson Website

Any time you see the Nelson web icon in your textbook, you can go to the Nelson website and find links to useful sources of information.

Go to Nelson Science

PRACTICE: Research Geothermal Energy

Brainstorm a list of questions on the topic of geothermal energy. Choose one of these questions to research. Identify several sources of information you could use, and evaluate them using the five points for evaluating Internet resources. Organize the information from your search results in a table. Make a conclusion.

3.J. Exploring an Issue Critically

An issue is a situation in which several points of view need to be considered in order to make a decision. A person's point of view, or opinion, about an issue is based on what he or she thinks is important or on what he or she values. Therefore, it is difficult to come to a decision that everyone agrees with. When a decision has an impact on many people or on the environment, it is important to explore the issue critically. This means thinking about all the possible solutions and trying to understand all the different points of view—not just your own point of view. It also means researching and investigating your ideas, and communicating with others. Figure 5 shows all the steps in the process.

Figure 5 The steps in exploring an issue critically

3.J.1. Defining the Issue

The first step in exploring an issue is to identify what the issue is. An issue has more than one solution, and there are different points of view about which solution is the best. Try stating the issue as a question: "What should…?" The issue can also include information about the *role* a person takes when thinking about an issue. For instance, you may think about the issue from someone else's point of view—you may take the role of a landowner, a government worker, or even a tour guide. The issue can also include a description of who your *audience* will be—will it be other students, a meeting of government officials, or your parents? Be sure to take into account role and audience when thinking about your issue.

3.J.2. Researching

The decision you reach must be based on a good understanding of the issue. You must be in a position to choose the most appropriate solution. To do this, you need to gather factual information that represents all the different points of view. Develop good questions and a plan for your research. Your research may include talking to people, reading about the topic in newspapers and magazines, and doing Internet research. For a land-use issue, you may also want to visit the site to make observations.

3.J.3. Evaluating

Evaluate your research and your sources. Are they reliable, accurate, and current? Watch out for biased information that favours only one side of the issue.

Review the relevant sections of this Skills Handbook to help you evaluate the sources you used. Were the sources valuable? Could you have found better information elsewhere?

3.J.4. Identifying Alternatives

There are always different solutions to a problem. For example, suppose that your municipal council is trying to decide how to use some vacant land next to your school. You and other students have asked the council to use the land as a nature park. Another group is proposing that the land be used to build a seniors' home because there is a shortage of this kind of housing. Some school administrators would like to use the land to build a track for runners and sporting events.

After defining the issue and researching, you can now generate a list of possible solutions. You might, for example, come up with the following choices for the land-use issue:

- Turn the land into a nature park for the community and the school.
- Use the land as a playing field and track for the community and the school.
- Create a combination park and playing field.
- Use the land to build a seniors' home with a nature park.

3.J.5. Analyzing the Issue

Develop criteria to evaluate each possible alternative. For example, should the solution be the one that has the most community support? Should it be the one that protects the environment? You need to decide which criteria you will use to evaluate the alternatives so that you can decide which solution is the best.

3.J.6. Making a Decision

This is the stage where everyone gets a chance to share ideas and information gathered about the issue. Then, the group needs to evaluate all the possible alternatives and decide on one solution based on the list of criteria.

Cost-Benefit Analysis A cost-benefit analysis can help you determine the best solution to a complex problem when a number of solutions are possible. First, research possible costs and benefits associated with a proposed solution. Then, based on your research, try to decide the level of importance of each cost and benefit. This is often a matter of opinion. However, your opinions should be informed by information you find in your research.

Once you have completed your research and identified costs and benefits, you may conduct the cost-benefit analysis as follows:

1. Create a table like Table 1.
2. List costs and benefits.
3. Rate each cost and benefit on a scale from 1 to 5, where 1 represents the least important cost or benefit, and 5 represents the most important cost or benefit.
4. After rating each cost and benefit, add up the results to obtain totals. If the total benefits outweigh the total costs, you may decide to go ahead with the proposed solution.

Table 1 Cost-Benefit Analysis of Using Vacant Land to Build a Seniors' Home with a Nature Park

Costs		Benefits	
Possible result	**Cost of result (rate 1 to 5)**	**Possible result**	**Benefit of result (rate 1 to 5)**
land cannot be used for sports	2	provides needed housing for seniors	5
expensive to maintain	4	park preserves some habitat for plants and animals	4
nature park will be very small	3	park increases value of seniors home	3
Total cost value	**9**	**Total benefit value**	**12**

3.J.7. Communicating

Choose a method to communicate your decision. For example, you could choose one of the following methods:

- Write a report.
- Give an oral presentation.
- Make a poster.
- Prepare a slide show.
- Create a video (Figure 6).
- Organize a town hall or panel discussion.
- Create a blog or webcast.
- Hold a formal debate.
- Write a newspaper article.

Figure 6 Making a video is a great way to communicate the results of a study.

Make sure to choose a type of presentation that will share your decision or recommendation in a way that is suitable for your audience. For example, if your audience is small, it might be easiest to present your decision in person (Figure 7). An oral presentation is a good way to present your decision to many people at one time. Creating a poster or a blog allows people to read your recommendation on their own, but you must find a way to let others know where to find this information. The most important thing is to choose a method of communication that will allow you to defend your decision in the best possible way. You must explain your case clearly and present your evidence in a way that will convince your audience that your recommendation or decision is the best. You can learn more about the different ways of communicating results and decisions in the section "Presentations in Science and Technology."

Figure 7 There are many different ways to communicate decisions. Engineers may explain their decisions by presenting blueprints and designs to other engineers or builders working on a project. Be sure to choose a method of communication that is appropriate for your audience.

3.K. Conducting Interviews and Surveys

One way to do research is to talk directly to people who are knowledgeable or have an opinion on the topic. For example, you might be interested in how we can conserve more energy when we heat our buildings in winter. You have two choices. You can either conduct an interview with one or two building engineers, who know a lot about the topic, or you can do a survey of many people who have an opinion on the subject.

3.K.1. Conducting an Interview

Before the Interview

- Prepare your questions before approaching the person you want to interview.
- Practise your questions with someone you know, so that you can see how long they might take to answer and whether they should be revised.
- Ask your teacher, your parents, or a librarian if you are not sure who to interview.
- Let your teacher or a parent know that you plan to conduct an interview. Make sure they know who you will be contacting and when.
- Make the initial contact by writing, e-mailing, or calling by phone for an appointment.
- Mention how long your interview might take. Give a specific amount of time, say half an hour. Then make sure you keep to that.
- State the purpose of the interview. For example, "I want to find out how we might save energy in our buildings in the winter for a project I'm doing at school."
- Ask the person to give you a time when they would like to be interviewed.
- Ask the person if they prefer phone interviews or face-to-face interviews.

During the Interview

- Have a list of questions prepared, even if you decide to ask a further question in response to one of the answers, or leave a question unanswered.

- Be polite, no matter how the person answers the questions.
- Keep your interview on track. Get as much information as possible from the person you are interviewing (Figure 8).
- Take careful notes, but also give the person audible feedback. For example, when the person gives an answer, you might say, "Yes, I see" or "That's interesting."

Figure 8 Conduct an interview to get information from someone who knows a lot about your topic.

After the Interview

- Thank the person and ask them if they would like a copy of your final paper.
- Send a follow-up e-mail or card to the person, thanking them again.

3.K.2. Conducting a Survey

Planning the Survey

- Establish the goal of your survey. One common goal is to find out what the majority of people think about a topic. Decide what your topic is.
- Decide how many people you want to survey. You probably need at least 20 or 30 people so that you can draw some general conclusions.
- Select the people who will complete the survey. Will you ask your fellow students? Their parents? Your neighbours?

- Decide how long the survey will be. If you keep the survey short (for example, 5 to 10 minutes), will more people be willing to complete it?
- Decide how you will find people to participate in your survey. If you want to survey the parents of your fellow students, will you ask your classmates to take the survey home with them?
- Explain your plans to an adult before you begin your survey. Let someone know who you will be surveying, how you will contact them, and how you plan to collect the completed surveys.
- Do not survey people you do not know without checking with an adult first.

Creating the Survey

- Decide on the type of questions for your survey (Figure 9). Will you use agree/disagree questions? Multiple choice questions? Or questions that ask people to choose on a scale of 1 to 5, from strongly disagree to strongly agree?

This survey is about how we can conserve energy in our houses and apartments in winter. For each statement, choose a response from strongly disagree to strongly agree.

1. The way we waste energy in our buildings in winter will be a serious problem for our environment in the long run.

   ☐ Strongly Agree   ☐ Agree   ☐ No Opinion

   ☐ Disagree   ☐ Strongly Disagree

2. The government should increase taxes on heating fuel so that they can give home owners and apartment building managers money to better insulate their buildings (for example, windows, attics, doors, etc.).

   ☐ Strongly Agree   ☐ Agree   ☐ No Opinion

   ☐ Disagree   ☐ Strongly Disagree

Figure 9 This survey asks people to rate how they feel about energy conservation in winter.

- Create a draft survey or questionnaire. For a survey 5 to 10 minutes long, you might want 10 questions.
- Pre-test or "pilot" your survey with some friends or family members. Does it take them too long to fill it out? Do they find the questions easy to respond to?
- Revise your survey based on the feedback from your pre-test or pilot. You want the survey questions and instructions to be clear and understandable for your participants.

Gathering and Analyzing Survey Data

- If you want 30 people to complete the survey, make 35 copies of your final draft. Not all people who agree to answer a survey will complete and return it, for one reason or another, even if they are good friends.
- Try to give out your surveys and collect them again in the same week.
- Analyze your collected surveys question by question. For example, suppose that of the 30 people who respond to the first question, seven people choose "strongly agree," eight choose "agree," seven choose "no opinion," three choose "disagree," and none choose "strongly disagree." Clearly, the majority of the people agree with the statement in the first question.
- Create a bar graph for each question to show how many people chose each option. (See "Using Mathematics in Science and Technology.")
- Prepare a report on your survey results. Can you write a one-sentence conclusion?

4. Technological Problem Solving

4.A. Thinking Like a Technologist or Engineer

Have you ever tried to fix a broken bicycle? When your computer needed updating, did you install the new programs yourself? Have you ever tried to invent a way to get your chores done faster? If you have done any of these things, or things like them, you have been thinking like a technologist.

• *Technologists and engineers notice problems in the world that can be solved by creating a new product or process.* These problems often involve meeting human needs. However, technologists and engineers also solve environmental problems. For example, we need to heat our homes in winter, but how can we do this without wasting energy? Or, suppose that your class wants to set aside part of the schoolyard as a natural area (Figure 1). How can you keep foreign plant species from invading and pushing out the natural species you are trying to grow?

How do you keep harmful insects out without using pesticides? And how do you water the area without wasting a lot of water? When you think like a technologist, you must consider both human needs and the environment.

• *Technologists and engineers consider a wide range of solutions and choose one that is beneficial, practical, and inexpensive.* Think again of the energy wasted in our homes. How can we reduce energy loss through windows in the winter? Perhaps the easiest solution is to cover the windows with an insulating material that can be removed again in the summer. Of course, windows come in all different sizes and shapes, so this proposed solution creates another series of problems. You learned how to analyze solutions and make decisions in the section "Explore an Issue Critically," and these skills can also be applied to technological problem solving. There are many steps in the process of technological problem solving, and planning ahead is very important (Figure 2).

Figure 1 Students working to create a natural area

Figure 2 Planning is one of the steps involved in technological problem solving.

4.B. Performing Technological Problem Solving

You use a variety of skills when you do technological problem solving or construct a technological product. Refer to this section when you have questions about how to use any of the following skills and processes:

- identifying a problem or need
- planning
- selecting equipment and materials
- designing
- testing
- modifying
- communicating

4.B.1. Identify a Problem or Need

Technology begins with identifying a problem that needs to be solved. This could be a personal problem like a broken bicycle (Figure 3).

It may also be a global problem, such as the lack of clean drinking water for people in developing countries (Figure 4). You need to decide on what problem you are most interested in, and then start researching more about the problem. (See "Scientific Research.")

> **PRACTICE: Identify Local Problems**
>
> Think of some problems or needs in your neighbourhood. You might want to brainstorm a list with a school friend or family member. If you do not know where to begin, think of things such as graffiti on walls, noise from a nearby highway, or garbage on the streets. After generating a list, make some priorities by placing "1" beside the problem or need that you think is most important, "2" beside the next one, and so on.

Figure 3 Many skills are involved when you solve technological problems.

Figure 4 These Canadian water filters provide drinking water to people in many countries.

4.B.2. Planning

Once you have identified the problem, your next step is to refine the problem, generate possible solutions to it, and then select one of the solutions to work on. The technology you are creating can be either a process or a product that will solve a problem, but the planning method is the same.

Suppose that your problem is how to reduce energy loss through the windows of your home in winter. You decide to create a product that will help insulate the windows. You might develop a list of questions before you begin:

- *Cost:* How much is your family prepared to spend on insulating the windows?
- *Durability:* Do you want the product you create to be usable next winter?
- *Time:* How much time do you want to spend on this project?
- *Ease of use:* How easy will it be to attach your product to the windows of your house?
- *Looks:* How will your product look when it is on the window?

You should consider things such as size, safety, and environmental issues when planning your product or process.

Now you are in a better position to begin thinking about possible solutions and selecting one. However, before answering these questions, you may have to do some research such as consulting a local hardware store and family members for their advice. You may also go to the library to research print sources, or look up Internet and other electronic sources. Once you have completed your research, you can decide on a plan—for instance, to prevent energy loss, you decide to make removable window frames covered with transparent plastic for your windows at home (Figure 5).

Figure 5 Installing the window insulator

The first thing you do after deciding on a solution is to write out a series of steps for your plan. In your plan, you should consider creating a list of criteria to evaluate your solution to the problem. You will know if your solution is successful if it meets these criteria. After you have created a plan, be sure to have your teacher check it before you carry it out.

PRACTICE: Developing Criteria

Suppose you were constructing insulating frames for your windows. Make a list of criteria you would use to test the first prototype frame that you make. What would you examine before you put it on a window? After it had been on the window for a while? (Suppose you made it for the window in your bedroom.)

If the problem you choose is a process, such as cleaning up a local park, you will also need to make a plan. What equipment and materials will you need? How will you dispose of the garbage? Do you need to make a diagram of anything? Since there could be dangerous materials in the park, such as broken glass, perhaps you should write out a numbered procedure showing each step you will take.

4.B.3. Selecting Equipment and Materials

One important aspect of technological problem solving is selecting appropriate equipment and materials. You may need to use specialized tools, such as drills, saws, tubing, and so on. For example, to build an insulating cover for a window, you may want to use a wood frame covered with transparent plastic. In that case, you will need tools for cutting the wood (like a saw), as well as for holding the wood secure while it is being cut (a vice or mitre box with clamp). You will also need to wear eye protection while you are cutting the wood. When selecting tools for any technology project, be sure that you are aware of any safety precautions. Make sure you go over your plans with an adult before using tools and other equipment. They might have some safety concerns you have not thought of.

Planning ahead and taking precautions are the best way to prevent accidents when you work with tools and equipment. Before you begin the construction phase of any product or action phase of any process, make a list of possible accidents and what you can do ahead of time to prevent them. Let an adult know before you start working with tools and equipment. Think about yourself, those around you, and the environment. How can you protect each of these areas? (Take a look at the section "Safety, Tools, and Equipment.")

PRACTICE: Think About Safety

Suppose your bicycle is not running very well (Figure 6). You find yourself pedalling as hard as you can, and you cannot get it to go any faster, even on a flat stretch of road. Write out a simple list of steps that you could do to inspect your bike and fix the problem. Then, make a list of things that could go wrong, possible accidents, and what you should do to protect yourself from each of these.

Figure 6 If your bicycle is not working well, the axles may need adjusting.

4.B.4. Designing

Once you have a solution in mind and have come up with a plan, it is time to design your prototype—an original model that exhibits the essential features of the solution you chose. It can be a device, or it can be a method that demonstrates a new or improved process.

You can start by making a working diagram or series of diagrams. (See "Technical Drawings.") These can be simple sketches, but you may want to make a drawing that shows specific measurements and moving parts.

The next step is to ensure that you have all of the equipment, tools, and materials to build your prototype. Examine any drawings you make to ensure that your list is as complete as possible.

Once you have all of your materials, write out the instructions that you will follow as you build the prototype. This is much like writing a procedure—be sure to write everything down and be clear in your instructions. As you write down each step, you may think of additional materials and equipment you need, or you may encounter problems that require a design change. Once you have the steps written down, it is time to build your prototype.

If your problem solving requires you to build something, this is the stage at which you make the product. For example, if you are making insulating frames for your windows at home, start with one model for one window. Purchase the materials for one frame and make that first. Then, after you have tested it and evaluated it (see "Testing"), you can go on to other frames.

Before you begin construction or implement the first steps of your plan, look over the safety notes you have made. Also, make sure you have plenty of time to carry out your plan. Refer to your plans while you are doing the construction (Figure 7). You want this phase to go as smoothly as possible.

Figure 7 Follow a plan when building your model.

4.B.5. Testing

When you have finished building your device, you need to test it. Be sure to use the criteria that you came up with to develop your test. There are two reasons for this. First, you want to see how well it solves your problem. Second, you may want to modify something in your plan and build a second model. Engineers and technologists often find that they need to build and test several prototypes before they settle on a final plan.

You also need to record the results of your test. You can do this in a variety of ways, such as using point-form notes, sentences, a paragraph, a data table, or labelled diagrams and graphs.

When you have finished the product or process and have tested it to see how it works, you need to evaluate the process.

- *Did you follow the problem-solving process and meet your criteria?* For example, in creating and testing the insulating window frame, did you go through all the steps described in this section? Did you identify a need, generate possible solutions, focus in on one, and make a plan? Did you use tools safely when building the model? Did you test the model thoroughly to make sure it works? Did your product or process meet all of your criteria?
- *What were the environmental, social, and economic impacts of your solution?* How will you dispose of the oil you use to make your bicycle parts function more effectively? Will the cost of your insulating window frames be more than your family's energy savings? It is important to consider all the different impacts of your product or process on the world around you. As you have learned, one of the core beliefs of technology is that, in meeting human needs, we should be careful not to endanger the environment.

4.B.6. Modifying

Once you have evaluated your solution, you can identify areas that need improvement. Should you have done more research before developing the plan? Did you test it sufficiently, or should you repeat the process? Could you have completed the project more safely? Thinking about questions like these will help you create a better plan the next time you try to solve a technological problem.

Once you have a list of modifications that you think might improve your solution, revise and reconstruct your prototype. Repeat this process until an effective solution to the problem has been developed (Figure 8).

PRACTICE: Evaluate a Process

Suppose your project was to develop a process for inspecting the parts of your bicycle to see how they can be made to function more effectively. How would you evaluate whether you had followed the problem-solving steps for that process? Write a list of questions you might ask yourself.

4.B.7. Communicating

When technologists and engineers make something new that meets a human need or solves a problem, they will share what they have found with others. There are certain things you should include in your report or presentation:

- *You should give a complete explanation of your product or process, including the materials you used and decisions you made.* For example, why did you decide to use certain materials in your insulating window frames, and how did that decision affect the end result?

- *You may need to provide a technical drawing of your device showing how it meets your criteria.* How does the insulating window frame keep warmth from escaping? The next section, "Technical Drawings," will give you some examples of these diagrams.

- *You should look over your writing to see if you have used correct scientific and technological vocabulary.* Did you provide the correct names to the materials you used to build your insulating frame? Do not just copy names off of containers. If they also have common names, you should include those, too. This will help make your explanation clearer to others.

Figure 8 Engineers have constructed many prototypes of solar-powered vehicles. (a) An early prototype of a solar car (b) A modern solar car created by students at Queen's University

4.C. Technical Drawings

When you are planning a technology project, you will often need to do a technical drawing. This might start out as a rough sketch. However, you may need a detailed drawing to follow so that your finished product is constructed correctly. You may also want to use the drawing to communicate to others what you are planning to do, and include it in your final report or presentation.

4.C.1. Creating a Sketch

Sketching out a plan for a device can help you find solutions to a problem. Sketches can also be useful to keep track of your ideas. Figure 9 is an example of a sketch for a game design. Notice how it is very simple, and has just a few things written on it, including a question that is still unsolved.

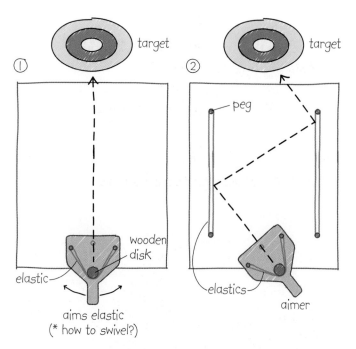

Figure 9 A sketch for a game design

4.C.2. Making an Isometric Drawing

If you plan to use your drawing to help build a product or device, you need to create a detailed and accurate drawing. Isometric drawings use straight lines drawn at 30° or 60° to represent the three dimensions of an object. Whenever three lines come together, they represent the height, width, and depth of the object (Figure 10). This method can be used to create a three-dimensional drawing of almost any device. In these drawings, you can use the real measurements, as in Figure 11. This will make it easy to re-create.

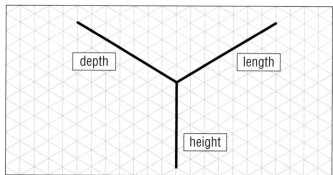

Figure 10 The parallel lines in an isometric grid run at 60° to one another.

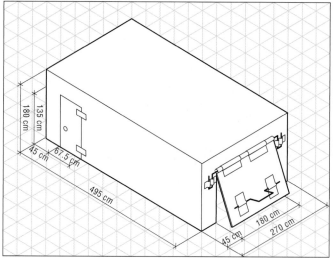

Figure 11 A model of a garage to be made from a shoebox

4.C.3. Making an Orthographic Projection

An orthographic projection allows you to look at each side of a model face-on (Figure 12). Each drawing is two-dimensional and includes all the details and measurements of the model. To understand how this works, think of placing your model inside a transparent box and looking at it from three different sides (Figure 13). Then, suppose you opened the box up and flattened the model out. You would get the three flat projections that you see in Figure 12. Orthographic projections should be drawn on graph paper.

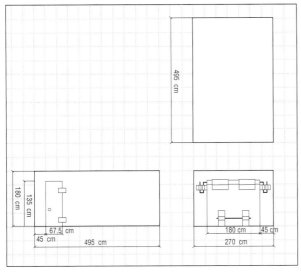

Figure 12 An orthographic projection.

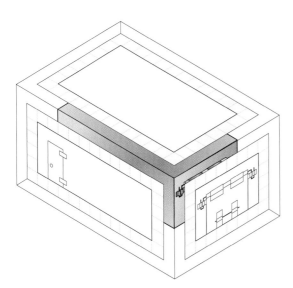

Figure 13 What orthographic projections would look like if they were assembled together in three dimensions

4.C.4. Showing Other Views of a Device

If you want to show what a device looks like inside, you can draw a cross-section (Figure 14).

If you are making a multi-component mechanical device and you want to show how the various components come together, you can draw an exploded view (Figure 15).

You can also take a small part of a drawing and enlarge it to show more detail (Figure 16).

Figure 14 A cross-section of a syringe

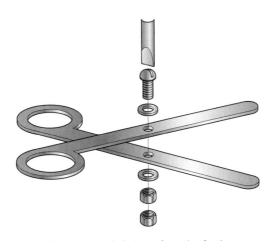

Figure 15 An exploded view of a pair of scissors

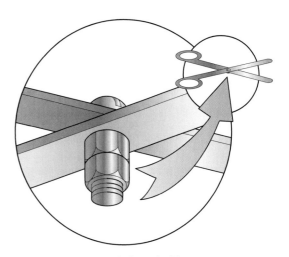

Figure 16 An enlarged view of a hinge

5. Safety, Tools, and Equipment

5.A. Getting Off to a Safe Start

Science and technology investigations can be a lot of fun (Figure 1). You have the chance to work with new equipment and materials. Investigations can also be dangerous, however, so you have to pay attention! As well, you have to know and follow special rules. Here are the most important rules to remember (Table 1).

Figure 1 You can enjoy science and technology investigations when you know and follow special safety rules.

Table 1 Working Safely in a Science and Technology Classroom

1. Follow your teacher's directions	2. Act responsibly	3. Be prepared
• Listen to your teacher's directions and follow them carefully. • Ask your teacher for directions if you are not sure what to do. • Never change anything, or start anything on your own, without your teacher's approval. • Get your teacher's approval before you start an investigation that you have designed yourself.	• Pay attention to your own safety and the safety of others. • Tell your teacher immediately if you see a safety hazard, such as broken glass or a spill. Also, tell your teacher if you see another student doing something that you think is dangerous. • Tell your teacher about any allergies or medical problems you have, or about anything else your teacher should know. • Do not wear contact lenses while doing investigations or activities. See your teacher about this. • Read all written directions carefully before you start an investigation or activity. • Clean up and put away any equipment after you are finished.	• Come prepared with your textbook, notebook, pencil, worksheets, and anything else you need for an investigation or activity. • Keep yourself and your work area tidy and clean. • Wash your hands carefully with soap and water at the end of the investigation or activity. • Never eat, drink, or chew gum in the science and technology classroom. • Wear eye protection or other equipment when instructed by your teacher. • Keep your clothing and hair out of the way. Roll up your sleeves, tuck in loose clothing, and tie back loose hair. Remove any loose jewellery.

5.B. Safe Science and Technology

Follow these instructions to work safely in the science and technology classroom.

Heat, Fire, and Electricity

- Never heat anything without your teacher's permission.
- Always wear eye protection when you are working with fire.
- Keep yourself, and anything else that can burn, away from heat or flames. Keep long hair tied back and do not wear loose clothing. Never reach across a flame.
- When heating a test tube, use a test tube holder and point it away from yourself and other students. Do not only heat the bottom of the test tube.
- Never heat a liquid in a closed container.
- Use tongs or heat-resistant gloves to pick up a hot object.
- Test an object that has been heated before you touch it. Slowly bring the back of your hand toward the object to make sure that it is not hot.
- Know where the fire extinguisher and fire blanket are kept in your classroom.
- Keep water away from electrical equipment. Never touch an electrical appliance or outlet with wet hands.
- Do not touch the top of a hot plate—a cold hot plate looks the same as a hot one.
- Do not heat Erlenmeyer flasks, Petri dishes, or wet objects on a hot plate.
- Do not pull on the cord to unplug an item; pull the plug itself.
- Switch off all electrical appliances immediately after use.

Chemicals

- Remain standing when performing experiments with chemicals.
- Prevent contact between chemicals and your eyes. Wear chemical splash-proof eye protection when appropriate.
- If you spill a chemical (or anything else), tell your teacher immediately.
- Never taste, smell, touch, or mix chemicals without your teacher's permission.
- Never put your nose directly over a chemical to smell it. Gently wave your hand over the chemical until you can smell it.
- Keep the lids tightly closed on chemicals that you are not using.
- Wash your hands well with soap after handling chemicals.
- Never pour anything into a sink without your teacher's permission.
- If any part of your body comes in contact with a chemical, wash the area immediately and thoroughly with water. If your eyes are affected, do not touch them; wash them immediately and continuously with cool water at the eye wash station for at least 15 minutes. Inform your teacher.

Living Things

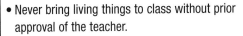

- Never bring living things to class without prior approval of the teacher.
- Treat all living things with care and respect.
- Never treat an animal in a way that would cause it pain or injury.
- Touch animals only when necessary. Follow your teacher's directions.
- Always wash your hands with soap before and after working with animals or touching their cages or containers.

Glass and Sharp Objects

- Handle glassware, knives, and other sharp instruments with extra care.
- If you break glassware, collect it with a dust pan and brush, never with your bare hands. Put the glass in the "Broken Glass" container, never in the garbage. Tell your teacher immediately if you cut yourself.
- Never work with cracked or chipped glassware. Give it to your teacher.
- Never point a knife or sharp object at another person.
- When cutting, make sure that you cut away from yourself and others. Be sure to use a cutting board or mat.

5.B.1. Caution Symbols

The activities and investigations in *Nelson Science and Technology Perspectives* are safe to perform, but accidents can happen. This is why potential safety hazards are identified with caution symbols and red type (**Figure 2**). Make sure that you read the cautions carefully, understand what they mean, and follow them. Check with your teacher if you are unsure.

 Never attempt to fix or test an electrical product without the help of a knowledgeable adult. Electrical shocks or fires could result.

Figure 2 Safety hazards are identified with caution symbols.

5.B.2. Safety Symbols

The safety symbols shown in Figures 3 and 4 are used throughout Canada to identify products that can be hazardous. Make sure that you know what each symbol means. Always use extra care when you see these symbols in your classroom or anywhere else.

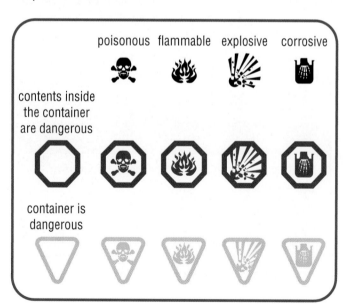

Figure 3 Hazardous Household Product Symbols (HHPS) appear on many products that are used in the home. Different shapes identify whether the contents of a container are dangerous or the container itself is dangerous.

 compressed gas

 dangerously reactive material

 flammable and combustible material

 biohazardous infectious material

 oxidizing material

 poisonous and infectious material causing immediate and serious toxic effects

 corrosive material

 poisonous and infectious material causing other toxic effects

Figure 4 Workplace Hazardous Materials Information System (WHMIS) symbols identify dangerous materials that are used in all workplaces, including schools.

PRACTICE: Make a Safety Poster

Make a safety poster for you and your classmates. Decide with a partner or group which rules and symbols are important enough to be highlighted and placed on the classroom walls. You could also include information about the route your class is supposed to follow to exit the building in case of a fire.

PRACTICE: Draw a Safety Map

Draw a map of your classroom or lab as seen from an aerial view. Show where the safety features are located, including the eyewash station, first-aid kit, fire blanket, broken glassware container, fire exits, and so on. Ensure that someone could find these safety features quickly and easily when looking at your map (make them stand out).

5.C. Working with Tools and Equipment

Follow these instructions to use science and technology tools and equipment safely in the classroom.

5.C.1. Personal Safety

When you are using specialized tools, equipment, and materials, you should always be wearing the following items (Figure 5):

- apron
- eye protection
- something to tie back long hair
- gloves if necessary

You should also be standing whenever you use equipment or tools in science and technology, unless you have permission to sit down.

Figure 5 Safe practices in science and technology

5.C.2. Working with Syringes and Tubing

When you are working with hydraulic equipment such as syringes and tubing, you need to take extra precaution not to spill water on yourself, your classmates, or the room. If possible, you should do this work over a sink.

5.C.3. Working with Glue Guns

Remember the following tips for the safe use of glue guns:

- Be sure to consult the "Personal Safety" rules before you work with glue guns.
- Use the glue gun near an electrical outlet so that the electrical cord is not in the way of yourself or other students.
- Use glue guns in well-ventilated, low-traffic areas.
- Make sure that you protect your work surface area (table or bench) before you start using the glue gun.
- You should be gluing at the level of your work surface area.
- Always hold your glue gun pointing down.
- If you need to move the object you are gluing, use a stick instead of your fingers to move it (Figure 6).

Figure 6 Safe use of a glue gun

5.C.4. Working with Sharp Tools

The following safety notes apply to hand tools such as drills, saws, knives, and hammers. Make sure you follow the "Personal Safety" rules, as well as these additional notes.

Drills

- Use a clamp to fasten the object that you want to drill a hole in.
- Use the drill in an upright position, drilling downwards into the object.

Saws

- Match the mitre box with the saw you use, and fasten it securely to the table or bench.
- Check that the blade of the saw is pointing away from you (Figure 7). Keep your fingers away from the blade.
- Saw with steady, even strokes, taking care not to dislodge the mitre box.

Figure 7 Safe use of saw and mitre box

Knives

- Wear gloves when using a sharp utility knife.
- Always use a metal ruler or straight edge to help you cut.
- Cut the object by holding the knife with the blade down and pulling the knife toward you.
- Always cut using light pressure, slowly, and under control.
- Carefully pull the blade back into the knife (with the button or lever) when you are not using it.

Hammers

- Begin hammering by gently tapping the nail in, so that it stands straight up. Then, remove your fingers, and hammer the nail on its head.
- If you have trouble keeping the nail straight, use a pair of needle-nose pliers to hold the nail in place while you are hammering it.
- Always work on a solid, flat surface.

Power Tools

- When working with power tools such as drill presses, wood lathes, power sanding belts, jigsaws, or skill saws, you need to take special precautions beyond the suggestions on this page. Consult your teacher for the safety instructions for each of the power tools before you begin to use them.

5.D. The Microscope

You must magnify cells and other small objects in order to study them in detail. A compound light microscope has two lenses and a light source to make objects appear larger (Figure 8). The object is magnified by a lens near your eye, called the ocular lens (sometimes called the eyepiece), and again by a second lens, called the objective lens, which is just above the object. The comparison of the actual size of the object with the size of its image is referred to as magnification. Table 2 lists the parts of a compound light microscope and their functions.

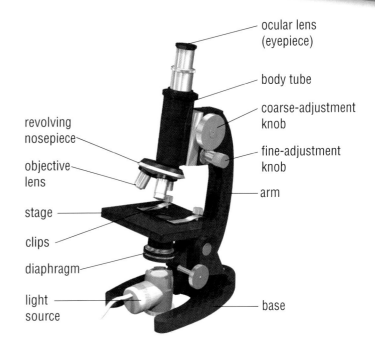

Figure 8 A compound light microscope

Table 2 Parts of a Compound Light Microscope

Structure	Function
stage	• supports the microscope slide • a central opening that allows light to pass through the slide
clips	• found on the stage and used to hold the slide in position
diaphragm	• regulates the amount of light that reaches the object being viewed
objective lens	• magnifies the object • usually three complex lenses located on the nosepiece immediately above the object • the low-power lens magnifies by 4× • the medium-power lens magnifies by 10× • the high-power lens magnifies by 40×
revolving nosepiece	• rotates, allowing the objective lens to be changed
body tube	• contains ocular lens • supports objective lenses
ocular lens	• magnifies the object, usually by 10× • also known as the eyepiece • this is the part you look through to view the object
coarse-adjustment knob	• moves the body tube up or down to get the object or specimen into focus • used with the low-power objective lens only
fine-adjustment knob	• moves the stage to get the object or specimen into focus • used with medium-power and high-power magnification • used only after the object or specimen has been located and focused under lower-power magnification using the coarse-adjustment knob

5.E. Using Other Scientific Equipment

You can do many experiments using everyday materials and equipment. Your science and technology classroom has many different pieces of equipment, including a few that you may not be familiar with. Below is a list of common science and technology equipment.

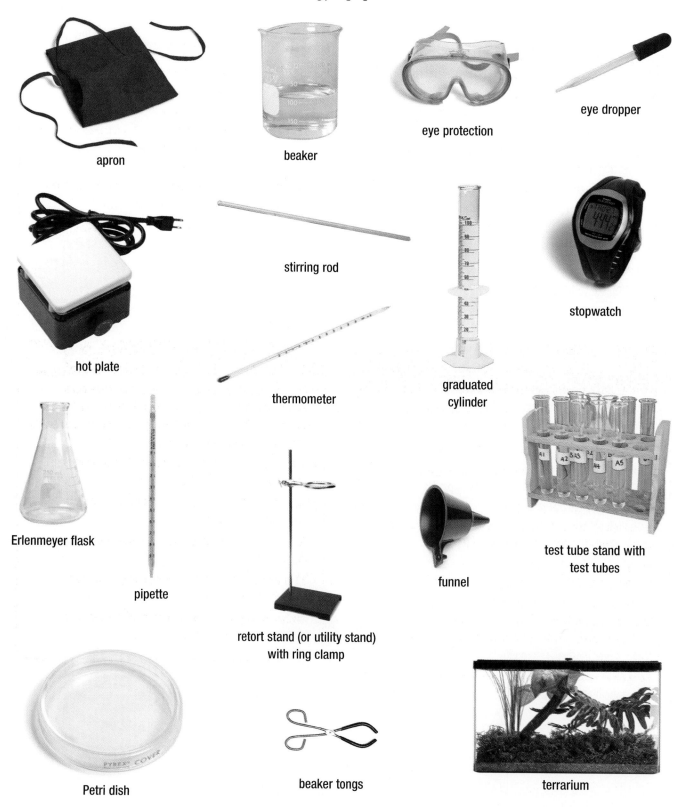

apron

beaker

eye protection

eye dropper

hot plate

stirring rod

thermometer

graduated cylinder

stopwatch

Erlenmeyer flask

pipette

retort stand (or utility stand) with ring clamp

funnel

test tube stand with test tubes

Petri dish

beaker tongs

terrarium

5.F. Safety at Home

When you do science and technology activities at home, you need to be just as aware of safety as in your school classroom. All the previous rules in this Skills Handbook apply to working at home. In addition, here are some things you need to remember.

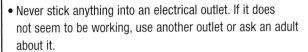

Electrical Safety at Home

- Never stick anything into an electrical outlet. If it does not seem to be working, use another outlet or ask an adult about it.
- Never unplug an electrical appliance by pulling its cord. Pull the plug itself.
- Always keep water away from electrical outlets, cords, and appliances.
- Never touch the electrical panel in your home by yourself.
- Never touch the electrical wires and outlets on the outside of your house or apartment.

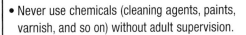

Chemical Safety at Home

- Never use chemicals (cleaning agents, paints, varnish, and so on) without adult supervision.
- Before using paints or varnish for a project, read the label on the container carefully, and consult with an adult. Never use containers without labels.
- When you are cleaning or working with chemicals, paint, or varnish, always keep the room well ventilated.

Safety with Tools and Sharp Objects at Home

- Never carry a pair of scissors or a knife with an open blade in your pocket.
- Keep scissors closed whenever you are not using them.
- Put all knives and other sharp tools away when you are not using them.
- When you work at home with hand tools such as drills, saws, knives, and hammers, follow the same rules as at school. Study the section "Working with Sharp Tools."
- When you work at home with power tools, always work with an adult, and always read the safety rules first.
- Handle glassware very carefully. If you break any glass containers, always consult with an adult about cleaning up the broken glass. Collect broken glass with a dustpan and brush, never with your bare hands.

Working with Plants at Home

- If you are planting, do not use seeds that have been coated with chemicals or fertilizers. Read the package or ask the supplier before purchasing them. Beans and seeds from a grocery store are usually safe to handle.
- Never eat any part of a house plant without consulting an adult. Some plants are poisonous.
- Find out whether you have any allergies to plants before you begin a project with them.
- Do not handle seeds or plants if you have cuts or sores on your hands.
- Often it is best to wear non-allergenic gloves when working with plants and soils.
- Always wash your hands with soap and water after working with plants or soil.

6. Using Mathematics in Science and Technology

6.A. Measurement and Measuring Tools

Measuring is an essential part of science. Measurements allow you to give exact information when you are describing something, so knowing how to measure things correctly is very important. Some common measurements are

- length
- volume
- mass
- time
- temperature
- force
- viscosity

Most countries in the world, including Canada, use the International System of Units (SI). The SI units for some common measurements are listed below in Table 1.

The three basic units of measurement have their origins in properties of Earth. The basic unit of length was originally defined in terms of the size of Earth. One metre is one ten-millionth of the distance between the equator and either pole. The basic unit of mass is related to the basic unit of length. One gram was defined to be the mass of a cube of water at 0 °C that measures exactly 1 cm on each side. The basic unit of time was originally defined in terms of the rotation of Earth. One second is one sixtieth of a minute, which is one sixtieth of an hour, which is one twenty-fourth of a day. One day is the time it takes for Earth to make one complete rotation on its axis.

Table 1 Common SI Units

Measurement	SI unit	Name	Related units	Relationship
time	s	second	hour (h) minute (min)	1 h = 60 min 1 min = 60 s
temperature	°C	degree Celsius	degree Kelvin (°K)	x °C = x °K + 273
mass	kg	kilogram	gram (g)	1 kg = 1000 g
length	m	metre	centimetre (cm) millimetre (mm) kilometre (km)	1 m = 100 cm 1 m = 1000 mm 1 km = 1000 m
volume	m^3	cubic metre	litre (L) millilitre (mL)	1000 L = 1 m^3 1 mL = 1 cm^3
density	kg/m^3	kilogram per cubic metre	gram per cubic centimetre (g/cm^3)	1000 kg/m^3 = 1 g/cm^3
force	N	newton		
work	J	joule	newton-metre (N·m)	1 J = 1 N·m
pressure	Pa	pascal	newton per square metre (N/m^2)	1 Pa = 1 N/m^2

Table 2 lists some common SI prefixes that can be applied to units of measurement.

To convert from one unit to another, you simply multiply by a conversion factor. For example, to convert 12.4 metres (m) to centimetres (cm), you use the relationship

1 cm = 0.01 m, or 1 cm = 1/100 m

> 12.40 m = ? cm
> 1 cm = 0.01 m
> $12.40 \; \text{m} \left(\dfrac{1 \; \text{cm}}{0.01 \; \text{m}} \right) = 1240 \; \text{cm}$

Once you know the conversion factor, you can convert between any quantities with the same base unit.

PRACTICE: Convert Units

(a) Convert 23 km to m and to mm.
(b) Convert 675 mL to L.
(c) Convert 450 g to kg and to mg.

6.A.1. Measuring Length

Length is the shortest distance between two points. Four units are generally used to measure length: kilometres (km), metres (m), centimetres (cm), and millimetres (mm).

10 mm = 1 cm	100 cm = 1 m
1000 mm = 1 m	1000 m = 1 km

You measure length when you want to find out how long something is. You also measure length when you want to know how deep, how tall, how far, or how wide something is. The metre is the basic unit of length (Figure 1). See the next page for some tips on measuring length.

Figure 1 Metric rulers are used to measure lengths in millimetres and centimetres, up to 30 cm. Metre sticks measure longer lengths up to 100 cm.

Table 2 Common SI Prefixes

Prefix	Symbol	Factor by which unit is multiplied	Example
giga	G	1 000 000 000	
mega	M	1 000 000	1 Mm = 1 000 000 m
kilo	k	1000	1 km = 1000 m
hecto	h	100	1 hm = 100 m
deca	da	10	1 dam = 10 m
		1	
deci	d	0.1	1 dm = 0.1 m
centi	c	0.01	1 cm = 0.01 m
milli	m	0.001	1 mm = 0.001 m
micro	μ	0.000 001	1 μm = 0.000 001 m
nano	n	0.000 000 001	1 nm = 0.000 000 001 m

Tips for Measuring Length

- Always start measuring from the zero mark on a ruler, not from the edge of the ruler.
- Look directly at the lines on the ruler. If you try to read the ruler at an angle, you will get an incorrect measurement.
- To measure something that is not in a straight line, use measuring tape or a piece of string (Figure 2). Cut or mark the string. Then, use a ruler to measure the length of the string. If you have a tape measure made from fabric, you could use this instead.

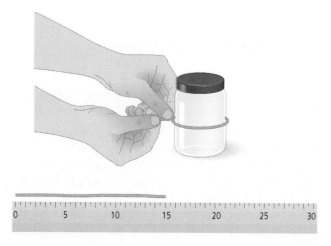

Figure 2 Use string to measure objects that cannot be measured in a straight line.

6.A.2. Measuring Volume

Volume is the amount of space that a three-dimensional object takes up. The volume of a solid is usually measured in cubic metres (m^3) or cubic centimetres (cm^3). The volume of a liquid is usually measured in litres (L) or millilitres (mL).

$$1000 \text{ mL} = 1 \text{ L} \qquad 1 \text{ L} = 1000 \text{ cm}^3$$
$$1 \text{ cm}^3 = 1 \text{ mL} \qquad 1000 \text{ L} = 1 \text{ m}^3$$

You can calculate the volume of a rectangular solid (Figure 3) by measuring the length, width, and height of the solid, and then using the following formula:

volume = length × width × height

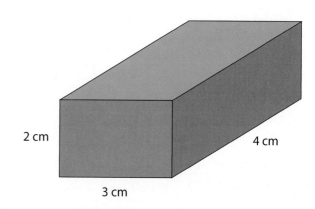

Figure 3 Multiplying length, width, and height will give you the volume of a rectangular solid.

You can measure the volume of a liquid using a special container, such as a graduated cylinder. See the next page for some tips for measuring volume with a graduated cylinder.

You can measure the volume of an irregularly shaped solid, such as a rock, using water (Figure 4). To do this, choose a measuring container that the irregular solid will fit inside. Pour water into the empty container until it is about half full. Record the volume of water in the container, and then carefully add the solid. Make sure that the solid is completely submerged in the water. Record the volume of the water plus the solid. Calculate the volume of the solid using the following formula:

> volume of solid =
> (volume of water + solid) − volume of water

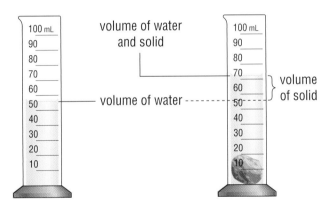

Figure 4 You can use a graduated cylinder to measure the volume of an irregular solid.

Tips for Measuring Volume

- Use a container that is big enough to hold twice as much liquid as you need. You want a lot of space so that you can get an accurate reading.
- Use a graduated cylinder to get the most accurate measurement of volume.
- To measure liquid in a graduated cylinder (or a beaker or a measuring cup), make sure that your eyes are at the same level as the top of the liquid. You will see that the surface of the liquid curves downward in the middle. This downward curve is called the **meniscus**. You need to measure the volume from the bottom of the meniscus (Figure 5).

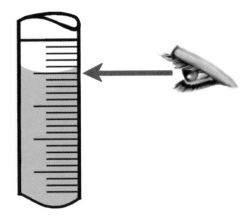

Figure 5 Reading the volume of a liquid correctly

PRACTICE: Determine Units of Volume

What volume of liquids do you drink in an average day? Use the illustrations of volume measurements to help you answer this question.

measuring cup	milk carton	tablespoon	pop bottle
500 mL	1 L	15 mL	2 L

PRACTICE: The Importance of Volume

Measuring accurately is a critical skill. For example, measuring medication doses accurately is very important. If the volume of a liquid medication is not measured accurately, the medicine may not be effective or could cause an overdose. Make a list of three everyday examples where accurate measurements of volume are important. Give reasons for your choices.

6.A.3. Measuring Mass and Weight

Mass is the amount of matter in an object. In everyday life, we often confuse weight with mass. When people state their "weight" in kilograms, they are really stating their mass! Weight is actually a force caused by the pull of gravity on a mass and is measured in newtons. Weight can vary depending on the location of an object—for instance, your weight on the Moon is one-sixth your weight on Earth. Mass is the same on both Earth and the Moon because the amount of matter in an object does not change with its location. The common units used to measure mass are grams (g), milligrams (mg), kilograms (kg), and metric tonnes (t).

> 1000 mg = 1 g
> 1000 g = 1 kg
> 1000 kg = 1 t

Scientists use balances to measure mass. Two types of balances are the triple-beam balance (Figure 6) and the electronic balance (Figure 7).

Figure 6 A triple-beam balance: Place the object you are measuring on the pan. Adjust the masses on each beam (starting with the largest) until the pointer on the right side is level with the zero mark. Then, add the values of each beam to find the measurement.

Figure 7 An electronic balance: Place the object you are measuring on the platform and read the measurement on the digital display. If you want to measure the mass of a substance without including the mass of the container that it is in, you can place the container on the platform and re-zero the balance. This resets the scale to zero. You can then measure the mass of the substance that you add to the container.

Scientists use spring scales to measure weight (Figure 8). Spring scales compare the force of gravity (and other forces acting on an object, like buoyancy) to the force applied by the spring. The spring scale shows you where these two forces balance, telling you how much force is exerted by gravity on the object.

Figure 8 Spring scales: First, let the spring hang vertically with nothing attached to it and fix the "zero" point. Then, attach the mass that you are measuring and note the point that it extends to. This measures the force of gravity acting on the mass. You can also use spring scales in a horizontal position to measure the force you are pulling something with horizontally.

Tips for Measuring Mass and Weight

- To measure the mass of a liquid, first measure the mass of a suitable container. Then, measure the mass of the liquid and the container. Subtract the mass of the container from the mass of the liquid and the container. Mass is measured in grams (g) or kilograms (kg).
- To measure the mass of a powder or crystals, first determine the mass of a sheet of paper. Then, place the sample on the sheet of paper, and measure the mass of both. Subtract the mass of the paper from the mass of the sample and the sheet of paper.
- To measure the weight of an object (that is, the force of gravity acting on the object's mass), place the object on a spring scale by hooking it or tying it to the scale, and observe the spring scale reading in newtons (N). To obtain an accurate reading, you should make sure that the spring scale reads 0 N before you suspend the object from it. You can usually adjust the spring scale to give this initial "0" reading.

6.A.4. Measuring Temperature

In science, temperature is generally measured in degrees Celsius. Some temperatures you may be familiar with include

0 °C = freezing point of water
20 °C = warm spring day
37.6 °C = normal body temperature
65 °C = water that is hot to touch
100 °C = boiling point of water

Each mark on a Celsius thermometer is equal to one degree Celsius. The glass contains a coloured liquid—usually alcohol. When you place the thermometer in a substance, the liquid in the thermometer expands or contracts to indicate the temperature (Figure 9).

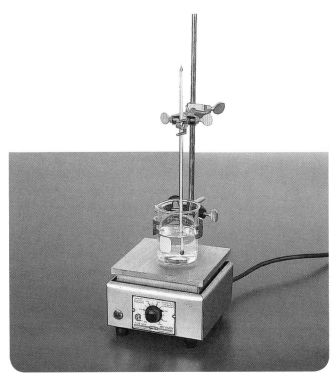

Figure 9 For accurate measurement, make sure that the bulb of the thermometer is in the middle of the water, not touching the bottom or sides, and not near the surface of the water.

Tips for Measuring Temperature

- Make sure that the coloured liquid has stopped moving before you take your reading.
- Hold the thermometer at eye level to be sure that your reading is accurate.
- Handle thermometers with care. Never shake or play with a thermometer.
- Return the thermometer to its storage case when you are finished working with it.

6.B. Solving Numerical Problems Using the GRASS Method

In science and technology, you sometimes have problems that involve quantities (numbers), units, and mathematical equations. An effective method for solving these problems is the GRASS method. This always involves five steps: **G**ivens, **R**equired, **A**nalysis, **S**olution, and **S**tatement.

Given: Read the problem carefully and list all of the quantities and their known values that are given. Remember to include units.

Required: Read the problem again and identify the quantity that the question is asking you to find.

Analysis: Read the problem again and think about the relationship between the given quantities and the required quantity.

There may be a mathematical equation you could use to calculate the value of the required quantity using the given values. If so, write the equation down in this step. Sometimes it helps to sketch a diagram of the problem.

Solution: Use the equation you identified in the "Analysis" step to solve the problem. Usually, you substitute the given values into the equation and calculate the required value. Do not forget to include units, and to round off your answer to an appropriate number of digits. (See the next section on significant digits and scientific notation for help.)

Statement: Write a sentence that describes your answer to the question you identified in the "Required" step.

SAMPLE PROBLEM: Determine Mechanical Advantage of a Pulley System

To lift a load 50 cm off the ground with a pulley system, 150 cm of rope had to be pulled. What is the mechanical advantage of the pulley system?

Given: input distance = 150 cm
             output distance = 50 cm

Required: mechanical advantage (MA)

Analysis: $MA = \dfrac{\text{input distance}}{\text{output distance}}$

Solution: $MA = \dfrac{150 \text{ cm}}{50 \text{ cm}}$

$MA = 3$

Statement: The mechanical advantage of the pulley system is 3.

6.C. Significant Digits and Scientific Notation

6.C.1. Using Significant Digits

Suppose you use a ruler to measure the length or height of something, such as the height of a plant that you are growing (Figure 10). You measure the height of a plant for four weeks. The measurements you get are as follows:

- 6 cm
- 7.5 cm
- 9 cm
- 9.9 cm

Figure 10 Measuring different lengths with the same accuracy

What is wrong with these measurements? You did not use the same accuracy for each measurement. If you decide to measure to one decimal place, the first number should be 6.0 cm, not 6 cm. If you wrote down 6 cm, it is most likely that you really measured 6.0 and not 6.1 or 5.9. Similarly, the third measurement should not be 9 cm but 9.0 cm. Your new list of numbers should be

- 6.0 cm
- 7.5 cm
- 9.0 cm
- 9.9 cm

All of these measurements have the same number of significant digits. They all represent the same accuracy of measurement. Accuracy is also important when manipulating numbers. Suppose you are multiplying values with a calculator and your final value is an eight digit number. You must make sure to record this value to the appropriate number of significant digits. Table 3 provides some guidelines for determining significant digits.

Table 3 Guidelines for Determining Significant Digits

Guideline	Example	
	Number	Number of significant digits
Count from left to right, beginning with the first non-zero digit.	345	3
	457.35	5
Zeros at the beginning of a number are never significant.	0.235	3
	0.003	1
All non-zero digits in a number are significant.	1.123	4
	76.2	3
Zeros between digits are significant.	107.05	5
	0.02094	4
Zeros at the end of a number with a decimal point are significant.	10.40	4
Zeros at the end of a number without a decimal point are sometimes significant (3030), but for a very large number are not usually significant (4 500 000 000)).	3030	4
	4 500 000 000	2
All digits in the coefficient of a number written in scientific notation are significant.	2.45×10^6	3

6.C.2. Using Scientific Notation

Sometimes in science and technology, we work with very small or very large numbers. Take, for example, the width of a water molecule in metres. As you might imagine, it is very small: 0.000 000 000 280 m. Or consider the number of cubic metres of fresh water that Canadians use in their homes and municipalities each year. It is enormous: 4 500 000 000 m^3. It's not easy to write these large and small figures. Therefore, we often use **scientific notation**, a type of mathematical abbreviation that omits large numbers of zeros, for numbers like these.

First, we decide on the number of significant digits for each measurement. The amount of fresh water Canadians consume each year, given as 4 500 000 000 m^3, has two significant digits. We assume that none of the 0's to the right of the 5 are significant but just represent the factors of 10. Therefore, the first part of the scientific notation is 4.5. Since we have to move the decimal point to the left past nine places to get 4.5 (there is an invisible decimal point to the right of the last zero in 4 500 000 000), the second part of the scientific notation is 10^9.

The amount of water used by Canadians in their homes and municipalities each year is 4.5×10^9 m^3 in scientific notation. The calculation would look like this:

4 500 000 000 =

$4.5 \times 10 \times 10 \times 10 \times 10 \times 10 \times 10 \times 10 \times 10 \times 10$

$= 4.5 \times 10^9$

Table 4 shows powers of ten and their decimal equivalents. Table 5 (on the next page) shows some examples of large and small numbers expressed in scientific notation.

Table 4 Powers of 10 and Decimal Equivalents

Power of 10	Decimal equivalent
10^9	1 000 000 000
10^8	100 000 000
10^7	10 000 000
10^6	1 000 000
10^5	100 000
10^4	10 000
10^3	1000
10^2	100
10^1	10
10^0	1
10^{-1}	0.1
10^{-2}	0.01
10^{-3}	0.001
10^{-4}	0.0001
10^{-5}	0.000 01
10^{-6}	0.000 001
10^{-7}	0.000 000 1
10^{-8}	0.000 000 01

The width of the water molecule, 0.000 000 000 280 m, is measured to three significant digits, as there is a 0 to the right of the 28. So, the first part of the scientific notation is 2.80. Then, since we have to move the decimal point to the right past 10 places to get 2.80, and each place represents a factor of 10, the second part of the scientific notation is 10^{-10}. The width of the water molecule is 2.80×10^{-10} m in scientific notation. Here is the equation for your conversion to scientific notation:

0.000 000 000 280 =

$$\frac{2.80}{10 \times 10 \times 10 \times 10 \times 10 \times 10 \times 10 \times 10 \times 10 \times 10}$$

$= 2.80 \times 0.000 000 000 1$

$= 2.80 \times 10^{-10}$

Table 5 Numbers Expressed in Scientific Notation

Large or small number	Common decimal notation	Scientific notation
124.5 million km	124 500 000 km	1.245×10^8 km
154 thousand nm	154 000 nm	1.54×10^5 nm
753 trillionths of a kg	0.000 000 000 753 kg	7.52×10^{-10} kg
315 billionths of a m	0.000 000 315 m	3.15×10^{-7} m

6.D. Data Tables and Graphs

6.D.1. Creating Data Tables

Data tables are a great way to organize your observations. Data tables can be used to record qualitative and quantitative observations, and they make it easy to convert your data into a graph for analysis (Figure 11). Creating a data table should be one of your first steps when conducting an investigation.

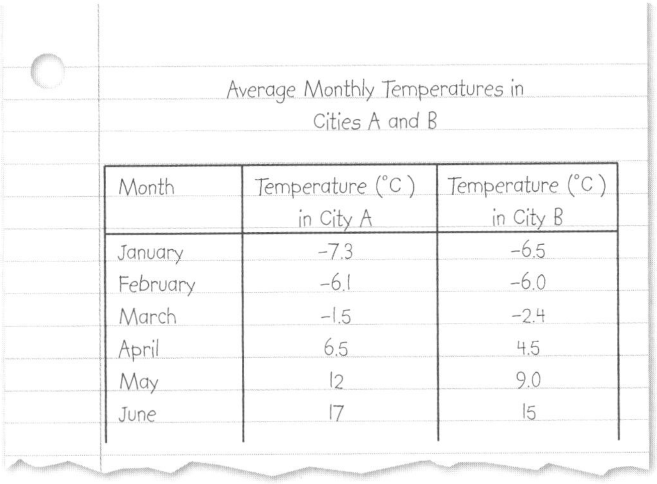
Average Monthly Temperatures in Cities A and B

Month	Temperature (°C) in City A	Temperature (°C) in City B
January	−7.3	−6.5
February	−6.1	−6.0
March	−1.5	−2.4
April	6.5	4.5
May	12	9.0
June	17	15

Figure 11 This data table records average monthly temperatures in two cities from January to June.

Follow these guidelines to make a data table:

- Use a ruler to make your table.
- Write a title that describes your data as precisely as possible.
- List the values of the independent variable in the left-hand column of your table. (In Figure 11, for each city, the independent variable is the month.)
- List the values of the dependent variable that you are measuring (the average monthly temperature) in the columns to the right of the column of the independent variable (month).
- Include the units of measurement for each variable.

6.D.2. Graphing Data

When you do scientific research or perform an investigation, you often collect a lot of data. Sometimes it is difficult to see patterns by looking at a data table. Look at Table 6. Can you see a pattern?

Table 6 Average Rainfall in Ottawa, Ontario

Month	Rainfall (mm)
January	15
February	16
March	32
April	58
May	75
June	77
July	88
August	92
September	83
October	70
November	63
December	33

One way to make patterns in your data easy to see and analyze is to turn your data into a graph. There are three common graphs that you will probably be familiar with:

- bar graphs
- line graphs
- circle or pie graphs

Each kind of graph has its own special uses. You need to identify which type of graph is best for the data that you have collected.

Bar Graphs A **bar graph** helps you make comparisons when one variable is in numbers (that is, rainfall) and the other variable is not (that is, month of the year). Bar graphs are useful for showing how data are distributed across categories. The following bar graph in Figure 12 was created from the data in Table 6. It clearly shows the rainfall in different months of the year, and makes it easy for the reader to see a pattern. You may have noticed that rainfall is lowest in January and highest in April from looking at the data table alone, but the *overall* pattern of rainfall over the course of the year is much easier to analyze when presented in a bar graph like Figure 12.

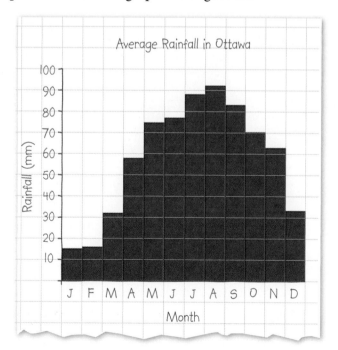

Figure 12 Bar graph

Tips for Drawing Bar Graphs

1. Draw and label the axes of your graph. Usually, the bars rise vertically from the horizontal axis. Therefore, label the quantitative variable (the amount of rainfall) on the vertical axis and the qualitative variable (the month) on the horizontal axis.

2. Before you place the numbers on the vertical axis, develop a scale. In the example above, the rainfall reaches a maximum of 92 mm in August. Therefore, you want your vertical axis to go up to 100. If there are 10 grid lines on your vertical axis, you would number by tens.

3. For the horizontal axis, if there are 12 months, choose 12 grid lines. Draw each bar up the middle of the grid line. To draw your bars, first use a ruler to draw straight lines for the two sides of the bar, and the top, and then shade the bars in.

4. Label each bar below the horizontal axis, using a short form if necessary (the first letter of the month).

5. Place a title at the top of your graph. The title should state clearly and concisely what your graph is showing.

Line Graphs A **line graph** is useful when you have two variables that are numerical quantities. It shows changes in measurement. It can also help you decide whether there is a trend or relationship between two sets of numbers: for example, "if this happens, then that happens." Table 7 (on the next page) gives the height of a plant over several weeks. The line graph for this data (Figure 13 on the next page) helps you see that the height of the plant increases over time.

Table 7 Plant Height Over Time

Time (weeks)	Plant height (cm)
0	0
2	3
4	4
6	8
8	11
10	14

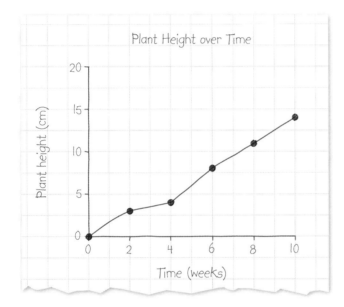

Figure 13 Line graph

Tips for Drawing Line Graphs

1. Decide which variable goes on which axis. Usually, the independent variable (time in weeks) goes on the horizontal axis, while the dependent variable (the plant height) goes on the vertical axis.

2. Develop a scale for each axis. For example, if you use a scale of 5 cm for every two grid lines on the vertical axis, you will need four or five grid lines to accommodate the 14 cm of total height attained by the plant.

3. Plot the points on the graph. For numbers that do not fit exactly on a grid line, such as 11 cm, place them between the 10 cm and 12.5 cm grid lines, as close as possible to where 11 would be.

4. Sketch a line through the points.

5. Place a clear and concise title at the top of your graph.

Circle Graphs A **circle graph** (or pie graph) shows the whole of something divided into all of its parts. A circle graph is round and shows how large a share of the circle belongs to different categories. You can use a circle graph to see how different things compare in size or quantity. It is a good way to graph data that are percentages or can be changed to percentages. The data in Table 8 has been graphed in Figure 14.

Table 8 Water Use in Houses in Canada

Type of water use	Daily consumption of water (L)
kitchen and drinking	40
laundry	80
cleaning	20
toilet flushing	120
showers and baths	140

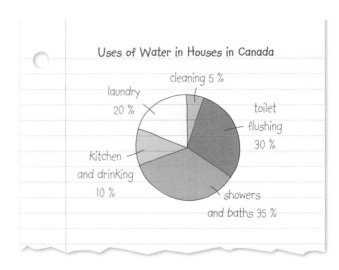

Figure 14 Circle graph

Tips for Drawing Circle Graphs

1. Use a circle graph instead of a bar graph when you can convert your quantitative variable to a percentage. You can do this when you know the total value of this variable. In Table 8, the total daily water usage adds up to 400 L. (Check this out by adding up the numbers in the right column.)

2. Change each value to a percentage of the total. For example, people use 40 L per day in the kitchen and for drinking, which is $\frac{40}{400}$ or 10 % of the total of 400 L.

3. Check that all of the percentage values add up to 100 %.

4. Convert each percentage to an angle of the circle by changing each percentage to a decimal and multiplying by 360°. For example, for kitchen and drinking, 10 % of $360° = 0.10 \times 360° = 36°$.

5. Draw a circle with a compass, and use a protractor to measure off the number of degrees for each section (for kitchen and drinking, this is 36°).

6. Shade each section of the circle a different colour. This makes the graph easy to read.

7. Label each section and title the circle graph.

6.D.3. Reading Graphs

As you have learned, graphing allows you to see patterns in your data that can help you understand the relationship between your variables. Here are some tips for reading and interpreting graphs:

- Identify the dependent and independent variables. Are they quantitative or qualitative?

- For quantitative variables, look at the units of measurement and the scale chosen for the graph. Could these affect the patterns you see?

- Determine the range of values on each axis (this is the difference between the highest value and the lowest value). What do these numbers tell you about the data?

- Look for trends or patterns in the data. Does the pattern tell you anything about the relationship between variables? Do the values of the dependent variable increase or decrease as the values of the independent variable change?

6.D.4. Graphing with the Computer

You can use a graphing or spreadsheet program on a computer to make your data table and create the graph that you want.

Making Data Tables Using Software Open the graphing or spreadsheet program to a new page and type your data table into the software. When you do this, you follow the same steps for creating a data table by hand.

Making Graphs Using Software Once you have the data table entered in the computer program, highlight the cells with numerical data in them. Then, click the graphing button or select this option from the menu. The following steps will help you create the final graph:

- When you are given graph options, select the type of graph you wish to create (you may have to select "Enter" or "Next" to move to the next choice).

- If you are asked whether your data or "series" is in columns or rows, select columns, since data tables are usually set up this way.

- Enter a title for your graph and labels for the axes.

7. Study Skills for Science and Technology

7.A. Reading Strategies

You can use different skills and strategies to help you read different types of material. Reading a science and technology book is different from reading a novel. When you are reading a science and technology book, you are reading for information. Here are some strategies to help you read for information.

7.A.1. Before Reading

Skim the section you are going to read. Look at the illustrations, headings, and subheadings. Ask yourself the following questions:

- *Preview:* What is this section about? How is it organized?
- *Make connections:* What do I already know about the topic? How is it connected to other topics I have already learned?
- *Predict:* What information will I find in this section? Which parts will give me the most information?
- *Set a purpose:* What questions do I have about the topic?

7.A.2. During Reading

Pause and think as you read. Spend time looking at the photographs, illustrations, tables, and graphs, as well as at the words. Ask yourself the following questions as you read:

- *Check your learning:* What are the main ideas in this section? How would I explain them in my own words? What questions do I still have? Do I need to re-read? Do I need to read more slowly, or can I read more quickly?
- *Determine the meanings of key terms:* Can I figure out the meanings of unfamiliar terms from context clues in words or illustrations? Do I understand the definitions of highlighted terms? Is there something about the structure of a new term that will help me remember its meaning? Are there terms I should look up in the glossary (Figure 1)?

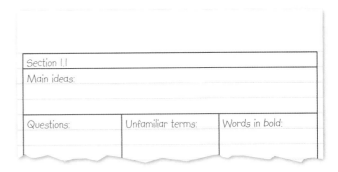

Figure 1 Making charts can help you organize your note taking.

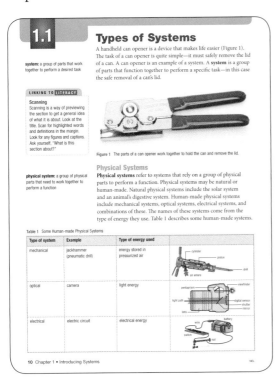

- *Make inferences:* What conclusions can I make from what I am reading? Can I make any conclusions by "reading between the lines"?
- *Visualize:* What mental pictures can I make to help me understand and remember what I am reading? Would it help to make a sketch?
- *Make connections:* How is this like the things I already know?
- *Interpret visuals and graphics:* What additional information can I get from the photographs, illustrations, tables, or graphs?

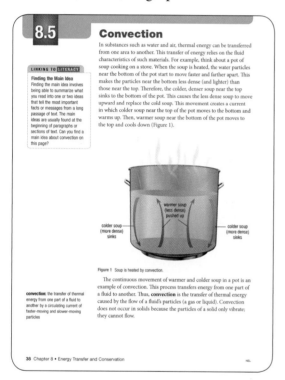

7.A.3. After Reading

Many of the strategies you use during reading can also be used after reading. In your textbook, for example, there are questions to answer after you read. These questions will help you check your learning and make connections.

- *Locate needed information:* Where can I find the information I need to answer the questions? Under what heading might I find the information? What page is it on? What highlighted terms should I skim for? What details do I need to include in my answers?
- *Synthesize:* How can I organize the information? What graphic organizer could I use? (See the next page for information on graphic organizers.) What headings or categories could I use?
- *React:* What are my opinions about this information? How does it, or might it, affect my life or my community? Do other students agree with my reactions?
- *Evaluate information:* What do I know now that I did not know before? Have any of my ideas changed as a result of what I have read? What questions do I still have?

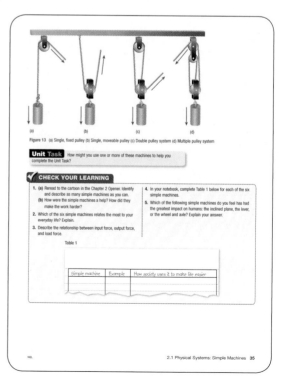

7.B. Graphic Organizers

Diagrams that are used to organize and display ideas visually are called **graphic organizers**. Graphic organizers are especially useful in science and technology studies when you are trying to connect together different concepts, ideas, and data. Different graphic organizers are used for different purposes:

- to show processes
- to organize ideas and thinking
- to compare and contrast

- to show properties or characteristics
- to review words and terms
- to collaborate and share ideas

To Show Processes

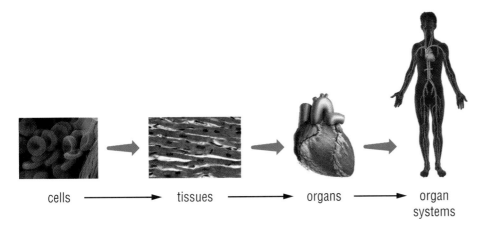

cells ⟶ tissues ⟶ organs ⟶ organ systems

You can use a **flow chart** to show a sequence of steps or a series of component relationships.

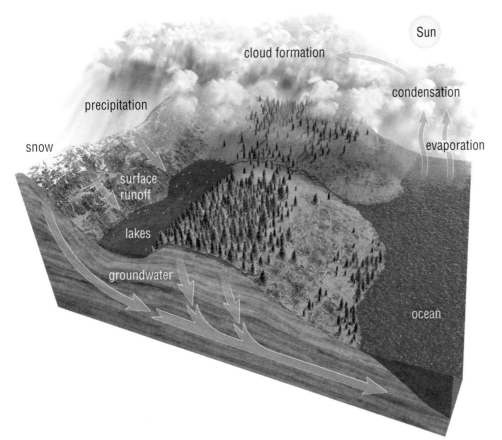

You can use a **cycle map** to show cycles in nature.

To Organize Ideas and Thinking

A **concept map** is a diagram showing the relationships between ideas. Words or pictures representing the ideas are connected by arrows and words or expressions that explain the connections. You can use a concept map to brainstorm what you already know, to map your thinking, or to summarize what you have learned. **Mind maps** are similar to concept maps, but mind maps do not have explanations for the connections between ideas.

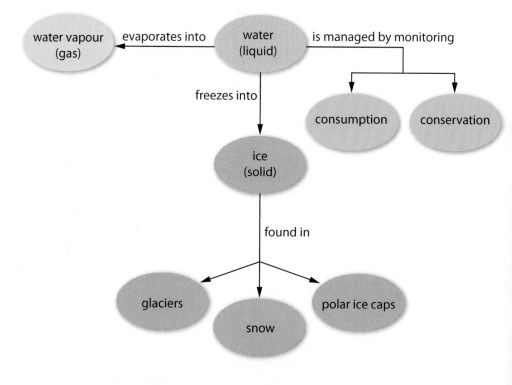

You can use a **tree diagram** to show concepts that can be broken down into smaller categories.

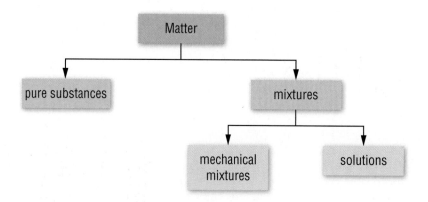

You can use a **fishbone diagram** to organize the important ideas under the major concepts of a topic you are studying.

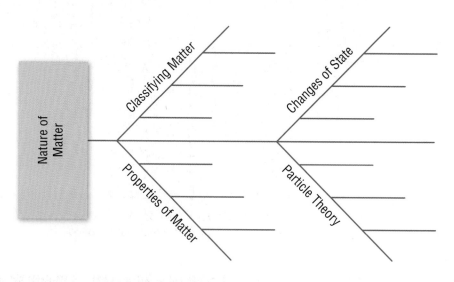

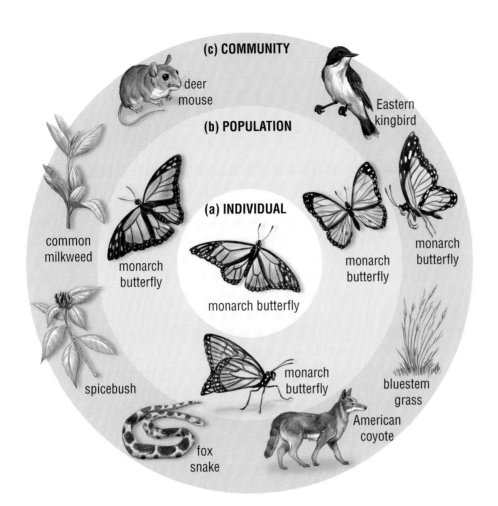

(c) COMMUNITY

deer mouse

Eastern kingbird

(b) POPULATION

common milkweed

monarch butterfly

(a) INDIVIDUAL

monarch butterfly

monarch butterfly

monarch butterfly

spicebush

monarch butterfly

bluestem grass

fox snake

American coyote

You can use a **nested circle diagram** to show parts within a whole.

What do we <u>K</u>now?	What do we <u>W</u>ant to find out?	What did we <u>L</u>earn?
The Sun provides warmth.	How do objects warm up and cool down?	One way thermal energy travels is through convection.
Objects can warm up or cool down.	How does thermal energy travel?	For example, air and water currents carry hot air and hot water to other locations.

You can use a **K-W-L chart** to write down what you know (K), what you want (W) to find out, and, afterwards, what you have learned (L).

To Compare and Contrast

You can use a **comparison matrix** to record and compare observations or results.

Comparison of the Three States of Matter

State	Fixed mass?	Fixed volume?	Fixed shape?
solid	✓	✓	✓
liquid	✓	✓	
gas	✓		

You can use a **Venn diagram** to show similarities and differences. Similarities go in the middle section.

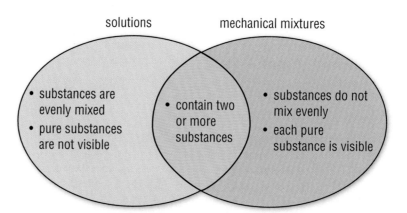

solutions

mechanical mixtures

- substances are evenly mixed
- pure substances are not visible

- contain two or more substances

- substances do not mix evenly
- each pure substance is visible

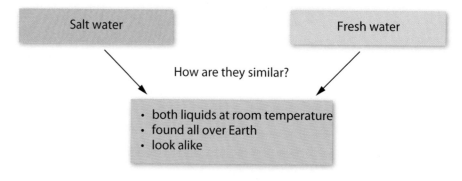

Salt water

Fresh water

How are they similar?

- both liquids at room temperature
- found all over Earth
- look alike

How are they different?

You can use a **compare and contrast chart** to show both similarities and differences.

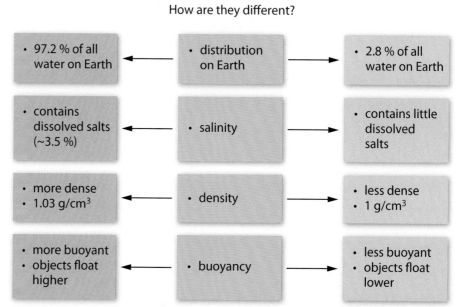

- 97.2 % of all water on Earth

- distribution on Earth

- 2.8 % of all water on Earth

- contains dissolved salts (~3.5 %)

- salinity

- contains little dissolved salts

- more dense
- 1.03 g/cm³

- density

- less dense
- 1 g/cm³

- more buoyant
- objects float higher

- buoyancy

- less buoyant
- objects float lower

To Show Properties or Characteristics

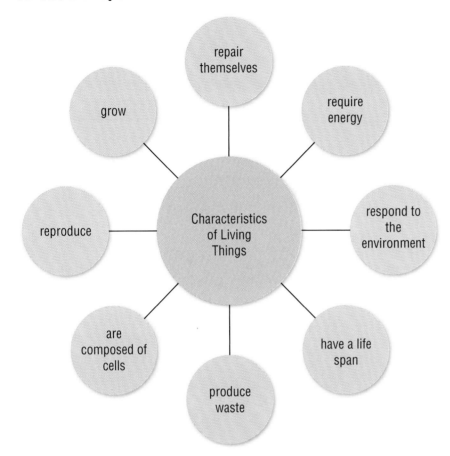

You can use a **bubble map** to show properties or characteristics.

To Review Words and Terms

You can use a **word wall** to list, in no particular order, the key words and concepts for a topic.

mechanical mixture

particle theory

saturated

solute

solution

sifting

heterogeneous

pure substance

concentrated

homogeneous

solvent

evaporation

insoluble

unsaturated

distillation

universal solvent

dissolve

filtration

dilute

WHMIS symbols

environmental impact

solubility

A **word splash** is more colourful than a word wall, and "splashes" key words of a topic on a page randomly.

To Collaborate and Share Ideas

Before:

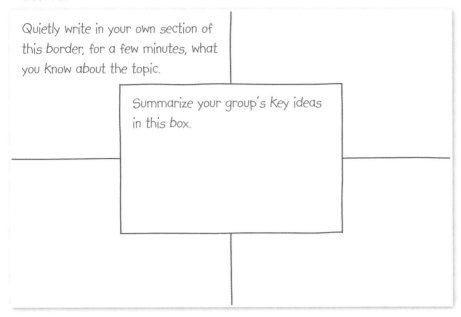

Quietly write in your own section of this border, for a few minutes, what you know about the topic.

Summarize your group's key ideas in this box.

A **placemat organizer** gives each student in a small group a space to write down what they know about a certain topic. Then, the group discusses their answers and writes in the middle section what they have in common.

After:

Fresh water: The world is running out of water. Canada has a lot of fresh water. Some of the world's water is stored as ice.

Fresh water: Canada has the most fresh water of any country in the world. We waste a lot of water.

Fresh Water and Canada's Role: Since Canada has a lot of fresh water, we have a responsibility to use it well.

Fresh water: The world will soon run out of water. How can we in Canada make sure that we will always have fresh water?

Fresh water: Will there be enough water in the future? Since Canada has so much, what should we do with it?

7.C. Working Together

Teamwork is just as important in science and technology as it is on the playing field or in the gym. Scientific investigations and technological inventions are almost always made by teams of people working together. Ideas are shared, experiments are planned, projects and processes are designed, results are analyzed and evaluated, and the completed projects are shared with other scientists and technologists. Group work is necessary and is usually more productive than working alone.

7.C.1. General Rules for Effective Teamwork

- Keep an open mind. Everyone's ideas deserve consideration (Figure 2).
- Divide the task among all the group members. Choose a role that is best suited to your particular strengths.
- Work together and take turns. Encourage, listen, clarify, help, and trust one another.

Figure 2 Team of students sharing ideas at the beginning of a project

7.C.2. Investigations and Activities

This kind of hands-on work is most effective when done by small groups. Here are some more suggestions for effective group performance during investigations and activities:

- Make sure that each group member understands and agrees to the role assigned to him or her.
- Take turns doing the work during similar and repeated activities.
- Safety must come first. Be aware of where other group members are and what they are doing. What are the hazards involved in the activity? What are the safety procedures? What would you do in case of emergency?
- Take responsibility for your own learning. Make your own observations and compare them with the observations of other group members.

7.C.3. Explore an Issue Critically

When there is research to be done, follow these guidelines:

- Divide the topic into several areas and assign one area to each group member.
- Keep records of the sources used by each group member.
- Decide on a format for exchanging information (for example, photocopies of notes or oral discussion).
- When the time comes to make a decision and take a position on an issue, allow each group member to contribute. Make decisions by compromise and consensus.
- Make communicating your position a group effort.

PRACTICE: Work Together

Your group is stranded in the middle of nowhere (Figure 3). It will be five days before you are missed and searchers come looking for you. Therefore, you have decided to make a long hike to a town marked on the map. The problem is your group will have to travel very light, and can only carry a few things. You have gathered your combined resources from your luggage.

As a group, review the following list and choose the five items that you feel are essential for survival over the five days. The final decision on the items should be reached by consensus. Share your decision with the rest of the class.

- flashlight and four batteries
- four hats
- 12 chocolate bars
- box of matches
- groundsheet
- six cans of beans
- fruit (four days' supply)
- knife
- pen, pencil, and paper
- comic books
- map of area
- rope
- calculator
- water
- books
- chewing gum
- Monopoly game
- compass
- first-aid kit
- can opener
- laptop computer

7.C.4. Team Feedback

When your team has finished the project, it is important to assess your work as a team and your individual contribution to the team. You may also want to give feedback to each other about how well you worked together. Do not blame others for problems or difficulties you experienced while working together. Remember to keep your feedback positive and constructive.

- What were some of the positive ways that your team worked together?
- What were some of the drawbacks of your work together as a team?
- What new ideas and perspective did you get from working as part of a team?
- What would you have done better if you were working by yourself?
- How would you change the "team rules" if you needed to work together with the same team on another project?

Figure 3 Planning to survive by working together with few resources

7.D. Setting Goals for Yourself

7.D.1. Look at Your Personal Strengths

Setting goals begins with taking an honest look at yourself. Think about last year. What did you do best at school? What things can you change for this year?

7.D.2. Make Goals that Are Realistic and Observable

Make sure you set realistic goals for yourself. Your best strategy is to focus on getting your projects and assignments done well, instead of focusing on your marks. Do the homework that is assigned to you, work hard on projects and activities, and complete your work on time. Whatever marks you get, everyone will be able to see that you are trying your best.

7.D.3. Share Your Goals

Sometimes it helps to discuss your goals with a good friend or family member. They can help you recognize your strengths and weaknesses, and support you as you work to improve. Hearing another person's perspective support will put you in a better position to achieve your goals.

7.D.4. Write Out a Detailed Plan

As with any other science and technology activity, accomplishing your goals will be easier if you create a detailed plan. Make a list of some actions you can take that will help you meet your goals (Figure 4).

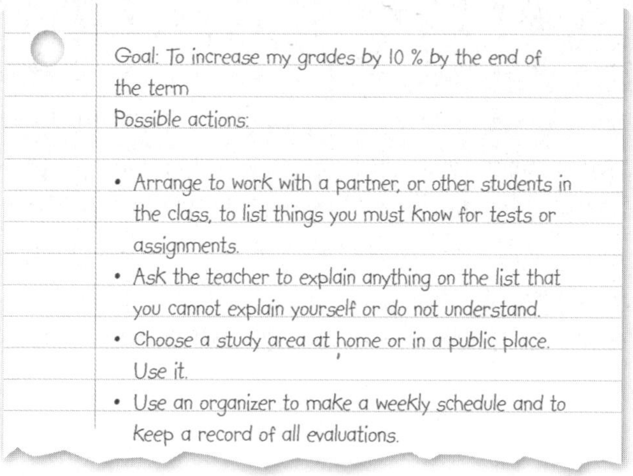

Goal: To increase my grades by 10 % by the end of the term
Possible actions:

- Arrange to work with a partner, or other students in the class, to list things you must know for tests or assignments.
- Ask the teacher to explain anything on the list that you cannot explain yourself or do not understand.
- Choose a study area at home or in a public place. Use it.
- Use an organizer to make a weekly schedule and to keep a record of all evaluations.

Figure 4 An example of one student's goals to increase grades

7.D.5. Set Target Dates

If you want to improve grades by 10 % by the end of the semester, how much time do you have? How many tests and assignments are scheduled between now and then? Work back from your target date at the end of the semester. Determine the dates of all the tests between now and then. These dates will give you short-term targets that, if you reach them, will make it easier for you to reach your overall target. A working schedule appears in Figure 5.

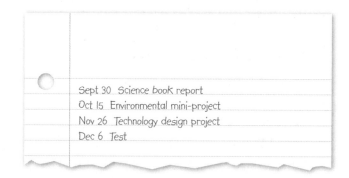

Sept 30 Science book report
Oct 15 Environmental mini-project
Nov 26 Technology design project
Dec 6 Test

Figure 5 Planning for tests and assignments ahead of time

7.D.6. Assess Your Progress

Every so often, you need to look at how you are doing with regard to your goals and targets. Are you handing in your assignments and projects on time? Are you studying for the tests? Are your marks improving? After you have assessed how you are doing, you may realize you need to work on your study habits. The next section has some useful tips for improving your study skills.

7.E. Study Habits

7.E.1. Working on Your Study Habits

Studying is an active process and can take many forms. The key thing is that you learn more and understand more about the subject. Also, it is important to hand in your assignments on time. Here are some suggestions.

Organize Your Work Area

- Find a quiet area to work where you will not be distracted by television, music, friends, or family members. If there are too many distractions at home, consider looking for a space at school or the public library.
- Make your work area suit you. What do you need to feel comfortable and make you more efficient in your study?
- Get organized. Find some files or drawers in which you can place your papers and assignments. Organize your textbooks and other resources that you use.
- Prepare ahead of time. Do you have your school assignments? Textbook? Classroom notes? Experiment observations? What about paper, pen, pencil, eraser, marker, and computer?

Improve Your Work Habits

- Review the notes you made in class. Do you want to revise anything? Take additional notes as you review the textbook, figures, and your class notes to help you summarize what you have learned.
- Study with a friend as long as you are both focused on what you are learning (Figure 6).
- Use graphic organizers. They can help you tie together the concepts you are learning.
- Make a schedule for yourself. When are you planning to study? In the afternoons, when classes are over? After supper?

- Use a daily planner. Your school may have given one to you. Keep it with you at all times. Write in it the times when you plan to study, as well as any test and assignment dates.
- Take a break from your study when you have achieved a certain goal. For example, you can take a study break when you have completed half your homework, or one out of two assignments.
- Make a checklist of the things you want to do every time you study, and keep a record of which things you have finished. You will find it very satisfying to cross items off your list!

PRACTICE: Plan Good Study Habits

Write out a checklist of three or four things that you know you need to plan for in science and technology. These may include finishing some homework, doing an at-home activity, doing some research on the Internet, reading a section from the textbook, studying for a test, or working on a project. Be specific. Write the due date beside each item.

Figure 6 Study with friends only if you can focus on your work.

7.F. Learning the Key Concepts

7.F.1. Fundamental Concepts and Big Ideas

Every subject has fundamental concepts that you need to learn. For science and technology, the fundamental concepts include matter, energy, systems and interactions, structure and function, sustainability and stewardship, and change and continuity. These concepts form the backbone of all science and technology knowledge.

They can also help you apply your understanding of science and technology to other areas.

Each fundamental concept can be described by big ideas. As you progress through your studies in science and technology, the big ideas are what you should remember from grade to grade. The big ideas for Grades 7 and 8 are listed in Table 1 and Table 2 (on the next page).

Table 1 Fundamental Concepts and Big Ideas, Grade 7

Unit	Fundamental concept	Big Ideas*
Pure Substances and Mixtures	Matter Systems and Interactions	• Matter can be classified according to its physical characteristics. • The particle theory of matter helps to explain the physical characteristics. • Pure substances and mixtures have an impact on society and the environment. • Understanding the characteristics of matter allows us to make informed choices about how we use it.
Interactions in the Environment	Systems and Interactions Sustainability and Stewardship	• Ecosystems are made up of biotic (living) and abiotic (non-living) elements, which depend on each other to survive. • Ecosystems are in a constant change of state. The changes may be caused by nature or by human intervention. • Human activities have the potential to alter the environment. Humans must be aware of these impacts and try to control them.
Heat in the Environment	Energy Sustainability and Stewardship Systems and Interactions	• Heat is a form of energy that can be transformed and transferred. These processes can be explained using the particle theory of matter. • There are many sources of heat. • Heat has both positive and negative effects on the environment.
Form and Function	Structure and Function Energy	• Structures have a purpose. • The form of a structure is dependent on its function. • The interaction between structure and forces is predictable.

* All wording of the Big Ideas comes from *The Ontario Curriculum, Grades 1–8—Science and Technology, 2007.*

Table 2 Fundamental Concepts and Big Ideas, Grade 8

Unit	Fundamental concept	Big Ideas*
Systems in Action	Systems and Interactions Continuity and Change	• Systems are designed to accomplish tasks. • All systems include an input and an output. • Systems are designed to optimize human and natural resources.
Cells	Systems and Interactions Structure and Function	• Cells are the basis of life. • Cells organize into tissues, tissues into organs, organs into organ systems, and organ systems into organisms. • Healthy cells contribute to healthy organisms. • Systems are interdependent.
Fluids	Matter Systems and Interactions	• Fluids are an important component of many systems. • Fluids have different properties that determine how they can be used. • Fluids are essential to life.
Water Systems	Sustainability and Stewardship Systems and Interactions Change and Continuity	• Water is crucial to life on Earth. • Water systems influence climate and weather patterns. • Water is an important resource that needs to be managed sustainably.

* All wording of the Big Ideas comes from *The Ontario Curriculum, Grades 1–8—Science and Technology, 2007*.

8. Presentations in Science and Technology

8.A. Written Presentations

In the working world, both individuals and companies often need detailed information on a particular topic to help them make informed decisions. In preparing to write your report, consider the purpose of your report. Are you presenting facts, presenting choices to your readers, or trying to change readers to your way of thinking? You should know your audience.

8.A.1. Research Reports

The purpose of a research report is to present factual information in an unbiased way. Your readers must be able to understand without being talked down to. Be sure to include a complete list of your sources.

8.A.2. Position Papers

A position paper is a report that expresses a particular viewpoint on a current issue (energy usage, for example). When planning a position paper, you may

- start with a position on the issue, and then conduct research to support your position
- start by researching the issue, and then decide on your position based on your research
- conclude by recommending some action for people to take on the issue

Once you have taken a position, support your arguments with evidence, reasoning, and logic.

8.A.3. Issue Reports

An issue report is similar to a position paper. It describes a current issue people are discussing (for example, what to do about songbirds disappearing from large cities in Ontario), and gives various viewpoints. Unlike a position paper, an issue report does not need to take one position on the subject or recommend only one kind of action.

Issues are controversial because there are various points of view. When preparing an issue report, consider the issue from many points of view.

8.A.4. Letters to the Editor

A letter to the editor of a newspaper or magazine is typically a shorter version of a position paper (Figure 1). Space is limited, so express your thoughts as briefly as possible. You do not have to support every point in your argument with scientific facts, but indicate that such support is available.

Figure 1 A letter to the editor of a local newspaper is a shorter version of a position paper.

8.A.5. Magazine Articles

Magazine articles are usually written in response to a request from the editor. The editor will tell you how long the article should be, so do not write more than you are asked for. As you write the article, try to focus on factual information. You must be prepared to support your statements if you are challenged.

8.A.6. Environmental Impact Reports

Environmental impact reports are a relatively new type of report. Until recently, the environment was not a consideration when developments or actions were planned. Today, we must consider, study, and explain the possible results of any intended action. Carrying out an environmental impact assessment begins with a listing of existing species, both plant and animal. If a similar development has taken place elsewhere, you may want to observe what is happening there. You may want to find out what experts think. All this information then must be brought together and presented in a report.

There is no single format for an environmental impact report. The following elements, however, should be included:

- an introduction stating what the report will contain
- a description of how data were collected
- an analysis of the data
- conclusions and a recommendation (if you have one)
- possible long-term results
- suggestions for further study to be conducted before a decision is made, including what additional information is needed
- detailed documentation of all your sources

PRACTICE: Read an Environmental Impact Report

Search the Internet for an environmental assessment or impact report related to new gas-generating projects in Ontario. Try to identify which parts of the report contain the elements listed above.

8.A.7. Posters

You may be asked to present your research in the form of a poster. A poster is a visual presentation of a written report or investigation. Before you start, you need to plan your display. Here are some hints:

General

- Avoid too much "stuff" on your poster. A simple title, six or seven sections, and some visuals are all that are needed.
- Use an attention grabber on your poster, such as an important photograph, chart, graph, or quotation. Most people look for a few seconds before deciding if they want to read more.
- For environmental reports, your sections can be organized into the elements described in the last section. For scientific inquiry and research, you can use the seven sections in the written report shown under "Communicating" in the section "Scientific Inquiry."

Layout

- Place your title in a central place with a large type size and a colour that stands out.
- Make your subheadings a medium type size.
- For the descriptive text, labels, and captions, use a smaller type size that is still readable at a distance.
- Use dark colours for the text. For the background, a soft colour is easy on the eyes, but be careful with yellows and reds.
- It is important to use well-constructed graphs and charts, as well as clear photographs.
- After you have printed off the text and visuals, try placing them in different arrangements around the poster, asking some classmates or family members to give you their opinions.
- The sections can flow downwards by column, or across by row, or clockwise around the title, which is placed at the centre of the poster.
- Place your results in a central position.
- Leave lots of white space.

8.B. Oral Presentations

You may be asked to make an oral presentation to role-play a situation, debate an issue, or present the results of an investigation. In an oral presentation, you are communicating with others using your voice. If you find this method of communication stressful, the following tips will help to reduce or eliminate your stress, improve your presentation, and help you effectively deliver your message to the audience:

- Plan your oral presentation well in advance. Waiting until the last minute increases stress levels dramatically.
- Find out how much time you are being given for your presentation.
- Write the key points of your presentation on cue cards or into a computer slide show.
- Practise your presentation in front of an audience to make sure that it fits into the allowed time.
- When you are giving the presentation, speak clearly and make eye contact with your audience.

8.B.1. Debating

A debate is basically an organized argument (Figure 2). One group takes a position on an issue, while another group takes a different position. Each group tries to persuade the audience that their position is the right one. The following suggestions may be helpful if you are taking part in a debate:

- Research the issue thoroughly. Make notes as you go.
- Pick four or five major points, with examples, to support your position. Write them out in point form.
- Present your argument logically and clearly, and within the allowed time period.

- Listen closely to the arguments presented by those who have taken the opposite position. Make notes on any points that you feel you can argue against in your rebuttal.
- Show respect for the opposition at all times. While you can question their evidence, never resort to name-calling or rudeness.

Figure 2 Student pairs practising for a classroom debate

If you are expected to vote on the issue at the end of the debate, you need to evaluate the arguments made by each side. The following questions may help:

- Which side seemed more knowledgeable about the issue?
- Which side presented the best evidence to support its position?
- Which side had the strongest arguments?
- Which side was better organized and had the better presentation?
- Were the arguments of one side persuasive enough to change your opinion on the issue?

8.B.2. Role-Playing

Role-playing is simply a variation of debating in which you are expected to take on the role of a "character." You then present an opinion, position, or decision from the point of view of that person in the form of a speech. Your goal is to convince the audience that your position or recommendation should be followed. Follow these guidelines as you prepare for and present your character's point of view:

- Research both your topic and your assigned or chosen character. Your arguments must appear to be those of your character.
- Include personal examples from your character's life to support the position you are taking and to make the experience realistic.
- Stay "in character" when presenting. Use "I" and "my" to convince your audience that you are indeed the character you are portraying.
- Relax and have some fun with your presentation.
- After the role-play, spend some time thinking about and discussing your experience. How did you feel and think during the role-play? Discuss the positive and negative aspects of the experience.

It is always valuable to switch roles and have a second round of role-playing. This will help you appreciate other points of view.

8.B.3. Town Hall Discussion

Sometimes there are controversial topics that concern many people, and there are many different opinions about how to fix the problem. In this case, you may decide to hold a town hall discussion. It is often helpful to invite one or more special speakers who are experts on the topic. Choose a moderator to lead the town hall discussion. The moderator must make sure that the speakers get a chance to share their knowledge, and that everyone else can share their opinions and ask the speakers questions.

8.B.4. Panel Discussion

Panel discussions are useful when you need to hear a variety of expert opinions on an issue. A moderator invites several panelists to join the discussion, and prepares questions ahead of time. During the discussion, the moderator ensures that all panelists have an opportunity to present their viewpoints. Near the end of the discussion, members of the audience may ask questions of the panel. They should ask questions of public interest. Panel discussions are good for large audiences where there are too many people for a town hall discussion.

8.B.5. Presenting Results

This is a very factual type of oral presentation (Figure 3). It must be clear and to the point. Your presentation should include answers to the following questions:

- What question were you trying to answer?
- What was your prediction or hypothesis?
- How did you carry out your investigation?
- What were your results?
- Were there any problems or other sources of error?
- What conclusion did you reach?
- Based on your results, is there another investigation that could be done?

Figure 3 Students presenting results

8.C. Electronic Presentations

8.C.1. Preparing a Presentation

Today, people often present their messages electronically, using DVDs, CD-ROMs, or multimedia presentations or by creating a website. Here are some suggestions to help you with electronic presentations:

- Think about who your audience will be and what medium is best to use.
- Write out some main goals for your presentation. What do you want to communicate to your audience?
- Write out an introduction and conclusion.
- Create a flow chart for the presentation. In this flow chart, do not just place information. Think about practical examples of what people can do with the information you give them.
- Create some storyboards (Figure 4). What do you want the audience to see?
- Review the draft outline. You probably need to revise it, and reduce it in length by taking out all unnecessary text.
- Decide on the format of your presentation. Choose graphics, colours, or other effects that will do two things: (1) help people remember your presentation, and (2) make the message you present more understandable.

8.C.2. Creating a Presentation Using Slides

Several software programs allow you to create a series of slides that can be projected onto a screen. You can even add sound, music, or your recorded voice to the presentation. These guidelines may help you prepare a multimedia presentation:

- Use a storyboard to write your slides as point-form notes.
- Limit yourself to no more than 10 lines of text on each slide.
- Use a font that is large enough to be read by the audience.
- Do not read directly from the slides when you are presenting. Text on the slides should simply summarize your main points.

8.C.3. Creating a Web Page

A web page is a way of communicating with anyone in the world who has access to the World Wide Web. Every page has its own URL and may include graphics, sound, animations, and video clips, as well as links to other web pages. If you think that a web page presentation would benefit others, ask your teacher for help in creating one.

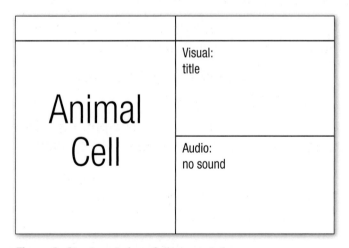

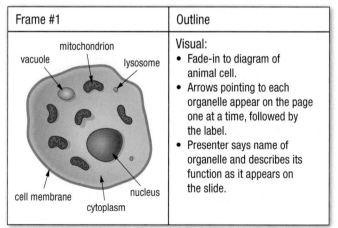

Figure 4 Storyboards for a Cells presentation

Glossary

A

abiotic [ay-bye-AW-tik] **element** any non-living component of the environment (p. 98)

active solar energy system a device that harnesses radiant energy from the Sun and converts it into a more useful form of energy (p. 244)

aesthetics [es-THET-iks] the concept of how visually attractive or beautiful something is (p. 325)

alternative energy source a source of energy that is not as common as conventional sources; alternative energy sources tend to be renewable and have few negative impacts on the environment (p. 242)

arch a curved structure used to span a space while supporting a load (p. 301)

B

bar graph [GRAFF] a type of graph used to make comparisons when one variable is in numbers and the other is not; useful for showing how data are distributed across categories (p. 400)

beam a horizontal structure designed to support a load (p. 295)

biodiversity [BYE-oh-dih-VUR-sih-tee] the variety of plant and animal life in an ecosystem (p. 152)

biofuel [BYE-oh-fyoo-uhl] a liquid fuel, such as ethanol, produced from plant or animal material (p. 248)

biotic [bye-AW-tik] **element** any living thing found in the environment (p. 97)

bubble [BUH-bul] **map** a graphic organizer that shows properties or characteristics (p. 409)

C

cantilever [KAN-tuh-LEE-ver] a beam supported at only one end (p. 297)

carnivore [KAHR-nuh-vawr] an organism that eats other animals only (p. 123)

cause-and-effect question a type of question that asks whether something is causing something else (p. 357)

cause variable see **independent variable**

centre of gravity the point around which an object's mass is equally balanced in all directions; the point where the mass seems to be concentrated (p. 290)

chemistry [KEH-muh-stree] the study of matter and its changes (p. 10)

circle [SER-kuhl] **graph** a type of graph that shows the whole of something divided into all of its parts; shows how different things compare in size or quantity; also known as **pie graph** (p. 401)

closed system a system in which the amount of matter remains constant over time (p. 135)

community a group of populations of different species in a given area (p. 97)

compare and contrast chart a graphic organizer that shows similarities and differences (p. 408)

comparison matrix [MAY-triks] a graphic organizer used to record and compare observations or results (p. 408)

competition [kawm-puh-TIH-shun] occurs when more than one organism tries to obtain the same basic resources in the same habitat (p. 107)

compression [kuhm-PREH-shun] an internal force that presses or squeezes the particles of an object together (p. 279)

concentrated solution [KAWN-suhn-TRAY-tid suh-LOO-shun] a solution with a large number of solute particles in a given volume of solution (p. 42)

concentration [kawn-suhn-TRAY-shun] the amount of solute present in an amount of solution (p. 43)

concept [KAWN-sept] **map** a graphic organizer that shows relationships between ideas; the ideas are connected by arrows and words or expressions that explain the connections (p. 406)

condensation [kawn-duhn-SAY-shun] the change in state of a substance from gas to liquid (p. 138)

conduction [kun-DUHK-shun] the transfer of thermal energy through a substance, or between substances in contact, by the collision of particles (p. 207)

consumer an organism that eats other living things for energy (p. 123)

controlled variable a condition that remains unchanged in an investigation; does not affect the outcome (p. 357)

convection [kun-VEK-shun] the transfer of thermal energy from one part of a fluid to another by a circulating current of faster-moving and slower-moving particles (p. 210)

conventional energy source a source of energy that has been widely used for many years (p. 234)

corrugation [kor-uh-GAY-shun] multiple folds in a material that provide additional strength (p. 296)

cycle [SYE-cuhl] a pattern in nature that repeats over time (p. 135)

cycle map a graphic organizer that shows cycles in nature (p. 405)

D

dead load a type of static load caused by the weight of the structure itself (p. 273)

decomposer [dee-kuhm-POH-zer] an organism that consumes and breaks down dead organisms or waste matter into simple substances (p. 124)

dependent variable the variable that is affected by a change in an investigation; the variable measured to see how it is affected by the independent variable; also known as **effect variable** (p. 357)

detrivore [DET-rih-vohr] an organism that feeds on large parts of decaying plant and animal matter and on waste material (p. 124)

dilute [dye-LOOT] **solution** a solution with a small number of solute particles in a given volume of solution (p. 42)

dissolve [dih-ZOHLV] to mix one type of matter into another type of matter to form a solution (p. 36)

dissolving mixing completely with a solvent to form a solution (p. 36)

distillation [dih-still-AY-shun] the process of separating liquids in a solution by heating the solution, trapping and cooling the gas, and collecting the resulting pure liquid (p. 69)

dome a shell structure that looks like the top half of a sphere (p. 302)

dynamic [dye-NAM-ik] **load** any load on a structure that is not caused by gravity; for example, wind or rushing water (p. 273)

E

Earth's energy balance the balance between the energy lost by Earth into space and the energy gained by solar radiation trapped by Earth's atmosphere (p. 238)

ecology [ee-CAWL-uh-jee] the study of relationships between organisms, and between organisms and their environment (p. 99)

ecosystem [EE-koh-sis-tum] the network of interactions that link the living and non-living parts of an environment (p. 98)

effect variable see **dependent variable**

electric generator a machine with moving parts that produce electricity when they spin (p. 75)

endangered species [SPEE-seez] species that are at risk of becoming extinct due to either reduction in numbers or an environmental threat (p. 152)

ergonomics [ur-guh-NAW-miks] the science of using knowledge of human characteristics to design structures and systems that are comfortable, safe, and efficient (p. 327)

evaporate [ih-VAH-puh-rate] change from a liquid to a gas (p. 67)

evaporation [ih-VAH-puh-RAY-shun] the process by which a sample of matter changes from a liquid to a gas (p. 68 Unit A: Pure Substances and Mixtures); the process in which a substance changes state from liquid to gas (p. 138, Unit B: Interactions in the Environment)

external force a force acting on an object or structure from the outside (p. 277)

extinction [ex-TINK-shun] the complete disappearance of a species from anywhere on Earth (p. 152)

F

filter a device with many small holes that trap solid pieces of a mixture but allow liquids and gases to pass through (p. 60)

filtration [fill-TRAY-shun] the process of passing a mechanical mixture through a filter to separate solid pieces from a liquid or gas (p. 60)

fishbone diagram a graphic organizer that shows the important ideas under the major concepts of a topic (p. 406)

floating [FLOH-ting] a separation technique in which a "lighter" component rises to the top of a liquid where it can be skimmed or poured off (p. 59)

flow chart a graphic organizer that shows a sequence of steps or a series of component relationships (p. 405)

food chain a sequence that shows how energy and nutrients are transferred from one organism to another in an ecosystem (p. 126)

food web a model that shows how food chains in an ecosystem are connected (p. 127)

force a push or a pull (p. 270)

form the shape and physical appearance of a structure (p. 268)

fossil [FOSS-uhl] **fuels** concentrated sources of chemical energy such as coal, oil (petroleum), and natural gas that were formed deep in Earth's structure over millions of years from decayed and compressed plant and animal material (p. 236)

frame structure a network of parts that supports loads (p. 274)

friction [FRIK-shun] a force produced when objects rub against each other (p. 231)

function [FUNK-shun] the task or purpose of a structure (p. 268)

G

gas a state of matter that does not have a definite volume or a definite shape; a gas takes the shape and volume of its container (p. 15)

geothermal [jee-oh-THUR-muhl] **energy** energy contained below Earth's surface (p. 208)

global warming an increase in Earth's global temperature due to changes in the atmosphere that enhance the greenhouse effect (p. 240)

graphic [GRAF-ik] **organizer** a diagram used to organize and display ideas visually; useful for connecting different concepts, ideas, and data (p. 405)

gravity the force of attraction between all objects; it is noticeable when at least one of the objects has a large mass; it is a non-contact force (p. 270)

greenhouse effect a rise in temperature resulting from certain gases in the lower atmosphere trapping radiant energy and warming Earth's surface (p. 238)

greenhouse gases gases such as water vapour, carbon dioxide, methane, and nitrous oxides that trap energy in Earth's atmosphere (p. 238)

H

habitat [HAB-uh-tat] the environment where an organism lives (p. 100)

heat the transfer of energy from the particles of a warmer object to the particles of a cooler object (p. 186)

herbivore [HUR-buh-vawr] an organism that eats plants only (p. 123)

heterogeneous mixture [heh-tuh-ruh-JEE-nee-uhs MIKS-cher] see **mechanical mixture**

homogeneous [hoh-muh-JEE-nee-uhs] **mixture** see **solution**

hypothesis [hye-PAW-thuh-sis] a prediction about the outcome of a controlled experiment along with an explanation for the outcome; may be written as an "if…then…because…" statement (p. 358)

I

I-beam a beam that is in the shape of the letter "I" when seen from the end (p. 296)

igneous [IG-nee-uhs] **rock** rock formed from magma that has cooled and solidified (p. 208)

independent variable the variable that is changed in an investigation; also known as **cause variable** (p. 357)

inference [IN-fer-uhns] a possible explanation of an observation; an educated guess based on experience, knowledge, and observations (p. 362)

insoluble [in-SOHL-yuh-buhl] unable to dissolve in a specified solvent (p. 41)

internal force a force acting between two parts of a body (p. 277)

invasive species [in-VAY-siv SPEE-seez] a species that has been introduced (accidentally or purposely) into an area where it did not exist before; often reproduces so aggressively that it replaces some of the original species (p. 153)

K

kinetic [ki-NEH-tik] **energy** energy that all moving objects possess; a particle has more kinetic energy when moving faster and less kinetic energy when moving slower (p. 187)

K-W-L chart a graphic organizer that shows what you know (K), what you want (W) to find out, and what you have learned (L) (p. 407)

L

law a general statement that describes a commonly occurring natural event; a law does not explain why or how a natural event occurs; it just describes what happens in detail (p. 351)

line graph a type of graph that shows changes in measurement when two variables are in numbers; shows a relationship between two sets of numbers (p. 400)

line of symmetry a line that divides an object in half; helps display symmetry (p. 323)

liquid [LIH-kwid] a state of matter with a definite volume, but no definite shape; a liquid takes the shape of its container (p. 14)

live load a type of static load caused by the weight of the objects it supports (p. 273)

load a force acting on a structure (p. 273)

M

mass the quantity of matter in an object, commonly measured in grams (g) or kilograms (kg) (p. 272)

matter anything that takes up space and has mass (p. 10)

mechanical mixture a mixture with different parts that you can see; also known as **heterogeneous mixture** (p. 24)

meniscus [muh-NIS-kuhs] the downward curve of the surface of a volume of liquid (p. 393)

metamorphic [met-uh-MOHR-fik] **rock** rock that is formed when heat and pressure change existing rock (p. 209)

micro-organism [MI-kro-OR-guh-nihz-um] a living thing that is small and must be viewed with the help of a microscope (p. 97)

mind map a graphic organizer that shows relationships between ideas; words or pictures representing ideas are connected by arrows; similar to a concept map, but does not include explanations for connections (p. 406)

mixture matter that contains two or more pure substances mixed together (p. 20)

mutualism [MYOO-chew-uhl-izm] an interaction between individuals of different species that benefits both individuals (p. 109)

N

native species [NAY-tiv SPEE-seez] species that occur naturally in an area (p. 153)

nested circle diagram a graphic organizer that shows parts within a whole (p. 407)

non-renewable energy resource a source of energy that could eventually be used up (p. 235)

nuclear [NOO-klee-er] **energy** the energy released when the particles of pure substances like uranium split apart (p. 75)

nutrient [NOO-tree-unt] a substance that an organism needs to grow and maintain its body (p. 102)

O

omnivore [OHM-nih-vawr] an organism that eats both plants and animals (p. 123)

organism a living thing (p. 97)

P

particle theory of matter an explanation of what matter is made of and how it behaves; the particle theory states that all matter is made up of tiny particles that are always moving, that attract each other, and that have space between them (p. 12 Unit A: Pure Substances and Mixtures); a theory that explains what matter is made of, and how it behaves (p. 185 Unit C: Heat in the Environment)

passive solar heating heating caused by the passage of radiant energy through the windows of a building (p. 244)

photosynthesis [foh-toh-SIN-thuh-sis] a process by which plants use water, carbon dioxide, and sunlight to produce sugars (food) (p. 122)

pie graph see **circle graph**

placemat organizer a graphic organizer that gives each student in a group space to write down what he or she knows about a topic; the group then discusses the answers and writes what they have in common in the middle section (p. 411)

plane of application an imaginary flat surface through which an applied force passes (p. 278)

point of application the location on an object where an external force is applied or concentrated (p. 278)

pollution [puh-LOO-shun] contaminants in the environment that could harm living things (p. 39)

population [paw-pyoo-LAY-shun] a group of organisms of the same species in a given area (p. 97)

precipitation [prih-sip-uh-TAY-shun] water in the liquid or solid state that falls to Earth (p. 138)

predator an organism that hunts other living things for food (p. 108)

prediction [preh-DIHK-shun] states what is likely to happen as the result of a controlled experiment; may be written as an "if…then…" statement (p. 358)

prey an animal that is hunted by a predator (p. 108)

primary succession [suhk-SESH-un] succession that develops a community of plants and animals in an area where no living things existed before (p. 148)

procedure a step-by-step description of how an investigation will be performed (p. 359)

producer an organism that makes its own food from non-living materials (p. 122)

pure [pyoor] **substance** matter that contains only one kind of particle (p. 20)

pyramid of numbers a model that shows the number of individuals at each level in a food chain or food web (p. 133)

Q

qualitative [KWAHL-ih-tay-tiv] **observation** an observation that describes characteristics that cannot be measured or expressed in numbers (p. 360)

quantitative [KWAHN-tih-tay-tiv] **observation** a measurable observation that can be expressed in numbers (p. 360)

R

radiant energy energy that travels in the form of electromagnetic waves through empty space; includes visible light, ultraviolet rays, and infrared rays (p. 214)

radiation [RAY-dee-AY-shun] the transfer of radiant energy by means of electromagnetic waves (p. 214)

radioactive [ray-dee-oh-ACK-tiv] a term used to describe pure substances whose particles naturally split into smaller particles, releasing energy as they break apart (p. 75)

renewable energy resource a source of energy that can be used indefinitely, without running out (p. 234)

repetitive strain injury damage, usually to the small muscles of the wrists or hands, from repeated activities over a long period of time (p. 329)

S

saturated solution a solution in which no more solute can dissolve (p. 43)

scavenger an organism that eats already dead animals (p. 123)

scientific inquiry [SI-ehn-TIH-fik in-KWI-ree] the process of exploring the world, asking questions, and searching for answers that increase our understanding (p. 348)

scientific notation a type of mathematical abbreviation that omits large numbers of zeros (p. 398)

secondary succession [suhk-SESH-un] succession that develops a community in an area after it has been disturbed (p. 150)

settling a separation technique in which a "heavier" component sinks to the bottom of a liquid, and the liquid can be poured off (p. 59)

sewage [SOO-ij] the mixture of water and waste that is flushed down toilets and sink drains (p. 64)

shear [sheer] forces acting in an object as a result of pushes and/or pulls in opposite directions; usually results in rips or tears in an object (p. 280)

shell structure a hollow structure with a curved shape providing high strength and rigidity (p. 275)

sieve [siv] a device used to separate the components of a mixture, with many visible holes that allow smaller solid pieces and liquids to pass through while blocking the larger solid pieces (p. 60)

sieving the process of passing a mechanical mixture through a sieve to separate the larger pieces of matter (p. 60)

solar energy radiant energy (mostly visible light and infrared radiation) produced at the Sun's outer surface and radiated out into space (p. 230)

solid a state of matter with a definite volume and a definite shape (p. 14)

solid structure an object that uses solid construction to support loads (p. 274)

solubility [SAWL-yuh-BILL-ih-tee] a measure of how much solute can dissolve in a certain solvent to form a saturated solution at a particular temperature and volume (p. 44)

soluble [SAWL-yuh-buhl] able to dissolve in a specified solvent (p. 41)

solute [SAWL-yoot] the smaller part of a solution; the part of a solution that dissolves in the solvent (p. 36)

solution a mixture that looks like a single pure substance; a uniform mixture of two or more pure substances; also known as **homogeneous mixture** (p. 25)

solvent the larger part of a solution; the part of a solution into which the solutes dissolve (p. 36)

sorting physically separating large pieces of a mechanical mixture so that similar pieces are together (p. 58)

species [SPEE-seez] a group of similar organisms that can mate and reproduce more of the same type of organism (p. 97)

stability the ability of a structure to remain in or return to a stable, balanced position when forces act on it (p. 290)

steward [STOO-erd] a person who carefully manages a resource by taking responsibility for their actions and educating others (p. 157)

structural failure the failure of a structure as a result of the structure, or part of the structure, losing the ability to support a load (p. 306)

structure [STRUK-cher] anything made of parts put together for a particular purpose (or purposes) (p. 268)

succession [suhk-SESH-un] a series of gradual changes that result in the replacement of one community of plants and animals by another (p. 148)

sustainable [suh-STAY-nuh-bul] something that can be maintained and used indefinitely (p. 136)

symmetry [SIM-uh-tree] an exact reflection on opposite sides of a line dividing an object in half (p. 323)

T

temperature [TEM-per-uh-cher] a measure of the average kinetic energy of the particles of a substance (p. 187)

tension [TEN-shun] an internal force pulling the particles of an object apart (p. 279)

theory [THEE-uh-ree] an explanation of an observation (p. 351)

thermal contraction a decrease in the volume of a substance caused by cooling (p. 189)

thermal energy the total kinetic energy and energy of attraction of all the particles of a material (p. 188)

thermal expansion an increase in the volume of a substance caused by heating (p. 189)

torsion [TOR-shun] internal twisting forces created in an object as a result of a twisting motion being applied to the object (p. 280)

tree diagram a graphic organizer showing concepts that can be broken down into smaller categories (p. 406)

truss a network of beams arranged in triangles (p. 300)

U

universal design an arrangement of the components of a structure or device resulting in the most user-friendly product possible (p. 332)

unsaturated solution a solution in which more solute can be dissolved (p. 43)

V

variable any condition that could affect the outcome of an investigation (p. 357)

Venn diagram a graphic organizer that shows similarities and differences (p. 408)

volume a measure of the quantity of space occupied by an object (p. 14)

W

weight [weyt] the force of gravity acting downward on an object, measured in newtons (N) (p. 272)

word splash a graphic organizer that "splashes" key words of a topic on a page randomly; similar to a word wall, but more colourful (p. 410)

word wall a graphic organizer that lists the key words and concepts for a topic (p. 410)

Index

Credits

Cover Image Source Photography/Veer

iv top left Dave Starrett; bottom left Jeff Morgan environmental issues/Alamy; bottom right TEK IMAGE/ Science Photo Library; v left Bill Brooks/Alamy; right Roderick Chen/All Canada Photos; vi top left Darwin Wiggett/All Canada Photos; bottom left Jeff Greenberg/ PhotoEdit; right Corbis RF/Alamy; vii left David Beaucage Johnson; right Rene Johnston/Toronto Star/ First Light; viii top left Steve Craft/Masterfile; bottom left Larry Williams/Corbis Canada; right mediacolor's/ Alamy; ix left Jim West/Alamy; right John Sylvester/ Alamy; x top left Larry MacDougal/First Light; bottom left Michelle D. Bridwell/PhotoEdit; right Chris Cheadle/ All Canada Photos; xi left Chien-min Chung/Getty Images.

Unit A

2–3 Dave Starrett; 7 Jeff Morgan environmental issues/ Alamy; 8–9 TEK IMAGE/Science Photo Library; 10 TongRo Image Stock/Alamy; 11 left Derek Capitaine Photography; centre © National High Magnetic Field Laboratory, Florida State University; right Courtesy of Dr. R. V. Lapshin, Institute of Physical Problems, Russia and Dr. S. A. Gavrilov, Moscow Institute of Electronic Technology, Russia; 14 Edward Kinsman/ Photo Researchers, Inc.; 17 top Creasance/Shutterstock; bottom Kevin Schafer/Photographer's Choice/Getty Images; 24 left Michael Boyny/MaXx Images; 25 top left Derek Capitaine Photography; top centre Organics image library/Alamy; top right Richard Hutchings/ Photo Edit; bottom left vnlit/Shutterstock; bottom centre kotik1/Shutterstock; bottom right Dorling Kindersley/ Getty Images; 28 left Jose Gil/Shutterstock; centre Robert Brook/Science Photo Library; 29 Dick Hemingway Editorial Photographs; 30 left Jose Gil/Shutterstock; right Robert Brook/Science Photo Library; 31 top left Derek Capitaine Photography; top centre Organics image library/Alamy; top right Richard Hutchings/ Photo Edit; bottom left vnlit/Shutterstock; bottom centre kotik1/Shutterstock; bottom right Dorling Kindersley/ Getty Images; 32 Edward Westmacott/Alamy; 33 left Derek Capitaine Photography; right Andrew Lambert Photography/Science Photo Library; 34–35 Bill Brooks/ Alamy; 35 Michael Newman/Photo Edit; 37 top Steve Rosset/Shutterstock; bottom CanStock Images/Alamy; 38 left JoLin/Shutterstock; right James Steidl/ Shutterstock; 42 P. Cross/Shutterstock; 45 left Randy Faris/Corbis Canada; right James King-Holmes/ CELLTECH R&D LTD./Science Photo Library; 49 Gusto Images/Science Photo Library; 50 top right JoLin/ Shutterstock; bottom CanStock Images/Alamy; 54–55 Roderick Chen/All Canada Photos; 58 FoodCollection/MaXx Images; 59 top FoodCollection/ MaXx Images; bottom Martin M. Rotker/Photo Researchers, Inc.; 60 top left Chris Priest/Science Photo Library; centre Marli Miller/Visuals Unlimited; 61 Derek Capitaine Photography; 64 PhotoAlto/Alamy; 65 top Dr. Jeremy Burgess/Science Photo Library; bottom Frithjof Hirdes/zefa/Corbis Canada; 66 Reuters/Corbis Canada; 67 top Philip and Karen Smith/Iconica/Getty Images; 68 Stuart Gregory/Photodisc/Getty Images; 71 Scott Kemper/Alamy; 72 John E Marriott/Alamy; 73 PhotoAlto/Alamy; 74 bottom Mashkov Yuri/ITAR-TASS/Landov; 76 ITAR-TASS/Fyodor Savintsev/Landov; 78 top left Food Collection/MaXx Images; top right Marli Miller/Visuals Unlimited; bottom left Reuters/ Corbis Canada; bottom right PhotoAlto/Alamy; 79 John E. Marriott/Alamy; 81 Scott Barrow/MaXx Images; 82 Jeff Morgan environmental issues/Alamy; 86 Henry Westheim Photography/Alamy.

Unit B

88–89 Darwin Wiggett/All Canada Photos; 90–91 Stuart O'Sullivan/Taxi/Getty Images; background Emanuel/Shutterstock; 91 BroadSpektrum/Alamy; 93 Jeff Greenberg/PhotoEdit; 94–95 Corbis RF/Alamy; 95 centre Tina's Groove © Rina Piccolo, King Features Syndicate; 96 top left Jupiter Images; bottom left Danita Delimont/Alamy; 98 Miles Ertman/Masterfile; 99 bottom right O. Bierwagen/Ivy Images; 100 top Doug Lemke/ Shutterstock; centre left David Nunuk/All Canada Photos; bottom left Tohoku Color Agency/Japan Images/ Getty Images; bottom right Taylor S. Kennedy/National Geographic/Getty Images; 101 Oli Gardner/Alamy; 102 top Stocktrek Images/Getty Images; bottom Dave Reede/ All Canada Photos; 103 top blickwinkel/Alamy; 104 Carolyn A. McKeone/Photo Researchers, Inc.; 106 left

Sheila Terry/Science Photo Library; right Arco Images GmbH/Alamy; 107 All Canada Photos; 108 Eastcott Momatiuk/National Geographic/Getty Images; 109 Nigel Cattlin/Visuals Unlimited; 110 Photograph by David Lui, Humber Institute of Technology and Advanced Learning; 111 Bill Ivy/Ivy Images; 112 centre CFP/Ivy Images; left David Young-Wolff/PhotoEdit; 113 Nickel Tailings #36, Edward Burtynsky Photography; 114 left Courtesy of Toronto Emergency Medical Services; right Benelux/ zefa/Corbis Canada; 116 bottom left blickwinkel/Alamy; bottom right Oli Gardner/Alamy; 117 top left Eastcott Momatiuk/National Geographic/Getty Images; top right Nigel Cattlin/Visuals Unlimited; bottom Bill Ivy/Ivy Images; 119 Dick Hemingway Editorial Photographs; 120–121 David Beaucage Johnson; 121 Robert Estall photo agency/Alamy; 123 left Michael Francis/Animals Animals; centre Paul Hobson/Nature Picture Library; right Michael Newman/PhotoEdit; 124 top David M. Dennis/Animals Animals; bottom FoodPhotography Eisin/MaXx Images; 125 Gabe Palmer/Alamy; 128 Leonard Lee Rue III/Photoresearchers/First Light; 129 Courtesy of Bridget Stutchbury, York University; 135 left John Cancalosi/Alamy; centre Biosphoto/Klein J.-L. & Hubert M.-L./Peter Arnold Inc.; right Terrance Klassen/ Alamy; 136 Michael P. Gadomski/Photoresearchers/First Light; 139 WorldFoto/Alamy; 142 left Michael Francis/ Animals Animals; centre Paul Hobson/Nature Picture Library; right Michael Newman/PhotoEdit; 146–147 Rene Johnston/Toronto Star/First Light; 147 Pat LaCroix/ The Image Bank/Getty Images; 148 top Jim West/Alamy; bottom Don Johnston/Alamy; 150 left Dr. John D. Cunningham/Visuals Unlimited; right Stockbyte/Alamy; 151 Robert Quinlan/Alamy; 152 left Lynn Stone/Animals Animals; right John Lemker/Animals Animals; 153 left Jim West/Alamy; right Larry L. Miller/Photo Researchers, Inc.; 154 top John T. Fowler/Alamy; centre Nigel Cattlin/ Visuals Unlimited; Jeff Daly/Visuals Unlimited; bottom David Sieren/Visuals Unlimited; 158 top Andrew McLachlan/All Canada Photos; bottom Derek Capitaine Photography; 159 top left joel zatz/Alamy; top right Kristin O'Connor, Hamilton Harbour Remedial Action Plan; bottom Dick Hemingway Editorial Photographs; 160 bottom Marilyn Angel Wynn/Nativestock; 161 Ross Frid/Visuals Unlimited; 162 Michael Klinec/Alamy; 164 left Robert Quinlan/Alamy; right David Sieren/

Visuals Unlimited; 165 top Marilyn Angel Wynn/ Nativestock; bottom Michael Klinec/Alamy; 167 Stone Nature Photography/Alamy; 168 (both) Mike Grandmaison/Grandmaison Photography; 171 amana images inc./Alamy; 172 Georgie Holland/A.G.E. Fotostock/First Light.

Text credit: 160 *Birdfoot's Grampa* by Joseph Bruchac, reprinted with permission of the author's representative, Barbara Kouts

Unit C

174–175 Steve Craft/Masterfile; 176 Ivy Images; 177 left Ashley Cooper/Alamy; right Courtesy of Ready Mixed Concrete Association of Ontario; 179 Kindra Clineff/ Index Stock/MaXx Images; 180–181 mediacolor's/ Alamy; 181 top THE CANADIAN PRESS/Sault Ste. Marie Star—Rachele Labrecque; bottom GeoStock/First Light; 182 top left Chase Swift/Corbis Canada; top right Marli Miller/Visuals Unlimited; bottom SuperStock/ Alamy; 183 Bill Freeman/Photo Edit; 184 maciej czajka/ Alamy; 187 top left CP PHOTO/Adrian Wyld; top right Donald Enright/Alamy; bottom doug steley/ Alamy; 192 top Lester Lefkowitz/Stone/Getty Images; bottom Photos by Tom Pantages; 195 top CP PHOTO/ Jonathan Hayward; bottom Chris Mattison/Alamy; 196 Marli Miller/Visuals Unlimited; 197 top right doug steley/Alamy; 198 left Tony Freeman/Photo Edit; centre Bon Appetit/Alamy; 199 Tony Freeman/Photo Edit; 200–201 Jim West/Alamy; 203 Floresco Productions/ Corbis Canada; 205 right Germany Feng/Shutterstock; 206 Dorling Kindersley/Getty Images; 208 top left Bill Ivy/Ivy Images; centre left Greg Vaughn/Alamy; centre right Gary Crabbe/Alamy; bottom Mark Schneider/ Visuals Unlimited; 209 top David Woods/Shutterstock; bottom left Ken Lucas/Visuals Unlimited; bottom centre ELEN/Shutterstock; bottom right Gerry Rousseau/ Alamy; 213 top Martin Fischer/Shutterstock; centre Martine Oger/Shutterstock; bottom Phil Degginger/ Alamy; 214 top Randy Lincks/All Canada Photos/Getty Images; bottom JG Photography/Alamy; 216 Corbis RF/ Alamy; 217 Ted Kinsman/Photo Researchers, Inc.; 218 top David R. Frazier Photolibrary, Inc./Alamy; bottom Kathryn Ivy/Ivy Images; 219 S. Callahan/Photri; 220 Carey High School, Carey ID, Sponsored by Radiant Foil,

Ketchum, ID, Art Carlson, Engineer; 221 Ken Straiton/ First Light; 225 top Greg Vaughn/Alamy; bottom left David R. Frazier Photolibrary, Inc./Alamy; bottom right S. Callahan/Photri; 226 top left foodfolio/Alamy; top right Photri; bottom WireImageStock/Masterfile; 227 Carlos Dominguez/Photo Researchers, Inc.; 228–229 John Sylvester/Alamy; 229 bottom right Ali Mazraie Shadi/Shutterstock; iStockphoto; 230 Science Source/ Photo Researchers, Inc.; 231 left Publiphoto/Photo Researchers, Inc.; right Rhoda Preacher; bottom Dex Image/Alamy; 232 Andy Caulfield/Riser/Getty Images; 233 bottom left imagebroker/Alamy; top right Courtesy of Enwave Energy Corporation; 234 top left REUTERS/ Gary Wiepert/Landov; bottom Courtesy of NASA; 235 CP PHOTO/Toronto Star–Dick Loek; 236 CP PHOTO/ Sarnia Observer/Glenn Ogilvie; 237 Visions of America, LLC/Alamy; 238 Paul Souders/Corbis Canada; 240 top David McNew/Getty Images; centre tbkmedia. de/Alamy; bottom Nigel Cattlin/Alamy; 241 D Trask/ Ivy Images; 242 Design Pics Inc./Alamy; 243 top Povl Eskild/Alamy; bottom Copyright 2007 Marine Current Turbines Ltd.; 244 left David Lyons/Alamy; right Bill Brooks/Alamy; 245 top Artist's conception, property of OptiSolar Farms Canada Inc.; bottom Michael Newman/Photo Edit; 246 ARCTIC IMAGES/Alamy; 248 David R. Frazier Photolibrary, Inc./Alamy; 249 Bill Ivy/Ivy Images; 250 left CP PHOTO/Sarnia Observer/ Glenn Ogilvie; centre ARCTIC IMAGES/Alamy; right David R. Frazier Photolibrary, Inc./Alamy; 251 top Paul Souders/Corbis Canada; centre D Trask/Ivy Images; bottom Design Pics Inc./Alamy; 252 Roderick Chen/ All Canada Photos/Alamy; 253 Sergey Dolzhenko/epa/ Corbis Canada; 254 Larry Williams/Corbis Canada; 258 Dick Hemingway Editorial Photographs.

Text credit: 229 "The Energy Blues", lyrics by George R. Newall, from *Schoolhouse Rock!* by Tom Yohe, published by Hyperion Books, NY, reprinted with permission. All rights reserved.

Unit D

260–261 Larry MacDougal/First Light; 262 background serg64/Shutterstock; Dick Hemingway Editorial Photographs; 263 Dick Hemingway Editorial

Photographs; 265 Michelle D. Bridwell / PhotoEdit; 266–267 Chris Cheadle/All Canada Photos; 267 top Xinhua/Landov; bottom Reuters/Corbis Canada; 268 left James Warwick/Stone/Getty Images; right CHRISTIAN CHARISIUS/Reuters/Corbis Canada; bottom Shutterstock; 269 left Jan Richter/imagebroker/ Alamy; top right Biosphoto/Balcaen Claude/Peter Arnold Inc.; centre right Jeffrey Greenberg / Photoresearchers/ First Light; bottom right KARIM SAHIB / AFP / Getty Images; 270 left Michael Nemeth/The Image Bank/ Getty Images; right Photodisc/Alamy; 271 left THE CANADIAN PRESS/Peter McCabe; right Xinhua/ Landov; 273 Image Alchemy/Alamy; 274 top left John E. Marriott/All Canada Photos; bottom left Dr. Donald Fawcett/Visuals Unlimited; bottom right Biczó Zsolt/ Shutterstock; 275 top Derek Capitaine Photography; bottom Roger Harris/Science Photo Library; 276 top Andy Sacks/Riser/Getty Images; bottom Bill Brooks/ Alamy; 277 Nick Kozak/Pictobank/Abaca Press/CP Photo; 279 top Buddy Mays/Alamy; bottom David R. Frazier Photolibrary, Inc./Alamy; 280 top TORU YAMANAKA/AFP/Getty Images; bottom Martin Jepp/ zefa/Corbis Canada; 281 top Bashford and Thompson Photo. PH Coll. 290.36 University of Washington Libraries. Manuscripts, Special Collections, University Archives Division; bottom PH Coll. 290.33c University of Washington Libraries. Manuscripts, Special Collections, University Archives Division; 282 Roger Ressmeyer/ Corbis Canada; 283 bottom Adrian Sherratt/Alamy; 284 left Shutterstock; right Jan Richter/imagebroker/ Alamy; 285 top left John E. Marriott/All Canada Photos; top right Roger Harris/Science Photo Library; bottom centre TORU YAMANAKA/AFP/Getty Images; bottom right Martin Jepp/zefa/Corbis Canada; 286 left cloki/Shutterstock; centre Danilo Ducak/Shutterstock; right Shutterstock; 287 Brian Koster/Scoopt/Getty Images; 288–289 Chien-min Chung/Getty Images; 289 Wikipedia; 294 Barry Lewis/Corbis Canada; 296 left Lester Lefkowitz/Stone/Getty Images; right Neil Rabinowitz/Corbis Canada; bottom Lester Lefkowitz/ Stone/Getty Images; 297 James Nazz/Corbis Canada; 301 top left Richard Broadwell/Alamy; top right PictureNet/ Corbis Canada; bottom John T. Fowler/Alamy; 302 Wilfried Krecichwost/Riser/Getty Images; 303 left epa/

Corbis Canada; right Visuals Unlimited/Corbis Canada; 304 Barrie Watts/Alamy; 306 top left Enigma/Alamy; top right Janet Horton; bottom left Dave Welcher/Hulton Archive/Getty Images; bottom right Derek Capitaine Photography; 307 Derek Capitaine Photography; 308 top YONHAP/AFP/Getty Images; bottom Robert Galbraith/CP Photo; 309 Ros Drinkwater/Alamy; 312 left Neil Rabinowitz/Corbis Canada; centre James Nazz/Corbis Canada; right Wilfried Krecichwost/Riser/Getty Images; 313 top YONHAP/AFP/Getty Images; bottom Ros Drinkwater/Alamy; 314 balaikin/Shutterstock; 315 top Piotr Lukasik/Shutterstock; bottom National Archives of Canada C-009766/CP PHOTO; 316–317 Bill Brooks/Alamy; 317 top CP PHOTO/Adrian Wyld; bottom Alan Marsh/First Light; 318 top Vstock/Tetra Images/Getty Images; bottom Lucas Oleniuk/Toronto Star; 319 left Tereshchenko Dmitry/Shutterstock; right Kim Steele/The Image Bank/Getty Images; 320 left Rolf Vennenbernd/dpa/Corbis Canada; right Kevin Dodge/Corbis Canada; 321 top Dennis Ku/Shutterstock; bottom Ivy Images; 323 top left Brownstock Inc./Alamy; top right Northrop Grumman/Via Bloomberg News/Landov; bottom left Eu Toch/Shutterstock; bottom right Susan McKenzie/Shutterstock; 324 Cameraphoto/Art Resource, NY; 325 left Tim Graham/The Image Bank/Getty Images; right FAN travelstock/Alamy; 326 Adam Crowley/Photodisc/Getty Images; 327 top Corbis Canada; bottom Janice Hazeldine/Alamy; 329 top left Werner Forman/Art Resource, NY; top right Courtesy of Stirex Innovation AB; bottom Marilyn Angel Wynn/Nativestock Pictures/Corbis Canada; 332 top left David Young-Wolff/PhotoEdit; top right Jerry Horbert/Shutterstock; bottom left BUILT Images/Alamy; bottom right Jupiter Images; 334 Dick Hemingway Editorial Photographs; 335 top Dorling Kindersley/Getty Images; bottom Charles Bowman/Alamy; 336 top left Lucas Oleniuk/Toronto Star; top right Kim Steele/The Image Bank/Getty Images; bottom left Cameraphoto/Art Resource, NY; bottom right Susan McKenzie/Shutterstock; 337 top left Janice Hazeldine/Alamy; top right David Young-Wolff/PhotoEdit; 338 Travstock/Alamy; 339 Dick Hemingway Editorial Photographs; 340 Realistic Reflections/Getty Images; 343 top right Stocktrek Images, Inc./Alamy; bottom (a) Ned Therrien/Visuals Unlimited; (b) Robyn Mackenzie/Shutterstock; (c) trailexplorers/Shutterstock; (d) Germany Feng/Shutterstock; 345 top right Erin Patrice O'Brien/Taxi/Getty Images; bottom (a) John Sylvester/Alamy; (b) graficart.net/Alamy; (c) Coquilleau/Shutterstock; (d) Tibor Bognar/Corbis Canada; 345 left Jaa/Shutterstock; right Robert Harding Picture Library Ltd./Alamy.

Skills Handbook

346–347 Elemental Imaging/Shutterstock ; 348 ©Estate of Fred Stein/Art Resource, NY; 349 left James King-Holmes/Science Photo Library; right Laguna Design/Science Photo Library; 350 left Mehau Kulyk/Science Photo Library; right Sue Cunningham Photographic/Alamy; 351 left Thomas Robinson; right zimmytus/Shutterstock; 352 right SRI International; 353 top rpixs/Shutterstock; bottom left david sanger photography/Alamy; bottom right Time & Life Pictures/Getty Images; 354 ©Brooklyn Production/CORBIS; 355 ©The Natural History Museum/Alamy; 366 left Andrey TTL/Shutterstock; right ©Rudy Sulgan/Corbis; 367 top U.S. Army Corps of Engineers, Detroit District; bottom Digital Vision/Alamy; 371 right Den Kou Images/Alamy; 374 left Tom Morrison/Getty Images; 375 left Steve Skjold/Alamy; right Canadian International Water Purification Ltd.; 377 Oleg Kozlov & Sophy Kozlova/Shutterstock; 379 left ©Yves Forestier/CORBIS SYGMA; right Idealink Photography/Alamy; 382 Michael Newman/Photo Edit; 388 bottom right Carolyn A. McKeone/Photo Researchers, Inc.; 394 top and bottom left Boréal; 405 left Scimat/Photo Researchers, Inc.; middle Dr. G.W. Willis/Visuals Unlimited; right SIU/Visuals Unlimited; 413 Yellow Dog Productions/Getty Images; 415 Miodrag Gajic/Shutterstock; 420 Michael Newman/Photo Edit; 421 Michael Newman/Photo Edit.

Additional Photography by

Dave Starrett
Ray Boudreau